*Aspinwall
personal*

THE BLUE GUIDES

Jarash: the Oval Precinct from the South Theatre

Please help us to keep the Blue Guide as up to date and accurate as possible by sending in your comments, suggestions and corrections for the next edition. Writers of the most helpful letters will be awarded a free Blue Guide of their choice.

BLUE GUIDE

Jordan

Sue Rollin and Jane Streetly

A & C Black
London

WW Norton
New York

First edition 1996

Published by A & C Black (Publishers) Limited
35 Bedford Row, London WC1R 4JH

A CIP catalogue record of this book
is available from the British Library.

ISBN 0-7136-4108-8

Published in the United States of America by
WW Norton and Company, Inc
500 Fifth Avenue, New York, NY 10110

Published simultaneously in Canada by
Penguin Books Canada Limited
10 Alcorn Avenue, Toronto, Ontario M4V 3B2

ISBN 0-393-31420-0

The authors and the publishers have done their best to ensure the accuracy of all the information in Blue Guide Jordan; however, they can accept no responsibility for any loss, injury or inconvenience sustained by any traveller as a result of information or advice contained in the guide.

Sue Rollin was tutor in Ancient Near Eastern History at University College, London, and has also taught courses at the School of Oriental and African Studies, London, and Cambridge. She has worked as an archaeologist on excavations in several countries and travelled widely in Europe, the Middle East and India. She currently works as a guide/lecturer in the Middle East, and also as a freelance interpreter.

Jane Streetly was born and brought up in Trinidad. She studied French and Spanish at university and has travelled widely in Europe, Latin America and the Middle East. She works as a freelance interpreter.

Publisher's acknowledgements. Thanks are due to the following for permission to reproduce illustrations: the Ministry of Tourism and Antiquities, Jordan (pages 50 and 169); the Henry E. Huntingdon Library and Art Gallery (page 127); *The Mosaic Map of Madaba* by H. Donner, the Kok Pharos Publishing House, (pages 138-9); K.D. Politis (page 129); the Bodleian Library, University of Oxford (page 252). The illustration on page 249 is after Mrs Herman Shapiro's drawing in *Deities and Dolphins* by Nelson Glueck, Cassell.

Printed and bound in Great Britain by
Butler & Tanner Ltd, Frome and London

CONTENTS

Maps and Plans

PREFACE

With its rich historical and cultural heritage Jordan is a fascinating country to explore. Petra is, of course, rightly famous, but there is much besides to see and do in Jordan. Sites range from the beautiful classical ruins of Jarash, to Byzantine church mosaics, early Islamic desert complexes, Roman forts and the spectacular Wadi Rum. Mountains run the length of the country affording opportunities for hiking, climbing and camping. There are beaches at Aqaba, and the experience of a swim in the Dead Sea should not be missed.

With four-wheel drive and a guide there are also plenty of rewarding sites to visit in the desert, but we cannot emphasise too strongly the care one should take when venturing off the beaten track. Often a Bedouin from the nearest tent you can find will be willing to come with you—presents or a sum of money should always be offered in return. Drive with extreme caution in the desert—a rock or a small wadi may look innocuous, but can ruin your day if not spotted in time. Rain can also be dangerous—flash floods occur with frightening speed in narrow wadis and can dislodge rocks and soil. Take care if clambering around Petra, where a stick is a useful aid on some of the steep climbs. Reasonably accurate road maps are on sale in Jordan and elsewhere, but not all historical sites and new roads are marked.

Things are changing fast in Jordan, and that includes entrance fees and telephone numbers. We have tried to ensure that information given here is accurate, but little can be done if prices and numbers are subsequently changed. The same is true for historical sites where excavations are constantly revealing more of the past. An Archaeological Park and the Apostles' Church are due to open shortly at Madaba and we have given some description of both sites. The recently discovered cuneiform inscription at Sela has not yet been published and doubtless there will be much more to research for the second edition.

Tourism is booming and with the opening of borders between Jordan and Israel visitors can now combine trips to both countries. We would, however, urge travellers to allow sufficient time on any visit to Jordan. From our own experience, we can say that it is well worth the effort.

Acknowledgements

Traditional Arab hospitality is renowned, and we have been fortunate enough to experience it time and again in the course of our work on Blue Guide Jordan. Above all we could not have written this book without the support and assistance of the Jordanian Ministry of Tourism and Antiquities who so generously provided us with transport, a driver and logistical help for our trips to Jordan. Both Dr Mohammed Adwan and his successor as Minister of Tourism and Antiquities, Mr Abdel-Elah Khatib, could not have been more helpful, as was Dr Ghassan Mufleh, then Secretary General at the Ministry. Our driver Mohammed Abed al Qader Ali constantly faced new challenges in the form of floods, desert tracks, wadi beds and missed lunches as we scoured the desert in search of obscure piles of stone. Fayez Hussain helped us at the airport as did Mahmoud Helalat in Aqaba and Sameer Khota at Wadi Rum. Our very special thanks must go to Faten Abboud who so efficiently and cheerfully organised our stays in Jordan and was always there when we needed her. We are equally indebted to Major-General Shafik Jumean for his kind interest and invaluable assistance with this project.

The Department of Antiquities with its network of inspectors across the country was a mine of information. Director Dr Ghazi Bisheh kindly updated us on recent excavations and provided us with letters of introduction which opened many doors. We were met with tremendous kindness and expert knowledge as we travelled. Inspectors everywhere accompanied us at the oddest times and well out of working hours to show us the newest sites and most recent discoveries. We cannot sufficiently thank former Acting Director Faisal Quelah, Dr Mohammed Waheeb, Atalla Laghawat, Mohammed Abd al-Aziz, Ibrahim Zubi, Ali Musa Ali, Ali Khayyat, Sultan Shraydi, Hekmat al-Ta'ani, Sawson Fakhri, Hazim Jasser, Nabil Begain and his driver Juma and Jihad Darwish whose family also showed us great hospitality in the Tafila District. Among archaeologists who spared precious time from their digs we would like to thank Suzanne Richards, Stephen Bourke, Jonathan Tubb, Rupert Chapman, Peter Dorrell and Peter Parr.

Elsewhere Abdullah Qassem thoroughly explored Umm Qais with us, both above and below ground; Ahmad Ma'ita at Lejjun managed to find Bshir fort for us; Amar Awad Eid al Suleiman showed us sites in the Hauran and Ahmad Isa Asad left his sheep to take us to Qasr Tuba. Thanks, too, to Haya Halassa, Zaid Qusoos, Fares al Jada, Basem Sabatini, Saleh Ahmad Suweilhiya, Nasser Awad and Sabah Atieeq, who showed us some of his favourite places around Rum and Disi. Countless Bedouin families invited us into their tents for tea, coffee and meals—they proved an invaluable source of local knowledge, taking us to sites which no one else could find.

In Petra Ahmad Moammar gave us much valuable information, showed us many sites and walked long distances with us up mountains and down valleys in search of Edomites and Nabateans. We would also like to thank the Moammar family, especially Sheikh Ali, as well as Hani Ali and his family for many meals and much hospitality. Khaled Twisi, formerly chief guide at Petra, accompanied us on several expeditions; Jameel Nawafleh and Mohammed Al-Hasanat gave us helpful tips and Awad Salameh shared with us his vast knowledge of the Petra region. Particular thanks go to Yousef al-Nawaflah for giving up a morning of work to accompany us to Umm al-Biyara, and to Haroun Awad al Bdul whose long stride exhausted us but got us to Sabra and much else in one day.

Among our sponsors in Jordan we would like to thank Richard Lyons and the Marriott Hotel, the management of the Forte Grand in Amman, Aref Abdul Rahman, also Abu Rami and Mahmoud Hillawi of Wadi Rum Resthouse and the management of the Ashtar Hotel, Ma'in Spa Village.

In the UK we have been equally fortunate—Gareth Williams, having been through it all himself, was full of useful suggestions; Nikkos helped with Greek inscriptions, and Hugh Kennedy very kindly lent us the manuscript of *Crusader Castles*. Thanks, too, for advice and help to Naomi Glubb, Margaret Oliphant, Ruth Baker, Deborah Morrison, Francis Miller, Mungo Tulloch and Michael Streetly and to other family and friends for their encouragement. We would particularly like to thank Neil Macfadyen for his illustrations, Mr Ahid Quntar, formerly of Royal Jordanian London for generous sponsorship and, of course, our editor Gemma Davies, who has calmly coped with our demands. Most of all, Emma Bodossian of Royal Jordanian has been a stalwart friend and helper throughout this time—we could not have done it without her unfailing kindness.

PRACTICAL INFORMATION

Sources of Information

Royal Jordanian offices provide information and advice on travel to and within Jordan (Tel: London 0171 734 2557; New York 212 949 0050). A reasonable road map published by the Royal Jordanian Geographic Centre is on sale in major hotels in Amman. Several maps of Jordan can be bought in the UK, among which the Bartholomews map of Israel and Jordan is the most detailed but only covers part of Jordan. Maps of Petra and of a limited area around Rum can also be bought in Jordan.

When to Go

The climate varies considerably within the country, but spring is the nicest time of year to visit: spring flowers will be out and while there may be some rain, the weather should be reasonable from mid-March onwards. Summer is long and hot, autumn is pleasant, but winter rains can start in November so take raingear for trips between November and April.

Average temperatures:

Amman	Jan.	8.1°C (46.6°F)	July 25.1°C (77.2°F)
Aqaba	Jan.	15.6 C°(60°F)	July 31.3°C (90°F)

What to Take

Raincoats, jerseys (it can be cold in the Petra mountains), good walking shoes and a small backpack as well as a stick (very handy in Petra), bathing suits, suntan lotion, mosquito repellent, basic medical kit to include aspirin, plasters, antiseptic ointment and an anti-diarrhoeal. Penknife, camera and film (more expensive in Jordan), binoculars and a torch should also be packed. Electric sockets vary and may take British plugs or two-pin European plugs. The current is 220 volts. American visitors will need transformers and adaptors. Women are advised not to wear sleeveless shirts or revealing dresses; a headscarf is required to visit mosques and is also good protection against desert sand. If planning to camp at Wadi Rum or Dana, please note that mattresses and blankets can be hired, but you may like to bring a sleeping bag liner. In general Jordan is a safe country for women travellers; harrassment is unusual, especially outside the main tourist centres (Aqaba or Petra), but sensible dressing and behaviour in a different culture are obviously advised. Travellers' cheques in UK£ or US$ are exchangeable in big hotels and banks as are other major currencies. It is also advisable to take cash, especially if heading off the beaten track. The standard road map can be bought in most major hotels.

Health

Polio, typhoid, tetanus and hepatitis vaccinations are recommended. See your doctor for advice. British Airways Travel Clinics and Trailfinders Travel Agency (Travel Clinic Tel: 0171 938 3999) in London offer advice and treatment for a fee. Bottled water is widely available and tap water is drinkable in the major hotels. Take something for stomach trouble like Lomotil or Imodium; if you observe reasonable precautions you should not need it. If you do have stomach trouble keep to plain food and yoghurt. Pack a basic medical kit (see above); health travel insurance is recommended.

Time
Jordan is two hours ahead of London and seven hours ahead of New York. Clocks also change in summer.

Customs and Allowances
200 cigarettes, one litre of spirits and two litres of wine. 200 grams of tobacco and personal items like camera, typewriter etc.

Currency
The Jordanian Dinar, known as the JD, is a convertible currency and can be bought outside Jordan. There are 1000 Fils to the JD, but Jordanians sometimes work in piastres—100 to the Dinar. Major credit cards are accepted in big hotels and shops, elsewhere cash is needed. Travellers' cheques in US Dollars or Pounds Sterling are recommended.

How to Get There

Formalities. A visa is required for non-Arab visitors to Jordan. The price varies according to nationality and can be expensive. Contact your local embassy for details. A single entry visa is valid for three months, but you must contact the police after two weeks if you wish to stay longer or risk paying a fine at the airport. Visas may also be issued on arrival at Amman airport where they are slightly cheaper, and at the Aqaba-Eilat crossing. Please note that a departure tax, currently 10 JD, must be paid on leaving. For group travellers visas and departure tax are arranged by the tour operators.

Travel agents like Trailfinders (Tel: 0171 938 3366/3939) can arrange your flight. Tour companies will organise your entire holiday. Companies which offer specialist tours include:

Tour Company	Telephone
Bales	01306 885991
British Museum Tours	0171 323 8895
Martin Randall	0181 742 3355
Swan Hellenic	0171 800 2200

By Air. To Queen Alia airport, c 40 minutes drive south of Amman, or to Aqaba airport. There are daily scheduled flights by Royal Jordanian and many other major airlines operate direct flights to Amman, e.g. British Airways, Air France, KLM, Alitalia. Royal Jordanian (Tel: London 0171 734 2557, New York 212 949 0050) also fly between Amman and Aqaba daily. Buses run regularly from the airport to Amman Abdali station. Alternatively, you can take a taxi, but always agree the fare first. Hotels may have a bus service or meet you on request.

By Land. Overland from Syria, Israel, Iraq and Saudi Arabia. If driving you will need an international driving licence and insurance to drive in Jordan. There is a bus service between Damascus and Amman and JETT buses operate from Jeddah to Amman. 'Service' taxis (shared taxis working a route) also run between Damascus and Amman and usually take 3–4 hours.

By Train. A weekly train runs between Damascus and Amman.

By Ferry. Between Nuweibeh in Egypt and Aqaba. Allow plenty of time as there are usually long delays on this crowded ferry which runs twice a day both ways.

Communications
The international code for Jordan is 962

Amman-06	Aqaba, Petra, Kerak-03	Irbid, Umm Qais-02
Jerash-04	Madaba-08	Zarqa-09

Where to Stay

Luxury hotels listed have all the usual facilities, although they may not be quite the same standard as European and American equivalents. Resthouses are no longer all owned by the Government, but generally provide a fair standard of accommodation with en suite bathrooms and restaurant. For Petra you are advised to book well in advance, particularly in spring and autumn. There are two spa hotels, one on the Dead Sea and one at Zarqa Ma'in. In general accommodation is expensive. When planning a holiday independent travellers should note that local tour operators can usually arrange cheaper accommodation.

(*** = Expensive ** = Moderate *= Cheap)

AMMAN

Forte Grand ***	Shmaysani. Friendly staff, spacious rooms and good service.	Tel: 06 696 511 Fax: 06 67426
Intercontinental ***	Between Second and Third Circle. Expensive option for rather poor service.	Tel: 06 641361 Fax: 06 645217
Marriott Hotel ***	Shmaysani. Pleasant, well-run hotel with good sports facilities.	Tel: 06 607607 Fax: 06 670100
Amra ***	Sixth Circle. Most floors recently renovated. Staff are very friendly and food is good.	Tel: 06 815071 Fax:06 814072
Bonita Inn ***	Near Third Circle. Six rooms only above Amman's best Spanish restaurant—this is a popular venue with long term visitors.	Tel: 06 615061 Fax: 06 615060
Regency Palace ***	Near Sports City on a busy road. Ask for a room at the back.	Tel: 06 660000
Torino ***	Sweifiyeh. Apartment hotel with a good Italian restaurant below.	Tel: 06 818637 Fax: 06 679304
Orchid **	Shmaysani. New hotel with good facilities; no alcohol.	Tel: 06 604 229 Fax: 06 606961
Hisham **	Near Third Circle. Smaller hotel in a quiet street with helpful staff.	Tel: 06 642720 Fax: 06 647540
Shepherd **	Near Second Circle. Lots of bars and a good fondu restaurant.	Tel: 06 639197 Fax: 06 639198
Caravan *	Near King Abdullah mosque downtown. Simple but clean.	Tel: 06 661195/7 Fax: 06 661196
Alia Gateway **	Near the airport south of Amman. Adequate, but hotels in Amman are preferable.	Tel: 08 51000 Fax: 08 51029

PETRA

Taybet Zaman ***	14km from Petra, this stylishly converted Ottoman village offers views of the Petra mountains, craft shops and swimming pool.	Tel: 03 336922/3

Petra Forum ***	Expensive, but conveniently close to Petra. Swimming-pool in summer.	Tel: 03 336266 Fax: 03 336977
Grand View ***	Luxury hotel on the road out of Wadi Musa. Only recently opened and expensive.	Tel: 03 336983/4 Fax: 03 652417
Petra Resthouse **	Includes a Nabatean tomb on site. Recently partly furnished and upgraded.	Tel: 03 336011 or 03 336014 Fax: 03 336686
Kingsway Inn **	Larger hotel at the top of town near Moses Spring.	Tel: 03 336799 Fax: 03 336796
Edom **	Conveniently near to Petra. Pleasant staff and good service.	Tel: 03 336994/5
Petra Palace **	Popular with tours, small but clean rooms within walking distance of Petra.	Tel:03 336723
Flowers **	Recently expanded, friendly staff, near the Petra Forum.	Tel: 03 336770
Anbat *	At the top of Wadi Musa. Cheap, but a long walk down.	Tel: 03 336265
Moses Spring *	Next to Moses spring, one of the cheapest—you can even sleep on the rooftop.	Tel: 03 336310

AQABA

Coral Beach ***	On the beach road a little way from the centre, with private beach.	Tel: 03 313521 Fax: 03 313614
Holiday *International* ***	Next to the Coral Beach Hotel. Most expensive in Aqaba, but pleasant.	Tel: 03 312426 Fax: 03 313426
Aquamarina 1 ***	On the beach road. Good sports facilities include diving, windsurfing and waterskiing.	Tel: 03 316250 Fax: 03 314271
Aquamarina 2 ***	Sister hotel to Aquamarina I, but not on the beach.	Tel: 03 315165 Fax: 03 315169
Aqaba ***	On the beach with rooms or bungalows.	Tel: 03 314091/2

KARAK

Karak *Resthouse* **	By the castle. Fifteen rooms with lovely views west down the Wadi Karak.	Tel: 03 351148 Fax: 03 813248
Towers *	Cheaper alternative down the road with pleasant manager.	Tel: 03 354293

AZRAQ

Azraq Resthouse **	2km from the fort. Twenty-four rooms around a courtyard with pool in summer.	Tel: 06 647610/1, ext 6

DIBEEN

Dibeen *Resthouse* **	National park in the pine hills above Jarash. Ring to make arrangements and check details in advance.	Tel. 04 452413

AJLUN

Ar-Rabad **	On the road up to the castle with good views.	Tel: 04 462202 Fax: 06 630414
Ajlun Hotel **	Nearby but cheaper; recently expanded, ask for one of the new rooms on the front.	Tel: 04 462524

SPA HOTELS

Dead Sea Spa ***	Near the springs of Kallirhoë with private beach and spa facilities. 6JD entrance fee for day visitors includes use of showers.	Tel: 09 802028 Fax: 09 688100
Ma'in Spa *Ashtar Hotel* ***	Spa Hotel with range of therapies. Swimming pool and outdoor thermal springs. Entrance fee charged for day visitors.	Tel: 08 545500

IRBID

Hijazi Palace **	The closest accommodation to Umm Qais, reasonable standard and in the town.	Tel: 02 279500 Fax: 02 279520

CAMP SITES

Wadi Rum *Resthouse*	Camping only, but good shower block and meals available from restaurant. Tents, mattresses and blankets provided.	Tel: 03 313930 Fax: 03 313948
Dana	RSCN run campsite with good facilities in beautiful mountain landscape. Tents, mattresses and blankets provided.	RSCN in Amman Tel: 06 830456

Getting Around

By Car. Most major car hire companies (Avis, Hertz, Budget) have offices in Amman and there are plenty of local companies too. You will need an international drivers' licence to hire a car. Amman is not the easiest town to drive in, but once outside the city the roads are fairly well signed; many road signs are given in English as well as Arabic. The standard issue map of Jordan is reasonably accurate, but the newest roads are not shown. If driving down the Dead Sea/Wadi Araba road fill up beforehand as petrol stations are few and far between. Flocks of sheep and goats crossing even major roads can be a hazard. Remember to drive on the right in Jordan.

By Bus. There are two main bus stations in Amman—Abdali covers the northern area, Wahdat southern destinations. Raghadan is for local destinations. JETT buses operate routes to Petra, Aqaba, Wadi Rum among others. The JETT information number is 894872 or 664146.

By Taxi. Hotel taxis tend to be more expensive than street taxis, service taxis are cheaper, shared and work a set route.

Tour Operators. Tours of Jordan can be also be arranged within the country by local companies:

	Telephone	**Fax**
Arab Falcon	06 685520/685525	06 683410
Dakkak	06 680704/601076	06 601077
International Traders	06 607014	06 669905
Petra Tours	06 667028/670267	06 681402

Airlines

Royal Jordanian:	Amman 06 678321	Aqaba 03 314477
Air Canada 06 630879	Air France 06 666055	Alitalia 06 625203

American Airlines 06 669068	British Airways 06 641430
KLM 06 622175	Qantas 06 862288/862299
TWA 06 623430/622684	United Airlines 06 641959

Useful Telephone Numbers
Embassies

| British 06 823100 | US 06 820101/64437 | Canada 06 666124 |
| Australia 06 673246 | Irish 06 630878 | New Zealand 06 636720 |

British Council: (on Rainbow St near First Circle) 06 636147.

Emergency Numbers

Police and tourist police 192   Ambulance 193   Operator 121

The *Jordan Times* publishes a list of telephone numbers including emergency numbers, duty doctors and chemists.

Tourist Information

The Ministry of Tourism (Tel: 642311), near Third Circle, supplies maps and information.
Aqaba Tourist Office Tel: 03 313363/313731. Petra Tourist Office Tel: 03 336020/60.

Churches Anglican Church: 06 630851, 06 628543, International Church: 06 652526.

Newspapers

The English language *Jordan Times* is published daily, the *Star* weekly. *Your Guide to Amman* is a bilingual monthly publication often provided in hotels which has useful numbers and a What's On section. Foreign papers can be bought, usually a day or two late, at major hotels.

Language

Arabic is a major world language spoken in over 20 countries. Like Hebrew and Aramaic, it belongs to the group of Semitic languages. While the Koran is written in classical Arabic, there are considerable differences in the colloquial language of each country. The major spoken and written medium, Modern Standard Arabic, is understood throughout the Arab-speaking world. Arabic is written in cursive script from right to left and short vowels are omitted. This can make it a difficult language to learn. Numbers are written from left to right. As Arabic has many sounds which do not exist in English, the transliterations given in this book are only approximate.

Numbers

One	*Wahad*	Seven	*Sab'a*
Two	*Ithnain*	Eight	*Thamaniya*
Three	*Thalatha*	Nine	*Tis'a*
Four	*Arba'a*	Ten	*'Ashara*
Five	*Khamsa*	Hundred	*Mi'a*
Six	*Sitta*	Thousand	*Alaf*

Greetings

Hello (formal)	*As-Salaamu-alaykum*	What is your name?	*Shu ismak?*
		Where is...?	*Wain...?*
Hello (in response)	*Alaykum as salaam*	I want...	*Awaz (m) Awza (f)*
		How are you?	*Kaif halak (m) halki (f)*
Hello (informal)	*Merhaba*		
Yes/No	*Aiwa/La*	I am very well.	*Bi khair, al-hamdulillah*
My name is...	*Ismi*		

Useful phrases

Please	*Min fadlak*	Petrol Station	*Mahattat benzeen*
Thank you	*Shukran*		
Don't mention it	*Afwan*	Petrol	*Benzeen*
How much...?	*Kam...?*	Oil	*Zait*
Do you speak English?	*Tatakallam al inglizi?*	Water	*My*
		Hotel	*Funduk*
I don't speak Arabic	*Ana ma atakallam al arabiya*	Room	*Ghurfa*
		Restaurant	*Mata'am*
I am from...	*Ana min...*	Bill	*Fattura*
I have...We have	*Aindi...Aindna*	Problem/No problem	*Mushkila/ Mush mushkila*
Do you have...?	*Aindak? (m) Aindki? (f)*		
		Family	*A'ila*
There is....is not	*Fi...Ma fi*	Mother/father	*Umm/Ab*
Town centre	*Wasat al-madina*	Sister/brother	*Ukht/Akh*
Bazaar	*Suk*	Daughter/son	*Bint/Ibn*
Post Office	*Maktab al bareed*	Big/small	*Kabir/Saghir*
		Hot/cold	*Harr/Barid*
Bank	*Bank*	Expensive/Cheap	*Ghali/Rakhees*
		Beautiful	*Jameel*

Directions

Left/Right	*Ash-shimal/ Al-yamin*	Mountain/hill	*Jabal*
		Valley	*Wadi*
Straight ahead	*Dughari*	Antiquities, ruin	*Athar*
Road	*Tareek*	Church	*Kanisah*
Castle	*Qasr*	Cistern	*Birka*
Tower	*Rujm*	Spring	*'Ain*
Ruins	*Khirbet*	Well	*Bir*

Food and Drink

Throughout the region Arab hospitality continues as a tradition. Any visitor will be treated as an honoured guest, welcomed, plied with tea or coffee, and offered food—the best place to sample Arab food is, of course, in an Arab home. The food is spicy, but not hot; and much use is made of olive oil. Starters, often a mouth-watering array of usually cold dishes, are an important part of the meal. The main meal often consists of lamb or chicken accompanied by rice or cracked wheat, vegetables and salad. Muslims never eat pork as the pig is deemed to be an unclean animal. Vegetarians should find a good selection of dishes from the starters, but if stuck can always ask for an omelette. Fruit and sweet desserts follow the main-course and a meal is rounded off with small cups of strong, sweet Turkish coffee. A long tradition of sweetmeats continues, typically these are pastries stuffed with pinenuts, pistachios and walnuts. *Jabri*, *Zalatimo* and *Ata Ali* are the best sweet shops. Snacks such as falafal and shawarma with salad in pitta bread are sold everywhere—in Amman, one of the best stalls is at Second Circle. During the month of Ramadan, when most Muslims fast in daylight hours, shops close earlier and many restaurants are empty at lunchtimes. Some may not serve alcohol.

A typical menu might consist of:

Starters (*Muqabbilat*)

Shorba	Soup
Hummous	Pureed chick peas
Zaytoon	Olives
Tabbouleh	Cracked wheat salad with lots of parsley and lemon
Waraq ainab mahshi	Stuffed vine leaves
Koosa mahshi	Stuffed courgettes
Mutabal bazanjan	Aubergine puree
Labanee	Thick yoghurt
Kibbeh	Cracked wheat stuffed with minced lamb
Fool	Broad beans
Jibneh	White cheese

Main Meals

Mansaf	The traditional bedouin dish. Lamb or chicken served with rice and pine nuts on bread with a sauce made from dried yoghurt.
Maqlouba	'Upside down'—chicken or lamb stewed with rice and aubergines
Shish kebab/ta'uk	Lamb/Chicken grilled on skewers
Koftah	Meatballs
Samak/Dajaj mishwee	Grilled fish/chicken
Shawarma	Sliced spit-roast lamb
Ruzz	Rice
Khoubz	Bread
Baytha	Eggs

Fruit and Desserts (*Halawiyat*)

Tuffah	Apple
Burtaqal	Orange
Muz	Banana
Mishmish	Apricot
Ainab	Grapes
Teen	Figs
Lawz	Almonds
Fistiq	Pistachios
Baklava	Pastry stuffed with nuts in syrup
Ruz bi laban	Arabic rice pudding
Halva	Sesame sweet

| Kanafah | 'Weetabix' sweet with nuts and syrup |
| Qatayif | Cake with a layer of mild soft cheese served hot with a syrup |

Drinks

Qahwa/Shai	Coffee/tea
Bi/Bidoon sukkar	With/without sugar
Shai bi nana/maramiya	Mint/sage tea
Haleeb	Milk
Aseer	Fruit juice
Arak	Arak (aniseed flavoured spirit)
Beera	Beer
Nabeeth	Wine
My	Water

Restaurants

AMMAN

Leonardo Da Vinci's	Shmaysani	Italian. Excellent service and good food.
Al-Bustan	North Amman	Arabic. One of the best for Arabic food, always busy.
Romero's	Near the Intercontinental	Italian. With its outdoor terrace a very pleasant place to eat in summer.
Bonita Tapas Bar	Near Third Circle	Popular, well-run venue also has a quieter restaurant. There are also a few rooms upstairs for accommodation.
Turino	Sweifiyeh	Italian. Good food and self-catering accommodation next door.
Kan Zaman	Towards the airport	Very nicely restored 19C buildings with handicraft shops, coffee shop and reasonably priced buffet restaurant.
Shepherd Hotel	Near Second Circle	Good fondue restaurant in the hotel.
Taiwan Turismo	Near Third Circle	Chinese. The best Chinese and not too expensive.
Milano's	Shmaysani near Jabri's	Cheerful, fast service offering pizza and salads. Popular with young Jordanians.
Al Waha	End of Garden Street	Excellent Arabic food, popular with locals, decor includes a traditional Bedouin tent.
Reem al-Bawadi	Next to Al Waha	Delicious traditional food in pleasant surroundings. Popular with Jordanians and visitors from other Arab countries.
Al Quds	Next to Jabri's downtown	Good simple Arabic food. A popular place, but no alcohol served.
Jabri	Downtown, Sixth Circle and Shmaysani	Mouth-watering sweets and pastries, ice cream and fast food.
Zalatimo	By the Amra Hotel	Long-established company offering fine sweets.
New Orient	Just behind Third Circle	Arabic food. Terrace in summer.

JARASH

Green House	On the Amman road	Nice place for lunch.
Lebanese House	Near Hadrian's Arch	Excellent Lebanese food.
Resthouse	On site, near South Gate	Reasonable fare, but pricey.

UMM QAIS

Resthouse	Stylishly converted Ottoman house on site	On the expensive side, but the wonderful views over Galilee compensate.

PELLA

Resthouse	Above the site with a pleasant terrace	Good food—fresh fish from the Jordan can be ordered in advance.

AQABA

Ali Baba	Downtown	Very popular and always busy.
Mina House	On a boat near the fort	Good fresh fish.
Petra International Hotel	Lovely views from the 'On Top Restaurant'	Expensive, but a good menu.
Ata Ali	Near Ali Baba	Jordanian sweets and ice creams.

Opening Hours

Offices usually open at 8/8.30 am; many shops open later. Post Offices are open all day. Banks usually close for lunch and reopen later. Ministries and Government offices close at 2pm. On Fridays shops, banks and Post Offices are closed. During Ramadan many places close early. Opening hours are longer in summer when the lunch break is also longer. Many museums are closed on Tuesdays, but some close on Fridays.

National Holidays and Festivals

1 May	Labour Day
25 May	Independence Day
10 June	Army Day
11 August	King Hussein's Accession to the throne
14 November	King Hussein's Birthday

In addition to these there are the Islamic religious holidays of which the festivals of Eid al-Fitr, celebrating the end of Ramadan, and Eid al-Adha, the feast of sacrifice, are the most important. As the Islamic calendar is based on the lunar year, these dates vary. The Jarash Festival is an international arts festival held on the site of Jarash each summer. Tickets for performances and programme details can be obtained from the Ministry of Tourism at Jarash and from various travel agents. The Jarash Festival Office can be reached on tel: 06 675199/686197.

Tipping

Tips are a way of life in this part of the world and are expected everywhere. Remember that wages are not high and tips help to compensate for this.

Shopping

The best place for shopping is Amman. Amman's main suq in the town centre sells everything from pots and pans to gold. For handicrafts, which include pottery, weaving, embroidery, glass-blowing and jewellery, there are a number of handicraft centres which are usually cheaper than the big hotel shops: *Bani Hamida*, just off Rainbow St, has beautiful traditional rugs woven by Bedouin women, and next door *River Jordan Design* sells cushion covers, wall hangings, embroidered waistcoats and quilts—both are sponsored by Save The Children Fund and are located in beautifully renovated old houses. The Queen Noor Foundation also sponsors craft centres; its head office is near Safeway. Outside Amman there is the *Hebron Glass Centre* in Na'ur and in Salt the Queen Noor Foundation backs a Handicraft Training centre in the Salt Cultural Centre.

South of Amman off the airport road is *Kan Zaman*, a carefully restored Ottoman complex with a variety of little shops, a café and restaurant. A similar development is due to open shortly in Salt. The airport shop stocks a range of crafts and Dead Sea mud and mineral cosmetic products.

Sport

There are plenty of possibilities for climbing, walking and also ballooning in Wadi Rum, and for hiking in Petra and the Dana Nature Reserve. For camel treks between Petra and Wadi Rum contact Awad Salameh in the Bdul village near Wadi Musa or ask at the Visitors' Centre in Wadi Musa. Scuba-diving, snorkelling and water-sports are all possible at Aqaba.

Diving. Royal Diving Centre: Tel: 03 317035 Fax: 03 314206, Aquamarina 1 Hotel: Tel: 03 316250 Fax: 03 314271
Ballooning. Jordan Tourism Investment Company: Tel: 06 668606, 03 316324
Royal Society for the Conservation of Nature (run Dana Campsite) Tel: 06 830456
Safari Trips from Aqaba: Wadi Rum Resthouse Tel: 03 313930

Departure from Jordan

Confirm flight bookings at least 48 hours in advance of your departure. Check-in is usually two hours before departure and an airport tax of 10JD must be paid. Royal Jordanian Flights leave from Terminal I, while most other airlines use Terminal II across the road; check which you need when reconfirming your booking. The departure lounge has a coffee-shop, various gift-shops and a Duty-Free shop.

BACKGROUND INFORMATION

The Land

A drive down the Jordan valley provides a glimpse into its exciting geological past—the great depression of the Jordan valley or Ghor (sunken land) and the Wadi Araba is actually a branch of the African Rift valley. The Dead Sea is the lowest point on earth at 435m below sea level—the sea bed itself is over 100m deeper. Although the Jordan flows into it and there is no outlet for water from the Dead Sea, the evaporation rate is high enough to prevent the water level from rising. Salinity is over 26 per cent, compared to 3–4 per cent for ocean water, which is why nothing sinks in it nor can anything live in it. Called the Asphalt Sea in ancient days because of the abundance of bitumen found there, its tar pits are mentioned in the Bible.

East of the rift rise the highlands. This was the land of the Ammonites, Moabites and Edomites. The highlands are crossed in places by the awesome gashes of the great wadis running westwards into the Jordan and Dead Sea—the Yarmuk, the Zarqa (River Jabbok), the Wadi Mujib (biblical Arnon) and the Wadi Hasa (the brook Zered) are the most impressive. South of the plains of Moab the mountains of Edom rise to 1600m. Continuing east are the expanses of desert or steppe which take up two-thirds of Jordan's territory, spreading out towards the borders with Syria, Iraq and Saudi Arabia. Historically this land on the edge of the desert is the land of the Bedouin, and while many have now been settled or 'sedentarised' their black tents and flocks of sheep and goats can still be seen here, although trucks and Mercedes have now replaced camels. In the north-east the land is dominated by volcanic black basalt while elsewhere in the north white limestone predominates, changing to sandstone further south. It is the weathering of these sandstones which has given rise to the fantastic scenery of Petra and the Wadi Rum.

The climate varies considerably. On the Red Sea, Aqaba is hot to warm all year round; Amman is a pleasant 55–73°F. Snow may fall in the highlands in winter. Spring is perhaps the loveliest time of year to visit Jordan—there may still be some showers in March, but the spring flowers are beginning to bloom. Summer is long and hot and the winter rains begin again in November and December; flash floods can be extremely dangerous because of the speed with which they occur in narrow wadis.

The capital Amman has a population of over 1.5million—other major towns are Irbid, Jarash, Zarqa, Salt, Madaba, Karak, Ma'an and Aqaba. Jordan's population in 1991 was 3.5 million, but there is a very high birth rate. Only a small part of the land can be farmed, much of it in the warm and fertile Jordan valley. Water is scarce: most farmers depend on rainfall although irrigation is increasing rapidly and water consumption has risen correspondingly in recent years. Olives, citrus fruit, grapes, wheat and tobacco are all cultivated.

Phosphates, potash, fertilisers, cement, and oil-refining are important industries—potash comes from the Dead Sea and the phosphate mines can be seen on the way down the Desert Highway. Jordan is dependent on imports of crude oil although there are a number of projects involving renewable energy sources underway. Following the Gulf War crisis in 1991, there was a severe shock to the economy as the United Nations sanctions against Iraq hit Jordanian exports and 400,000 people returned to Jordan from Kuwait and other Gulf States, with a corresponding loss of remittances from abroad. Tourism also suffered in the aftermath of the war, although with the advent of peace to the region it has recovered and is booming again.

People Past and Present

The land east of the Jordan features regularly in **biblical history**: it was home to those much-cursed enemies of the Israelites the Ammonites, Moabites and Edomites. The biblical rivers, Jabbok, Arnon and the brook Zered (today's Wadis Zarqa, Mujib and Hasa), served as rough boundaries for the Ammonites in the north, Moabites in between and Edomites to the south. Lot and Abraham knew the land. Lot grazed his sheep here, before the area south of the Dead Sea became infamous as the land of Sodom and Gomorrah and his wife was turned to a pillar of salt. Strange salt formations can still be seen here and a church at 'Lot's sanctuary' at 'Ain Abata is currently being excavated. Having lost his birthright to his wily brother Jacob, Esau came here with his flocks. He is said to be the ancestor of the Edomites who are therefore kin to the Israelites. On his way to Canaan, having led his people out of enslavement in Egypt, Moses sought permission to pass through Edom; the account of the request and its refusal given in Numbers 20: 14–21 actually mentions the King's Highway. It was from Mount Nebo/Pisgah in the land of Moab that God showed Moses the Holy Land (Deut. 34). Deuteronomy 3 details the apportioning of land on this side of the Jordan to the tribes of Reuben, Gad and half of Manasseh. Wars between the Israelites and their Transjordanian neighbours rage throughout the Old Testament and the Israelite prophets rained down curses upon them: 'Moab is my washpot, over Edom will I empty out my shoe' rants Psalm 60:8. David sought refuge from Saul's jealousy across the Jordan (his ancestress Ruth was a Moabite) but turned against his neighbours when he became king. Solomon's port of Ezion Geber lay on the Red Sea coast not far from the modern port of Aqaba.

In the New Testament, the river Jordan was the setting of Jesus' baptism and the story of the Gadarene swine took place in the Decapolis city above Lake Galilee now known as Umm Qais. It was in Herod's fortress at Mukawir that John the Baptist was imprisoned and Salome danced for his head. Some believe that Paul visited Petra—after his conversion he says, in Galatians 1:17, 'I went into Arabia'. When Christianity became the official religion of the Roman empire churches sprang up throughout the land, many of them with fine mosaic floors. Some towns in Jordan still have a sizeable Christian population.

Much of the land, particularly the fringe between the 'desert and the sown', has been and is still inhabited only by pastoral nomads. The Arabic word *Bduw* (Bedouin) means desert dwellers, but the Bedouin call themselves Arabs. In fact, much of Jordan's population is today of **Arab Bedouin origin**. The first Islamic dynasty, the Umayyads (p 86), built many fine residences on the edges of the desert in Syria, Palestine and Jordan, perhaps in order to maintain close relations with their Bedouin cousins. Nowadays, and despite some sedentarisation, the visitor to Jordan can still expect to see the black tents of the Bedouin, looking much as they did 1000 years ago but for the pickup parked outside. The tent, the *bayt shar* (house of hair) is traditionally woven from goat hair. Nowadays the woven strips which the tents are made up of can be bought, but many women still weave their own. They also continue to embroider their dresses, a tradition which is dying out in towns. Life is simple, but their famed hospitality and generosity is no myth—the unexpected visitor will be invited into the men's section, although subject to close scrutiny through any holes in the curtain dividing it from the women's section! The men are responsible for welcoming guests and making the coffee, a traditional ritual which is part of the code of hospitality. The Bedouin are also the best people to ask for directions to more out of the way sites and are often willing to accompany one there—payment may not be demanded, but some recompense should always be offered. The flocks of sheep and goats also provide yoghurt, cheese, milk and meat, while other essentials such as flour, tea, coffee and sugar are bought in from nearby towns.

In the late 19C many Muslim **Circassians** fleeing religious persecution in the Caucasus by Tsarist Russia were settled in Jordan as part of a policy intended to introduce an element of stability. Tribal unrest and feuding was then endemic in parts of the country. The Circassians were good farmers and brought with them their own cultural traditions, some of which they have kept despite their integration into Jordanian society. Salt, Amman and Jarash were among the towns settled by them between 1878 and 1909, although with the huge growth in population since the Second World War they are now a minority. The black and white checked Abu Darwish mosque, visible from the Amman citadel, was built by Circassians.

Another group who fled to Jordan more recently are the **Druze**. An offshoot of the Ismaili sect, itself a form of Shi'ism, this is a mysterious and esoteric form of Islam which believes the Fatimid Caliph al-Hakim (996–1021) to have been the embodiment of God. Following war in the Lebanon in the mid 19C and again in Syria in 1925, when they rose up against the French, the Druze fled into the north of Jordan in 1926–27. Azraq, for example, is a Druze village. However, their numbers were dwarfed by the enormous number of **Palestinian refugees** who have poured into Jordan with each war against Israel since the British withdrawal from Palestine in 1948. Half a million fled to Jordan at that time. Many still live in the refugee camps on the outskirts of Amman where UNRWA (the United Nations Relief and Works Agency) runs aid programmes.

Flora

The range of climate and terrain in Jordan gives rise to a corresponding diversity of plant life, some of it Mediterranean and some adapted to the harsher conditions of the desert or mountains. In biblical times much more of the land was forested: according to 2 Sam. 18:6–18 David fought the forces of his son Absalom in a forest in Gilead, north-west Jordan. Much of the tree cover has now been lost, although there are still pine woods in the northern highlands, and scrub or evergreen oak with some deciduous oak.

Spring is the time to visit for flowers. Many farmers do not use herbicides, with the result that the fields are also full of flowers: poppies, daisies, grape hyacinths and clumps of mallow make splashes of colour in the wheat. White broom grows everywhere, blue irises precede the anemones which stain the ground red at Jarash. On the dry hills asphodel, anchusa and giant fennel flower. Hollyhocks grow in the hills above Pella and Jordan's national flower, the black iris, grows by the roadsides south of Madaba. The cliffs of the Yarmuk Gorge are a mass of spring colour and even the basalt country of the Hauran has patches of bright green. Mimosa and other acacias flower along the roads—by July they are lined with the yellow flowers of verbascum and huge mauve thistles. At the end of summer the land is brown and bare, waiting for the winter rains to fall and the cycle to begin again.

Jarash was famed for its pomegranates in Classical times and the many fruit stalls on the new road between Jarash and Amman are filled with figs, apricots, grapes and apples in summer, before the pomegranates ripen in autumn. In spring, the fruit trees blossom while the ground beneath is still green and spread with spring flowers. The fertile soil and heat of the Jordan valley support citrus and banana plantations as well as tomatoes and water-melons. Olives are grown on the higher land and harvested in summer when you see women in brightly coloured clothes climbing the trees and laying the olives out on the ground. On the Moabite plateau wheat and tobacco grow and most houses have a vine to shade the terrace.

In Petra the ground is carpeted with poisonous sea squill and broom; tamarisk and juniper also grow there. South of the Dead Sea, flat-topped thorn trees grow in the desert and there are fringes of willow or oleander and cane brakes along the wadis. Azraq's oasis, with its reedy marshes, is both a stopover for migrating birds and home to indigenous species although numbers have declined drastically as the pools have shrunk since water pumping began. Even the sandy desert floors in Wadi Rum are full of shrubby bushes, greener after the winter rains when little white flowers may also bloom in the red sand, filling the air with scent. Herbs are used in teas and cooking: wormwood abounds, but thyme, sage, mint and rue are also plentiful. Many of these plants are used by the Bedouin. Gertrude Bell was struck by their knowledge of plant lore: 'With the leaf of the utrufan they scent their butter, from the prickly kursa'aneh they make an excellent salad, on the dry sticks of the billan the camels feed, and the sheep on those of the shih (wormwood), the ashes of the gali are used in soap boiling.'

Chronological Tables

BC

c 1,800,000–20,000		Paleolithic Period
c 20,000–8300		Epipaleolithic Period
c 8300–6000		Pre-pottery Neolithic Period: settlements at Ain Ghazal
c 6000–4500		Neolithic Period
c 4500–3200		Chalcolithic Period: fortress at Jawa and settlement at Teleilat Ghassul
c 3200–2000		Early Bronze Age; Sa'idiyah, Khirbet Iskander, 'Cities of the Plain'
c 2000-1550		Middle Bronze Age
c1550–1200		Late Bronze Age; Sa'idiyah and Deir 'Alla
c 1200–539		Iron Age
	c 1020–1004 King Saul	Kingdoms of Ammon, Moab and Edom
1000	c 1004–965 King David	
900	c 965–931 King Solomon	
	c 900–612 Neo-Assyrian Empire	853 Battle of Qarqar (Shalmaneser III)
800	c 876–869 King Omri	
	c 869–850 King Ahab	
	c 850 King Mesha of Moab	
700		734–732 Tiglath Pileser III conquers region
600	612–539 Neo-Babylonian Empire	612 Fall of Nineveh
		587 Nebuchadrezzar II conquers Jerusalem
500	539–332 Persian Empire	552 Nabonidus removes Edomite monarchy

400		
		332 Alexander conquers Syria and Palestine
300	323–64 Hellenistic period	323 Death of Alexander
		312 Nabateans first mentioned by Diodorus
200		323–198 Ptolemies and Seleucids contest Transjordan
		198 Antiochus III victorious over Ptolemy III
	NABATEAN KINGS	167 Start of Jewish revolts
	c 168 Aretas I	
100	[Rabbel I?]	
	c 100–96/92 Aretas II	
	96/92–86 Obodas I	64 Pompey makes Syria a Roman Province
	86–62 Aretas III Philhellenos	
	62–30 Malichus I	
	30–9 Obodas II	Herod the Great 37–4 BC
AD	9 BC–AD 40/44 Aretas IV	
	40/44– 70 Malichus II	
	70–106 Rabbel II	
	ROMAN EMPERORS	
100	98–117 Trajan	106 Trajan annexes Nabatea and creates the Province of Arabia
	117–38 Hadrian	111–114 Via Nova Traiana completed
	169–80 Marcus Aurelius	
200	193–211 Septimius Severus	
	211–217 Caracalla	
		272 Fall of Palmyra
	284–305 Diocletian	
300	286–305 Maximian	
	306–337 Constantine	313 Edict of Milan grants Christians freedom of worship
		337 Constantine baptised on his deathbed
		395 Roman Empire divided into two
400		
500	527–565 Justinian	
600	610–641 Heraclius	622 Mohammad goes to Medina—start of the Islamic era
		629 Muslims defeated at battle of Mota
		632 Death of Mohammad
		636 Muslim victory at battle of the Yarmuk
		638 Fall of Jerusalem
		639–42 Islamic conquest of Egypt
	UMAYYAD DYNASTY	658 First Islamic Civil War
	661–80 Mu'awiya	661 Death of Ali, start of Umayyad Dynasty
	680–83 Yazid I	
	683–84 Mu'awiya II	
	684–85 Marwan I	
700	685–700 'Abd al-Malik	
	705–715 al-Walid I	
	715–17 Sulayman	
	717–20 'Umar ibn 'Abd al-Aziz	
	720–4 Yazid II	
	724–43 Hisham	
	743–44 al Walid II	
	744 Yazid III	
	744 Ibrahim	

	744–50 Marwan II	750 Defeat of Umayyads by Abbasids
		762 Baghdad founded by Caliph Al-Mansur
800		
900		969 Fatimids establish Shi'ite Caliphate in Cairo
1000		1070–80 Seljuks move into Syria and Palestine
	CRUSADER KINGS	1095 Urban II preaches First Crusade
	1099–1100 Godfrey of Bouillon	1099 Jerusalem falls to Crusaders
1100	1100–1118 Baldwin I King of Jerusalem	1115 Baldwin founds Montreal Castle
	1118–1131 Baldwin II	1118 Knights Templar founded
	1131–1143 King Fulk	
	1131–1152 Queen Melisende	1144 Loss of Edessa to Zengi
	1152–1163 Baldwin III	1147–1148 Second Crusade
	1163–1174 King Amalric	1174 Saladin takes Damascus
	1174–1185 Baldwin IV	
	1185–1186 Baldwin V	
	1186–1192 Guy of Lusignan	1187 Defeat of Crusaders at Battle of Hattin
		1190–1192 Third Crusade
		1193 Death of Saladin
1200		1204 Fourth Crusade sacks Constantinople
		1217–1221 Fifth Crusade
		1250–1260 Mamlukes take power from Ayubbids
		1258 Mongols take Baghdad ending Abbasid Caliphate
	1260–1277 Baybars Mamluke Sultan	1260 Mamlukes defeat Mongols at Battle of 'Ain Jalut
		1271 Baybars takes Crac des Chevaliers
		1291 Acre falls to Mamlukes
1300		
1400		1400 Timur in Syria
		1453 Constantinople falls to the Turks
		1492 Fall of Moorish Granada
		1498 New route to India discovered by
1500		Vasco Da Gama
		1517 Ottomans conquer Syria and Palestine
1600		
1700		1798–1801 French in Egypt
1800		1869 Opening of the Suez Canal
1900		1908 Completion of the Hijaz Railway
		1916 Arab Revolt begins
		1917 Balfour Declaration
		Nov 1921 Abdullah becomes Emir of Transjordan
		15 May 1923 Britain formally recognises Transjordan
	HASHEMITE KINGS	May 1945 Establishment of the Arab League in Cairo
	25 May 1946 Emir Abdullah becomes King of Transjordan	Independence Day
		April 1948 British withdraw from Palestine
		Establishment of the State of Israel

Fighting erupts between Jews and Arabs
1949 Fighting in Palestine leaves Egypt
in Gaza and Jordanian forces in West Bank
Half a million refugees flee to Transjordan
1950 Hashemite Kingdom of Jordan
expands to include West Bank

20 July 1951 King
Abdullah assassinated,
King Talal succeeds him.
1953 King Hussein
succeeds on abdication of
King Talal

1956 Sir John Glubb, last British
Commander of the Arab Legion, leaves
Jordan
1964 PLO founded
June 1967 Six Day War
1973 Yom Kippur War
1982 Israel invades Lebanon
1990–91 Gulf War
26 Oct 1994 Peace Treaty signed between
Jordan and Israel

History of Jordan

Although it is only a small country, Jordan's geographical position on the land bridge between Africa and Asia has meant that it has played a modest, but nevertheless important role in the history of the Near East. Never itself the centre of a great civilisation like its neighbours Egypt and Mesopotamia, it has seen empires come and go, and as a regular corridor for commerce and conquest it has been profoundly influenced by peoples and cultures from east and west. Through the ages trade has been vital for Jordan's people and it was the Nabateans, merchants and middlemen par excellence, who gave Jordan perhaps its most distinctive culture and left behind monuments which are among the jewels of antiquity.

Already in the **Paleolithic period**, over 250,000 years ago, early man roamed the hills and valleys of Jordan hunting the larger game such as elephant and deer that lived in the savannah-like ancient environment. Stone tools left behind by these early hunters, mainly flint hand axes, have been found scattered in many parts of the country. Some time after 20,000 BC important changes took place. Camps and campsites of this **Epipaleolithic period** show that hunters were using composite tools, and hunting not just the larger mammals but many smaller creatures including rodents and birds. Some sites of the Epipaleolithic Kebaran culture show a remarkable concentration of certain animals. At Wadi Madamagh near Petra for example, nearly 82 per cent of the bones recovered are from wild goats, which suggests that people had already discovered how to herd these animals. Animal husbandry was a remarkable step forward in human development as it meant an assured food supply. Between 10,000 BC and 8500 BC, during the **Natufian period**, further progress was made. Camp sites were still seasonal, but round huts were made of stone and wood, and their occupants used agricultural tools such as sickles and querns, pestles and mortars. By collecting and using wild grains, the Natufians had moved one step towards cultivation and another important landmark in the history of mankind.

Jordan is one of the countries in the area of the Middle East known as the '**Fertile Crescent**', which describes an arc from Syro-Palestine to Mesopotamia. It was here that early experiments with food resources led to the first 'Agricultural

Revolution', without which complex societies and civilisations could never have developed. By the end of the 8th millennium BC, at **Pre-Pottery Neolithic sites** such as Beidha and 'Ain Ghazal, people were living in some of the world's first real villages, where they cultivated grains and other plants and herded goats. Pottery was soon 'invented' to store foods, people began to exchange luxury items with their neighbours and build special 'houses' to worship their gods.

During the 4th millennium BC Jordan witnessed early experiments in **metal-working**. At Teleilat Ghassul in the Jordan valley, a large agricultural village, the inhabitants have left us not only early copper tools, but also some of the earliest known wall paintings. Copper ores, lumps of refined copper and small objects such as awls and beads from Tell Maquss near Aqaba suggest copper working on the site. Jordan's main copper deposits at Feinan some 150km to the north were exploited throughout antiquity and were among the land's most important natural resources.

Soon man learned how to alloy copper with tin to produce bronze, a much harder and more useful metal, and easier to cast. During the **Bronze Age** (3200–1200 BC) complex, literate civilisations and empires appeared in Egypt, Mesopotamia and Anatolia and Syro-Palestine was inevitably involved in the power politics of the day. Walled cities, which appear throughout the area in the Early Bronze Age, reflect a concern with security and defence. Around 2300 BC many of these cities were violently destroyed, a catastrophe often attributed to the arrival of a new people, the Amorites. Five Early Bronze Age sites south of the Dead Sea, which were destroyed at this time, have been linked with the biblical story of Lot and tentatively identified with Sodom, Gomorrah and the other 'Cities of the Plain'. Most scholars, however, would date Abraham and Lot several centuries later.

There is little evidence for the **Middle Bronze Age** (2000–1550 BC) in Transjordan, except for some tombs from Amman, although this was an era of great city states in Syria to the north and Canaan to the west. Mari, Yamhad (Aleppo), Byblos, Megiddo and Hazor all flourished, to name but a few. This was also the age of the biblical patriarchs. With the advent of the **Late Bronze Age** (1500–1200 BC) Syro-Palestine became closely involved for the first time in the rivalries of the great powers around it: Egypt under the Pharaohs of the Eighteenth and Nineteenth Dynasties, the kingdom of Mitanni across the Euphrates in north-east Syria and the Hittites in Anatolia. Palestine and part of Syria came under Egyptian military control, local rulers took oaths of allegiance to the pharaoh and Egyptian governors regulated business between the pharaohs and their vassals. Tell as-Sa'idiyah in the Jordan valley may have been a border post of the Egyptian empire in Canaan, a large Egyptian-style public building there could have been a governor's residence.

At the end of the Bronze Age the whole of the Middle East experienced a period of turmoil. In Anatolia the Hittite empire collapsed, wealthy Syrian city states like Ugarit were destroyed and Egypt withdrew behind its own natural borders where it was threatened with attacks from the Libyans and groups of foreigners described as '**Peoples of the Sea**'. These peoples, who are shown on the move with their families and possessions on Egyptian reliefs, created havoc in the Eastern Mediterranean. Among them were the Philistines (Peleset of the Egyptians records) who settled on the south coast of Palestine and gave the land its name. This is also the period of the Exodus and the Israelite conquest of Canaan under Joshua. After passing through Sinai, Moses and the Israelites skirted Edom, through which they were refused passage, and camped in the plains of Moab opposite Jericho. Before he died and after appointing Joshua as his successor to lead the Israelites across the Jordan, Moses climbed Mount Nebo to view the Promised Land.

Some time after 1200 BC, during the **Iron Age**, the three kingdoms of Ammon, Moab and Edom arose in Transjordan, while to the west the Israelites consolidated their hold on Canaan. Israel, Ammon, Moab and Edom shared a common cultural heritage, but as each state sought to defend and expand its borders there were bitter regional struggles. Under King David Israel flourished briefly as a major military power and grew into an empire dominating almost the whole of Syro-Palestine. Ammon, Moab and Edom were reduced to vassaldom and had to pay heavy tribute. According to the Old Testament, David's General, Joab, slaughtered the entire male population of Edom except those who managed to flee to Egypt (1 Kings 11:15), then garrisoned the whole country. Northern Moab came under direct Israelite control and the Ammonites were subject to forced labour. During this period the Transjordanian states were probably not yet unified monarchies but ruled by various petty kings and tribal chieftains.

It may have been Israelite aggression which acted as a catalyst to the unification of Ammon, Moab and Edom. After King Solomon's death (c 930 BC), the empire disintegrated and in its place arose two kingdoms, Israel in the north and Judah in the south. During this period of upheaval Israelite control over Transjordan weakened, but was reasserted by Omri and his son Ahab. A certain Mesha, from Dhiban, who describes himself as king of Moab, managed to liberate his country when Ahab died (853 BC). There are accounts of the war in 2 Kings and on the Moabite stone, a black basalt stela set up in the Moabite capital Dhiban, recording Mesha's achievements. This is the longest inscription in Moabite, a Semitic language akin to Hebrew, Ammonite and Edomite, and is of major historical and linguistic importance.

TEXT OF THE MESHA STELA

I am Mesha, son of Kemosh[.], King of Moab, the Dibonite. My father ruled over Moab for thirty years, and I ruled after my father. I made this high place for Kemosh in Qarhoh...because he saved me from all the Kings and caused me to triumph over all my enemies. Omri king of Israel oppressed Moab for many days because Kemosh was angry with his land. His son succeeeded him and he also said 'I will oppress Moab'. In my days he said this but I triumphed over him and his house and Israel utterly perished for ever. Omri had taken possession of the land in Madaba and lived in it during his days and half of the days of his son, forty years; but Kemosh returned it in my days. I built Baalma'on and made the reservoir in it and I built Qaryaten. Now the men of Gad had always lived in the land of Ataroth and the king of Israel has rebuilt Ataroth for himself. But I fought against the city and took it and killed all the people of the city—a satiation for Kemosh and for Moab. I brought back from there the altar hearth of its... and dragged it before Kemosh in Qaryat. I settled in it the men of Sharon and of Maharith. Now Kemosh said to me 'Go take Nebo from Israel'. So I went by night and fought against it from dawn until noon. I took it and killed everyone—7000 native men, foreign men, native women and concubines, for I devoted it to Ashtar-Kemosh. I took from there the vessels of Yahweh and dragged them before Kemosh. Now the king of Israel had built Yazah and lived in it while he was fighting against me, but Kemosh drove him out from before me. I took from Moab 200 men, its entire unit. I took it up against Yazah and captured it to annex it to Dibon. I built Qarhoh, the walls of the parks and the walls of the acropolis. I rebuilt its gates and I rebuilt its towers. I built the palace and made the retaining walls of the reservoir for the spring inside the city. Now there was no cistern in the city so I said to all the people 'Make you every man a cistern in his house'. I dug the channels for Qarhoh with the Israelite prisoners. I built Aroer and made the highway at the Arnon, I rebuilt Bet Bamot because it had been torn down. I built Bezer—because it was in ruins— with 50 men of Dibon, for all Dibon was obedient. I ruled over hundreds in the cities which I had annexed to the country. I built Madaba, Bet Diblaten and Bet Baalma'on and I took up there the .. of the land. And Hawronen lived in it...Kemosh said to me 'Go down, fight against Mawronen.' So I went down...and Kemosh returned it in my days.

Ammon may also have regained its independence and coalesced into a united kingdom at this period. As for Edom, its people probably remained largely nomadic somewhat longer, for there is little evidence for permanent settlement before the end of the 8C BC. By the mid 9C BC the great military power of **Assyria** had appeared in the area. Assyria's advance was checked at the Battle of Qarqar on the Orontes in 853 BC, when Ammon may have fought in a coalition of 12 states in an alliance against Shalmaneser III. Victory was but temporary, for with the accession of Tiglath-Pileser III (745–727) a systematic policy of territorial expansion in the region began. Ammon, Moab and Edom all became Assyrian vassals but retained their independence in return for annual tribute. Under Assyrian suzerainty all three states enjoyed stability, prosperity and protection. Edom in particular ran a lucrative trade in various luxury items, particularly frankincense and other spices and aromatics from Arabia.

In 612 BC the Assyrian empire fell to the Medes and **Babylonians**, and the Babylonians inherited its territories in Mesopotamia and the west. For some decades Ammon, Moab and Edom remained client kingdoms, but in 582 BC Ammon and Moab were reduced to the status of a Babylonian province by Nebuchadrezzar II, who had sacked Jerusalem in 587 BC. It was probably Nabonidus who removed the Edomite monarchy in 552 BC on his way to Arabia. The Babylonian kings may have wanted direct control of the lucrative Arabian trade. In 539 BC the Persians under Cyrus took over the Babylonian empire and Transjordan became part of the vast Persian satrapy of Abarnahara ('across the river', i.e. west of the Euphrates).

Two hundred years later one of history's most brilliant generals put an end to Persian rule. In May 334 BC **Alexander of Macedon**, still only 21 years old, crossed the Dardanelles to embark on his extrordinary campaign of conquest in Asia. Following his victory in November 333 BC over the forces of the Persian king Darius III at the battle of Issus in south-east Turkey, Alexander marched south and took Syria and Palestine on his way to Egypt. Alexander's conquests were great, but his life was short—when he died in Babylon in 323 BC his empire stretched from Greece to India and comprised two million square miles. The period after his death is described as **Hellenistic**, it reflects an amalgam of Orient and Occident for, in bringing Greece to to the East, Alexander indelibly stamped the face of Greek culture on the ancient Orient. After Alexander's death, his generals struggled for power; initially Seleucus took Mesopotamia, then most of Syria, while Ptolemy held Egypt, Palestine, Lebanon and Transjordan. A bitter contest followed during which border areas in Palestine and Jordan changed hands several times until Antiochus III was finally victorious over Ptolemy III in 198 BC and the area came definitively into the Seleucid realm.

While the great powers were locked in conflict a people of Arab origin, the **Nabateans**, had moved into the former land of Edom, where they established their capital at Petra. We first hear about the Nabateans from Diodorus Siculus, who relates that in 312 BC one of Alexander's former generals, Antigonus the One-Eyed, sent his officer Athenaeus against the Nabateans, who at the time were still nomadic. It is likely that they were already famed for the wealth they had accumulated from their involvement in the Arabian trade, for Athenaeus waited until most of the Nabateans had gone to a festival, leaving their women, children and possessions on a strong, unwalled rock. He then attacked the rock, killed some of the Arabs and made off with vast quantities of myrrh, frankincense and silver. Soon the Nabateans overtook him, massacred most of his men and then sent an angry communication to Antigonus.

By the mid-3C BC, some 50 years after Antigonus' operations, the Nabateans were also established in and around the Hauran, an area of volcanic black basalt near the modern Syrian-Jordanian border, which became one of the most important and affluent regions of later Nabatea. They also moved west into the Negev and Sinai and south of Edom they inhabited the northern Hijaz region of Arabia at least as far as their city of Hegra (Meda'in Saleh) and their port of Leuke Kome on the Red Sea. At their zenith in the 1C BC and 1C AD, the Nabateans amassed immense wealth from their trading activities—bitumen from the Dead Sea for the mummification process in Egypt, silk from India and above all balsam, myrrh and frankincense from Arabia, an essential component of ritual and worship throughout the civilised world. They used their wealth to embellish their extraordinary city of Petra with its splendid monuments, watercourses and gardens.

We know of several **Hellenistic cities** in the north of Jordan such as Philadelphia (Amman), Gadara, Pella and Jarash, but their monuments have largely been obliterated by Roman and later rebuilding. An influential Hellenised Jewish family, the Tobiads, administered the Amman area under first the Ptolemies and then the Seleucids. One of their scions, Hyrcanus, created a delightful country estate with a palace in Wadi as-Sir, west of Amman, in the early 2C BC, when he judiciously fled Judaea after having quarrelled with his half-brother. By the mid-2C BC there was growing opposition to Hellenism in Judaea. When ultra-orthodox groups began riots against wealthy Hellenising Jews, Antiochus IV marched on Jerusalem, massacred 80,000 people, looted the Temple and banned the Jewish cult. Resistance soon flared into open rebellion, led by Mattathias, a priest of the **Hasmonaean family** and his five sons. After Mattathias died in 166 BC, his son Judas Maccabaeus became commander of the army. An excellent tactician, he won several victories against the Seleucids and took control of Palestine and north Jordan with most of the Hellenistic cities. Although the Seleucids eventually resumed control and Judas was killed, their empire was disintegrating. After the death of Antiochus VII in 129 BC, Judea became a more or less independent state and a Hasmonaean dynasty was established under John Hyrcanus, son of Judas' brother Simon. In 103 BC the Hasmonaean ruler Alexander Jannaeus moved eastwards and occupied most of the Hellenistic cities east of the Jordan. At the same time the Iturean Arabs were raiding from their bases in Lebanon and Upper Galilee and the inhabitants of Damascus appealed to the Nabatean king Aretas III for help. Aretas held the city for about 13 years until 72 BC when suddenly the Armenian king Tigranes swept down from the north and took it for himself, although he withdrew two years later. **Rome**, whose power had been growing steadily in the East, decided that it was time to intervene and impose law and order. In 64 BC Pompey took Damascus and subsequently annexed Syria for Rome. He 'liberated' the

Hellenistic cities and restored their autonomy, although they henceforth came under the aegis of Rome. Around this time a group of these Hellenised cities and the region where they were located became known as the Decapolis or 'ten cities'. Under the stability and prosperity fostered by the Pax Romana, Decapolis cities such as Jarash, Pella and Philadelpia grew in size and witnessed much rebuilding. Gadara suffered for a while when Augustus decided to present it to his protégé Herod the Great, but soon recovered after Herod's death in 4 BC.

Alongside the Decapolis cities the Nabateans prospered as faithful clients of Rome. Then in AD 70 their king Rabbel II moved the capital north from Petra to Bosra, possibly in response to shifting patterns of trade. Rabbel was the last king of Nabatea. On his death in 106 the Roman emperor Trajan peacefully annexed the Nabatean kingdom and created the **Province of Arabia**, thereby forging the last link in the imperial chain, completing the circle of Rome's possessions around the Mediterranean basin. Bosra became the capital of the new province. Nabatean troops were incorporated in the Roman army as *cohortes Ulpiae Petraeorum* and, in order to remove any potential for rebellion, were moved out of Arabia and distributed among the eastern provincial armies. A grand trunk road, the *Via Nova Traiana*, which ran between Bosra and the Red Sea, was completed between 111 and 114. It formed the backbone of the new province and served for the movement of traders and armies. Forts were built roughly 20km apart along the road. For Roman Arabia the 2C and early 3C was a Golden Age. Many of the grand monuments we see in Decapolis cities were built at this time and the emperor Hadrian honoured Jarash with a visit on his way to Palestine and Jerusalem. Septimius Severus, whose wife Julia Domna was Syrian, started a line of 'Syrian' emperors with a family interest in the eastern provinces. In Arabia, Severus paid particular attention to the upkeep of the extensive road network and the fortification of the Azraq area at the outlet of the Wadi Sirhan, a major transit route to the Arabian peninsula.

In response to the increased threat of raids by nomadic Arabs during the later 3C and the need to fill the vacuum created by the fall of Palmyra in the Syrian desert in 272, **Diocletian** (284–305) supervised the building of new forts including the great legionary fortress of Lejjun, a further repair of the road system and the construction of a new road, the *Strata Diocletiana*, which ran from Azraq to Damascus and on to the Euphrates. Trade routes to the Arabian peninsula took on a renewed importance with the fall of Palmyra and commercial caravans carrying myrrh, frankincense, silk and other luxury products passed in greater numbers through Roman Arabia and Palestine. The port of Aila (Aqaba) on the Red Sea flourished. As Ammianus Marcellinus writing in the 4C tells us: 'Arabia ... has among its towns some great cities, Bostra, Gerasa and Philadelphia, strongly defended by mighty walls.'

In the **early Byzantine period**, under Constantine, power shifted eastward to Constantinople (the New Rome) and Christianity became the official state religion. Palestine, the cradle of the new religion, was no longer a provincial backwater. Imperial patronage on a grand scale was extended to the region, Syrian towns prospered and many churches were built. A visit to Jerusalem by Constantine's mother Helena in 326 helped to set a trend for Holy Land pilgrimage; the Madaba area was the focus for such pilgrimage east of the Jordan. Another religious development affecting the Jordan valley was monasticism which from its beginnings in Egypt soon spread elsewhere. With official recognition and the support of rich patrons, the Church was rapidly becoming wealthy and replacing pagan and classical institutions. On the death of Theodosius in 395 the Roman empire was divided.

Traditionally this dates the start of the **Byzantine empire**. When the imperial army began to lose control at the fringes of their territory local powers emerged such as the Ghassanids, a confederation of Christian Arab tribes who held the frontier regions for the Byzantine Emperor. In the east, the Persians were locked in a power struggle with Byzantium—Antioch was sacked in 540 and Syria invaded in the 6C and again in the 613–628 war. The Byzantine victors, weakened by continuous war, were unable to take advantage of their ultimate victory in 628, while a new power was rising in the south and making its presence felt. Thus the development of **Islam** coincided with a decline in the two great empires to the north. Both had alienated the tribes on their southern borders who might otherwise have resisted the Muslim advances more strongly.

There had been waves of immigration northwards before as population pressure made itself felt—the Nabateans were an early example of this. What was new was the religious dimension. The followers of the Prophet swelled in number and **Mohammed** himself led a few raids to the north. Soon some frontier tribes were paying tribute to the Muslims, but it was not until after the Prophet's death in 632 that the Muslims pushed successfully north to *Bilad ash-Sham* (Greater Syria), having first suffered a setback at the battle of Mota' in September 629 where the three martyrs Zaid, Jafar and Abdullah lost their lives. The first blow fell on the Persians who, riven by internal power struggles and anarchy, were unable to respond effectively. Then, in 633–634, Muslim forces moved north into Syria and Palestine and, though halted at the Yarmuk, they defeated Byzantine forces at Ajnadain and Pella before besieging Damascus in 635. The emperor Heraclius raised another army on the fall of Damascus later that year only to be routed at the decisive battle of the Yarmuk in 636.

Victory abroad for the Muslims was mitigated by strife at home, following the murder of Caliph Umar and appointment of a weak successor in 644. In 656 Uthman was murdered and Ali, son-in-law of the Prophet, became caliph amid controversy. He was opposed by Mohammed's widow A'isha and later by Mu'awiya, Governor of Damascus. Civil war broke out and although Ali's forces had the upper hand both sides agreed to arbitration which probably took place at Udruh, in Jordan, in 659. In obscure circumstances Ali lost his case and the forces of the Governor of Syria, Mu'awiya, gained control. Ali himself was murdered in 661 and Mu'awiya, founder of the **Umayyad dynasty**, established his capital at Damascus. This was a significant shift of power, bringing the Muslims northwards into a new world: Jordan and Syria were now at the centre of an empire which proceeded to expand at a phenomenal rate. At its peak it extended into North Africa, Spain, India, Arabia, Persia and the Middle East. The Umayyad complexes scattered around the desert fringes in Syria and Jordan were built at this time as were seminal buildings such as the great mosque in Damascus and the Dome of the Rock in Jerusalem. The empire was tolerant of other religions and churches were still being built in Jordan in the early Islamic period.

Equally important was the **schism**, brought about by the civil war and Ali's death, between the Sunni or orthodox majority and the Shi'at 'Ali, party of Ali, or Shi'ites, as they have come to be known. In a second civil war in 680 Ali's son Hussein was killed, becoming another martyr to the Shi'ite cause. This division and other forms of religious dissent it has spawned have continued to dog the Islamic world since then. It played a part in the revolt against the Umayyads, overthrown in 750 by a new dynasty, the **Abbasids**. A new capital, the round city of Baghdad, was built by the Abbasid caliph al-Mansur in 762–63, heralding the eastward shift of power. Although the Abbasids retained the Caliphate until the Mongols arrived in 1258, after the peak of Haroun al-Rashid's reign (786–809) a slow decline set in during which local dynasties like the Persian Buyids and Samanids emerged, growing more powerful than the Caliphate which was a mere figurehead by the 10C. A new force appeared from the east with the arrival of the **Seljuk Turks** in the late 10C. They soon converted to Islam and by 1058 were governing from Baghdad as Sultans, although the Caliphate retained religious leadership. The Shi'ite Fatimids from Tunisia, with a rival Caliphate, had established themselves in Egypt in 969 and gained control over Palestine and Syria before themselves losing the region to the Seljuks by 1086. At the battle of Manzikert in 1071 the latter also defeated the Byzantine forces, even capturing the Emperor. There was trouble too from the Assassins, a fanatical offshoot of the Ismaili sect, whose leader was known as the Old Man of the Mountain. Their name derives from their supposed use of hashish, though it is now associated with their tactics. From their fastnesses in the Lebanese mountains they emerged to murder carefully selected targets.

It was at the end of this century that the **Crusaders** arrived in Palestine. Pope Urban II first called for a Crusade to reclaim Jerusalem and the holy places in 1095, and the response was excellent. Feuding between Seljuk heirs to Syria made their passage swifter and the First Crusade had won Jerusalem by 1099. At its 12C peak Outremer, as their territory was known, extended from Edessa in the north to Jerusalem and across the Jordan down to Aqaba. With the Crusaders came the Italian city state traders and trade through the Mediterranean ports flourished. The lordship of Oultre Jourdain, with its castles of Montreal (Shobak) and Karak, was a prize. It overlooked the trade and pilgrimage routes and from here the notorious Reynald de Chatillon pounced on his prey with rich reward. Concerted Muslim resistance took shape under Zengi, the *atabeg* (regent) of Mosul and Aleppo. His son and successor, Nur ad-Din, sent a young Kurdish officer called Saladin to Egypt where he deposed the Fatimid caliphs in 1171, returning to Damascus on the death of his master to take power himself. Uniting the Muslims behind him he attacked the Crusaders and dealt them a fatal blow at the battle of Hattin, near Lake Tiberias, in 1187. After this rout Crusader holdings fell like ninepins, although the garrisons at Montreal and Karak held out valiantly for a year. Richard the Lionheart recovered some territory in the Third Crusade and came close to winning back Jerusalem. In fact, for a short period Jerusalem did once more come under the Christians, but they were unable to hold out and their last outposts on the mainland fell to the Mamlukes in 1291.

After his death in 1193, Saladin's dynasty the **Ayubbids** ruled until 1250. Internal divisions developed, however, and after considerable conflict and confusion, particularly in Syria where the Ayubbids hung on, the **Mamlukes** seized power.

> The word Mamluke literally means *owned*. However, the Mamlukes were no common slaves, but a military elite. Bought as slaves from abroad, preferably of Turk or Caucasian origin, and trained as soldiers, their lack of family or tribal ties meant that their allegiance to their master was assured. Their own children could not inherit Mamluke status. Writing in the early 15C, the Frenchman Gilbert de Lannoy describes the system: 'The sultan draws his bodyguard only from among these slaves, and gives them women and castles, horses and clothing...rewarding each according to his merits... in this way one may rise to become emir of Jerusalem.'

The most famous Mamluke was **Sultan Baybars**, a Kipchak Turk from the south Russian steppes, who was bought cheaply in Aleppo market because of an eye defect. He rose to pre-eminence under the Ayubbids at a time when the region was shaken by the arrival of the Mongols, who swept into Baghdad bringing an end to the Abbasid Caliphate in 1258. The Egyptian Mamlukes under Baybars managed to withstand the Mongol onslaught, defeating them at the battle of 'Ain Jalut (Goliath's spring) near Lake Tiberias in 1260. Baybars became Sultan after the murder of the incumbent and was an energetic ruler who regained much Crusader territory and ruled till 1277 when he died, possibly poisoned by an enemy. The last Crusader possessions on the mainland fell to the Mamlukes at the end of the 13C. The Mamlukes ruled from Egypt until the 16C, but the sacking of Damascus by Timur (Tamerlane) in 1400–01 was a blow to them as was the discovery by the Portuguese explorer Vasco Da Gama of an alternative route to India via the Cape of Good Hope since much of their wealth came from trade up and down the Red Sea. But another power was already on the rise. It originated as a principality under the Seljuks in north-west Anatolia and was to be known as the **Ottoman empire** after its prince, Uthman/Osman. In 1453 Constantinople fell to the forces of Mehmet II and the last Byzantine emperor died in battle. The Ottomans now began to look southwards. The Mamlukes, who had been slow in adapting to the use of firearms, which they scorned, were no match for them. Syria and Egypt fell in 1516–17 and were to remain a part of the Ottoman empire for the next 400 years.

After a while the seemingly inevitable process of decline began again. By the 18C corruption, the bloated state and loss of trade were taking their toll and there was growing anarchy on the fringes of the empire. Turkey was becoming the 'sick man of Europe', unable to keep up with the technological advances of the rapidly developing Western European nations and their New World riches. Western European traders had long established themselves in the important towns and ports in the Middle East: the Capitulations—trading and other privileges including freedom of worship and security of property—were first granted to the French in 1535; military encroachments began with Napoleon's invasion of Egypt in 1798. It was after the departure of the French from Egypt that an Albanian called Mohammed Ali came to power there, but despite gaining a considerable degree of autonomy he was unable to break free from the chains of empire. His troops occupied Syria and Arabia for a while and caused considerable damage on their retreat. The Suez Canal opened in 1869. Steamboats plied the Red Sea and trade in the region began to recover from a long period of stagnation. Circassians, who had been persecuted in Russia for their Muslim faith, were settled in Jordan in the late 19C to farm the land and add an element of stability after unrest there. Inland the French were building railways in Syria and Palestine, and work began on the Hijaz railway. Its route was to follow the *Darb el-Haj* (Pilgrim's Way) from Damascus to Medina, but it was also an attempt to reassert Ottoman control over these areas and was completed in 1908. The use of local timber for fuel led to extensive deforestation along its route.

The turn of the century was a time of change, affecting even the most conservative societies, and it was now that Arab nationalism began to emerge as a force, prompted both by European intervention such as the British occupation of Egypt and by the general decay of the Ottoman empire. This coincided with increasing Western interest in the region following the discovery of the Iranian oil fields. The **First World War** brought the Ottoman empire into conflict with the British and French. The British in Egypt, anxious to foster what opposition they could to Turkey, entered into contact with the Emir of Mecca and offered support in the event of a revolt. The Arab uprising began in 1916 and moved northwards from the Hijaz, taking Aqaba, skirmishing along the Hijaz Railway and finally moving up to Damascus. The revolt was led by the Emir's son Feisal, famously aided on the British side by T.E. Lawrence.

After the war the British and the French had to reconcile their bilateral agreement on spheres of influence in the Middle East with Arab demands for the promises which had been made to them for independence to be honoured. Feisal first claimed Syria, which the French refused him, before becoming King of Iraq. The British ruled Palestine under a mandate which included Transjordan, but the Balfour Declaration of 1917, which had promised the Jewish people a home in Palestine, was already casting its shadow over the land and there was growing unrest between the Palestinian Arabs and Zionist immigrants. In 1921 Feisal's brother Abdullah arrived in Transjordan and was accepted as ruler there by the British who formally recognised the country as an Emirate in 1923. British officers were still in charge of its defence force, the Arab Legion, which was run from 1939 by Sir John Glubb. The country attained full independence in May 1946 when Emir Abdullah became king. In Palestine, increasing Jewish immigration, particularly after Hitler came to power, exacerbated tensions between the Arab and Jewish communities. After the Second World War the conflict flared up again. The United Nations Special Committee on Palestine proposed partition of Palestine but their plan was rejected by the Arab League. On the termination of their mandate on 15 May 1948, the British immediately withdrew. The state of Israel had been declared a few hours before and fighting broke out immediately between the Arabs and the Jews. Troops from neighbouring Arab countries fought with the Palestinians and hundreds of thousands of Palestinians fled—half a million of them to Transjordan, whose troops had managed to hold the territory now known as the West Bank. Israel, however, had gained considerable amounts of land.

In the spring of 1950 Jordan and the West Bank united to form the **Hashemite Kingdom of Jordan**. Against a background of unrest King Abdullah was assassinated at Friday prayers in the al-Aqsa mosque in Jerusalem on 20 July 1951. He was succeeded briefly by his son, King Talal, who abdicated in favour of his son, King Hussein, in 1953. The problem of Palestine has continued to cause strife in the region since then and has provoked a number of wars. The **Six Day War** of 1967, when Israel pre-empted Arab action by striking first, led to the loss of the West Bank, the Golan Heights, the Gaza Strip and Sinai. It was followed by the '**Yom Kippur' War** in 1973 when initial Egyptian successes were countered by an Israeli offensive.

In Jordan, unrest in the 1950s culminated in a couple of abortive coups and in February 1958 Jordan entered into a short-lived alliance with Iraq called the **Arab Federation**, partly in response to the United Arab Republic formed by Egypt and Syria. At an Arab League Conference in Cairo in 1964 the Palestine Liberation Organisation (PLO) was established and the first Palestine National Congress was held in Jerusalem later that year. The relationship between the PLO and Jordan was not easy—by 1970 there was considerable unrest in Jordan as a result of Palestinian incursions into Israeli-held territory from within Jordan and subsequent Israeli reprisals. PLO activities were destabilising the country: there was trouble in the refugee camps and clashes between the Jordanian army and Palestinian fedayeen (commandos). Restrictions were imposed on PLO activities culminating in its forced departure from Jordan in July 1971. In 1974 the United Nations General Assembly recognised the PLO as the 'sole legitimate representative of the Palestinian people'. Following the Camp David Agreements of 1978 a peace treaty was signed between Egypt and Israel in 1979, although the PLO had rejected the Agreements. Trouble came from another quarter in 1990–91 when Iraq, a neighbouring ally and chief supplier of oil to Jordan, invaded Kuwait. The dilemma of the Gulf War was handled skilfully by King Hussein, while coping with the return of large numbers of Palestinians from the Gulf and corresponding loss of remittances. Tourism to the region was also badly affected, but has since recovered and is booming with the signing of the historic peace agreement between Jordan and Israel on 26 October 1994. Borders are now open between the two countries. On 28 September 1995 Israel and the PLO signed a further agreement on self-rule for the major Arab towns of the West Bank.

Nineteenth-century Travellers

The 19C witnessed a boom in the number of visitors to the Holy Land, and for affluent Victorians it became a fashionable extension to the Grand Tour, spiced with a hint of the exotic and dangerous. The way was paved by a few hardy explorers who ventured far off the beaten track, rediscovering lost cities of the past and charting the desert. Foremost among them was **Jean-Louis Burckhardt** (p 243), who rediscovered Petra in 1812, but there were many others too. Even before Burckhardt **Ulrich Seetzen** had visited Jordan in 1806, finding the ruins of Jarash. Disguised variously as a beggar, 'an Arab Schech of the second rank' or a Christian Arab, he also saw Amman, Karak, Salt and Umm Qais and walked around the Dead Sea. Naval captains **Irby** and **Mangles** visited Palmyra, discovered the ruins of Iraq al-Amir and saw Petra in 1818. Two Frenchmen, **Léon de Laborde** and **Linant de Bellefonds**, visited Aqaba and Petra in 1828 and produced an illustrated account of their travels. Soon Petra was becoming quite an attraction, albeit an inaccessible one. **Richard Burton** braved extreme danger to get to Mecca disguised as a pilgrim. He was followed by the eccentric **Charles Doughty** whose travels through Jordan with the *haj*, or holy pilgrimage to Mecca, are detailed in *Arabia Deserta*.

There is no doubt that to many travel was a means of escaping from the constraints of an increasingly repressive society. As **Gertrude Bell** explained: 'To those bred under an elaborate social order, few such moments of exhilaration can come as that which stands at the threshold of wild travel.' For Victorians raised on the stories of the *Arabian Nights* and the Bible, this idea of escape combined with a romantic vision of the exotic Orient and the more familiar biblical-historical associations to produce an irresistible cocktail. The Romantics contributed to this view: **Byron**'s *Childe Harold* longed for the desert in order to forget the human race. In response, Alexander Kinglake wrily commented 'Practically, I think, Childe Harold would have found it a dreadful bore to make "the desert his dwelling place", for at all events if he adopted the life of the Arabs, he would have tasted no solitude.' Nonetheless, a yearning for the wild loneliness of the desert persisted. **Isobel Burton** saw the desert as a place 'to recover the purity of my mind...to be regenerated', and many were attracted to the Bedouin whose fierce tribal loyalties, outdoor life and masculine society appealed to the Victorian public schoolboy ethos.

After the explorers came the artists whose task, in the days before photography, was to capture the imagination of the armchair traveller. Those avid consumers of illustrated albums and accounts of exotic travel were also potential buyers of their paintings. Hotel rooms in Jordan are today almost uniformly decorated with prints of the work of **David Roberts** who produced a great number of paintings and engravings, particularly of Petra. Fewer people know that **Edward Lear** also made an expedition there to paint and wrote an amusing journal about his stay which included the customary show-down with the local inhabitants, determined to extract every last penny from the hapless artist. In 1854 the conscientious Pre-Raphaelite **Holman Hunt** painted *The Scapegoat* in the blazing heat on the western shores of the Dead Sea.

With such publicity tourists began to turn in increasing numbers to the Holy Land, braving certain hardships and accompanied by vast amounts of baggage and the inevitable Dragoman, who acted as assistant and 'interpreter'. **Alexander Kinglake**, who wrote one of the most delightful accounts of a journey in the Middle East, commented acerbically that 'the intervention of the Dragoman is fatal to the spirit of conversation'. The Holy Land was also popular with Americans—**John Lloyd Stephens**, later famous as a Central American explorer, and **Mark Twain** both published witty travel journals. **Baedeker** and **Thomas Cook** began printing guides to cater for the burgeoning tourist market. The latter was 'so clearly printed as to be read without difficulty, either on horseback or in the dim light of the tent'!

These early visitors performed a useful service for later historians and archaeologists. In their private journals and notebooks they methodically listed and described the sites they visited, many of which have since deteriorated and even disappeared. The fascination with biblical history and research in the cradle of civilisation attracted scientists and archaeologists as it became clear that a great deal remained to be discovered. The **Palestine Exploration Fund** was established in the 1860s for scientific research—at its request the Amman area was surveyed by **Captain Claude Conder** twenty years later. **Canon Henry Tristram** explored and documented both sides of the Jordan and later expeditions were undertaken by Gertrude Bell and **T.E. Lawrence**. **Selah Merrill**, archaeologist of the American-Palestine Society, travelled in Jordan between 1875 and 1877 while the Princeton Expedition under **H.C. Butler** documented sites and published valuable findings on several in Jordan. The Germans **Brünnow** and **Domaschewski** published their masterful study *Die Provincia Arabia* in 1904–09.

There were many strands to the attractions which Palestine and Transjordan held for the 19C visitor. A sense of the past and the link with the Bible history so familiar to them encouraged many to go. Looking down from above at the Dead Sea, Mark Twain explained that the panorama was 'so crowded with historical interest that if all the pages that have been written about it were spread upon its surface, they would flag it from horizon to horizon'. In many ways Petra exemplifies the appeal of the East to visitors of the last century: hidden away in the mountains of the desert, it remains remote, exotic and mysterious.

Glossary of Architectural Terms

ACROTERION. Statue plinths placed on the three points of the pediment

ADYTON. Inner sanctuary of a temple

APSE. Semicircular end or recess, especially of church or chapel

ARCADE. Arches borne on piers or columns

ASHLAR MASONRY. Large, hewn rectangular stones in horizontal courses

ATRIUM. Open court or entrance to Byzantine church; also open inner courtyard of a Roman villa

ATTIC. Storey above an entablature

ARCHITRAVE. Lowest of the three main components of the entablature; also a lintel resting on columns or piers

BAPTISTERY. Often separate part of church containing the font

BASILICA. Originally a Roman public hall, rectangular and apsed, the form adapted in Christian architecture to become an aisled church

BETYL. Literally 'House of God', aniconic representation of a god, usually in stone

BICLINIUM. Reception room with two couches

CAISSON. Decorative sunken panel in ceiling

CASTELLUM. Roman fort, diminutive of castrum, usually a small Late Roman fort with towers

CARDO. Colonnaded main street of a Roman city, usually north-south

CAVEA. Theatre auditorium

CAVETTO. Concave moulding, quarter circle in section

CELLA. Hall of a classical temple containing the cult image

CHANCEL. East end of church, reserved for the clergy and choir, site of the altar

CIBORIUM. Canopy or dome raised over the altar

CLERESTORY. Upper part of church walls above the aisle roofs, usually with windows

COLONNADE. Row of columns bearing arches or entablature

CORBEL. A projecting block which supports a horizontal beam

CORNICE. The upper element of the entablature; also moulding running along the top of a wall, arch etc

DECUMANUS. Main street of a Roman town at right angles to the cardo

DIACONICON. Byzantine architecture: room attached to a church, used to receive the offering, also as vestry, library or sacristy

DIAZOMA. Horizontal landing in a theatre auditorium

EMBRASURE. Recess for door or window; also wall opening in fortifications wider on the inside than outside

ENGAGED COLUMN. Column attached to, partly set into a wall

ENTABLATURE. Upper part of the order, consisting of architrave, frieze and cornice and resting on the columns

FINIAL. Ornament crowning pediment or apex of a building

FRIEZE. Middle part of the entablature, between the architrave and cornice

GLACIS. Sloping ground from below castle parapet downwards.

HYPOCAUST. Underground heating system allowing hot air to circulate underfloor

HYPOGEUM. Underground vault for tombs

IWAN. Middle Eastern architecture, bay, niche or reception area with pointed arch, often facing a courtyard or serving as entrance

KEEP. Also called the donjon, the main tower of a castle

LINTEL. The horizontal beam over an opening

LOCULUS. Recess carved in a tomb to place a body in

LUNETTE. Semicircular space between a doorway and its arch above, flat similarly shaped surface

MACHICOLATION. Military architecture: projecting parapet with holes below, through which to drop missiles, boiling oil etc

MAUSOLEUM. Large tomb, named after that of Mausolus at Halicarnassus.

METOPE. Plain space in a Doric frieze between two triglyphs

MIHRAB. Islamic architecture: point, usually a niche, in the qibla wall of a mosque which directs prayer to Mecca

MINARET. Tower from which the muezzin calls the faithful to prayer.

MINBAR. Islamic architecture: pulpit of a mosque, usually to the right of the mihrab.

NAOS. Shrine, or cella of temple.

NARTHEX. May be inner or outer in a Byzantine church—transverse vestibule west of nave and aisles.

NAVE. Central stretch of western section of church, usually flanked by aisles.

NYMPHAEUM. 'Sanctuary of the nymphs'—usually a fountain decorated with statuary and niches.

OBELISK. Tapering shaft of stone with pyramidal apex, especially in Egypt

ODEON. Small theatre or concert hall, sometimes roofed

OPUS SECTILE. Decorative stone or marble paving, cut and laid in geometric shapes

ORCHESTRA. In a classical theatre, the semi-circular paved area before the stage

PALMETTE. Fan-shaped, plant motif

PARADOS. Area between the stage and auditorium in a theatre which provides side access to the orchestra

PEDIMENT. Low pitched gable over a portico, door or window

PENDENTIVE. A means of supporting a dome over a square room with spandrels from the corners leading to the base of the dome

PERISTYLE. One or more rows of columns around a courtyard or building.

PIER. Square or rectangular free-standing support

PILASTER. Engaged pier which projects slightly from the wall

PORTICO. Roofed porch or walkway, often with pediment or columns

PORTICO IN ANTIS. Portico receding into a temple

PRAETORIUM. Roman military architecture, residence of Roman governor or barracks building

PRINCIPIA. Roman military architecture, headquarters of Roman camp

PRESBYTERY. Part of the church where the altar lies

PRONAOS. Porch or vestibule in front of a temple.

PROPYLAEUM. Monumental entrance gateway to temple precinct.

PROSCENIUM. Raised platform of the stage in a classical theatre.

QUADRIBURGIUM. A four-towered Roman fort.

SCENAE FRONS. Decorated façade at the back of the stage of a Roman theatre

SHAFT GRAVE. Vertical burial shaft

SOFFIT. The underside or lower surface of an architectural element

SPANDREL. Space between two arches or triangular space to the side of an arch

SQUINCH. An arch or arches placed, like a pendentive, in the corners of a room to bear a dome

STYLOBATE. Substructure beneath a colonnade. More specifically, the top step of a Greek temple

SYNTHRONON. Byzantine architecture, the clergy benches around the line of the apse

TABULA ANSATA. Decorative panel, usually containing an inscription

TEMENOS. Sacred enclosure to a temple

TETRAPYLON. Monumental four-sided arch, usually at an important intersection

THERMAE. Public baths consisting of a number of rooms of varying temperatures

THOLOS. Circular structure

TRICLINIUM. Roman dining-room with three couches

TRICONCH. Trefoil shape, e.g. of church

TRIGLYPH. Block of three vertical grooves between the metopes of a Doric frieze

TYMPANUM. Semi-circular space between lintel and arch

VAULT. Arched roof of varied design: barrel vault being the simplest, groin or cross vault consisting of intersecting barrel vaults

VESTIBULE. Entrance hall

VOLUTE. Spiral scroll on a capital

VOMITORIUM. Passageway into a theatre auditorium

VOUSSOIR. A wedge-shaped stone which forms part of an arch

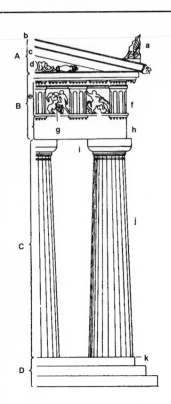

THE DORIC ORDER

A Pediment
B Entablature
C Column
D Crepidoma
a Acroterion
b Sima
c Cornice
d Tympanum
e Frieze
f Triglyphs
g Metopes
h Architrave
i Capital
j Shaft
k Stylobate

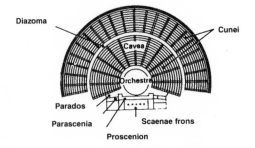

THEATRE

NABATEAN TOMB FAÇADES

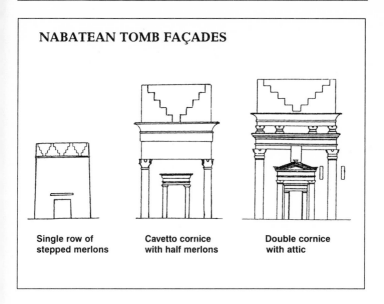

Single row of stepped merlons

Cavetto cornice with half merlons

Double cornice with attic

Primary Sources

Herodotus (484–420 BC). The 'father of History', a Greek historian from Halicarnassus in Asia Minor who travelled extensively from Egypt to Europe. His critics called him the 'Father of Lies', but his inquiring mind produced lively and well-researched works.

Polybius (c 200–after 118 BC). Greek historian who wrote a *Universal History* in 40 books on the period 220–145/6 BC. All of the first five books survive and parts of the later ones

Diodorus Siculus. Author of a 40-book world history written between 60 and 30 BC and covering the period from early times to Caesar's Gallic War (54 BC).

Strabo (64/3 BC–AD 21). Greek historian and geographer from Pontus in Asia Minor who travelled widely in the Roman East. His geography of the Roman Empire extends to 17 books and includes lively historical descriptions.

Josephus. Early Jewish historian (37–c AD 95), author of *The Jewish War* and *The Jewish Antiquities*. A commander on the rebel side in the Jewish Revolt (66–70), captured by the Romans, he then accompanied the future emperors Vespasian and Titus on their campaigns against the Jews.

Ptolemy of Alexandria. Mathematician and prolific writer (fl. AD 127–148) best known for his *Geography*. Its eight books were only superseded by the discoveries of Copernicus in the 16C.

Peutinger Table. 3–4C AD, world map, of which a 13C copy was bought by a scholar from Augsburg named Konrad Peutinger. Consisting of 11 sections of parchment, it ranges from Britain to India with the names of selected towns, roads, mountains and rivers and was intended for the use of travellers.

Eusebius (c AD 260–340). Bishop of Caesarea. Early church leader and writer on church history, author of Life of Constantine, whom he knew well.

Ammianus Marcellinus (c 330–395). A Roman officer who served in the East and subsequently wrote a *History* which only survives for the years 353–378. This is an invaluable source of information on military affairs in the East.

Notitia Dignitatum. A list of 'dignitaries' written after AD 395. It records all commanding officers of the Roman imperial army, giving their units and locations.

Select Bibliography

Bell, G. *The Desert and the Sown*. London 1907

Bienkowski, P. *The Arts of Jordan*. Alan Sutton 1991

Bowersock, G.W. *Roman Arabia*. Harvard University Press 1983

Browning, I. *Jerash and the Decapolis*. Chatto and Windus 1982

Browning, I. *Petra*. Chatto and Windus 1986

Cambridge Ancient History

Cresswell, K.A.C. *Early Muslim Architecture*. Oxford 1989

Donnan, G. *The Kings Highway*. Jordan, 1994.

Glueck, N. *Deities and Dolphins*. Cassell 1966

Grabar, O. *The Formation of Islamic Art*. Yale 1987

Hammond, P.C. *The Nabateans, their history, culture, archaeology*. Studies in Mediterranean Archaeology Vol. XXXVII, Paul Astroms Forlag, Sweden 1973

Helms, S.W. Jawa. *Lost City of the Black Desert*. London 1980.

Hourani, A. *A History of the Arab Peoples*. London 1991

Josephus. *The Jewish War*. London (Penguin) 1981

Kennedy, D. and Riley, D. *Rome's Desert Frontier from the Air*. London 1990

Kennedy, H. *Crusader Castles*. Cambridge 1994

Khouri, R. *Al Kutba Jordan Guides Series*.

Khouri, R. *Jerash: A frontier city of the Roman East*. Longman, 1986

Khouri, R. Petra: *A guide to the capital of the Nabateans*. Longman 1986

Khouri, R. *The Antiquities of the Jordan Rift Valley*. Jordan, 1988

Kinglake, A. *Eothen*. OUP, 1991.

Kraeling, C.H. *Gerasa, City of the Decapolis*. Connectictut, 1938

Lankaster Harding, G. *The Antiquities of Jordan*. London 1990

Lawrence, T.E. *Seven Pillars of Wisdom*. Penguin 1962

Lewis, B. *The Arabs in History*. Oxford 1993

Maalouf, A. *The Crusades through Arab Eyes*. London1984

Mackenzie, J. *The Archaeology of Petra*. British Academy Monographs in Archaeology No. 1, Oxford 1990

Mellaart, J. *The Neolithic of the Near East*. London, 1975

Michell, G. *Architecture of the Islamic World*. London, 1987

Miller, F. *The Roman Near East 31BC–AD337*. London, 1993

Miller, F. *The Roman Empire and its Neighbours*. New York, 1981

Parker, T. *Romans and Saracens*. American Schools of Oriental Research 1986

Piccirrillo, M. *The Mosaics of Jordan*. American Center of Oriental Research 1993.

Runciman, S. *A History of the Crusades*. 3 vols. London 1990

Salibi, K. *The Modern History of Jordan*. London 1993

Studies in the History and Archaeology of Jordan Vols 1–IV. Jordan

Talbot Rice, D. *Islamic Art*. Thames & Hudson, London 1975

Twain, M. *Innocents Abroad*

Ward-Perkins, J.B. *Roman Imperial Architecture*. The Pelican History of Art, Penguin 1981 and 1987

Wilson, J. *Lawrence of Arabia*. William Heineman Ltd 1989

AMMAN AND AROUND AMMAN

Most visitors who travel to Jordan by air arrive in **AMMAN**, capital of the Hashemite Kingdom and a vibrant, modern city. On the Transjordanian plateau, over 800m above sea level, Amman has cold winters and summers which are hot and dry, although the heat may be tempered by a cool breeze, especially in the evenings. In 1921, when Amman became capital of the Emirate of Transjordan, the city spread over seven hills; in recent decades the conurbation has expanded to cover 20 hills or more and houses almost half of Jordan's population. Amman is a clean city, with wide boulevards and predominantly whitish buildings, either of concrete or faced with the local limestone, especially in the wealthier areas, in compliance with municipal law. Except in the centre it is a city for driving around rather than walking. Areas in West Amman are located in relation to a broad thoroughfare with 'circles' (roundabouts) numbered from 1st to 8th at major intersections. Most roundabouts have recently been removed in favour of traffic lights and the crossroads renamed, but locals still refer to First, Second, Third Circle etc. Although the impression is of a modern town, Amman has a long history and a number of ancient monuments and museums well worth visiting. It is also an ideal centre for excursions in northern and eastern Jordan and the Jordan Valley and offers the visitor a wide choice of good hotels and restaurants.

History

Amman's long and varied history begins over 9000 years ago, when a people with a Pre-Pottery Neolithic culture settled at 'Ain Ghazal in Wadi Zarqa, alongside the modern Amman–Zarqa road. What began as a small hamlet grew into one of the largest Neolithic settlements so far discovered in the Near East. Its inhabitants were farmers, who lived in houses of several rooms with plastered and painted walls, and buried their dead beneath the floors or courtyards. Some of the oldest known statues in the world come from 'Ain Ghazal, human figures up to 90cm high made of lime plaster. During the Bronze Age (3200–1200 BC) Jabal al-Qal'a (citadel hill) in central Amman was fortified for the first time, with a wall and glacis (c 1800 BC), establishing a long tradition. Bronze Age tombs have been found near the citadel and elsewhere. A Late Bronze Age temple (c 1300 BC) on the old Amman airport site yielded a rich selection of finds including Mycenean and Cypriot pottery and Egyptian scarabs reflecting commercial links with other areas of the Eastern Mediterranean. Hundreds of fragments of burnt bones, mostly human, may suggest human sacrifice. Some time after 1200 BC Amman was settled by the Ammonites, who according to biblical tradition were descended from Abraham's nephew Lot (p 128). They made the city their capital, calling it Rabbath Ammon, the 'Great City of the Ammonites', also described in the Bible as 'the city of waters' (2 Sam.12:27). Rabbath Ammon is mentioned frequently in the Old Testament, for the Ammonites were often in conflict with their western neighbours. In the early 10C BC King David and his general Joab captured the city, and the Ammonites, who put up a fierce resistance, were subjected to forced labour (2 Sam.12:26–31). Uriah the Hittite, one of Joab's soldiers, was killed in the front line of battle, placed there at David's express request. David coveted Uriah's very beautiful wife Bathsheba and had already

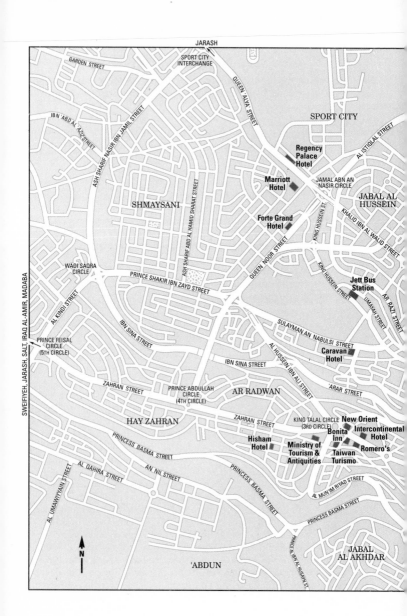

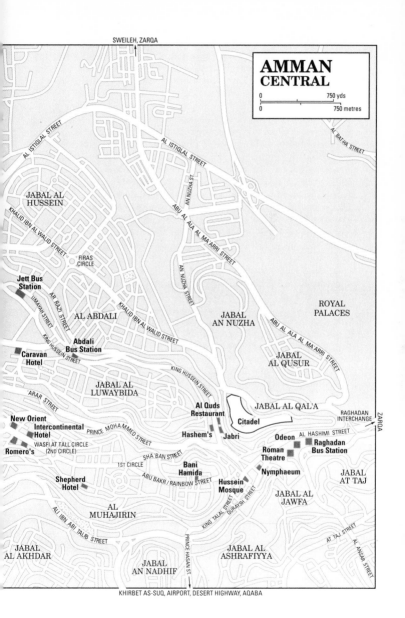

SWEILEH, ZARQA

AMMAN
CENTRAL

0		750 yds
0		750 metres

AL BATHA STREET

AL ISTIQLAL STREET

AL ISTIQLAL STREET

ABU AL ALA AL MA'ARRI STREET

AN NUZHA ST

KHALID IBN AL WALID STREET

JABAL AL
HUSSEIN

FIRAS
CIRCLE

AN NUZHA STREET

Jett Bus
Station

UMAYAH STREET

AR RAZI STREET

KHALID IBN AL WALID STREET

AL ABDALI

JABAL
AN NUZHA

ROYAL
PALACES

ABU AL ALA AL MA'ARRI STREET

KING HUSSEIN STREET

Abdali
Bus Station

Caravan
Hotel

JABAL
AL QUSUR

JABAL AL
LUWAYBIDA

KING HUSSEIN STREET

'ARAR STREET

JABAL AL QAL'A

RAGHADAN
INTERCHANGE

ZARQA

Al Quds
Restaurant

Citadel

New Orient
Intercontinental
Hotel

PRINCE MOHAMMED STREET

Hashem's

Jabri

Odeon

AL HASHIMI STREET

Raghadan
Bus Station

Romero's

WASFI AT TALL CIRCLE
(2ND CIRCLE)

1ST CIRCLE

SHA'BAN STREET

Bani
Hamida

Roman
Theatre

Nymphaeum

JABAL
AT TAJ

Shepherd
Hotel

ABU BAKR / RAINBOW STREET

Hussein
Mosque

JABAL AL
JAWFA

AL
MUHAJIRIN

ALI IBN ABI TALIB STREET

KING TALAL STREET

QURAYSH STREET

AT TAJ STREET

AL ANSAR STREET

JABAL
AL AKHDAR

JABAL
AN NADHIF

PRINCE HASAN ST.

JABAL AL
ASHRAFIYYA

KHIRBET AS-SUQ, AIRPORT, DESERT HIGHWAY, AQABA

committed adultery with her (2 Sam. 11). Later she became one of David's wives and mother of Solomon (2 Sam.12:24). By the mid 9C BC Ammon had regained its independence from Israel and the citadel was refortified. Now the great military power of Assyria appeared in Syro-Palestine. Twelve states including Israel and perhaps also Ammon allied against Shalmaneser III at the battle of Qarqar on the River Orontes in 853 BC. Although the Assyrians claimed victory their advance was temporarily checked. Just over a century later, however, Ammon and the other Transjordanian kingdoms became Assyrian vassals, but retained their independence in return for annual tribute and occasional labour and military service. Under the Pax Assyriaca Ammon enjoyed stability and prosperity, but with Assyria's successors, the Babylonians, the situation changed. In 582 BC Nebuchadrezzar II reduced Ammon to the status of a Babylonian province and when the Persians took over the Babylonian empire in 539 BC it became part of the Persian satrapy of Abarnahara ('across the river', i.e. west of the Euphrates).

Alexander the Great occupied Syro-Palestine in 332 BC and after his death nine years later the former kingdom of Ammon became a hotly contested border region as the generals struggled for power. First it was occupied by Ptolemy, then taken by Seleucus and reconquered by Ptolemy II Philadelphus, who rebuilt Rabbath Ammon and renamed it Philadelphia. An aristocratic family, the Tobiads, related to some of the influential nobility in Jerusalem, administered the Amman region for the Ptolemies. They continued to do so for the Seleucids, whose king Antiochus III incorporated Palestine and Transjordan into his empire after defeating Ptolemy III in 198 BC. During the later 2C BC and early 1C BC Syro-Palestine was in considerable turmoil. Philadelphia was probably occupied by the Nabateans for a short time and local 'tyrants' like Zeus Cotylas and his son Theodorus may have been Nabatean vassals. Pompey created the Roman Province of Syria in 63 BC to restore order to the region. Philadelphia retained local autonomy under the aegis of the governor of the new province. After the annexation of Nabataea by Trajan in 106 it became part of the Province of Arabia. Under Roman rule Philadelphia flourished as the southernmost of the great classical cities of the Decapolis (p 74). Situated on the Via Nova Traiana (p 174), the city benefited from trade and commerce along the great highway and was embellished with colonnaded streets, plazas, temples, theatres and other public buildings. A monumental stairway connected the lower city to the acropolis which was surrounded by fine fortifications.

Philadelphia was the seat of the bishopric of Petra and Philadelphia during the Byzantine period and boasted a number of churches. Like the rest of Transjordan it passed in 635 to Arab rule. Under the Umayyads (p 86) (661–750), who ruled from Damascus, the city became known as Amman, thus retaining part of the name of the ancient Ammonite capital. As capital of the Balqa district it was an important centre of administration and the pala-tial complex built on the citadel was probably the residence of a governor. With the fall of the Umayyads and the shift of power eastwards to Baghdad under the Abbasids, Amman's fortunes began to wane. Abandoned by the Mamluke period, it was described by the Arab author Abu al-Fida c 1321 as 'a very ancient town ... ruined before the days of Islam ... there are great ruins here and the river az-Zarqa flows through them'. In Roman times this river, known locally as Seil Amman, had been covered with a series of barrel vaults and paved. Merrill, archaeologist of the American Palestine Exploration Society, who visited Amman in 1876–77, noted some evidence of this. In his day the stream was well stocked with fish: 'They have yellow bellies and are very slimy compared with fish in our American streams. I tried to shoot some but did not kill any. The Arabs killed quite a string of these fish with stones—a method of fishing I never heard of before'.

Not long after Merrill's visit the Ottomans settled Circassian emigrants in Amman (1878) and the city's fortunes began to revive. Since becoming the capital first of the Emirate of Transjordan (1921) and then of the Hashemite Kingdom of Jordan (1947) Amman has continued to grow, and is now one of the most important cities in the region.

Central Amman

Amman's antiquities are spread over a wide area, but the main monuments are downtown, on and below Jabal al-Qal'a (citadel hill), the best place to begin a city tour. Be sure you have transport up the hill, otherwise it is a long climb!

CITADEL

Jabal al-Qal'a, at the heart of ancient and modern Amman, rises 850m above sea level and comprises three main terraces. On the two upper terraces, which together form the acropolis of the ancient city, there are several buildings of interest and an archaeological museum, the lower terrace has no visible remains except some sections of wall. Although archaeological investigations have shown that the citadel was inhabited from the Neolithic period (pottery sherds from the lower terrace) and fortified by the Middle Bronze Age, extant remains are mainly Roman, Byzantine and early Islamic.

On reaching the top of the hill the first area on the left encloses the **Roman Temple of Heracles**, a demigod and one of the most popular Greek heroes, who came from Tiryns and performed his 12 labours for the king of Argos. In fact it is not certain that the temple was dedicated to Heracles. Identification is based on the frequent occurrence of the demigod on Roman coins of the city and two fragments (an elbow and a hand) of a colossal statue found in the precinct, which would have been about 9m (30ft) high. These are now exhibited before the museum entrance. A fragmentary inscription dates the temple to the reign of Marcus Aurelius (169–180). It was a massive building on a podium, facing east, with a broad stair-case leading up to a colonnaded pronaos. Three columns have been re-erected. Inside the cella an area of bare rock is exposed, probably a sacred rock of great antiquity incorporated into the Roman building. It is believed there was an Iron Age temple or altar on the site in the 9C BC, dedicated to the Ammonite god Milcom. Pottery found there goes back to the Early Bronze Age (c 3000 BC).

A rectangular temenos enclosed the temple, its main gate in the south-eastern corner at the top of a monumental stairway which connected the acropolis with the lower city. There are no remains of the staircase, but an excellent view from the gateway of the city below. Note Amman's splendid Roman theatre, the smaller odeon and the nymphaeum further west. Looking west from here you can also see a well-preserved section of the citadel's **fortifications.** Here the Roman wall was repaired in the early Islamic period—the tower is Abbasid architecture, otherwise rare in Jordan.

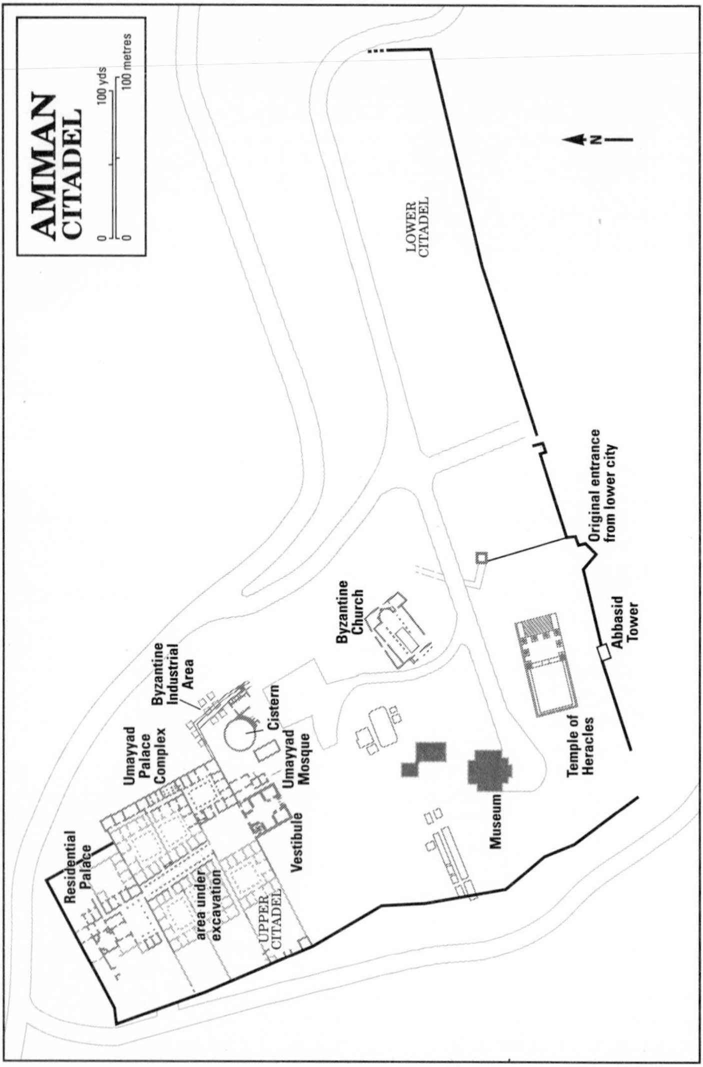

AMMAN CITADEL

100 yds
100 metres

N

LOWER CITADEL

Original entrance from lower city

Byzantine Industrial Area

Byzantine Church

Umayyad Palace Complex

Cistern

Umayyad Mosque

Residential Palace

Vestibule

area under excavation

UPPER CITADEL

Museum

Temple of Heracles

Abbasid Tower

Across the road from the Temple of Heracles and slightly further east is a small 5C–6C **Byzantine Church**. It is an ordinary single-apsed basilica, slightly irregular in plan, with two rows of columns, some re-erected, separating the nave and aisles. Several column bases and other building blocks were reused from the temenos of the neighbouring Roman temple. A mosaic pavement of geometric designs, quatrefoil rosettes and florets covered the nave, the aisles were paved with stone slabs. In the Umayyad period, probably after the collapse of the church in an earthquake, the buildings were reused.

Detail of the vestibule in the Umayyad Palace, Amman

Follow the path north-west of the church past recently excavated Byzantine buildings to a huge circular **cistern**, 5m deep and 16m across. It was built under the Umayyads, with much reuse of older materials including column drums and capitals in the inner face. Rainwater was channelled to the cistern from the roof of the vestibule of the palace complex to the west. Between the cistern and palace there is a small **Umayyad mosque** and north of the cistern was a **Byzantine industrial area** which included an olive press.

Dominating the northern terrace of the citadel is an extensive **Umayyad Palace Complex**. It incorporates an earlier **Roman temenos** comprising an artificial platform, where there may have been a temple, and a walled precinct bisected by a north-south street. Probably the Umayyad complex was the residence of the governor of Amman (720–750) and seat of provincial administration. It continued in use in the Abbasid (750–969) and Fatimid (969–1171) periods. Of the standing remains the most prominent is the entrance vestibule preceded by a courtyard to the south. Inside it has the form of a Greek cross, a central space which may have been domed, and four equal arms, two barrel vaulted and two with semi-domes. Decoration is typical of the period: geometric and foliate patterns and blind arches with dogtooth mouldings framed by engaged colonettes. Originally the entire interior was stuccoed and painted; in places traces of paint can still be seen. Two corner chambers accessed from the south arm may have been guardrooms or waiting rooms, for we can imagine that a visitor's credentials were thoroughly checked here before he could proceed further into the palace. Beyond the vestibule there is a second courtyard, then the colonnaded street, originally Roman, which leads to the main residential complex on the northern edge of the citadel. Flanking the courtyard and street are typical Islamic 'bayts', groups of rooms around a central court forming individual units. While the area to the east of the street has been well cleared, excavations are still underway on the other side. East of the 'bayts' note a niche and part of the wall of the earlier Roman temenos.

At the end of the colonnaded street a door passes through the north wall of the Roman precinct, decorated with a row of niches, to the third courtyard and

Umayyad residential palace. Much of this area is still to be cleared, though work is progressing fast. The main feature is a large hall with side doors, originally barrel-vaulted, leading to a room of cruciform plan with doors in the four arms, which was probably domed. In all likelihood this was a diwan or throne room in the Sassanid Persian tradition, where the Umayyad governor would have held audience. Step outside the diwan to look over the north end of the citadel. A massive retaining wall of the Roman period, with buttresses at the corners, supports the artificial platform on which the Islamic palace was built. Down below is the opening, covered with a grating, of a large underground reservoir which could be reached through a tunnel in the fortification walls. It is believed to be Iron Age or earlier in date and may be the cistern mentioned by Polybius who describes how the

Limestone statue of Yerah 'Azar, king of Ammon,
Archaeological Museum, Amman

Seleucid ruler Antiochus III captured Rabbath Ammon in 218 BC by blocking the tunnel which gave access to the town's water supply.

Follow the path south of the Umayyad palace to Amman's **Archaeological Museum** (open 9.00–17.00 or 10.00–16.00 on official holidays, closed Tuesdays). Though small, this museum houses a wealth of interesting objects from all over Jordan and should not be missed. Follow the arrows to the right on entry for a 'chronological' tour. Prehistoric finds include Pre-Pottery Neolithic statues from 'Ain Ghazal, plastered skulls from Jericho, a child burial from Chalcolithic Teleilat Ghassul, a Middle Bronze Age burial with grave goods from Jericho and a delightful reconstructed box inlaid with carved ivories from Middle Bronze Age levels at Pella. Showcases around the walls on the other side of the room contain Ammonite and Moabite objects including a limestone statue of Yerah 'Azar, king of Ammon, holding a lotus flower, found on the Amman citadel. He bears the distinction of being the only Ammonite king whose portrait we have. A larger statue wearing a conical crown with side plumes may represent Milcom, the Ammonite national deity. Roman and Byzantine objects from many different sites fill other showcases. Of the sculpture on display note two capitals from a Byzantine church at Aila (Aqaba) showing the soldier saints Theodorus and Longinus and a marble bust of Tyche of Amman wearing a crown in the shape of a hexagonal fortress. It was discovered near the temple of Heracles but perhaps came originally from the lower citadel where she is thought to have had a shrine. A room at the back of the museum contains a unique Chalcolithic wall painting from Teleilat Ghassul depicting a group of people in front of a shrine and Nabatean sculpture from Khirbet Tannur and Petra. Atargatis as vegetation goddess, her face and body adorned with leaves and surrounded by swirls of acanthus, vines, figs and pomegranates is the centrepiece. Alongside is a room with fragments of the Dead Sea scrolls and the Balaam text from Deir Alla. In two side rooms off the main room note in particular the 12C BC Balu' stela, which may represent a local Moabite prince or chief between a god and goddess, an inscribed capital of a water gauge recording the building of the cistern at Muwaqqar in 723 and several anthropoid clay coffins from Amman and Dhiban similar to those associated with the Philistines on the southern coast of Palestine.

ROMAN LOWER TOWN

Much of ancient Philadelphia has been obliterated by modern Amman, but painstaking archaeological investigations are gradually revealing the plan of the great Classical city. Topography dictated the layout, which was confined by the two narrow valleys running south and west of the acropolis. Two major colonnaded streets formed the backbone of the town centre, the **Decumanus Maximus**, running more or less south-west to north-east between the citadel and the Seil Amman and describing a curve in line with the stream, and the **Cardo**, which branched off the decumanus at right angles to follow the side valley west of the citadel. Amman city centre's two main streets now overlie the ancient thoroughfares. Of Philadelphia's remaining monuments, the best preserved is the **Theatre**, mostly built into the hillside with some blocks of seating at the sides supported on vaults. Completed in 169–177, under Marcus Aurelius, it is the largest theatre in Jordan and could accommodate an audience of almost 6000. Oriented 9° west of north it guaranteed the least possible sunlight in the spectators' eyes. Access to the seating was via grand staircases at the sides of the building and vaulted passageways.

When Merrill was in Amman in 1877 the theatre was in a sorry state: 'I spent a part of one night in the great theatre, when the moon was shining with all its intensity. The sense of desolation was oppressive. Kings, princes, wealth and beauty once came here to be entertained, where now I see only piles of stones, owls and bats, wretched fellahin and donkeys, goats and filth...' Now the lovely building has been cleared, small sections of the auditorium and the stage have been rebuilt and today the theatre with its excellent acoustics is once more used for performances, usually music and dance. Above the auditorium, in the centre, is a small shrine flanked by decorative niches. Its dedication is unknown. Athena has been suggested on the basis of the discovery of a broken statue of the goddess during clearance of the orchestra.

Rooms on either side of the stage house two small museums. To the left as you enter is the **Jordanian Museum of Popular Traditions**. Three rooms display a lovely collection of Jordanian and Palestinian costumes and accessories—headdresses, bags and jewellery. There is an interesting selection of different stones carried or worn by the bedouin for their curative properties or power to prevent

Amman Nymphaeum from East of Jordan *by Selah Merrill*

illness. Down steps right of the entrance is a room of mosaics found at Jarash (mostly from the Church of Elias, Mary and Soreg) and Madaba (mainly from the Church of the Virgin Mary).

Exhibits in the **Amman Folklore Museum** opposite include figures in traditional costume performing various activities, musical instruments, weapons and a bedouin tent. Opening hours for both museums are 9.00–17.00 or 10.00–16.00 on official holidays, closed Tuesdays.

In antiquity Philadelphia's **Forum** was in front of the theatre where now there are the remains of a colonnade and a public square. Among the largest of Roman fora (c 7620 square m) it was bordered by porticoes on three sides and the curve of the stream and decumanus to the north. To make sure the forum was kept dry the area was artificially raised above the level of the stream, provided with a drainage system of terracotta piping below the pavement and probably connected to the decumanus by bridges. Doughty in the 1880s saw 'a Roman bridge of one great span' which has since disappeared. Alongside the east portico of the forum a small free-standing **Odeon** with a seating capacity of around 500 is being reconstructed. It belongs to the 2C and was probably covered over.

From the area of the forum and theatre there is a good view of the citadel hill with the newly erected columns of the Temple of Heracles on the skyline. North of the decumanus at the foot of the citadel, a short distance west of the forum, there was once a **Propylaeum** which preceded the monumental stairway up to the temple precinct. Although there is now no trace of this building, its remains were recorded by several early travellers. It seems to have been a triple-arched gate, highly decorated with columns, pilasters, niches and statuary.

Further south-west along the decumanus, just before the intersection with the cardo, was Philadelphia's **Nymphaeum**, at the junction of the Seil Amman and a branch stream which flowed beneath the fountain. Currently under excavation, this was a truly monumental building. It was two storeys high and shaped like a half octagon, with three large exedrae, of which two remain, flanked by smaller niches. A colonnade of Corinthian order ran in front of the façade. Like the Jarash nymphaeum it was highly decorated, the façade was faced with 18 different marbles and statues filled the niches. A basin has been cleared in front of the north exedra. In the area of the nymphaeum the Seil Amman, which is now channelled through a culvert beneath the road, was sealed off on both sides with a retaining wall, covered with barrel vaults and paved. Remains of the vaulting was recorded by several early travellers.

Here by the nymphaeum you are in the heart of downtown Amman with its busy streets and markets. Take time to stroll around the colourful suqs to absorb the atmosphere of a modern Middle Eastern city. Note Amman's older houses covering the steep hillsides, which can only be reached by steps. Not far from the nymphaeum is the **Hussein mosque**, believed to date originally from the 7C but rebuilt earlier this century by Emir Abdullah and recently restored by King Hussein. If you are feeling hungry head for the junction of King Hussein and Prince Mohammad Streets—ask for *Hashem's*, up a side alley, a simple place with a

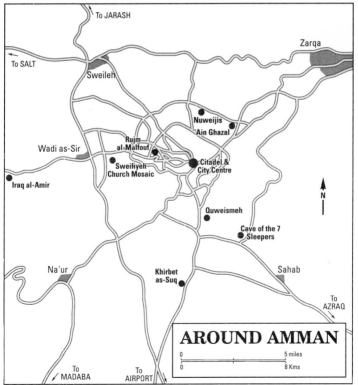

To JARASH

Zarqa

To SALT

Sweileh

Nuweijis

'Ain Ghazal

Wadi as-Sir

Rujm al-Malfouf

Sweifiyeh Church Mosaic

Citadel & City Centre

Iraq al-Amir

N

Quweismeh

Cave of the 7 Sleepers

Na'ur

Khirbet as-Suq

Sahab

To AZRAQ

AROUND AMMAN

| 0 | | 5 miles |
| 0 | | 8 Kms |

To MADABA

To AIRPORT

few tables outside which has some of the best snacks in town, or nearby *Al Quds* restaurant which serves good, standard food but no alcohol. A few doors down *Jabri*'s sells delicious sweets and pastries.

West Amman

Take the main road from the city centre towards Sweifiyeh. Between Third and Fourth Circles, south of the road and adjacent to the Department of Antiquities Offices, **Rujm Al-Malfouf** is the most accessible of several so-called Ammonite towers in and around the city. It is a round building, 20m in diameter, constructed of large, rough blocks with a rubble infill and has a series of rooms on at least three storeys, one of which is underground. An associated walled structure is adjacent to the tower. Although only 1C–3C Roman pottery has been found in the tower, many scholars believe it was first built in the 7C BC. Current excavations should help to clarify the problem.

Over 20 such massive stone towers, some round, others rectangular, have been recorded in the Amman region. Several have been excavated and yielded 7C–6C BC Iron Age pottery as well as later Hellenistic, Roman, Byzantine and even Umayyad wares. Some are sited on hilltops, others on sloping terraces at the heads of wadis with good views to the opposite bank and the next valley. Although opinions differ, it is generally assumed that most were built towards the end of the Ammonite kingdom and may have served as watch towers and signal stations integrated into a regional security system.

AMMON

Ancient Ammon, which extended from the Zarqa river (biblical Jabbok) to the plain of Madaba, is the least well known of the three Iron Age kingdoms which arose east of the Jordan sometime after 1200 BC. Its capital Rabbath Ammon, fortified with a thick stone wall, was on the site of modern Amman. Subject to Israel under David and Solomon, Ammon may have regained its independence in the 9C and allied for a while with Israel and other states against the threat of Assyria from the east. In the 8C, with Moab and Edom, it became an Assyrian vassal state, but was allowed to retain its independence on payment of tribute. Several Ammonite kings are known from biblical and Assyrian sources and one of a number of charming Ammonite statuettes depicts King Yerah 'Azar, son of Zakir, son of Sanipu' holding a lotus flower, a royal attribute. Ammonite statuary shows clear Egyptian influence, several figures wear a conical crown with side pieces, reminiscent of the Egyptian atef-crown usually borne by gods. Ammon's national god was Milcom, who had a temple in Rabbath Ammon, perhaps on the same site as the later Temple of Heracles on the citadel. According to the Old Testament, when King David captured the city 'he took the crown off Milcom's head; it weighed one talent of gold, and in it was set a precious stone which went on David's head instead' (2 Sam.12:20). Ammon and Milcom were constant targets for the wrath of the Old Testament prophets: 'I shall make the war cry ring out for Rabbah-of-the-Ammonites. She will become a desolate mound ... Shriek, daughters of Rabbah! Wrap yourself in sackcloth, raise the dirge, run to and fro among the sheep-pens! For Milcom is going into exile with all his priests and princes' (Jer. 49:2–3). In a way Jeremiah's prophecy came true, for like Israel and Judah Ammon was absorbed into the Babylonian empire in the 6C BC and was never again an independent kingdom.

A short distance from the Amra Hotel is the **Sweifiyeh Church Mosaic**, one of the few mosaics to be seen in Amman. Coming from the centre of town turn left at Sixth Circle, take the first right, then left and then the fourth right. The church, now enclosed for protection, was discovered in the garden of a house in 1969. It is open 8.00–14.00 and closed on Fridays.

Only the left hand part of the mosaic, dated to the second half of the 6C, remains. By the entrance and outside the border is a tree with two facing peacocks, symbols of the immortal soul. Vine tendril roundels enclose typical scenes: a boy with a laden donkey, a bearded man with a camel, a hunter and ibex, archer and horse and eagle and antelope. At the top is part of a two-line inscription in Greek including a reference to Bishop Thomas. The wide border is divided into smaller roundels containing a variety of animals, including hare, deer and birds. Human faces peer out from the foliage in the corners.

South Amman

Take the road to the airport past Al Wahdat refugee camp and Middle East Circle and a short distance after the Azraq turning you reach the suburb of **Khirbet as-Suq**. Little remains of what was probably originally a sizeable Romano-Byzantine settlement. By the roadside on the left (east) is a 2C–3C Roman mausoleum, now partly below street level. Steps lead down to an arched entrance, not bonded to the main structure. Open now to the sky, the mausoleum was once covered with a barrel vault. Its walls have an upper cornice and are over 1m thick. Heading back north towards Amman, take a left turn up the hill less than 1km from the mausoleum towards a red and white pylon. Near the pylon is a Roman temple later converted into a church. It is fenced around and the gate locked but you can see in from the outside. Two columns with Ionic capitals are still standing, others lie on the ground. When the building was excavated traces of a mosaic floor were found.

Continue on the main road to Amman and 2km after the Azraq turning bear right towards Sahab for c 3km **Cave of the Seven Sleepers**. Ask for Ahl al-Kahf as the area is locally known. According to legend seven Christian youths who were persecuted for their faith hid in the cave and then fell asleep for hundreds of years before miraculously awaking, a story also given in the Koran, Sura 18. Other sites, including Ephesus, lay claim to this anecdote.

On the hillside west of the modern mosque is the tomb of the Seven Sleepers. Subsequently a church was built over it which was later converted to a mosque. The column bases of the nave are still clear although the mosque entrance was made in the east end, presumably where the apse was. The *mihrab* of the mosque is over the tomb; later the area in front of the cave entrance was enclosed and a *mihrab* niche incorporated into the south wall. Over the narrow doorway to the tomb itself are five medallions, the left two badly weathered and the central one with a Greek cross. On each side there are semi-engaged columns, a shell niche and a capital without a column between them. Immediately inside the cave are two arched recesses with three sarcophagi on each side. A hole in one on the right reveals a few bones inside. Pass under an arch to the inner chamber—on the right a shaft leads up to the church above. The sarcophagi are decorated with carved motifs: egg and dart and bead and reel patterns surround the arch.

Return to the Amman–airport road and some 2km north of the Sahab junction, in the suburb of **Quweismeh**, there is a well-preserved Roman mausoleum in a garden. Look for the blue Department of Antiquities sign outside and knock for the guardian who should be around, at least in the morning, to let you in. Quweismeh mausoleum is built of well tooled limestone blocks, most with a central boss, the walls are plain on the outside with an upper cornice. Note the lion's head spout which drained rainwater from the roof on the west side. Steps lead up to the entrance where there are two column bases. Over the door is a 'window' with a large circular opening surrounded by four smaller ones. Inside the chamber, blackened by smoke, is barrel vaulted, with weathered writing on the lower two courses of the vault. There are still four sarcophagi inside, and outside the building, in the garden, are rock-cut graves.

North Amman

For **Qasr Nuweijis**, Amman's finest Roman mausoleum, head north out of the city, take the main highway to Zarqa and the site is a short distance south of the road near the Tariq intersection. Qasr Nuweijis is built on a podium and its walls, of well-dressed limestone blocks, stand for the most part to their original height. Pilasters at the corners have Ionic capitals, above which are a series of cornices decorated variously with line patterns, egg and dart and acanthus with people and animals. Inside the mausoleum is cruciform in plan with a central dome supported on arches and pendentives. The keystone is carved with a rosette. There are windows in each arm of the cross and four loculi in the walls. Outside, the dome is crowned with an urn finial.

To Iraq al-Amir

17km west of Amman in the lovely Wadi as-Sir lies the Hellenistic palace called **Qasr al-Abd** (Fortress of the Servant) at the site known as Iraq al-Amir (Caves of the Prince). There is a fine drive through the valley to get there which also passes a couple of other sites of interest on the way.

From Eighth Circle follow signs to Wadi as-Sir, a town once settled by Circassians. Continue through the town and beyond it. After a sign to Iraq al-Amir a track leads off to the left just before the road crosses the wadi. Follow it for 500m and then scramble up the slope to the curious building called **ad-Deir** (the monastery), the façade of which is visible across the valley from the road. Carved into the rock with a ground level entrance on the right and various windows, the cave inside is a mass of small triangular niches which may either have served to hold candles or as a dovecote. Ledges divide the two interconnected chambers into storeys.

Return to the road and continue on, noting the remains of an aqueduct on the right immediately after crossing the wadi. The valley is beautiful, full of olive, fig and pomegranate trees, while cypress and oleanders grow along the stream. After 2km, just past a fork in the road, look for a mosque up on the right. Near a large oak tree below it is a blocked cave in which part of a pedimented façade is visible. A further 4km down the road on the right is the cave system which gave the site the name of **Iraq al-Amir**. There are a number of smoke blackened caves on two levels, the upper storey connected by a ledge. Two of them bear the Hebrew inscription TBWH (Tobiah) near the entrance, providing the link with the Tobiad dynasty mentioned in the Old Testament. The Jewish historian Josephus describes these caves, adding that their entrance was made deliberately narrow so as to make them easier to defend from within. Shortly after this point the road descends and there is a good view of the **Qasr al-Abd** below.

One of the leopard fountains on Qasr al-Abd

History

The site was occupied long before the Tobiad family built their palace there: archaeologists have found traces of Early Bronze Age settlement on the mound to the north-east now partly covered by the modern village. Excavations have also produced evidence of 11C BC occupation before a long gap until 3C–2C BC, and some speculate that this was Ramath-Mizpeh of the Bible. Its present name Qasr al-Abd (Fortress of the Servant) may come from a reference in Neh. 2 10:19 to Tobiah, the servant; in the 6C BC a certain Tobiah was appointed governor of Ammon. Josephus gives a very accurate description of the palace 'of white stone to the very roof ... animals of a prodigious magnitude engraven upon it ... round a great and deep canal of water' (Ant. XII, 4). The building is important as a rare example of Hellenistic architecture in Jordan. The Tobiad family were supporters of the Ptolemies and Hyrcanus, son of Joseph, was accordingly sent to Egypt in his youth. On his return some time around the end of the 3C or early 2C BC he built this palace, then called Tyros, choosing to keep a safe distance from the power struggle between the Ptolemies and the Seleucids. This name Tyros survives in the modern name Wadi as-Sir. Work on the palace may have stopped on the death of Hyrcanus in 175 BC. It suffered earthquake damage in the 4C, but was reoccupied in the Byzantine period when it may have been part of a monastic settlement.

The two-storey building is impressive; its massive white limestone blocks quarried in the hills to the west measure up to 6m in length. The lion carvings on the upper façade were once surmounted by eagles—part of one from a corner of the palace can be seen among the blocks on the ground before you reach the building. On the long walls the first course of blocks was laid horizontally, followed by a second course placed vertically with gaps between for the seven windows and a final horizontal course to cap the whole. The building, much of which had fallen in an earthquake, was restored by French archaeologists in 1980. It was never finished: the carving on a lion block found near the south-west tower was only roughed out and other decorative elements are incomplete. The best preserved lions are on the south-west corner; the long sides also have limestone breccia leopard fountains at ground level. The entrance to the Qasr al-Abd is to the north, where a vestibule lies behind two columns and two half-columns over which a loggia repeats this design. At the opposite end is a similar vestibule—a wall with three windows c 2m high lies behind it, the upper storey with semi-engaged colonettes. Stairs in the south-east corner rose from here to the first floor. High up on the north-east side a carved lioness suckles her cubs.

The lioness carving on Qasr al-Abd

Qasr al-Abd was at the centre of a walled court of which little remains, and around it was an irrigated area and artificial lake, still full of water in spring; an aqueduct has been traced north to the cliffs and a water source beyond. Hyrcanus' residence has been aptly described as a sort of Hellenistic 'Roman villa' offering pleasure and comfort at the centre of a large estate.

If the entrance is locked the guardian with the key should be nearby—enter and turn through a small door on the left. The entrance had five flights of stairs leading to a north gallery and probably a terrace roof over all or part, a design which some believe is more in keeping with a temple. Emerge from the stairs into the main area and you will see that there is now no floor, only the foundations; by looking at the door sills it is possible to see that the floor level was just below the windows. Some second floor colonettes are still in situ.

To reach the monumental gate, excavated in 1976, walk 200m back down the road, turn right and it is on your right. It was also decorated with eagles and lions and aligned with a road, not the Qasr itself.

To Salt

A pleasant way to spend a morning is to drive north-west out of Amman from Sweileh Circle. Take the Sweileh road and continue on to 14km **Salt**, former Ottoman administrative capital of the region and still a prosperous town. In the centre you will find many old Ottoman houses built by prosperous traders in yellow limestone and with wrought-iron balconies. Abu al-Fida, Prince of Hama, (1273–1331) mentions the gardens of Salt and its famous raisins and in more recent times many prominent Jordanian families have come from here. Identified with Gedora of the Bible, it was capital of the land of Peraea. The large mosque on the citadel hill was once the site of a Mamluke castle, already ruined when Gertrude Bell visited here and now vanished. Circassian immigrants fleeing persecution in Russia were settled in Salt in the 1880s, but the once dominant town declined when Amman became the Transjordanian capital under King Abdullah. This may have been a blessing in disguise as the town has not suffered from the worst ravages of modern development and has preserved many of its 19C houses.

A visit to Salt can also be combined with a trip to the Hellenistic palace at Iraq al-Amir or en route to the Jordan valley.

As you drive down to the town, note the milestones in the central reservation of the road. On the left across the road at the lights are the offices of the Department of Antiquities and Ministry of Tourism. The former houses a small museum (open 8.00–16.00, closed Fridays) with a collection of coins, pottery, glass, a large jar discovered in recent excavations at Khirbet as-Suq and some mosaic panels from the Byzantine church at Tell Nimrin. A five minute walk towards the town centre is the Salt Cultural Centre, housed in a modern complex which includes an ethnographic museum (open 8.00–17.00, closed Fridays) and the showroom for the Queen Noor Foundation Training Centre downstairs which produces and sells ceramics and weaving.

Across the junction and 50m along on the right is the *Beit Touqan* (the House of the Touqan family)—the large houses mostly bear the names of the families who built them. Restored a few years ago it now belongs to the local authority, but you can ask to see around it. Walk back down to the Cultural Centre and head uphill. Branch off to the right to walk up a busy market street with some lovely, if dilapidated, old houses along its length and you will come to a square of sorts at the top, opposite which are more Ottoman houses built by wealthy families but now divided into apartments. A 'Salt Zaman' centre has recently opened in Salt with a restaurant and craft shops selling a variety of products.

From Salt you can continue straight on and down to the Jordan valley passing Zai National Park in the hills on the right, which is good for picnics, or take the Wadi Shu'aib road down from the museum towards the King Hussein bridge passing 4km **Khirbet as-Suq** where excavations have unearthed Roman and Byzantine tombs on both sides of the road and a wine and an olive press.

JARASH AND THE NORTH

Between Amman and the Syrian border are the hills and valleys of northern Jordan, inhabited from prehistoric times and during the Classical period the heartland of the Decapolis (p 74). **Jarash,** the best known of the Decapolis cities, is probably Jordan's most popular historical site after Petra; north of Irbid are the ruins of **Capitolias** and **Abila.** After the Romans came the Arabs. **Ajlun** castle, strategically located on a remote hilltop, is a rare example of medieval Arab military architecture, while the Crusaders occupied **Araq al-Habis**, an enigmatic complex of caves overlooking the Yarmuk gorge.

JARASH

Jarash is one of the most beautiful and best-preserved provincial Roman cities in the Middle East. Prosperous and cultured, its inhabitants spent lavishly on their city, erecting splendid buildings in a distinctive 'oriental baroque' style. Jarash is in a high valley, surrounded by hills, 50km north of Amman, on the road to ar-Ramtha and the Syrian border, and can easily be visited in a day trip from Amman by car or by bus.

■ Minibuses and service taxis leave Amman from Abdali bus station. The bus station in Jarash is by the East Baths. JETT buses run daily round trips from Amman during the Jarash festival.

To reach the site, drive north-west out of Amman on the road to Salt and at the Sweileh junction take the exit north, signposted Jarash. On the outskirts of the city the road descends steeply and at the bottom of the hill on the right hand side is the Baq'a camp, one of the largest Palestinian refugee camps in Jordan, which has grown into a small bustling town. Past Baq'a the road begins to climb into the mountains and below to the left, c 40km from Amman, is the Zarqa river, the biblical Jabbok, and the modern King Talal dam. In biblical times the river Jabbok marked the northern border of the kingdom of Ammon, beyond which rose the mountains of Gilead. It was near the river Jabbok, in the Jordan valley further west, that Jacob wrestled with God and was given the name Israel (Gen. 33). Jacob then named the spot Penuel, 'before God', sometimes equated with Tell Deir 'Alla (p 122). Jarash is 8km from the bridge over the Zarqa river; from the main road take the South Jarash exit which is also marked by a brown Ajlun/Jarash sign and follow the Chrysorhoas river valley to the archaeological site, where there are ample car parking facilities.

■ There are no hotels in Jarash, but the small town has shops and restaurants. Around the car park are kiosks selling postcards, film, batteries and souvenirs. Up some steps is a *resthouse* with clean toilets, a bar and a restaurant which serves snacks and a buffet lunch. Check prices of food beforehand as it can be rather expensive. Alternatives are the *Green Valley Restaurant*, by the Amman road, where you can watch 'taboun' bread being made and the *Lebanese House Restaurant*, signposted off the Amman road. Both cater for groups and have good food. There are several other restaurants in Jarash town, along the valley road below the site.

During the popular Jarash festival, held every year for 2–3 weeks in July and August, there are stalls in and around the site selling a variety of food, drinks, handicrafts and other souvenirs, and evening performances of music, dance and drama in the South Theatre, 'Forum' and other venues. Tickets for these events can be purchased at outlets in Amman (Jarash Festival Administration Offices—tel: 675199, 686197 for information) or at the site.

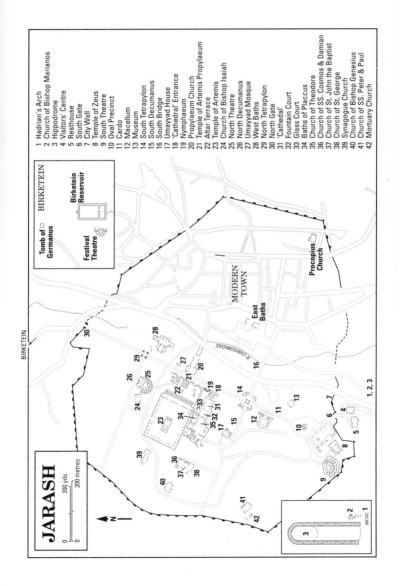

1 Hadrian's Arch
2 Church of Bishop Marianos
3 Hippodrome
4 Visitors' Centre
5 Resthouse
6 South Gate
7 City Wall
8 Temple of Zeus
9 South Theatre
10 Oval Precinct
11 Cardo
12 Macellum
13 Museum
14 South Tetrapylon
15 South Decumanus
16 South Bridge
17 Umayyad House
18 'Cathedral' Entrance
19 Nymphaeum
20 Propylaeum Church
21 Temple of Artemis Propylaeum
22 Altar Terrace
23 Temple of Artemis
24 Church of Bishop Isaiah
25 North Theatre
26 North Decumanus
27 Umayyad Mosque
28 West Baths
29 North Tetrapylon
30 North Gate
31 'Cathedral'
32 Fountain Court
33 Glass Court
34 Baths of Placcus
35 Church of Theodore
36 Church of SS. Cosmos & Damian
37 Church of St. John the Baptist
38 Church of St. George
39 Synagogue Church
40 Church of Bishop Genesius
41 Church of SS. Peter & Paul
42 Mortuary Church

History

Jarash, ancient Gerasa, is one of the great classical cities of the Near East. It is situated in the hills of Gilead, a fertile region described in the Bible as producing cereals, olives, vines, oak and pine, which has attracted settlers for many thousands of years. Palaeolithic hand axes and Neolithic bone and stone tools were found near the site and Bronze and Iron Age pottery has been excavated within the city walls.

Jarash came to prominence during the Hellenistic period and in Roman times it was a prosperous city of the Decapolis. Later tradition ascribes its foundation to Alexander the Great or his general Perdiccas, but the archaeological evidence favours a Seleucid date, most likely Antiochus IV (175–164 BC) after whom it was named Antioch on the Chrysorhoas or 'Golden River'. There is little archaeological evidence for the Hellenistic city, which was probably centred around the Temple of Zeus and Museum Hill. It adopted typical Greek institutions and classical forms of architecture and its citizens spoke Greek, the lingua franca of the towns and cities of the Hellenistic world. Aramaic was spoken in the countryside; the name Gerasa is a variant of the Aramaic 'Garshu'.

At the beginning of the 1C BC Jarash and other Decapolis cities were subject to the Hasmonaean dynasty of Judaea. This was a time of considerable upheaval in the area—Seleucid authority was collapsing, the Ituraean Arabs were raiding from the anti-Lebanon, the Nabateans briefly held Damascus and the Armenians moved south to oust them. The Romans decided to take matters into their own hands and in 64 BC Pompey marched into Syria. Jarash was 'liberated' and regained its local autonomy although it came under the overall aegis of the new Roman province. The city declared a new Era, issued a new coinage and benefited from the growth and stability fostered by the Pax Romana. There was an upsurge in building activity and during the 1C AD the basic town plan of Jarash as we see it today was laid out. The city was enclosed by a wall; it was given a grand colonnaded main street, the Cardo, intersected by two colonnaded side streets; the South Theatre and a new temple of Zeus were built; and there were additions to the Temple of Artemis, the city goddess.

Trajan instigated a further reorganisation of the Roman East when in AD 106 he annexed the Nabatean kingdom and created the Province of Arabia, with Bosra as its capital and several of the Decapolis cities including Jarash within its boundaries. Jarash was linked by a branch road to the Via Nova Traiana, which ran from Bosra to the port of Aila on the Red Sea. Trajan's successor Hadrian visited Jarash in 129/30 and its inhabitants must have been proud to entertain their first imperial guest. His visit stimulated more building activity—as well as a monumental arch erected in his honour outside the walls the city centre was given a facelift with the widening of the main street, rebuilding of temples and expansion of civic amenities.

The 2C and early 3C was the 'Golden Age' of Jarash, which was promoted to the privileged status of colony by Caracalla and had a population of perhaps 20,000–25,000. Rome suffered major setbacks, however, during the 3C, largely connected with the threat of the Parthians and Sassanians from the east and Jarash's prosperity suffered accordingly. Constantinople's inauguration as the new capital of the Eastern Roman empire in 330 and the proclamation of Christianity as the official religion revived the fortunes of the eastern provinces. The Holy Land witnessed a profusion of church building; no fewer than 15 churches graced Jarash alone. The last church, of Bishop

Genesius, was built in 611, three years before the Persian invasion which so weakened the empire and 25 years before the Muslim conquest of 636.

Jarash was still inhabited in the early Islamic period but the transfer of power from Damascus to Baghdad in 750 with the advent of the Abbasid caliphate, and a series of bad earthquakes in the mid-8C, marked the end for the city. It was more or less deserted for over 1000 years. 'So complete is the general desolation of this once proud city', wrote the English traveller J.S. Buckingham in 1816, 'that Bedouin Arabs now encamp in the valley for the sake of the spring there...'. In 1878 Circassians were settled there by the Turks and they still form the majority of the inhabitants of the small town which has since grown up on the east bank of the river, covering most of the remains of the residential area of the ancient city.

Hadrian's Arch, Jarash

On the approach road from Amman the first monument is **Hadrian's Arch**, built outside the city to commemorate the visit of the emperor to Jarash in AD 129/30 as recorded in an inscription on the north façade, now removed. Hadrian travelled widely with his entourage throughout the empire to encourage economic stability and military security. As a philhellene he had a special interest in the hellenised East. The triple archway has a wide central opening flanked by two smaller ones with niches above and two side buttresses which were added perhaps up to 100 years later. Probably the arches had wooden doors. They are flanked by engaged columns with a calyx of acanthus leaves around the base, an unusual feature which is mirrored on the South Gate of the city. Hadrian probably wintered in Jarash in 129/30 and gave jurisdiction while he was there.

Some 30m north of the arch are the foundations of the small **Church of Bishop Marianos**, a simple structure built in 570 and originally floored with geometric mosaics. Several rock-cut shaft graves are associated with the church.

Across the street, which ran from Hadrian's Arch to the South Gate, three rooms in the walls of the Hippodrome were reused as the deacon's house.

The **Hippodrome** was built into the east side of a valley, with a high vaulted substructure, now collapsed, supporting the long west side. Of unknown date and poorly preserved, it is currently undergoing restoration. Although smaller than the hippodromes of great cities such as Rome and Antioch, Jarash's hippodrome could accommodate around 10,000 spectators. Sixteen rows of stone seats, some of which are still visible at the north-west corner, were supported on arches, below which were shops and storerooms. There were entrances in the east and west walls and a main entrance, leading to a ramp, in the semi-circular north wall. At the south end were ten stalls, with altars on top, flanking a central pavilion above which was the magistrate's tribunal. Here began the chariot races, so popular in the Roman world. Horses competed under the colours of the different factions: the Greens, Blues, Whites and Reds, associated with earth, water, air and fire. Pantomimes and circuses were also staged in the Hippodrome. At some point, perhaps during the late 4C or early 5C, the Hippodrome was divided by a semi-circular retaining wall. The excavators of the site suggest that the north part continued to be used for games while in the south part there were a number of pottery kilns and workshops. A later earthquake which caused the collapse of the cavea buried at least eight unfortunate individuals; their skeletal remains were found west of the north entrance.

■ Beyond the Hippodrome is the car park. In the Visitors' Centre alongside, where the Tourist Police have their office, is a model of the ancient city. The ticket office (JD2 pp) is opposite the entrance to the site, which is open from 7.30am until sunset.

Jarash is entered through the **South Gate**, of a similar design to Hadrian's Arch and probably built at the same time. The road from Philadelphia passed through both gates to enter the city. Part of the 3.5km long **city wall** is well preserved by the South Gate. Almost 3m (10ft) thick and with over 100 square towers, the existing wall is a 4C structure replacing a 1C wall little more than half its width. Passing through the gate, where a deep sounding (now refilled) provided a stratigraphic record dating from the Middle Bronze Age (c1600 BC) to the 1C AD, there is an area on the left which was perhaps used as a market in the 2C and 3C. In an underground room with steps leading down are the remains of a 3C olive press made partly of reused column sections.

Recent excavations have revealed different levels of the street which leads to the Oval Precinct past the beautifully restored vaulted substructure of the lower temenos of the **Temple of Zeus**, built in 162/3, on the left. A broad staircase gives access to the terrace, which was surrounded by a covered portico decorated with engaged columns and blind arches. On the northern part of the terrace are the remains of an earlier 1C sanctuary. This probably replaced the 2C BC Hellenistic temple where the ruler of Philadelphia, Zeus Cotylas, and his son Theodorus, placed some of their treasure for safekeeping when the region was under threat from the Hasmonaeans. According to an inscription the construction of the 1C temple of Olympian Zeus was partly financed by Zabdion son of Aristomachos, priest of Tiberius Caesar, in 22/3. Early in the 1C the Imperial cult was thus functioning at Jarash, although no shrine to the emperors has yet been located.

From the lower courtyard a monumental staircase, now partly buried beneath collapsed masonry, leads to the 2C temple, which stood on a high podium within an upper temenos. It was a simple peristyle temple with 12 x 8 columns. Those now standing have been re-erected, unfortunately incorrectly. Fragments of the entablature are lying in the vicinity. Niches adorn the outer walls of the cella; inside there are simple engaged pilasters. Within the thick entrance wall were steps to the roof and a small doorway in the north wall led to the adjacent South Theatre. This is a good spot to get an idea of the size of Roman Jarash; in the modern town to the east, part of the ancient city wall is visible in a gap between buildings to the left of a red and white pylon.

Pomegranates and grapes—detail of carving near the Temple of Zeus, Jarash

One of the earliest extant theatres in Syria, the much restored **South Theatre** is the larger of the two theatres within the city walls. It was built under the emperor Domitian (81–96) as recorded by two dedicatory inscriptions which are now kept under glass outside the theatre on the side facing the Oval Precinct. The longer inscription is dated AD 90 and mentions Lappius Maximus, who was governor of Syria 90–94; the shorter inscription, which is identical but stops after the list of imperial titles, is dated one year later. A third inscription discovered after the first two is shorter still and dates to AD 92. Probably the monument was dedicated but not finished in AD 90 and as other sections were completed inscriptions in the relevant places recorded the progress made. Domitian's name has been subsequently hacked out of all the inscriptions, probably reflecting general odium of a tyrant who had murdered so many, overruled the Senate and virtually accorded himself semi-divine honours.

Construction of the theatre was partly financed by some of Jarash's wealthy citizens, whose munificence was duly recorded. On the podium at the western end of the auditorium a beautifully cut inscription honours the retired *decurio* Titus Flavius Dionysius for his donation of 3000 drachmae to build a block of seats. Again Domitian's name has been erased. All cities depended on such benefactors to finance their building projects, civic amenities and religious cults. Usually donors came from three or four wealthy families who vied with each other for power and prestige. Their rivalry was matched by keen rivalry between cities to outdo each other in the magnificence of their buildings. There was a lack of a middle class to fill the gap between the rich and poor, although some, including veteran soldiers like Titus Flavius, athletes and retired gladiators, enjoyed a certain upward mobility.

Among the events staged in the South Theatre was an annual festival in honour of Trajan. At the beginning of the 2C, according to an inscription on a cylindrical block now on the museum steps, Titus Flavius Quirina Gerrenus, who held the office of *agonothetes*, was responsible for defraying the costs of the celebrations. For his munificence the 'sacred guild of the ecumenical, victorious, crowned artists in the service of Dionysus' placed a statue of Titus Flavius in the theatre, which was to be ceremonially crowned at future performances. At the time of the festival Titus Flavius was also *gymnasiarch*, a six-monthly office involving further heavy expenditure. Honour and status were only achieved at a price! During such festivals—the 'holidays' of the ancient world, which continued for days, even weeks in the agricultural off-season—the citizens could enjoy drama, pantomime, music, oratory and all manner of competitive sport. Many temples, public buildings and houses were hung with garlands and festivals were often combined with colourful local fairs.

Dionysus, the popular god of the theatre and of wine and revelry, was said to be the son of Zeus and Semele, daughter of the king of Thebes. Encouraged by jealous Hera, Semele, when six months pregnant, contrived to view the true divine nature of Zeus, but was struck dead when he appeared as thunder and lightning. Hermes saved the baby by sewing him into Zeus's thigh and he was born three months later. Pursued by Hera, the child was finally entrusted to the nymphs of Nysa, who protected and raised him. Dionysus discovered wine in Nysa, and when he reached manhood he spread this gift throughout the world.

Over 3000 spectators could enjoy performances in the South Theatre. The lower seats, built into the hillside and accessible through two paradoi that lead into the orchestra are separated by a diazoma from the upper seats, which are supported on arches and reached through four vomitoria. Greek letters are carved on some of the lower tiers in the eastern and western sections: probably influential citizens could reserve these 'numbered' seats. Acoustics in the theatre are excellent: the circular depressions in the podium act as soundboxes.

Behind the stage, which probably had a wooden floor but has been repaved in stone, is the elaborate scaenae frons, with the usual three doors from backstage and niches for statues. Most of the second storey has collapsed. Arched and pedimented niches and beautiful 'Amazon's shields' carved in relief decorate the front of the stage. In the centre is an inscription from Domitian's reign, later recarved and with the emperor's name erased. It refers to the pavement of the theatre, dedicated by the city.

One of the most distinctive features of Jarash is the **Oval Precinct**, often referred to as the 'Forum'. It was probably constructed during the 1C, around the same time as the first Roman Temple of Zeus and the South Theatre, and is delineated by a beautiful Ionic colonnade, characteristic of that era. Greek names carved on columns at the south-east end record benefactors who paid for individual sections of the arcade.

Stone slabs pave the precinct, following the curve of the ellipses, and there is a raised pavement alongside the colonnade. On the west the intercolumniations are slightly wider at two points, suggesting some feature behind. In the centre the remains of a square podium may have supported a statue: the column has been erected for the present-day Jarash festival. A tank was built around this structure in the 7C and water channelled into it through ceramic pipes which crossed the precinct from the north and west, the lines of which are still visible. At that time small houses covered much of the precinct, constructed of materials robbed from elsewhere and the stone seats, perhaps from the South Theatre, may have been reused at this period. An elegant architectural device, the Oval Precinct harmoniously linked the Zeus sanctuary and the street leading from the South Gate with the Cardo, the grand boulevard of classical Jarash.

Originally laid out in the Ionic order in the mid-1C (39–76), the **Cardo** runs for over 800m from the Oval Precinct to the North Gate. During the remodelling of the city in the 2C it was widened as far as the Temple of Artemis with new Corinthian columns, though with much reuse of older shafts and bases. To allow for the widening of the street the two columns at the north end of the east colonnade of the Oval Precinct were moved closer together. Where the Precinct joins the Cardo there are two piers on each side of the main street. They may have been joined by arches leading to the passage behind the oval colonnade: one collapsed arch is lying in the Precinct just before the Cardo.

Along the Cardo the colonnade supports a continuous architrave, and wherever there is a public building, the columns are higher. From the pavement alongside the street steps led up to the covered porticoes of the colonnade where pedestrians could stroll protected from the elements and visit the shops behind. The street itself was paved with diagonally laid blocks alternating with horizontal courses, and beneath ran a central drain accessible through round, stone man-hole covers. Ruts worn by centuries of wheeled traffic are a reminder of how crowded and animated the Cardo once was.

A short distance along the Cardo four higher columns on the left mark the entrance to the food market or **Macellum** (Gk. agora) of ancient Jarash, which is surrounded by *tabernae* or shops. At this point the pavement is higher, marking later Byzantine remodelling, as elsewhere in the city. Apparently the macellum, built in the first quarter of the 2C, was either a gift to the city by the provincial governor Tiberius Julianus Alexander or built in his honour. Through a triple gateway flanked by two-storey shops is an octagonal courtyard with a central fountain and exedrae in the four corners, behind a double colonnade. In the south-west exedra are four supports or 'legs' carved with a forward-facing bull or lion and a massive limestone 'tabletop'. Originally there was a mensa or table in each exedra; one is now at the macellum entrance. Perhaps these mensae were used for money changers and for commercial deals rather than as food stalls. It is easy to imagine the market in antiquity—financial transactions in the exedrae, *tabernae* well stocked with foodstuffs and other goods, and traders and customers haggling over prices. Outside the macellum note the inscription αγορεω[v] (notaries) on a column which must have been paid for by the notaries of Gerasa. Beside the pavement north of the macellum is a Byzantine stone trough below a Roman lion's head fountain dedicated to Julia Domna, the Syrian wife of Septimius Severus (193–211).

Opposite the macellum steps lead up to the small **Jarash Museum** (open Wed–Mon 8.30–17.00 in summer, 8.30–16.00 in winter, Tues 8.30–12.00). On exhibition are a few sections of mosaic and sculptural fragments, including an inscription mentioning the engineer who built the lower terrace of the Temple of Zeus. Around the walls are showcases with pottery, glass, lamps, metal and flint implements from the Neolithic to Mamluke periods, in chronological order. Central showcases have coins, jewellery and other small items as well as recent discoveries.

Some 50m beyond the museum steps is the intersection of the Cardo with the South Decumanus. In the 2C the original simple crossroads was redesigned. In the centre, four pedestals, with shell niches on the sides, each supported four granite columns, probably crowned by an entablature and roofed. No doubt they held statues, perhaps of local dignitaries. There are several broken sections of the granite columns nearby. At the same time as the tetrapylon was built the angles of the crossroads were probably cut away to create a circular plaza bordered by two-storey shops.

The **South Decumanus** slopes from west to east, as is strikingly clear from the incline of the entablature atop the colonnade, and crossed the River Chrysorhoas on the South Bridge, recently restored but blocked to both pedestrians and vehicles.

Excavations north of the colonnade west of the Cardo have revealed the foundations of an **Umayyad House** dated to around 660, with at least ten rooms around a central courtyard. It may have had a second storey. Below the courtyard is the drainage system which emptied into the main drain beneath the Decumanus. In the mid-8C the house was subdivided into three smaller units which continued in use until the site was abandoned in the early Abbasid period.

North of the junction with the South Decumanus begins the central and widest part of the Cardo. The water trough and raised pavement are 6C Byzantine and the niches may have held statues or even lamps, although street lighting was rare in the ancient world. By the end of the 4C the main streets of Antioch and Ephesus were illuminated but most cities were not so well appointed. After about 100m eight taller columns on the left mark the 'Cathedral' entrance, believed to be a rebuilding of the propylaeum of the 2C **Temple of Dionysus**.

Fountain basin in the Nymphaeum at Jarash

Beyond, marked by two pairs of massive columns, is the **Nymphaeum**, built towards the end of the 2C. It was dedicated to the water nymphs, daughters of Zeus, young unmarried women who loved dancing and music and inspired mortals with poetry and prophetic power. The splashing waters of the fountain, one of the most splendid monuments of Jarash, must have been a delightful reminder of these lissom spirits of nature. A semi-circular recess with two storeys was built into the hillside and originally covered by a half dome. Green cipollino marble faced the lower storey and the upper storey was plastered and painted with green and orange geometric designs, of which there are traces in the semi-circular niche on the top left. Small Corinthian columns framing the niches carried a finely carved entablature with half pediments on the upper storey. Statues in the lower niches probably held vases from which water flowed into the basin. Note the holes through which the water came. From the basin the water splashed through lions' heads in the retaining wall into shallow circular basins in the step below carved with charming motifs of fish and dolphins, their eyes serving as drainage holes. The large red granite laver is a later Byzantine addition.

Beyond the nymphaeum the east side of the Temple of Artemis precinct is marked by four huge columns with thirteen lower ones on either side.

Starting in the east of the city the **Sacred Way** to the temple crossed the Chrysorhoas at the North Bridge (now destroyed). From there a monumental staircase led to a triple arch and colonnaded street ending in a trapezoidal shaped plaza which opened onto the Cardo opposite the four great columns before the Temple of Artemis Propylaeum. On each side of the plaza entrance were four spirally twisted columns. Their architrave now rests on the wall and has a beautifully carved inscription dated to 150, commemorating the establishment by the consul designatus L. Attidius Cornelianus of fountains, probably those which flowed into the troughs flanking the plaza façade.

During the 6C, when the cult of Artemis had declined at Jarash and Christianity was the dominant religion, the plaza and Sacred Way to the arch were ingeniously converted into a church, known as the **Propylaeum Church**. At the triple gateway, which had probably suffered earthquake damage, was the apse, and the columns of the former street separated the nave and aisles. Within the apse were clergy seats and in front was the altar and a basin for ablutions. The plaza became the atrium of the church.

Part of the inscription of L. Attidius Cornelianus opposite the Propylaeum of the Temple of Artemis, Jarash

From the Propylaeum church you can see the columns of the great Temple of Artemis. A devotee of the goddess walking the Sacred Way would have crossed the Cardo to the triple gateway of the temple **Propylaeum**, which is flanked by rows of two-storey shops. In the tympanum above the central doorway was a dedicatory inscription dated to 150 of the same consul designatus L. Attidius Cornelianus who was responsible for the elegant layout on the opposite side of the Cardo. The ornate decoration of the Propylaeum is best seen framing the niches above the smaller side arches on the outer and inner faces of the entrance wall. An elaborate entablature and pediment crowned the gateway, part of which is on the pavement of the Cardo opposite.

Through the Propylaeum a monumental staircase of seven by seven steps between flanking walls is 1930s rebuilding. At the bottom of the staircase are two doors which gave access to the upper storey of the gateway. The staircase rises steeply to an **Altar Terrace** where there are the foundations of a open air altar. On the flanking wall to the north is a little votive altar dedicated by Diogenes Leonidas. Beyond the Altar Terrace and stretching the full width of it three more flights of steps led to a colonnade in front of the east wall of the temple precinct. Only the scant foundations are now visible. In antiquity the temple was concealed behind this colonnade and worshippers passing through one of the three doorways into the temenos must have been duly awestruck at the sight of the most splendid of all the monuments of Jarash, the **Temple of Artemis**.

Artemis, daughter of Zeus and sister of Apollo, night huntress of the forests and hills, who protected women and bestowed fertility, was the patron goddess of Jarash. Her temple complex was huge and designed to impress. The colonnades which surrounded the 160 x 120m open precinct are still being excavated; to the north column drums and capitals stick whimsically out of the earth. Shepherds now graze their goats among the fallen limestone blocks and columns. In front of the temple are the foundations of a second open-air altar much obscured by the ruins of later Byzantine and Umayyad pottery kilns and workshops. There are also the foundations of a small 6C church in the southern part of the temenos. Most rituals and festivals connected with the cult of the goddess would have been celebrated in this great courtyard, as only priests could enter the sanctuary proper (oriented east–west and slightly off centre).

Artemis' temple stands on a high podium with underground vaults and has wings projecting east which originally framed the broad staircase leading up to the entrance portico—the present small staircase is modern. A peristyle of 11 x 6 columns, 13 metres high and crowned by capitals which are masterpieces of carving, surrounds the cella. A key or penny slotted between the drums will move gently up and down, demonstrating that the columns sway imperceptibly in the breeze.

Entered through a doorway flanked by niches, the cella was clad inside with marble slabs; the walls are dotted with dowel holes for the hooks to which they were attached. At the back of the cella steps lead up to the niche which housed the image of Artemis. Surprisingly, her grand temple may never have been completed, as no element of either entablature or roofing has been found.

Beyond the north wall of the Temple of Artemis precinct a track leads back to the Cardo past the **Church of Bishop Isaiah**, dedicated in the mid-6C. Currently it is closed to the public but looking from outside you can see the nave and aisles and the remains of a chancel screen. Its fine floor mosaics have been reburied for protection. Alongside is the **North Theatre**, which can be entered from the back at this level. Constructed in the mid-2C as a small odeon, the theatre originally comprised the 14 rows of seats to the diazoma wall which is decorated with shell niches and has five vomitoria.

During the first quarter of the 3C the theatre was enlarged by adding the eight rows of seats of the upper auditorium, which doubled the audience capacity to around 1600. Vomitoria were constructed in the new outer wall leading to an internal vaulted passageway which gives access to the cavea. Some seats below the diazoma have Greek names inscribed on them (e.g. Apollo, 5th row down in the centre), a number of which are prefaced by ΦΥΛ, probably alluding to the tribes (phyloi) that voted in the boule or city council. This council would have comprised 50 representatives from each of 10–12 tribes who may have held their meetings in the theatre. During meetings and performances the theatre could be covered by an awning; post holes are visible on the lowest row of seats. Although much of the theatre's statuary and decoration has been lost or removed there remains enough to give an idea of its original splendour. Red, green and grey marble paved the orchestra, and the scaenae frons, partly reconstructed, had niches for statues framed by columns with elaborate capitals. On the pilasters at each end of the orchestra wall are charming reliefs of musicians: a chubby boy with pipes, a seated figure with a lyre, a woman with pipes and a woman with a staff and round object (tympanum?).

Best viewed from the North Decumanus, the theatre forecourt was laid out on a grandiose scale. On the north side of the Decumanus four 12m high Corinthian columns were flanked by two engaged columns and pilasters and across the street, at the top of a broad flight of steps, this was matched by another towering colonnade, the eastern part of which is still standing, although rather precariously. Double engaged columns at the ends were attached to the side walls of the theatre portico behind. Steps flanking the portico led to the back of the stage.

The theatre complex continued in use until the 5C but subsequently suffered serious damage, perhaps after the earthquake of 551. Stones were robbed for other structures and in the 7C and 8C there were Umayyad pottery kilns and squatter occupation among the ruins.

Return to the Cardo down the dirt road from the back of the North Theatre and on the opposite side behind the colonnade are the ruins of a small **Umayyad mosque**, distinguishable by the mihrab facing south (a reused Roman conch) and paved area strewn with column drums in front. This is the only known mosque in Jarash.

Detail of the West Baths complex, Jarash

To the north, across the dirt service road, are the unexcavated ruins of the huge **West Baths** complex which comprised the usual changing rooms, cold and hot baths and two flanking rooms to the north and south. To the north is a room with two columns in front which has a well preserved domed roof supported on four arches.

Not far from the West Baths, at the junction of the Cardo and the North Decumanus, is the **North Tetrapylon**, built during the remodelling of the city towards the end of the 2C. Arches on all four sides lead into a circular interior which may originally have been domed. Pedestals flank the east and west arches on the outside and inside there are shallow niches and brackets for statues. The **North Decumanus**, which is currently being cleared, has beautiful diagonal paving and Ionic colonnades.

From the North Tetrapylon the **Cardo** continues to the North Gate. This is the only remaining section of the main street as it was in the 1C, narrower and with Ionic colonnades. According to an inscription the **North Gate** was built in 115, under Trajan's legate C. Claudius Severus, who also rebuilt the road from Jarash to Pella. This road met the Cardo at an angle of 18°; cleverly to disguise the turn and have both façades at right angles to the road the gate is wedge-shaped. Bastions on either side are later Byzantine additions.

To explore the main ecclesiastical complex return along the Cardo to past the nymphaeum. Behind eight tall columns is the finely carved 'Cathedral' gate, believed to be a 4C rebuilding of the propylaeum of the Temple of Dionysus. While the temple probably faced west, the church faces east, so the staircase through the gate leads to the outer apse wall, relieved by the little **Shrine of St Mary**, a shell niche below which the names 'Michael, Holy Mary, Gabriel' were painted in red. Traces of Mary and Gabriel are still visible.

The early Syrian church inherited a strong emphasis on the female principle from the pre-Christian era, when the cult of the Syrian Goddess spread across the Graeco-Roman world. By the 4C Syrian devotion for Mary was flourishing, long before it became widely popular elsewhere. Michael and Gabriel, archangels and guardians of doorways and entrances, are in appropriate context, as entry to the **Cathedral** was along passages to the north and south of the shrine. There were doors in the north and south walls of the building and three main doors in the west wall leading into a nave and aisles separated by columns reused from an earlier 2C building. West of the apse, which had seats for the clergy, was a chancel screen and there were two screens across the aisles in front of the diaconica. Pale pink limestone still paves the aisles.

At some point the church was made smaller by building a wall across the nave and aisles, and during the 6C the **South West Chapel** was attached, encroaching on the south passageway and the colonnade of the adjacent **Fountain Court**. Named from the square fountain in the centre, the Fountain Court was the colonnaded atrium of the 4C Cathedral. Now the western colonnade is covered by part of the later Church of St Theodore, accessed by stairways to the north and south and connected to the fountain by a vault borne on two arches. Older Corinthian columns were reused for the eastern colonnade, which was paved with red and white opus sectile and formed the porticoed entrance to the cathedral. The other colonnades were of lower, Ionic columns and paved with mosaics. Water from the reservoir at Birketein, north of the city, was channelled to the fountain through lead piping below the paving of the courtyard.

According to the 4C Roman historian Epiphanius the feast of the miracle of Cana, when Jesus turned water into wine, took place every year at a fountain in Gerasa; the most likely venue for the celebrations is the Fountain Court. As the cathedral is probably built over the Temple of Dionysus, the god of wine, there may be a connection with a pre-Christian festival.

Behind the Fountain Court to the north east is the small **Glass Court**, used for glass-making during the Muslim period. Over 120lb of coloured glass pieces were found during the excavations. Originally part of a Roman building, it was twice floored with mosaics during the Byzantine period and probably associated with the church complex.

Left of the Glass Court a stairway leads to a stepped side street which runs between the ecclesiastical complex and the Temple of Artemis. Walking west up the street the **Baths of Placcus**, built by Bishop Placcus in 454–5, are on the left followed by a residential complex which may have housed some of the clergy. Behind is the **Church of St Theodore**, one of the great 'soldier saints' of the East. It was dedicated in 496 according to an inscription on the lintel over the main west entrance. A nave and aisles are flanked by passages and ancillary rooms including a baptistery to the south. A broad colonnaded atrium spans the front of the building. The nave and aisles were floored with coloured marble and stone while the upper walls and semi dome over the apse sparkled with glass mosaics. Mosaic floors adorned the colonnades of the atrium and various ancillary rooms.

Very different concepts are expressed in the architecture of the Christian churches and the adjacent Temple of Artemis. The Artemis complex was on a truly grandiose scale and was matched by the Temple of Zeus at the other end of town; both were designed to be seen from afar and dominated the city. Worship was outside, crowds thronged the vast open courtyards. In the case of the Christian buildings, hemmed in by other structures, it would have been impossible to get a clear view of the basilicas; worship was inside the church, as were the glitter and the trappings. Nevertheless the churches of Jarash are impressive, in their size and their number (15 are known so far).

Along a path west of St Theodore's is a group of three churches built between

529 and 533 which share a common atrium and have interconnecting doors. Fine mosaics in the **Church of SS Cosmos and Damian** which is closed to the public can be viewed from above over a modern wall. Cosmos and Damian, twin brothers and patrons of medicine and pharmacy, were born in Arabia, studied in Syria and became famous doctors who charged no fee to their patients. They were probably martyred under Diocletian at the beginning of the 4C and from the 5C their cult became very popular.

The mosaics show diamonds and squares with geometric designs, birds, animals and donor portraits. Below the chancel screen is the dedicatory inscription dated 533 which names the patron as Bishop Paul. It is flanked by portraits of Theodore the paramonarius or 'church warden' holding an incense burner and his wife Georgia, her hands upraised in prayer. Below Georgia are the bases for the three columns that held up the pulpit and the portrait of a donor named Calloenistus. Below Theodore is John, son of Astricius; both men carry baskets, symbolising giving. Between the two an inscription records the gift of the apse by Dagistheus, one of Justinian's generals. Glass mosaics adorned the apse and the walls were decorated with painted plaster.

South of the apse was a baptistery which also served the adjacent **Church of John the Baptist**, a centralised church with exedrae in the four corners and an apse extending to the east. It was dedicated in 531 under Bishop Paul and sponsored by Theodore, foster son of Thomas, according to the inscription originally before the chancel screen. Fragments of the fine mosaics are still in situ: geometric, floral, animal and vase motifs. Other mosaics are in the Amman Museum of Popular Traditions. The **Church of St George** is similar in plan to SS Cosmos and Damian; fragments of mosaics in situ show repaired iconoclastic damage and include geometric patterns in the north aisle and roundels with plants and animals in the south aisle.

North of SS Cosmos and Damian is the 6C **Synagogue Church**, built over an earlier building with an atrium to the east which was probably a synagogue. Mosaic decoration in the synagogue vestibule included a seven-branched candelabrum (menorah) and the Jewish ritual objects associated with it—a palm branch (lulah), citrus fruit (ethrog), a ram's horn (shofar) and a censer (shovel). Also depicted was the story of Noah and his family leaving the ark after the flood. When the building became a church the orientation was reversed, a new geometric mosaic was laid, and the apse of the church protruded into the former atrium. The structure is very ruined but the ground plan is clear.

South of the Synagogue Church, the **Church of Bishop Genesius**, constructed in 611, was the last church to be built in Jarash, as far as we know. It is badly ruined. Unlike other churches in Jarash the chancel screen extended into the aisles.

In the south-west of the town near the city wall is the **Church of SS Peter and Paul**, a basilica with a nave and aisles and a side chapel attached to the north. The remains are very overgrown.

Close by is the **Mortuary Church**, a small single hall structure built into the hillside with an undercroft to the south cut into the solid rock. An inscription found in front of the chancel records that the church was built by an unknown founder in honour of his parents, perhaps as their mortuary chapel. It is the last resting place of the British scholar G. Lankester Harding, for 20 years Director of the Department of Antiquities in Jordan, 'a great man and archaeologist who loved Jordan' as his memorial plaque records.

East of the river Chrysorhoas most of the buildings of ancient Jarash have been destroyed or covered by the modern town. Still standing to an impressive height are some walls of the **East Baths** and up the hill on the edge of town, opposite the police station, is the **Procopius Church**, so-called after its main benefactor. It was decorated with geometric mosaics, but now only some wall foundations, column bases and partly re-erected columns are visible. Opposite the church is a part of the city wall and an impressive section runs behind and beyond the police station. North of the Procopius Church was the **Chapel of Elias, Maria and Soreg**, now covered by houses, and beside the Chrysorhoas River was the **Church of the Prophets, Apostles and Martyrs**, also destroyed. Mosaics salvaged from the two churches are in the Jarash Museum and the Amman Museum of Popular Traditions.

East of the road c 200m north of the North Gate is another church, octagonal in shape with a large rectangular forecourt or atrium, like the basilica church at Umm Qais.

About 1.5km beyond is **Birketein**, which means 'two pools' in Arabic, where in a small shady valley there is a huge double reservoir, restored in 1962, divided by a thick wall with a sluice gate which regulated the level of water in the larger northern basin. Frogs croak loudly in chorus among the thick weed of the pools. A processional way linked Jarash to Birketein, which was the venue for the annual Maiumas festival, a popular licentious feast with water amusements sporadically banned by the authorities. Along the western edge of the reservoir ran a colonnade and built into the hillside beyond, overlooking the water, is the small **Festival Theatre**, which could seat around 1000 spectators.

North of Birketein, along the route of the processional way is the picturesque **Tomb of Germanus**, once an impressive 'temple tomb' with square cella, underground vault and pillared portico, probably dating to the mid 2C. Three pillars still stand before the overgrown, ruined walls, tumbled stones and open sarcophagus which probably once contained the body of Germanus, son of Molpon, wealthy centurion of an auxiliary cohort who sponsored the reconstruction of the Temple of Zeus Epicarpius, a building only known from a fragmentary inscription found nearby at the turn of the century.

THE DECAPOLIS

During the early Christian era a group of Hellenised cities and the area of Roman Syria where they were located became known as the Decapolis or 'ten cities'. According to the 1C writer Pliny these were Damascus, Raphana, Hippos, Dion, Canatha (all in modern Syria), Scythopolis (on the West Bank), Philadelphia, Gadara, Pella and Gerasa (in Jordan). Later authors include other cities within the Decapolis, among them Abila and Capitolias. Affluent, elegant and cosmopolitan, the Decapolis cities seem to have enjoyed a semi-independent status under Rome and their citizens could take their complaints to the Roman authorities. An equestrian official serving under the legate of Syria supervised the region. Excavation at several Decapolis sites has revealed some of the grandest cities of the Graeco-Roman East: Philadelphia's theatre seated 6000, Gadara's baths at Hammath Gader were compared with the splendid imperial baths of Baiae near Naples and the Temple of Artemis at Gerasa could rival the best.

Christianity is early associated with the Decapolis; according to Mark's gospel, Jesus passed through the area on his return from Tyre and Sidon (7:31) and the healed Gadarene madman, whose devils were driven into a herd of pigs, proclaimed his story in the Decapolis (5:20). Describing the crowds that followed Jesus at the start of his ministry in Galilee, Matthew says that some came from the Decapolis

(4:25). Christian communities were well established by the 2C and during the late 5C and 6C dozens of churches changed the face of the Decapolis cities. Byzantine supremacy, however, was short-lived; in 636 the Muslim armies conquered the region and most of the cities declined, with one notable exception, Damascus, which lived on to become the captial of the Ummayyd Caliphate.

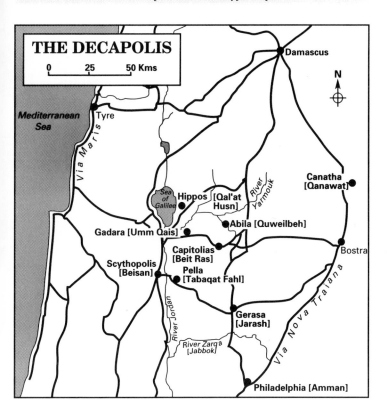

From Jarash to Ajlun and Dibeen

A pleasant 40 minute drive through the hills to **Qala'at ar-Rabadh-Ajlun Castle** combines well with a visit to Jarash. From Hadrian's Arch turn west and continue up through pine woods and olive groves. Look for the photogenic castle on a distant hilltop once you reach the top. Bear right in 20km Anjara, left by the old mosque in Ajlun and head straight up to the castle. Its spectacular position gives wonderful views of the countryside. In Ajlun the old mosque has a minaret, the square base of which is 14C or older. On the way up to the castle there are two hotels where lunch can be taken and a resthouse is being built just below the castle.

History

Built in 1184–85 by Saladin's cousin Izz ad-Din Usama, Ajlun is a rare example of a wholly Islamic castle. It was intended to check Crusader expansion—Belvoir castle faces it across the Jordan valley as a reminder of the Frankish presence. It may also have guarded the iron deposits of the Ajlun hills and was a stopover for the pigeon post which could relay messages from Baghdad to Cairo in 12 hours. Ironically the Crusader threat disappeared within only a few years of Ajlun's construction with their defeat at the battle of Hattin (1187). An inscription on the South Tower records that later work strengthening its defences was completed in 1214–15 under the energetic Izz ad-Din Aybak. According to a 13C Arab historian, the Mongols 'threw down the battlements' when they took it in 1260. Surrendered by them after defeat by the Mamlukes at the battle of 'Ain Jalut, it was repaired and became an administrative centre, but suffered earthquake damage in the 19C. The views are wonderful in all directions—look for the hump of Mt Tabor to the west— and on weekends it is always busy.

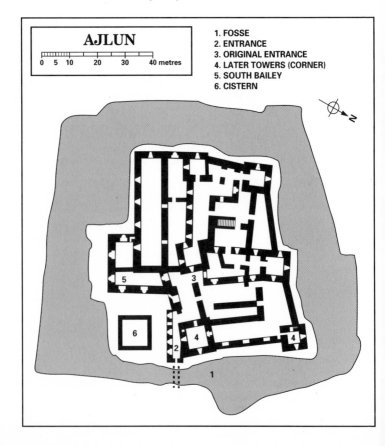

AJLUN

0   5   10   20   30   40 metres

1. FOSSE
2. ENTRANCE
3. ORIGINAL ENTRANCE
4. LATER TOWERS (CORNER)
5. SOUTH BAILEY
6. CISTERN

Originally the castle was probably square with four two-storey towers; the present entrance (2) and the two towers on its right (4) were added after the battle of Hattin, as was the fosse which was required to improve defences. The early masonry is rougher than the later work. Water was stored in a large cistern (6) left of the entrance and there were five smaller cisterns inside. Cross the footbridge and walk up the passageway to a second entrance, where there are some crudely carved birds over the arch and a machicolation. The original entrance (3) now lies ahead and inside the confusion of the different building phases becomes apparent. A good view can be had by climbing to the top of the tower nearest the entrance. An inscription on the long **South-West Tower** says it was added under Sultan Baybars in 1262–63.

SALADIN

Al-Malik al-Nasir Salah ad-Din Abu'l Muzaffer Yusuf ibn Ayyub ibn Shadi is the full name (including honorific titles) of the man better known to the West as Saladin. His dynasty, the Ayyubids, took its name from his father. Born in 1137–38, he was actually of Kurdish descent, and suffered discrimination because of this, being brought up in Syria. His father was an official in the service of the atabeg Zengi, who struck the first serious blow against the Crusader cause by taking Edessa from them in 1144. On his murder in 1146, Zengi's son Nur ad-Din succeeded him. Saladin's uncle Shirkuh rose in his service and was despatched to Egypt during factional fighting there in 1164. Saladin went with him. Egypt was then ruled by the Shi'ite Fatimids—a thorn in the side of the orthodox Sunnis. After some years of intrigue and fighting, Shirkuh became vizier in 1171 and brought the country back to the Orthodox fold by giving the order to pray for the Abbasid (Sunni) caliph at Friday prayers. A few weeks later Shirkuh died and Saladin was elected to replace him. On Nur ad-Din's death in 1174, fighting broke out over his succession. In response Saladin marched up from Egypt, married his widow and took command. The Crusaders were prevented from profiting in the interregnum by the death of their own king Amalric and Saladin now began working to unite the Muslims behind him in a *jihad* (holy war) against the Crusaders. Once he had succeeded in this task he needed only a *casus belli*. The opportunity arose when the infamous Reynald of Chatillon launched a raid from his stronghold at Karak against a Meccan caravan in violation of a truce—this affront was too much for the upright Saladin who mustered his army and set off for Palestine.

The battle of Hattin took place on 4 July 1187. It spelt catastrophe for the Crusaders who had squabbled over tactics and ended up overnighting without water. Exhausted and dehydrated, they were an easy target for the Arab forces although they put up a brave fight. The king, Guy of Lusignan, and many knights were captured and while Saladin was as chivalrous as ever to the king he personally struck off the head of Reynald of Chatillon. Hattin turned the tide of the conflict against the Crusaders and a domino effect followed as castle after castle fell or surrendered to Saladin. By mid-1189 the Crusaders held only Tyre, Tripoli and Antioch, although they did recoup some of their losses during the Third Crusade under Richard the Lionheart's able leadership.

Saladin died of a fever on March 1193 at the age of 54. He left barely enough money for his funeral, having died as simply as he lived. Nor did his line survive long after him as the Mamlukes ousted the Ayyubids in 1260. Saladin, however, lived on as a legend in the West. Finding it hard to reconcile his principled greatness with their own vision of the Saracen, he was made an honorary Westerner and seen as the embodiment of Christian virtues despite his religion. The French even claimed he must be of their blood to have been so great a knight and gave him a French grandmother! Dante put him in the first circle of hell—a limbo for good heathens—and Sir Walter Scott painted a glowing, romantic portrait of him in *The Talisman*. Strangely he was less popular among Muslims than the Mamluke Sultan Baybars, the Caliphate having always been rather wary of him.

From Ajlun you can either return to Jarash or continue down to the Jordan Valley by turning left immediately after the Ar-Rabad Hotel. This is a lovely drive in spring when the country road is lined with wild flowers and takes c 45 minutes, emerging south of Pella.

Also not far from Jarash is **Dibeen National Park** where there is a *resthouse* with accommodation. Phone ahead to make arrangements if you want to stay, or take a picnic, as many Jordanians do, and enjoy the landscape of hills and pine woods in which the resthouse is located. To reach Dibeen from Jarash turn right at Hadrian's Arch, then immediately left and keep on, passing the Lebanese House Restaurant. After 11km, bear right at a sign for the 2km resthouse or stop to picnic on the way.

Jarash to Irbid

From Jarash to Irbid on the shortest route it is c 35km via 30km **al Husn**, a small town notable for the number of its churches and the magnificent tell, some 40ft high (12m), which dominates the settlement. Tell al Husn is unexcavated, but a tomb discovered 1km to the south was first used at the beginning of the Bronze Age (c 3000 BC), suggesting the site may already have been settled then. Surface finds and architectural fragments attest Roman and Byzantine occupation.

IRBID
Irbid, Jordan's third largest city after Amman and Zarqa, has grown around an ancient tell which is now largely covered by modern buildings. Surveys and salvage excavations have shown that the site was occupied from the Chalcolithic period (c 3500 BC). Irbid has been identified with Roman/Byzantine Arbela, mentioned in Eusebius' Onomasticon, but the remains of classical antiquity recorded by 19C travellers are no longer visible. There are plans to convert an Ottoman building on the tell, formerly used as a prison, into a museum. Irbid already has one of the best archaeological museums in the country, the **Museum of Jordanian Heritage**, sponsored by the Federal Republic of Germany, which is in the vast campus of the **Yarmuk University** on the southern outskirts of the town. One of the foremost universities in Jordan, Yarmuk University was inaugurated in 1976.

■ There are several entrances to the university campus; coming from Amman turn left at the roundabout by the stadium, then right after c 500m, around the stadium, and there is an entrance by a museum sign with opening hours (Sat–Wed 10.00–17.00) c 500m along on the left. If you drive in you should first contact the authorities in a building on the right just inside the gate; they will tell you how to reach the museum, which is part of the Institute of Archaeology and Anthropology.

Exhibits are arranged over two floors, in more or less chronological order, and accompanied by photographs and detailed descriptions. On the ground floor are four main rooms and a temporary exhibition hall, to the right of the entrance desk, which often focuses on recent excavations. Jordan's prehistory is the theme of **Room 1**, which features Palaeolithic hunter-gatherers and the development of farming and village life in the Neolithic period. Notable are clay figures of the 7th millennium BC from 'Ain Ghazal near Amman, among the earliest 'statues' known. In **Room 2** are finds from the early city states of the Bronze and Iron Ages including Ammon, Moab and Edom. **Room 3** concentrates on the Nabateans and the Decapolis; a special section exhibits finds, including jewellery and leather sandals, from a cemetery excavated at Queen Alia Airport, Amman. **Room 4** looks at Jordan as part of the Islamic world; among reconstructions are a traditional pharmacist's shop, a potter's workshop and a blacksmith's forge. Rooms around the courtyard represent local rural life and architecture. On the **upper floor** are excellent displays of the development of different crafts and technologies such as stone, metals, glass and textiles.

About 1km from the university, in the Department of Antiquities building on Al Ma'amun Street, is the smaller **Irbid Archaeological Museum** (open 8.00–14.00 except Fridays) with cases containing pottery, glass, figurines and jewellery from the Irbid area and Jordan Valley. Mosaic panels along the walls and in the corridor come from various sites including Hallabat.

North-east of Irbid

Around Irbid the countryside is beautiful, especially in spring, when many areas are covered in flowers. To the north-east is the lovely Wadi al-Shallaleh, with fig trees and olive groves, on the western edge of which is the site of **Zeiraqun**, c12km from Irbid. Follow signs to Sal east of Irbid, continue through the village, c1.5km after the end of the asphalt road bear left on a dirt track along the side of the wadi, keep left at the fork after 2km and c 500m further Zeiraqun is on a rise to the left.

Zeiraqun, which has been excavated in two areas, is one of the largest Early Bronze Age sites in Jordan. Surrounding the settlement was a massive 7m-wide wall with projecting towers and bastions, which has been partly cleared in both the upper and lower town. There is a bent axis gateway in the upper fortifications, and behind the city wall south of the gate is a temple complex consisting of a circular structure, probably an altar, and rectangular rooms, all surrounding an open courtyard. A permanent water supply was ensured by stepped shafts leading to the water table in the valley bottom from inside the town.

Looking north down the valley from Zeiraqun is the unexcavated **Tell as-Subba**, where Chalcolithic pottery has been collected and across the wadi to the north-east on a high spur is c1km **Tell al-Fukhara**, reached by continuing down the same road to the valley bottom and up the other side, bearing left at the fork and left again just before the site. Excavations here have revealed a Hellenistic 'villa' surrounded by a wall, with stone silos in several rooms; deep soundings have given a sequence from the Early Bronze to the Iron Age.

Capitolias, Abila and Araq al-Habis

North of Irbid are the Decapolis cities of Capitolias and Abila, the latter well worth a visit. Take the Umm Qais road and after c 3km turn left past a petrol station in the modern village of **Beit Ras**, ancient **Capitolias**.

History

Capitolias is not mentioned as one of the Decapolis cities in Pliny's description of the area in the 1C, but is included in the expanded list given by the 2C geographer Ptolemy. Named after Jupiter Capitolianus, it was a walled Roman city by the end of the 1C and grew in importance during the Byzantine period when it was represented at the early Church Councils of Nicea (325) and Chalcedon (451). Like Gadara and Abila it was famous for its wine, which was exported as far as the Hijaz. Capitolias peacefully adapted to the Islamic invasions and flourished during the Umayyad period when Caliph Yazid II had a palace there. It was still noted as a town under the Abbasids and some occupation probably continued until the present day.

There are few remains of ancient Capitolias. A short distance down the hill on the right surrounded by modern buildings are the rubbish filled remains of a large reservoir, probably originally Roman although reused in later periods and further along, up the hill on the right, is a second reservoir cut into the bed rock, which was connected to the first by a tunnel.

Continue along the main Umm Qais road and where there is a left fork for Umm Qais keep straight on towards the Yarmuk. After c 7km the road turns left to descend to the luxuriant green Wadi Quweilbeh, filled with pomegranate trees. In the valley bottom is 'Ain Quweilbeh, a strong perennial spring. About 1km beyond the spring fork right and turn right again by the first olive grove towards the columns of a Byzantine church some 500m along. **Quweilbeh**, ancient **Abila**, is a huge site, comprising two mounds, Umm al-'Amad (to the south) and Tell Abila (to the north) with the lower town between them and an extensive cemetery across the valley to the east.

History

In antiquity, as now, Abila was in a favourable position, well watered and surrounded by fertile agricultural land, and excavations have shown that the site was occupied at various times from the Neolithic to the Umayyad period and later. Like Capitolias, Abila is first mentioned as a Decapolis city by the 2C geographer Ptolemy; it flourished in Roman and Byzantine times and declined after the Umayyad period, perhaps as a result of the severe earthquake in the area in 746.

On **Tell Umm Al-'Amad**, which means 'mother of columns' in Arabic, excavations revealed a 7C triapsidal church with two rows of 12 columns, alternately limestone and basalt, flanking the nave, and a pillared porch to the west. Many of the columns have been re-erected; the limestone capitals are decorated, some with a cross, the basalt capitals are plain. Geometric mosaic decoration was found in the porch and the nave and side aisles were paved with opus sectile. **Tell Abila** to the north, the city's acropolis, was surrounded by a substantial wall. A trench on the northern slope showed that the wall was added to in the Byzantine and Umayyad periods and its lower courses date to the Hellenistic and Iron Ages. On the acropolis a 6C triapsidal **basilica** has been excavated, built over an earlier church or temple and reused during the Umayyad period. A deep sounding by the church goes back to the Early Bronze Age.

In the depression between the two mounds was the commercial centre of the city, at least in Roman and Byzantine times. Clearly visible is what appears to be the cavea of a **theatre**, in which a large Umayyad building was subsequently

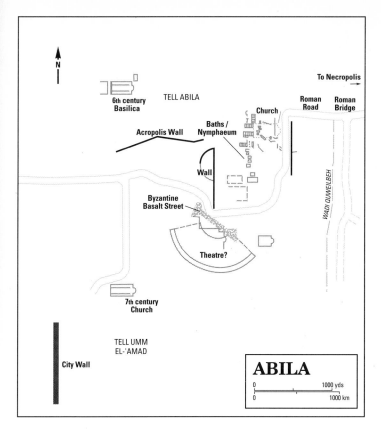

6th century
Basilica

TELL ABILA

Church

Roman
Road

Roman
Bridge

Baths /
Nymphaeum

Acropolis Wall

Wall

WADI QUWEILBEH

Byzantine
Basalt Street

Theatre?

7th century
Church

TELL UMM
EL-'AMAD

City Wall

ABILA

0 — 1000 yds
0 — 1000 km

constructed. In front of the cavea is a well-preserved section of Byzantine basalt street, laid over earlier limestone paving, and to the east are the foundations of a third **basilica church**. North of the cavea is a large building with vaults which may have been a **nymphaeum** or baths complex. Two *qanats* or underground aqueducts which run from 'Ain Quweilbeh below Umm al-'Amad may have fed this installation. Beyond is another church, near the old east–west road which crosses the wadi over an ancient **bridge.**

Several cemeteries have been investigated at Abila; in the **necropolis** on the eastern side of Wadi Quweilbeh, opposite the site, you can visit several beautiful painted tombs, probably the last resting place of some of Abila's wealthier citizens.

Either walk across the valley and climb up to the tombs or return to the Irbid road and turn left at the junction where you descended the valley. Park after c 700m, take a torch with you and walk left across the fields to the cliff edge. There should be a guard around to show you the tombs, most of which date from the Late Hellenistic, Roman and Byzantine periods; if he is not there they may well be open anyway. Along the cliff to the north is a very large tomb with a door and arched entrance and 20–30 loculi inside. Walls and ceilings were frescoed but the painting is quite damaged; in the vaulting towards the back of the tomb is a portrait of a lady. From this tomb crawl into the one alongside which contains a number of sarcophagi and better preserved frescoes: portrait busts of women wearing Phrygian caps, flowers, pomegranates, birds and dolphins to guide the deceased to safe havens on the other side. Retrace your steps and climb further down to visit a third tomb which can be difficult of access because of the thistles. It has a beautifully carved solid stone door with a knocker and inside are some of Abila's most charming paintings. In an alcove to the right a lady with a key hanging from her girdle holds open a book, to the left an inscription on a tomb painted in a tabula ansata reads 'Courage, no-one is immortal, she died six years old'.

To visit the caves of **Al-Habis**, one of the strangest Crusader sites in the Middle East, return to the road and continue on bearing right at a fork to 3km Hartha. Cross the roundabout and keep on for 4km, turning right at a track into an olive grove just before a checkpoint. From a dip to the south of the army observation post which overlooks the Yarmuk gorge (do not take photographs) you can see the caves at the top end of Wadi Habis—a 15-minute walk away on a narrow goat track running along its steep western slope. In spring the cliffs are covered with flowers and even if you do not get to the caves it is a beautiful picnic area.

History

The caves of Al-Habis Jaldak, as they are called by Arab historians, were probably first used in the Byzantine period. Early in the 11C they were occupied by the Crusaders, to whom they were known as Cava de Suet, and subsequently they changed hands several times. They are included in various treaties and were obviously of considerable strategic importance. Perched above the Yarmuk the occupants could keep a watchful eye over events below and retreat into their caves if necessary. William of Tyre gives an account of psychological warfare conducted by the Crusaders who, having lost the site to 70 Saracens, began to dig down from above. Fearing that the ceilings would collapse the latter surrendered after three weeks.

Nowadays the only occupants are goats below and hawks above. A small niche with a cross just above the upper caves is most easily seen from a distance. The rock shelf below the caves is now covered in a thick layer of dried goat dung and the lower caves, over which there are some petroglyphs, may be full of kids. Climbing equipment is needed to get to the upper storeys since part of the rock face has fallen away, but the 'Church Cave' can be reached by scrambling up a few rocks. Inside two bays flank the entrance and there are also a couple of niches. The ceiling is cross-vaulted; the lack of decoration may imply that this was used as a church during the Iconoclastic period. Apparently the three levels of caves were linked by wooden stairs and chimneys, and water was stored in cisterns.

EAST OF AMMAN

In the desert east of Amman lie a number of interesting sites which attest to the historic importance of the region. In Roman times this was frontier land and a number of forts, such as that at **Azraq**, built to hold the line and guard trade routes, still remain. The great trade route up the Wadi Sirhan led to Azraq; from there other routes continued to Syria and the Mediterranean marked by settlements which developed along their way. Various Umayyad desert complexes, among them **Qasr Kharana**, and the decorated baths at **Qusayr Amra**, can also be included in a round trip; it is possible to combine this route with a tour of the Hauran sites (p 97). Excursions can also be made to the nature reserve at **Shaumari** near Azraq and, with four-wheel drive and a guide, to the isolated **Qasr Burqu** and the forts at **Aseikhin** and **Uweinid.**

Some 20km from Amman en route to Kharana the large **reservoir** at **Muwaqqar** lies just south of the main road and is still in use. Not much remains of the former Umayyad complex on the hill above. Some capitals have been incorporated into modern village houses and the capital of a 10m stone water gauge with a carved Kufic inscription is now in Amman Archaeological Museum. This dated the reservoir in which it was found, and possibly the entire complex, to the time of Yazid II (720–724). When Gertrude Bell paid a visit to the site early this century a vaulted structure with columns and carved capitals was still partly standing, now all that remains is a jumble of rubble, some low walls and some paving between the village houses.

Excursion to Qasr Mshash

A four-wheel drive vehicle is needed for the last section of the trip to **Qasr Mshash**, one of the less well known of the Umayyad desert complexes. From Muwaqqar take the second road left and shortly after fork right. Head east for 16km on a paved road, then bear left on a track to cross the wadi to the north bank and continue eastwards a further 2km. Mshash stands on the very edge of the wadi and blends into its environment making it hard to spot. First you will reach the **reservoir** right of the track and half-buried in the sand—only the southern wall and plastered settling tank which runs into the west end are now visible. Continuing east you will come to the rectangular four-roomed **baths complex** and pool. The brick stokehole of the furnace can be seen at the north end, as can part of a bench in the adjacent long room. The baths were plastered and had marble floors. Mshash itself is a small (26sq m) building with 13 rooms around a **courtyard** and an entrance in the east. No signs of decoration remain and its precise function is unknown—it was probably a stop on the way from Azraq to Amman. The large number of cisterns and reservoirs built here imply agricultural activity as well. With four-wheel drive it is possible now to cross the wadi and head south-east to the main Amman–Azraq highway, otherwise you must take the long way back to Muwaqqar before continuing to 35km Kharana.

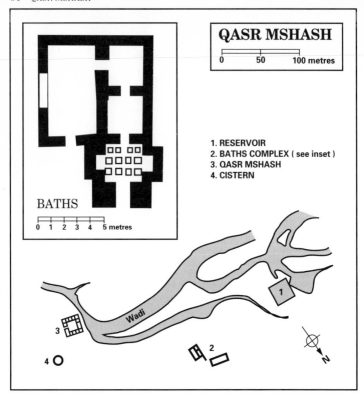

QASR MSHASH

0   50   100 metres

1. RESERVOIR
2. BATHS COMPLEX (see inset)
3. QASR MSHASH
4. CISTERN

BATHS

0 1 2 3 4 5 metres

Wadi

KHARANA

History

Of all the Umayyad desert complexes this small, striking building looks most like a castle. Lying just south of the main road and now unfortunately close to a radio mast and pylons, Kharana is extremely well preserved. Its looks belie its purpose, for it was not built as a fort. The 'arrow' slits in its walls are angled wrongly, set too high and are too narrow inside for archers to have used nor could the solid towers have been manned. The wadi Kharana is a tributary of the Wadi Sirhan, the great wide valley which was one of the trade arteries from Arabia to Azraq, and Kharana may have functioned as a stopover on trade routes between Amman, Qasr Tuba and Bayir or to Damascus, or possibly as a meeting place where tribal matters and differences could be discussed and settled. The building shows both Syrian and Iraqi influences, but the second storey appears to be unfinished. It is thought to have been built in the late 7C with later work dating to the 720s—an inscription scribbled over one of the doorways gives a date of 710.

Kharana is only 35m sq, with round **corner towers** and semi-circular **interval towers** in the north, west and east walls. The south wall entrance has flanking **quarter-towers** and a window surmounted by a decorative strip of five palmettes. Built of limestone rubble and mortar, the top courses were finished in larger, whiter

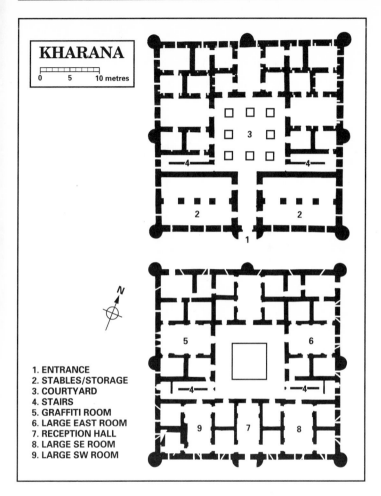

KHARANA

0   5   10 metres

1. ENTRANCE
2. STABLES/STORAGE
3. COURTYARD
4. STAIRS
5. GRAFFITI ROOM
6. LARGE EAST ROOM
7. RECEPTION HALL
8. LARGE SE ROOM
9. LARGE SW ROOM

limestone blocks. Three sets of window slits provide ventilation and between the top two is a band of diagonally placed bricks, a decorative element still seen locally on garden walls. The towers have an additional band of this decoration at a lower level.

Enter through the arched passage (1) which has two large rooms on either side thought to have served as stables and storage (2). The **courtyard** (3) had an underground cistern and an open, plastered drain led out to the south. A portico ran round the courtyard with arches borne on eight square pillars—traces of the arches can still be seen on some walls. The downstairs rooms are plain and divided, like those upstairs, into *bayts* (suites of rooms). This is a typically Umayyad feature found in other desert complexes like Tuba and Mshatta. There were two distinct stages of building at Kharana: first the ground floor and elaborately decorated west side upstairs and, at some later date, the rest.

Flights of stairs rise on the left and right sides (4); the little rooms behind them on the first floor were once thought to have been latrines. This is now doubted because the west side is in the direction of the prevailing wind and the drain outfall would have spilt into the room below! The first floor has six large rooms with a number of smaller chambers off each. The stairs continue up to the rooftop.

Climb the west (left) stairs and step into the first room to your left, minding your head on the very low lintel. The plaster rosettes decorating the walls here were made in moulds, but others on the south side are thought to have been stamped into the wet plaster in situ. The famous **graffiti room** (5) is next—so-called because of the scrawled **inscription** directly below the squinch over the north-west doorway. Though now very faded it reads 'Abd al-Malik the son of 'Ubayd wrote it on Monday three days from Muharram of the year 92' (24 November 710). Sadly modern graffiti has now joined it in this extremely ornate room with its blind arcades, rosette friezes and semi-domed ceiling. Kharana was innovative in its construction techniques; the placing of the dome on squinches and pendentives was later to become a notable feature of Islamic architecture. The rosettes here and in nearby rooms are typical of the early stage of building. All six large rooms upstairs have blind arcades and arches supported by groups of engaged colonettes. Pass through the possibly unfinished north side which is open to the sky. The large room on the east (6) is plainer with no rosettes, but a simple dog's tooth pattern for decoration. The south side is distinct in having three large rooms, the central one possibly a **reception hall** (7). It has a row of little windows over the courtyard door, fewer colonettes supporting arches and may have been dome-covered. The last large room (9) has larger rosettes at cornice level and a semi-dome with four arched windows framed by engaged colonettes over the door and stepped recesses above.

Water supplies to Kharana probably came from wells sunk in the gravel bed of the wadi, a system still in use today. No other contemporary buildings have been found in its vicinity, leaving it something of an enigma among the Umayyad residences of Jordan.

THE UMAYYADS

The Umayyads (AD 661–750) are the first Islamic dynasty. On Mohammed's death a leader, the Caliph, had been chosen by a Council. This custom continued for a while until power struggles broke out with the appointment of Caliph Uthman and subsequently worsened under his successor, the Prophet's son-in-law, Ali. After his victory in the ensuing civil war, the first Umayyad ruler Mu'awiya moved the capital north to Damascus where he had been Governor: a shift of power from the Hijaz northwards.

The Umayyads presided over a tremendous expansion of the Muslim world: to North Africa, Spain and Central Asia. It was a time of dynamic development, but it also saw the beginnings of dissent and schism within Islam—the Shi'ite movement (from Shi'atu Ali, the party of Ali) developed after the death of the Prophet's son-in law Ali in 661 (briefly caliph before being deposed in favour of Mu'awiya) and of his son Hussein in 680. Ultimately this conflict and tribal feuding was to lead to the downfall of the Umayyad house, but in the 90 years of Umayyad rule their achievements were considerable: they forged a new Islamic administration capable of running an empire which by then stretched from India to Morocco. Aesthetically they stood for a fusion of styles from which a truly Islamic art was forged. In Syria the Arabs entered a region with its own artistic and cultural heritage and were influenced both by Persian and Eastern Mediterranean (Graeco-Roman and

Byzantine) art and iconography. Hence the importance of the Umayyad monuments found in Jordan, Syria and Palestine: buildings like the Dome of the Rock in Jerusalem, or the Great mosque in Damascus paved the way for later developments in Islamic art.

On a more personal level there are the 'desert complexes', expressions of a more private side to their lives, but which stand today as prime examples of early, secular, Islamic art. Showing great variety in their construction and functions (the Amra baths, enigmatic Kharana, the splendid, but unfinished palace of Mshatta) one of their hallmarks was a wealth of decoration: mosaic, fresco, stone or stucco carving, depicting events, people, animals and sometimes just pure pattern. These complexes, often inaccurately called castles, are located on the edge of the desert and have aroused much speculation among scholars, who first saw them as retreats for the Umayyad rulers. Certainly they may have been built there in order to maintain a close relationship with the tribes whose support they needed, but there are other explanations: some were on well-used trade routes and may have served transient visitors, some may have had some defensive or agricultural purpose, while yet others were there purely for pleasure and as an escape from city life for a dynasty with close links to the bedouin and desert life.

It became increasingly difficult for the Umayyads to hold their empire together, weakened as it was with feuding and religious dissent. The Shi'ite movement was gaining support from disaffected converts to Islam, disgruntled at tax burdens and perceived discrimination. A further shift in the centre of power was heralded by the ascendancy of the Abbasid dynasty east of Baghdad. The last of the Umayyads, Marwan II, was killed in Egypt and his head sent back to the man who had by then been proclaimed Caliph, Abu'l Abbas, descendant of a relation of the Prophet. A branch of the Umayyads hung on in Spain until the 11C, but Syria and Jordan were never again to be so close to the centre of power. Nonetheless the monuments of the Umayyads still stand in the desert as reminders of the early days and achievements of Islam.

QUSAYR AMRA

From Kharana it is possible to reach Qasr Tuba (p 186) on a desert track southwards. Four-wheel drive and a guide are essential for this. Continue through the desert to 15km **Qusayr Amra** which lies just north of the road.

History

The baths complex at Qusayr Amra lies by the Wadi Butm, named after the terebinth trees which still grow there. Amra is thought to have been built by the Caliph Walid 1 (700–715), builder of the famous mosque at Damascus. The limestone building is in good repair, but its real attraction is its extensive wall paintings which represent a formative stage in the development of Islamic art. Figures and even erotic scenes are portrayed, showing late Hellenistic and Persian influences, illustrating the Umayyad use of borrowed iconography. A fascinating contrast to more formal, official statements, Amra affords us a glimpse of a private life. The master of Amra, whoever he was, withdrew here for relaxation and leisure and its walls provide a pictorial record of these pursuits. The baths also lie on an old trade route linking Azraq with Amman. They were carefully restored in the 1970s by a team of Spanish archaeologists.

Before entering note the remains of the **water system**: the cistern, the well and *saqiya* system (turning circle) for the ox are north of the entrance and the **furnace** is adjacent to the domed steam room. The tradition of the baths, offspring of the classical baths, but with an added religious dimension of ritual cleanliness, continues today in the Muslim world. Usually there is a cold room/frigidarium in which to acclimatise before moving to the hot room/caldarium for a sweat and returning to the warm room/tepidarium for a soap and massage. Rest was taken in the entrance room/undressing room/apodyterium.

Central aisle, 'Throne Room' and side rooms. Enter from the north into the **hall**, comparable to the Roman apodyterium, but larger. The walls and ceilings are covered in wall paintings depicting a great diversity of scenes, not all discernible despite the excellent conservation work. The tunnel-vaulted central aisle and two side-aisles lead down to two alcoves and the 'Throne Room' at the back. The wall painting over the entrance shows a barely discernible bed, the foot of a woman, two figures around the bed and two women by the windows at the side; there is also a fish in the lunette above. On the side spandrels of these arches are more figures: on the left as you face the entrance a naked lady crowned by Victory welcomes visitors and on the right are a woman with a flute, a young man with a lute and a dancer. The **central vault** depicts scenes of court life: figures are surrounded by game-birds and a man on horseback on the north-east side may be St George (a popular legend here too). At the far end the arch over the **'Throne room'** has a frieze of figures on balconies and there are leopards on the side spandrels at this end. The soffit of the west arch shows a naked woman, matching that on the other side of two women and a medallion with a man's portrait.

Inside the throne room there are depictions of three women who may represent fertility, with cornucopia and trees in the arches and more courtiers. Overhead is a pattern of foliage. On the back wall is a ruler, perhaps Walid himself, under a baldaquin; the inscription is almost illegible. He is waited on by two attendants each with fly whisks, one appears to be more richly dressed and may be a dignitary. A band of partridges frames the scene. The two small **side chambers** are similarly decorated with a design of grapes and vine leaves, pomegranates and acanthus and a mosaic floor worked in a geometric pattern. The east chamber apse shows a lotus flower within a circle and there is a small pool in the north-east.

The **side aisles** of the main hall contrast with each other, the decorative scheme of the west aisle being mainly devoted to women while the east wall depicts masculine activity. Near the throne room end of the west aisle wall a woman reclines on a couch under an awning with a young man, a seated woman and a bearded man who appears in a number of the murals and is assumed to be the Master of Amra: the woman may well be his favourite concubine. Above the figures are two peacocks and an inscription in Greek (θAPA NIKH) referring to a victory. This probably relates to the nearby mural of the Six Kings on the west wall which dates the baths to after AD 711. The Greek and Kufic inscriptions are now illegible: on the left is the KAISAR (the Byzantine Emperor); behind him is RODORIKOS, the last Visigoth King of Spain who ruled in the year 711 and was defeated by the Umayyads; in the middle at the front is COSROES, the Persian Emperor, with the NEGUS (King of Abyssinia) behind him and on the right two others who may represent the Chinese Emperor and the King of India. While much of the work at Amra is in the tradition of Hellenistic Syria this depiction of the enemies of Islam holding their hands in a gesture of submission or homage shows Persian influence. Next to this scene is the concubine bathing naked in a pool, watched by onlookers on the left and a servant on the right. Moving right again, the bearded man watches male gymnastics, with above a hunting scene of beaters driving onagers into nets—hunting was obviously a favoured occupation at Amra.

The hunting theme continues on the **east wall** where a pack of saluki hounds are hunting down onagers; the Master of Amra is also present as they are chased, killed and skinned. Overhead are scenes of two couples and a lion which the excavator suggests may tell the story of Good and Evil. Hellenistic influences again appear in the two lunettes alongside the window of the south wall, on the left the muses of History (ICTOPI) and Philosophy and, on the right, the personification of

The Caldarium at Qusayr Amra

A Ursa Major	K Leo
B Ursa Minor	L Cancer
C Cepheus	M Gemini
D Draco	N Orion
E Perseus	O Dolphinus
F Andromeda	P Capricorn
G Cygnus	Q Sagittarius
H Hercules	R Scorpio
I Ophiucus	S Erichthonius
J Bootes	T Aquarius

Poetry (ΠΟΙΗC). Overhead the ceiling is divided into caissons showing metal-workers, carpenters, masons and stonemasons.

The **baths** are reached through a doorway in this wall. The style of decoration changes here. It is thought that two artists worked on the wall paintings at Amra, one of whom was responsible for the main hall, the other for the baths. The first room, probably the tepidarium, had a marble floor and the benches on the south and east sides would have been marble-clad. Over the entrance is a reclining lady with an admirer and attendant cupid while on the south and north walls a diamond grid contains figures—note the dancing lady, the flautist and the bear playing a lute while the monkey to its left claps its hands. The smoke-blackened ceiling depicts the three ages of man. The present window is larger than the original, in the lunettes there are three figures. Look at the **hypocaust system** in the caldarium next door: the floor was raised on brick piles so that hot air could circulate below and up flues in the walls; it also has a water basin. The roof is cross-vaulted and in the tympanum over the entrance to the first room are the figures of three women bathing, one of whom holds a child in her arms. Another woman with a cauldron stands to the right. On the west wall she is pouring water from the cauldron and over the door to the third room the child is about to be lowered into the basin. A vine decoration with men and animals covers the vault and niche on the north.

The last room, another **caldarium,** contains one of the earliest representations of the sky on a domed surface. The circumpolar constellations shown have been transposed left to right: presumably the artist was using a sketch based on a globe where the sky is seen from outside looking down rather than from inside looking upwards. The map is centred on the north star; Ursa Major and Ursa Minor are top centre with part of Draco's tail between them. Nearby with arms outstretched is Andromeda, Cygnus and Cassiopeia are below. Lower down Ophiucus the Serpent-holder wrestles with the snake. Identified with Aesclepius by the Greeks, the snake is a symbol of healing, but he is also believed by some to be the thirteenth sign of the zodiac. Upside-down Hercules has his foot on Draco's head—this was the dragon that guarded the golden apples of the Hesperides. Part of Leo, Sagittarius and the legs of the Gemini twins opposite lie on the red band which represents the zodiac. There are two basins in here, but most of the plaster has disappeared apart from the ceiling. Coloured glass tesserae found here imply some mosaic decoration. To the east is a passage way linking the furnace and stoke-room, above it was the tank for the hot room.

300m north-west beyond the boundary fence and just through a gate are the remains of a small watchtower.

AZRAQ

Return to the road and head for 27km Azraq. The government *resthouse* in Azraq provides meals and accommodation, has air-conditioned rooms and a pool in summer. Mosquito repellent is definitely recommended. To reach it turn left at the T-junction in Azraq Shishan village and left again in 3km. There are several other places to eat in Azraq. The castle is 3km north of the resthouse in Azraq Druze village.

History

Azraq is located on the southern edge of the basalt country and at the top of the Wadi Sirhan, the great trade route up from the south. Its pools of fresh water, now sadly much depleted, made it the largest oasis in this part of the desert and second only to Palmyra in the Syrian desert—Azraq means blue in Arabic. The discovery of large numbers of Paleolithic hand axes while some marshland was being drained is proof that it was an important centre long before the Romans built a fort there, later renovated under the Ayubbids. The earliest inscription found at the fort was a basalt altar referring to Diocletian, which dates the fort at latest to the late 3C. It may also have been rebuilt during the reign of Constantine. The Third Cyrenaica Legion probably had a garrison here: defences at the top of Wadi Sirhan were vital to guard the trade route and the **Strata Diocletiana** ran north from here.

Old aerial photographs show a larger rectangular outline extending behind the fort which could be the plan of an earlier fort. The strategic importance of the site, and the fact that the small forts of Uweinid and Aseikhin were both occupied in the 3C as well, hints at earlier Roman military occupation. Rebuilt by the Ayubbids in the 13C Azraq had acquired an infamous reputation by the start of this century: one visitor was told by the headman of the Arabs living in the fort that his first task in the job had been to cut down the remains of his predecessor hanging over the gate! The Druze settled here in the 1920s fleeing trouble with the French in Syria and made a living making salt from the briny water of the local salt pans. Traditionally this was done by families in the summer months, but the job has now been taken over by a cooperative. The main freshwater pools of the oasis were just south of the castle and in Shishan village 6km south, where there is also a large peculiarly-shaped ancient reservoir on the eastern edge of the village. Formerly the marshes and mudflats attracted huge numbers of migrating birds as well as indigenous species, but now that water is pumped away the numbers have fallen drastically as the pools have dried up. However, if you visit in the early spring after a wet winter you will see sheets of water covering the flats and stretching away into the distance.

Azraq is much changed since Lawrence described it as: 'the blue fort on its rock above the rustling palms, with the fresh meadows and shining springs of water' and spoke of its 'unfathomable silence'. Now the road runs by it and a village has grown up around it. Enter through the **bent entrance gate** in the south wall, noting the massive **basalt door** which still swings on its hinges and the **machicolation** and **inscription** overhead recording rebuilding by Ayubbid occupants under the governor Azzadin Aybak in 1237. The basic structure of the fort remained unchanged, however, and some of the original Roman masonry is still there.

Inside the gatehouse on the left are a few carved stone panels of animals including gazelle, a horse, and a lion and a zebu around a date palm which were found in Shishan reservoir and are probably Umayyad. The corbelling overhead is typical of the basalt architecture of the Hauran. T.E. Lawrence wintered in the room above and complained of the leaking roof—as no mortar was used it must be very damp in winter. Chapter 79 of *Seven Pillars of Wisdom* has a dramatic account of his stay here with tales of ghostly dogs howling outside at night! The ancient Druze guardian, whose father was here then, will whisper his name at you if he is around. Opposite the entrance are a couple of milestones and various **inscribed blocks**: one on the left is a basalt altar broken in two. The almost illegible lower part is in Greek, the upper half, in Latin, is the earliest inscription found here. Referring to the Tetrarchy, it uses the pseudonyms Ioviorum and Herculiorum for the emperors Diocletian and Maximian, who assumed these titles, according to

Gibbon; 'from a motive either of pride or superstition...the motion of the world was maintained by the all-seeing wisdom of Jupiter, the invincible arm of Hercules purged the earth from monsters and tyrants.' Next to this and dated by experts to 326–333 is a block mentioning Constantine and repair work done to the building ([IN]CURIAEVETUSTATE...CONLAPSUM).

Basalt door at Azraq

In shape the fort is almost square with slightly projecting rectangular **corner towers** and **interval towers** in the north and south walls. The towers may have been three-storey, rooms along the walls two-storey. Two **flanking towers** in the centre of the east wall suggest that the original entrance lay here. A large structure, most likely the **Principia**, projects from the west wall just left of the **postern** with the 3 ton basalt door mentioned by Lawrence who says that the whole west wall shook when it clanged shut. The **courtyard mosque** with arched roof and *mihrab* is probably Ayyubid. Water came from a well near the north-east corner tower. Stables with stone mangers ran along the north wall—one look at the misshapen arches will show that modern repairs have been done here. Some rooms in the west and south walls also have palm tree rafters replacing missing basalt slabs; the Druze have also rebuilt some rooms.

Azraq to Shishan Reservoir, Shaumari Nature Reserve and the Roman fort at Uweinid

From Azraq it is a short journey south to the nature reserve at Shaumari. Head south at the junction with the road from Amra, passing **Shishan reservoir** on the left. Here in groves of cane and tamarisk at the pumping station are the remains of an unusually shaped reservoir with 2m basalt walls. After 7km turn right at a sign for Shaumari. The small Roman fort of **Uweinid** (four-wheel drive needed) lies on the tip of a low basalt spur c 4km right of the road and overlooking the Wadi Butm which bends around it, providing good natural defences on the north and west sides. Turn off the Shaumari road after c 2km and head towards the end of the basalt ridge—there is a desert road in the wadi, but if you cannot find it you will need to walk the last kilometre across the wadi. In plan Uweinid is irregular with a **tower** in the south-west corner and a small **entrance** in an angle of the west wall. Between the entrance and the tower lies the **inscribed lintel** which mentions Septimius Severus and L. Marius Perpetuus, Governor of Arabia 200–202. Its presence here implies a Roman military presence in Azraq by then, but no proof of this has yet emerged. The inscription is still clear, as is the deliberate obliteration of the fourth, fifth and sixth lines, possibly done to erase the name of the Emperor Geta, assassinated by his brother Caracalla in 212. A further inscription, now lost, referred to the building of a baths for a vexillation (detachment) of the Third Cyrenaica legion.

Unlike the fort at Aseikhin, water cannot have been a problem for the soldiers here. In spring the wadi is full of white broom and there are larks overhead; even in summer there is some water there. Another smaller **tower** stands in the wadi a few hundred metres west of the fort, its walls still 3–4m high. Although full of sand a door can be seen in the partition wall inside. The purpose of this tower is unclear, but it may have been built to guard a cistern. Uweinid appears to have been abandoned in the 4C.

Return to the road and continue on. Ahead in a grove of trees is **Shaumari nature reserve**. Since 1975 it has been run by the Royal Society for the Conservation of Nature who have a breeding programme for oryx which now number 167 head here. Shaumari is open daily, entrance is 300 fils and there is a playground, picnic area and viewing platform; the 22km square reserve also has onager, ostrich and gazelle although the latter are particularly shy and difficult to see. Predators like the wolf and hyena are now extremely rare, but jackal are still seen on occasion. Inside the gate on the right is a display room and the staff will also be happy to provide further information. There is also a reserve at Azraq, until recently an important stopover for migrating birds, many of whom now land further west since pumping has drained the pools of Azraq.

Excursion from Azraq to 'Ain as-Sil, Aseikhin and Burqu

1km north of Azraq fort turn right onto the old Safawi road and continue for 1km. The farmhouse of **'Ain as-Sil** lies near the pine trees down a track on the right. Built in Umayyad times over what was possibly a Roman fortlet the entrance in the east wall leads to a courtyard with seven rooms around it. Two bread ovens were found in the north-east corner room and in the adjacent rooms are a millstone and a basalt press. A partly excavated **baths complex** was later added along the west wall; plaster and some piping can still be seen there.

From Azraq take the road up to the junction at as-Safawi, passing the fort of **Aseikhin** distinguishable on a hill-top to the right c 15km north of Azraq fort. Again four-wheel drive is needed for the ascent to this superbly located fort. The easiest way to reach it is to get onto the old road running to the right of the new one at the 13km quarry. In 1.5km turn right onto a track heading north-east and circle round a further 7km to approach on the east. It is worth the scramble up the steep slope from here for the wonderful views, but it cannot have been the nicest place to be stationed—out on the frontier and with no assured water supply. Built of basalt with rooms around a square **courtyard**, the entrance is on the east side where the **gatehouse** and an arch still stand. Internal arches supported the ceilings of the rooms and still stand in the east, south and west centre rooms. There is no evidence of a second storey of rooms and no inscriptions have been found here, but there are signs of earlier occupation of the site in the form of flints, a boulder wall and kites (pens used in game hunting) nearby. Water provision was clearly a

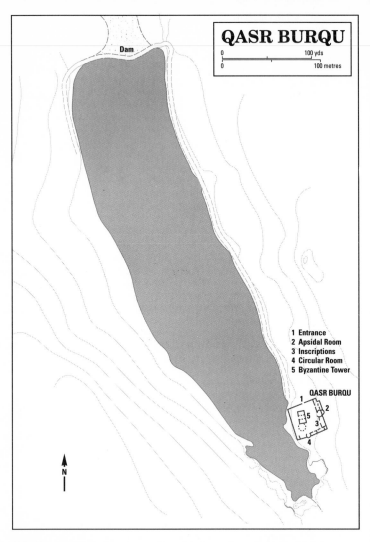

QASR BURQU

0 — 100 yds
0 — 100 metres

Dam

1 Entrance
2 Apsidal Room
3 Inscriptions
4 Circular Room
5 Byzantine Tower

QASR BURQU

N

difficulty: it seems to have been collected and stored in a hollow on the north side which was blocked by a dam wall. Doubtless this disadvantage was compensated for by the commanding position and prior to the Romans Aseikhin may have been occupied by the Nabateans.

Return to the road and at c 30km Safawi junction turn right onto the road to Iraq. Drive for c 1 hour to the check point at Muqat where **Burqu Islamic Palace** is signed left 18km. This rarely visited but worthwhile site requires a four-wheel drive vehicle. Take a Bedouin guide from here or from 10km Ruweiyshid village for the 20km trip north-west as the way across sand flats and past wadis is not clear.

History
The small basalt fort, consisting of a square courtyard with rooms on two sides and a tower, lies by a lake on the wadi Minqat created by the building of a dam 2km to the north. It may well have been built to guard this water supply for passing caravans. Burqu may have become a monastic settlement in the Byzantine era. Spring is a lovely time to visit when the water laps at the foot of the fort walls, poppies and iris are blooming among the wormwood and birds congregate attracted by the water. The earliest inscription found here, now in a Chicago museum, was in Greek from a tomb and was dated to the 3C, later Arabic inscriptions dating to 700, 1380 and 1409 have also been found. On this evidence it is thought that the tower may have been built in the 3C and the larger enclosure added in the Umayyad era.

Enter by a door in the north-west wall. On the north-east side the longest room bears an **inscription** on the lintel, not in its original setting, which dates it to 700: 'Oh God! Bismillah. This is what Amir al-Walid, son of the commander of the faithful, built: these rooms. In the year 81 [700]'. A second scrawled inscription above this, dated AD 1409, says that Haroun read the Kufic inscription. The small **apsidal room** on the left with a pointed arch has niches left and right. It may have been the reception hall although there is also some speculation that it was a chapel. A cross decorates the lintel of the **circular room** on the south-west which is not bonded into the wall and may represent an earlier building phase. This room also has engaged pilasters on two sides. Between it and the tower in the courtyard is a **cistern**; the **tower** is an earlier building and more finely built. A very small door on the south-west side is now blocked; this lends credence to the theory that the tower was the first structure built, since the small entrance was obviously easier to defend in an isolated watch-tower. Scramble up the sides to look in—there are three ground-floor rooms of which not much beyond an arch is now visible. The walls still stand c 8m high and there were probably three storeys of rooms.

Azraq to Qasr Hallabat

From Azraq head back towards Amra, fork right onto the Zarqa road (30km), turn right 54km from Azraq and left soon after—the baths of **Hamman as-Sarah** are almost immediately on the left by the road. Smaller than the Amra baths the attractive limestone building has been partly restored. From the road you will first come to the **water system**: well, tank and turning circle for the animal to raise the water. Remains of a late Ottoman mosque are also nearby. The entrance to the baths lies behind the building to the south. Here there was an **entrance hall** and pool or basin with traces of plaster still visible and to the east an **alcove** and two **side rooms** with latrines; the drains are still there. Almost nothing remains of the mosaic, marble and mural with which the baths were decorated. Inside is the **apodyterium,** a cross-vaulted **tepidarium** showing the **hypocaust system** and flues up the walls as well as a small recess and, next to the furnace at the north end, a semi-domed **caldarium** with two water basins and raised floor.

2km on from the baths is **Qasr Hallabat**, one of the largest of the Umayyad desert complexes. Situated on a rise to the left of the road, it is now in a poor state of repair.

History

It is now known that Hallabat was one of a number of Roman forts built in the 2C to guard the road linking Azraq to the Via Nova Traiana (p 174). Subsequently it was enlarged: a Latin inscription refers to extension work done 212–215 and, according to a Greek inscription, restoration work was carried out in 529 under Justinian. It may have been abandoned after the Persian invasion in 614. The Umayyads rebuilt it, but to the same plan, adding a mosque, baths and water system. They also decorated many of the rooms with mosaic floors.

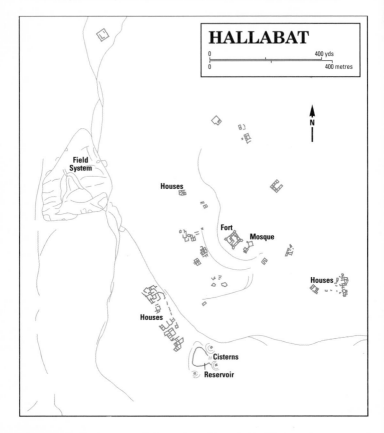

The **mosque** lies just east of the castle and is probably 8C. A portico ran round three sides and there were three entrances to it, the principal one in the north wall, opposite the *mihrab*. Between the mosque and the castle are the remains of a round structure which may have been built over as the fort expanded. On the other side of the entrance, by the north-east tower is a water tank. The **fort** is square with square **corner towers**; basalt was used in later extension work so its walls are now a blend of limestone and basalt particularly striking from outside. Turn left inside the castle and skirting the huge piles of rubble in the flagged courtyard, look over the doorway to the room left of the entrance: the great number of **inscribed**

blocks in it were perhaps taken from Umm al-Jimal or Khirbet as-Samra and are part of an inscription of the edict of the Emperor Anastasius reordering the Province of Arabia. Many rooms here have these blocks in the walls. In the rooms on the south wall there are still fragments of the marble cladding visible. The Umayyads added many mosaic floors, including fine depictions of animals and birds as well as geometric patterns; wall paintings and carved stucco completed the decorative scheme. If you scramble up to look out from the west wall you will see a **cistern** and house remains slightly to the left. Further away there is a large **reservoir** and several other cisterns while to the right the old agricultural area and two small mounds can be seen. The original 16m square Roman fort built of limestone was in the north-west corner of the present building. In the north-east corner a plastered stone water channel leads to the tower; water was collected on the roof, channelled around the castle and outside.

From here either retrace your steps to the main road or continue on and turn left and then right to rejoin the Zarqa road further on.

The Hauran

An alternative route north and east of Amman takes in the Hauran area of Jordan, a prosperous and thriving region in Roman and Byzantine times as attested by the numerous small churches, forts, provincial towns and smaller settlements along the way. Under the basalt stones which cover this treeless area the volcanic soil is fertile and productive—the Hauran was known for its grapes and indeed the area was sacred to Dionysus, Greek god of wine. Many Roman roads, including the Via Nova Traiana and the Strata Diocletiana, ran through the area and within the security of Roman military strength towns grew up and flourished along them. Interestingly, church inscriptions from the early Islamic period show that Christianity persisted here for a while. Some sites, like Umm al-Jimal, are well preserved enough to give a good idea of life in the Hauran in the Roman-Byzantine era; in others all that remains is the odd lintel inscribed with a cross and now incorporated into a modern building.

The industrial city of **Zarqa** lies some 20km north-east of Amman. There is not much to see here beyond the little Haj fort (closed Fridays) known as the **Qasr Shabib** which now lies in the grounds of a school near Shabib Hospital. From Ragadan Bus Station in Amman go straight to Zarqa and after 23km turn left at traffic lights down Prince Feisal Street. The partly restored 14m square building is well placed on the hill top at the end of the street. Enter from the north noting the **machicolation** between arch and door. Water was kept in two cisterns to the east and one by the doorway. Inside the single chamber is barrel-vaulted and the thick walls have *iwans* (arched bays) narrowing to flared slits for light and ventilation. Steps on the left wind upstairs where there are now only remains of walls and the stairs to the roof-top. In origin this fort is probably Mamluke and may have been built under the energetic 13C Sultan Baybars, perhaps to guard against attack by the Mongols. Charles Doughty called here while travelling with the Haj pilgrims from Damascus and gives a brief description of it in *Arabia Deserta*.

Continue north through Zarqa bearing right for Mafraq in 2km and then left in a further 2km at a sign for al-Hashemiya. Follow this road for 14km past a refinery and through the hills turning right at a sign for 7km **Khirbet as-Samra**. Cross the railway and drive up the hill to the gate on the left near the extensive ruins covering the hilltop.

History
This is ancient Hattita of the Peutinger Table, a town which prospered under the Romans; its location on the Via Nova Traiana midway between Amman and Bostra made it a suitable caravan stop. At the end of the 4C the *cohors I miliaria Thracum* was garrisoned here. A small fort east of the town may have been a watchpost on the Roman road. Like other Hauran towns, Byzantine Hattita fell within the Archbishopric of Bostra in Syria and is notable for its churches; eight have been excavated here, most had mosaic floors though none can now be seen in situ.

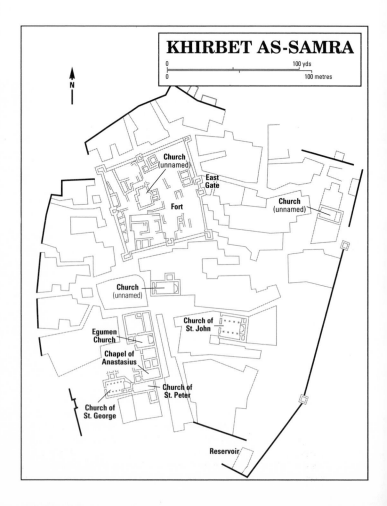

Begin with the **Roman fort** on the top of the hill which is probably 3C. A Latin inscription found here refers to 4C restoration work. The west wall is best preserved, together with its central gate, the north-west tower and the large **East Gate** with two flanking towers. The churches are mostly south of the fort, the largest, that of **St John**, is distinguished by the use of white limestone, unlike the rest which are built of basalt. Of particular interest was the 7C mosaic floor found here which, despite considerable iconoclastic damage, contained two intact representations of walled cities, now in the Amman Museum of Popular Traditions. An earlier representation of the same motif in the 6C church of SS Peter and Paul at Jarash identifies the towns as Alexandria and Memphis. In the south-west sector is a three-church complex which includes the **Church of St George**, built in 637 after the Islamic victory at the battle of the Yarmuk. A large cemetery now under the modern town which has moved east was remarkable for the great number of Christian stelae found. Marked with crosses, some were written in Aramaic. Half a kilometre east of the fort and just south both of the modern road and of a stretch of ancient road is a smaller, nearly square building which may have served as a watch-station over the Via Nova.

Return to the main road and continue on c16km, turn right to Mafraq, passing through **Rihab**, now a small village, where to date ten churches have been found. Two had mosaic inscriptions dating them to the period of Persian occupation in the early 7C, but the earliest, St Mary's, dates to 533. Five kilometres from the turn-off bear left along a small track towards the hangar protecting the **Church of St Menas**. It is possible to peer in if locked to see the rather faded mosaic of geometrical patterns with an **inscription** in the first intercolumnar space on the north side which mentions the benefactress Kometissa and gives a date of 635, during the brief Persian occupation. Across the road a reservoir is visible in the valley below, and south of the church a stone building incorporating earlier lintels, including one with part of a Greek inscription, houses another church.

Retrace your steps through Rihab turning left to 13km Mafraq in 1km. The little town of **Mafraq** has offices of the the the Department of Antiquities and a small archaeological museum is planned there, but not yet complete. Take the highway north a short distance turning right at a sign to Zubeidiyeh. Keep straight on at the junction in this village and 11km from the highway on the outskirts of **Ba'ij** look for the particularly fine stretch of **Via Nova Traiana** which crosses the modern road. This particular section is between milestations 13 and 14 and is constructed of rough stones contained within parallel side curbs and a central spine. In Roman times this foundation would have been surfaced with beaten earth. About 1km east of the road, in Ba'ij village, a late Roman fort was built in 411, which was recorded earlier this century and included a chapel, but almost all trace has been destroyed or covered by the modern village.

Excursion to Umm as-Surab and Sama

Turn left at the roundabout in Ba'ij crossing the Roman road again as you leave the village and head for 7km **Umm as-Surab** (mother of mirages). The tumbled basalt blocks of the site cover both sides of the road in the village. A tower on the north side marks the site of the **Church of SS Sergius and Bacchus**, converted to a mosque when the entrances and apse were blocked. To the north is a large plastered cistern and behind that a complex of rooms around a courtyard, in one of which is an arch and capitals on pilasters. The room next to this appears to have been a stable. 20m south-west of the church is another courtyard with rooms off it, one with a Nabatean inscription on the arch. South of the road are two more churches and a stable block. Look for a decorated lintel with a Greek cross which was once in position over the west door. The apse is almost buried under the rubble of basalt blocks.

Keep on for 8km **Sama as-Sarhan** and in the village turn left at the roundabout to look for the black basalt **Church of St George** on the hilltop by the roadside. Its main extant feature is the square minaret appended to the north side of the apse when the church was converted to a mosque and the apse walled off. Just north of the minaret a block with a Greek inscription has been reused as a lintel. There are further ruins scattered throughout the village.

UMM AL-JIMAL

From Mafraq bear right at Ba'ij roundabout and right again at a fork out of Ba'ij for 6km **Umm al-Jimal** which in antiquity was linked to the Via Nova by a branch road. Umm al-Jimal is the best-preserved of the ancient Hauran towns. Built entirely of the local black basalt, the jagged ruins are striking against the skyline. Although the dark stone gives a sombre impression, take one to two hours for a leisurely wander and the atmosphere will grow on you. Umm al-Jimal was not an elegant, cosmopolitan city like Jarash or Bostra but an ordinary provincial town with winding streets and alleys and irregular houses where people and animals lived side by side. Its Arabic name means 'mother of camels' and you may see some beautiful white camels, which apparently belong to the local sheikh, wandering in the ruins.

History

As Umm al-Jimal's ancient name is unknown, there are no literary sources which throw light on the history of the town and its people. What we know has been gleaned from archaeology and from Umm al-Jimal's general historical and geographical context. Bostra, the most important town in the southern Hauran, which could be visited in a one day round trip from Umm al-Jimal, became the capital of the Nabatean kingdom under its last king Rabbel II (71–106). It was during his reign, or somewhat earlier, that Umm al-Jimal was settled. There are few visible remains of the Nabatean/early Roman village, which lay to the east of the ruins we see today, but several Nabatean inscriptions, mostly from tombstones, have been reused in later buildings. When the Nabatean king Rabbel II died in 106 the Roman emperor Trajan incorporated his kingdom into the Roman empire. Umm al-Jimal was linked to Trajan's grand imperial highway, the Via Nova Traiana, and from the late 2C to the early 4C the town developed a military function. It was enclosed by a city wall, along the eastern side of which a military fort or castellum was constructed c 300 and was thus incorporated into the fortified Roman frontier defensive system.

The Roman military presence guaranteed stability and the civilian population of Umm al-Jimal began to expand. Between the 5C and 8C it was a prosperous agricultural and trading settlement. Most of the surviving buildings belong to the 6C, when Umm al-Jimal was predominantly Christian and numerous churches were built. When the Byzantine empire fell to the Arabs in the 7C occupation continued at Umm al-Jimal although on a reduced scale. Earthquakes in the 8C caused considerable damage, the town was not rebuilt and its inhabitants gradually left. The ruins lay abandoned for more than

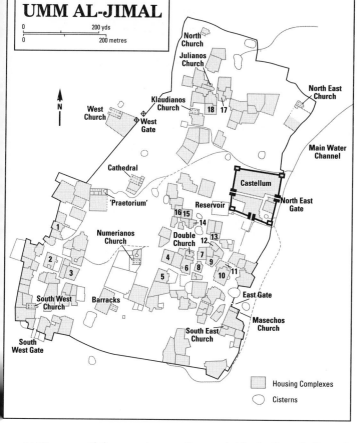

UMM AL-JIMAL

0   200 yds

0   200 metres

North Church

Julianos Church

North East Church

N

West Church

Klaudianos Church

West Gate

18   17

Main Water Channel

Cathedral

Castellum

'Praetorium'

Reservoir

North East Gate

1

16   15

14

Numerianos Church

Double Church

12   13

4   7

2

6   8   9

3

5

10   11

South West Church

Barracks

East Gate

South West Gate

South East Church

Masechos Church

Housing Complexes

Cisterns

1100 years until they were temporarily occupied by the Druze in the early 20C. Now the Druze have in turn left, but since 1950 a Jordanian village has grown up around the ancient town.

Arriving from Ba'ij, the first building you see is the **West Church**, outside the city walls, where the four intact arches between the nave and southern side aisle create a striking silhouette. Much of the wall above the aisle roof is also standing, with two of the clerestory windows. Note the crosses in the soffits of the arches and on the doorways beside the apse, which was partitioned off to make a separate room when the building was no longer used as a church. Just beyond the church is the **West Gate**, where the branch road from the Via Nova entered Umm al-Jimal. An inscription found in 1905 but since lost dated this gate to the co-regency of Marcus Aurelius and Commodus (177–180). South-east of the gate, in the west town, is the **Cathedral**, constructed in 556. Clamber up the fallen stones to look at an inscription mentioning Valens, Valentinian and Gratian, co-emperors in 371, on a stone

The 'West Church', Umm al-Jimal

reused as a door lintel. A short distance south-west is the so-called **'Praetorium'**, perhaps a Roman civic building, which is currently under restoration. There are three doorways in the finely-cut masonry of the southern façade: the central door leads into a court which was partly open to the air and to the east is a cross-shaped room with well-finished barrel vaulting and a central corbelled ceiling which originally had straight, flat beams covering the opening. Those now in situ were put there by the Druze.

In the south-west corner of the town are several blocks of houses, some of which back onto the city wall. In the inner courtyard of one of these, **House 1**, lies an inscribed stone, perhaps an altar, with a Greek-Nabatean bilingual inscription. In Nabatean it reads: 'This is the sacred stone which Masik, son of Awidha, made for Dushara.' In Greek it reads: 'Masechos, son of Aweidanos, to Dousar Aarra'. This provides a link with Bosra where the local deity A'ra was assimilated with the Nabatean god Dushara and became Dushara-A'ra. Built into the west wall of the courtyard is the reused Nabatean half of another bilingual inscription which reads:

'This is the tomb of Fihr
Son of Shullay, the tutor of Gadhimat,
The king of the Tanukh.'

This is an interesting and important inscription, as Gadhimat must be the same as the Arab Jadhima, the ruling sheikh of the tribal confederation of the Tanukh in the time of Queen Zenobia of Palmyra. Jadhima came into conflict with Zenobia and Arab sources attribute his demise to a clever ruse of the Palmyrene queen. She persuaded him to come to her and then cut his veins so that the blood would collect in a golden basin. Not surprisingly he died. Roman sources ascribe the destruction of Zenobia's kingdom in 272 to the Emperor Aurelian and his troops, but from the

Arab perspective it was 'Amr ibn 'Adi, Jadhima's successor, who eliminated Zenobia as an act of revenge for the death of Jadhima. In fact it was probably a coalition of Roman and Arab forces that was responsible. Jadhima's teacher was presumably a Nabatean Arab and a native of Umm al-Jimal.

Entered from the south side of **House 2** is a building with a triple doorway which had a columned porch. It may have been a Late Roman civic building or even a temple. The roof and interior arches are Druze reconstruction. Walk behind House 2 and alongside **House 3** (with the remains of a staircase to the upper floor and a circular window with a cross carved overhead, which acts as a lintel relieving device), to the large building known as the **Barracks**. Based on a lost inscription the Barracks are dated to the 5C, about 100 years after the first military fort or castellum, which is five times the size. It is not clear whether both were occupied at the same time or whether the Barracks housed a smaller military unit which replaced the castellum's 4C military garrison. There is a main gate in the eastern wall, a single basalt slab which still moves on its hinges with a machicolation above. Inside is a large courtyard surrounded by rooms, somewhat modified by French soldiers who camped here after World War One and built the crude pathways and platforms. Two towers protect the fort, the south-east tower stands six storeys high and the machicolations over the upper windows are inscribed with crosses and the names of the four archangels Michael, Gabriel, Raphael and Ouriel. Several Christian inscriptions in Greek may be the work of Christian soldiers, unless the building was converted for monastic use before the Arab conquest. Evidence of rebuilding includes a chapel attached to the east of the barracks and probably also the three-storey tower in the middle of the west wall. During the 6C the Romans were withdrawing troops and abandoning forts along the Arabian frontier and some of these abandoned structures were apparently used by monastic communities.

North of the Barracks is another of Umm al-Jimal's many churches, called the **Numerianos Church** because it was built to fulfill a vow by Numerianos, Joannes and Maria. In the courtyard of the badly ruined building is a large covered cistern which you can see if you climb up onto the walls. Cross the main track, follow the path between Houses 4 and 5 and turn left around House 6 to reach the **Double Church**, built into a housing block like many of Umm al-Jimal's churches. In the northern church, the better-preserved of the two, the arches between the nave and side aisles rested on columns rather than piers. Walk between Houses 7 and 8 to look at the entrance to **House 9**. Originally the outer doorway had a lockable double door while a simple arched opening gave access to the courtyard, now obscured by Druze rebuilding. Between the two is a fine example of ceiling corbelling, cantilevered supports designed to carry stone beams. Basalt corbels can carry heavy loads and beams can be up to 3m long. Corbels also functioned as stretchers at Umm al-Jimal, tying the two faces of the rubble filled walls together.

From House 9 cross to **House 10**, known as the 'Sheikh's House' because of its size, which you can enter through a door in the western wall. As you come into the large courtyard note the stairway to the left and the twin stairways opposite which make a V shape. Two different lintel-relieving methods can be seen in the doorways in the western wall; one has a small square window above it and the other a little segmental arch deflecting the weight onto the doorposts. In the eastern wall is the arched double window which has become Umm al-Jimal's emblem. Leave the courtyard by the main south entrance and continue left around the building past an impressive rock-cut cistern to get a better view from outside. Below **House 11** alongside is a domestic reservoir, once roofed, and an entrance which still has its

Basalt corbelling at Umm al-Jimal

massive single slab door. Continue round to look at the northern wall of the house. The doorway had a porch roof of which the plaster join remains; the lower masonry courses of the tower to the right are composed of unusual interlocking blocks. Follow the path between Houses 12 and 13 to another rock-cut cistern and a deep domestic reservoir with impressive roofing arches in **House 14** beyond.

Most of Umm al-Jimal's inhabitants were farmers, whose animals were kept in the ground floor rooms off the courtyard. **House 16**, reached through the court-yard of House 15, had good stabling facilities. Cows or horses were stabled in the western room, which has a row of mangers and is separated from the northern room, probably for sheep and goats, by a stone screen with air vents. In the corner of the northern room are a basin and small cubicle, perhaps a latrine, although there is no septic system. Built against the screen wall is a Druze arch.

From House 16 you can return to the West Gate or explore the north part of town. North-east is a very large **reservoir**, replastered earlier this century, fed by one of the two main aqueducts which channelled water to Umm al-Jimal from the hills to the north. Beyond is the very ruined **Roman castellum**, 100m square with square corner towers and rectangular towers flanking the four gates. Inside, sections of the barracks and the *principia* with the *aedes* (shrine of the standards) have been cleared and the **North-East City Gate** is well preserved. Follow the track between the barbed wire and the last building on the right is the **North-East Church** in fair condition with a small window in the apse and part of the synthronon. Across the town, in the north-west corner, the **North Church** is by a football pitch. From there take the path between the housing blocks past the ruined **Julianos Church** and **House 17**, with a row of mangers, and round to the front of the **Klaudianos Church**. On the door lintel is a Greek inscription with a name and a cross. From here it is a short walk to the West Gate.

Drive round the site to the east and continue to **Umm al-Quttein**. Its strategic position between the Via Nova and the Strata Diocletiana, and between Bostra and Azraq, made it an important town, although much has disappeared under the modern village. Old aerial photographs have shown that there may have been a large fort here, a possibility supported by the discovery of an inscription in one of its churches which refers to a cohort, probably the *III Augusta Thracium equitata*. To see the church turn left in the village and head for the mosque north-east of the road. The church has been reconstructed and used for animals with a modern door built into the apse, but the broken **inscription** is still visible at the base of the far arch on the south side. Nearby to the south-east the apse of a very ruined church is just visible and elsewhere old blocks, some with crosses, have been reused in the basalt houses.

THE STRATA DIOCLETIANA

Diocletian (284–305) undertook a major reorganisation of the Roman frontier in the east, in an attempt to solve some of the problems which had plagued the empire in the 3C, notably invasions from Sassanid Persia and raiding by Arab tribes who are called *Saraceni* in Roman inscriptions. Palmyra, which under its extraordinary queen Zenobia had dared to challenge the might of Rome, was finally defeated by Aurelian in 273. To fill the vacuum and protect central and southern Syria, Diocletian constructed a new defence in depth; its backbone was the **Strata Diocletiana**, which ran from Sura on the Euphrates via Palmyra to Damascus with an extension southward to Azraq. Soldiers garrisoned *castella* erected at intervals along the road, which more or less follows the 100mm rainfall line along the edge of the desert. On the southern extension of the Strata Diocletiana an important fort at Deir al-Kahf guarded the south-eastern Hauran and a castellum was built at Azraq to strengthen the vital defences at the outlet of the Wadi Sirhan, the great desert route to central Arabia.

Return to the road and head east to 26km **Deir al-Kahf** where there is a Roman fort built of basalt and dated by inscription to AD 306. Situated on the Strata Diocletiana between Azraq and Bostra this was doubtless a site of considerable importance. Its name (Kahf means cave) has led some to associate it with Speluncae where, according to the Notitia Dignitatum, the *equites promotae indiginae* were stationed. An inscription found here gave the date of 306 while a second, found on the south wall outside, referred to building repairs and expansion 367–375.

An entrance has now been made in the west wall, but the original entrance, where a huge basalt gate is embedded in the ground, was in the east. The fort is

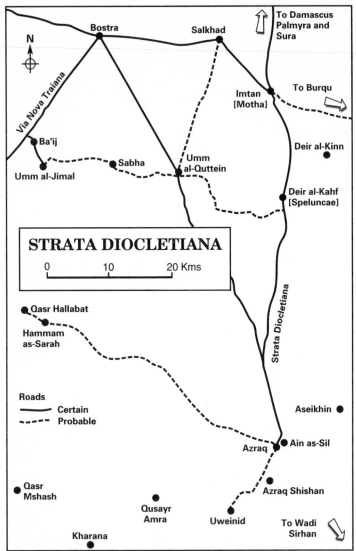

almost square with square projecting **corner towers** and two **interval towers** in the north and west walls. The curved line of the **apse** of a church added at a later stage can just be seen in the courtyard near the plastered cistern. Around the courtyard were two storeys of rooms, with stables on the ground floor, and the towers rose to three storeys. In the south wall a small **postern**, now blocked, led to a walled and covered cistern. A Greek inscription found over the lintel here referred to the prefect Agrippa. A nearby reservoir provided an additional supply of water. The fort appears to have been abandoned in the late 5C for unknown reasons.

Just beyond the fort a road left leads to the village of **Deir al-Kinn**, with the remains of a Roman reservoir and very ruined fort. From here a four-wheel drive and preferably a guide are needed to reach the remarkable ruins of c 7km **Jawa**, a unique Chalcolithic fortress town over 5000 years old. Continue for 2km past Deir al-Kinn and turn right off the road by a small settlement. Keep the Wadi Rajil on your left and after 5km of rough track Jawa's massive black basalt walls loom ahead on a steep, rocky ledge alongside the wadi. Jawa is an enigmatic site—its construction was an enormous undertaking, yet the people who built it, their origins unknown, abandoned their town after less than 50 years. Walk up the ridge on the north-west around a reused ancient reservoir to the top of the hill to begin exploring the site.

Jawa was divided into an **upper and a lower town** each surrounded by a massive wall of roughly coursed basalt with a rubble core, enclosing c 10ha. Strongest were the upper fortifications which still stand up to 6m above the bedrock. The lower fortifications were constructed somewhat later; it is suggested that the lower town, which is divided into three sectors, grew out of a temporary labour camp which housed the local workers recruited to build the upper fortress. Walking south along the upper west wall, built along a natural rock scarp, you come to Jawa's **main gate** (UT1), which projects from the wall and has a single internal chamber. Probably it was closed by two sets of double leaf doors. Later the main gate area was strengthened by an inner fortification wall and an inner gate, visible in the excavation trenches. Jawa has more gates than any prehistoric settlement yet discovered, at least six in the upper town and eight in the lower; the **best-preserved gate** in the lower town is to the south (LT4), with two internal chambers and three doors, one double leaf and two single. On either side of the gate is a true casemate wall, something which does not appear commonly on Near Eastern fortifications until over a millennium later.

Both upper and lower towns were densely packed with **irregular-shaped houses**, often partly subterranean with stone foundations, mud brick substructures, mud floors, plastered walls and roofs made of oak beams from the Jabal Druze covered with reeds and mud. There are excavated houses behind the main gate in the upper town and the south-west corner.

Perhaps the greatest skill of the Jawaites was **hydrology**. In such a bleak environment where springs are rare and access to ground-water virtually impossible it is crucial to harness the winter rains. Over 8km of stone canals, diversions, dams and reservoirs at Jawa and along the Wadi Rajil attest to the complex and efficient water system devised by the Jawaites. Rainwater was deflected into canals at three points which brought the water to circular reservoirs, several of which are clearly visible to the west and south of the town.

A few decades at most after the fortress and water system were built, Jawa was attacked—in many areas the walls were breached and the archaeological evidence suggests widespread disaster. Some people (the Jawaites or their attackers?) continued to occupy the site for a short time, but without proper upkeep the water system failed and Jawa was abandoned.

Over a millennium later it was reoccupied on a small scale by different peoples. In the upper town is a rectangular building, the 'Citadel', divided into cells and three transverse corridors. Many of the basalt roof beams are still in situ and there are traces of an upper storey. Around the 'Citadel' were a number of outbuildings. The excavator suggests that this complex was a Middle Bronze Age caravanserai, a stopping place on the route between Syria/Mesopotamia and Arabia and Palestine.

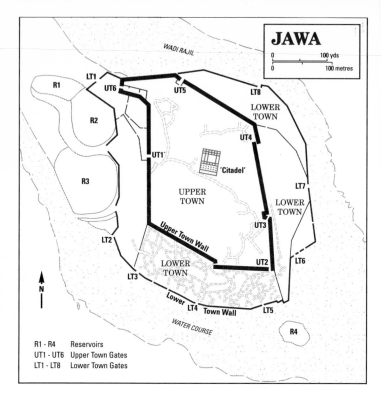

After this was abandoned Jawa was never resettled and for some 4000 years it has remained a bleak and silent enigma of the 'Black Desert'.

THE JORDAN RIFT VALLEY AND THE DEAD SEA

One of Jordan's most dramatic geographical features is the **Jordan Rift Valley**, part of the Great Rift Valley which stretches for some 6000km from East Africa to southern Turkey. Originally the whole valley up to Lake Galilee was beneath the Red Sea, but around 100,000 years ago a detached inland lake was created which eventually split into the two separate lakes we see today, Lake Galilee and the Dead Sea. Between them the River Jordan meanders through the wide Jordan Valley, where the climate is sub-tropical and humid and the land fertile. Fruits and vegetables are produced in abundance and benefit from agricultural development and irrigation schemes. This has always been one of the most densely populated areas of Jordan, and dozens of mounds or tells along the valley floor bear witness to thousands of years of human occupation. In biblical times, according to Genesis, the valley was 'irrigated everywhere ... like the Garden of Yahweh or the land of Egypt' (13:10) and lions roamed through the dense vegetation on the high river banks.

Near where the River Jordan flows into the **Dead Sea** is the lowest point on the earth's surface, over 365m below sea level. Here the sun can be fiercely hot and due to modern irrigation schemes the Dead Sea is shrinking; its waters are evaporating more quickly than they are being replenished. It was the 2C Greek traveller Pausanius who first coined the name Dead Sea because the lake is so brackish that nothing can live in it; at other times it has been called Salt Sea, Sea of Asphalt and Sea of Sodom. The climate is oppressive and the landscape desolate and rocky except for patches of bright green which mark sulphurous springs; the mountains of Moab rise steeply from the eastern shore.

South of the Dead Sea is **Wadi Araba**, a broad semi-desert valley fringed with sand dunes. Despite its inhospitable climate Wadi Araba has always been important as a communications route and mining centre. Rich copper deposits were exploited as early as 4000 BC and archaeological survey has shown that in antiquity the foothills supported terraced agriculture where today much of the land is barren.

The Jordan River Valley

From Amman to the Jordan Valley there are three main roads; south-west via Al-Adasiyya to King Abdullah Bridge and the Dead Sea and north-west via Salt from where one road goes to South Shuna and another to Muthallath al-Arida, south of Deir 'Alla. All roads descend steeply and offer lovely views across the green valley to Jericho and the mountains beyond. It is also possible to cross to the Jordan Valley from Jarash and Ajlun and there are roads from Irbid, to near Pella, to North Shuna or via Umm Qais.

UMM QAIS—GADARA

Alongside the modern village of **Umm Qais**, on the edge of a limestone plateau with magnificent views over the Sea of Galilee and the dramatic Yarmuk gorge to the Golan Heights beyond are the ruins of the ancient city of **Gadara**, famous as the setting for the biblical story of the Gadarene swine. On a clear day you can see the dark green rift of the Jordan valley and the town of Tiberias on the western shore of the lake. Gadara can be reached either from 28km Irbid or from the Jordan valley. West of the modern village, on the turn of the main road, a track leads past some rock-cut tombs to a parking place and the historical site, much of which is still covered by the deserted late Ottoman village of Umm Qais with its striking black basalt and white limestone houses.

History

Gadara, founded by the Ptolemies as a military colony after the death of Alexander the Great, changed hands several times. At the beginning of the 2C BC the Seleucids, rivals for the control of Greater Syria, took the city, and some 100 years later it was conquered by the Jewish Hasmonaean leader Alexander Jannaeus. The 10-month siege caused serious damage. Like the rest of Syria it was 'liberated' by the Roman general Pompey in 64 BC. Fortune favoured Gadara; as it was the home town of one of his favourite freedmen, Demetrius, Pompey personally saw to the rebuilding of the city. Gadara inaugurated a new era with Pompey—it adopted a new calendar and began to mint its own coins. It became one of the leading cities of the Decapolis (p 74).

In 30 BC the emperor Augustus gave Gadara to his friend and ally King Herod of Judaea, but the Gadarenes do not seem to have been too happy with the arrangement and sent delegations to complain to the emperor. When their attempts to discredit Herod failed some of the Gadarenes committed suicide rather than undergo the torture they assumed would otherwise be their fate. Those who were left must have been glad when Herod died in 4 BC and Gadara regained its autonomy under the aegis of the Roman province of Syria. Under the Pax Romana Gadara prospered, and with the creation of the Roman province of Arabia by Trajan in 106 stability was assured. For the Decapolis the 2C was a Golden Age; most of the standing Roman structures at Gadara were built at this time.

Christianity was firmly rooted among the Gadarenes by the 4C, when it had become the official religion of the Roman empire. The city was a bishopric until the 7C when after the Battle of Fihl (635) and the Battle of Yarmuk (636) it became part of the realm of Islam. During the 7C Gadara was renowned for its fine wines, but from the 8C onwards it went into rapid decline, precipitated by a series of earthquakes.

As was the custom in the Graeco-Roman world, Gadara buried its dead outside the city walls. Wooden or stone sarcophagi were placed in niches inside multiple chamber tombs. There are two well-preserved **Roman tombs** in a hollow on the left just after the turn-off from the main road. According to the inscription on the lintel the first tomb belongs to **Quintus Publius Germanus** and his relative **Aulus Germanus Rufus**. Now painted white, the basalt masonry façade imitates a temple. A few metres to the west is the tomb of **Lucius Sentius Modestus**, described as the Holy Herald (*Hierokeryx*) of the city. This was a priestly office connected with sacrifice. His inscription is within a wreath with its end strings tied in a Heracles knot, a common decorative element in Gadara. Solid basalt doors

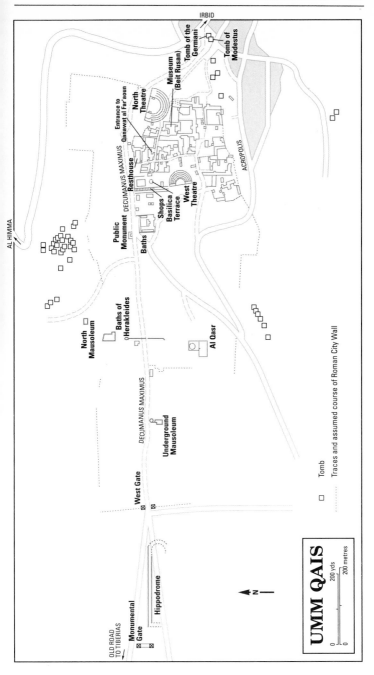

UMM QAIS

IRBID

Tomb of the Germani
Tomb of Modestus

Museum (Beit Rusan)

North Theatre

Entrance to Qanawat al Far'aoun

DECUMANUS MAXIMUS

Resthouse

ACROPOLIS

Public Monument

Shops

West Theatre

Basilica Terrace

Baths

AL HIMMA

North Mausoleum

Baths of Herakleides

DECUMANUS MAXIMUS

Al Qasr

Underground Mausoleum

West Gate

Monumental Gate

OLD ROAD TO TIBERIAS

Hippodrome

N

0   200 yds
0   200 metres

□ Tomb

······ Traces and assumed course of Roman City Wall

Tomb door at Gadara, a drawing from East of Jordan by Selah Merrill

which swung on massive hinges closed the tombs. The interiors are rather dank and malodorous and of no special interest. 19C travellers reported peasants living in them and they have been much altered inside.

Gadara's tombs are referred to in the curious **biblical incident of the Gadarene swine** narrated by Matthew, Mark and Luke. Jesus crossed Lake Galilee by boat, calming a storm which had arisen in transit and, according to Matthew:

'When he reached the territory of the Gadarenes on the other side, two demoniacs came towards him out of the tombs—they were so dangerously violent that nobody could use that path. Suddenly they shouted, "What do you want with us, Son of God? Have you come to torture us before the time?" Now some distance away there was a large herd of pigs feeding, and the devils pleaded with Jesus, "If you drive us out send us into the herd of pigs." And he said to them, "Go then," and they came out and made for the pigs; and at that the whole herd charged down the cliff into the lake and perished in the water.' (8:28–32)

The people of Gadara found the incident most disturbing and begged Jesus to leave their city right away. Which is perhaps not surprising as according to Mark (5:13) the Gadarene swine numbered about 2000, and they certainly performed an extraordinary feat; to reach the Sea of Galilee they would have had to run for over eight kilometres and leap over the deep gorge of the River Yarmuk!

By the car park the semi-circular shape of the **North Theatre** is still visible in the hillside, but most of the stones were robbed for re-use in the Ottoman village. Follow a well-paved path towards the site and after c 100m a broad flight of steps leads up to the terrace of what used to be the girls' school of Umm Qais, now converted into a *resthouse*.

■ Snacks, meals and refreshments are available at the *resthouse*; also there are clean toilet facilities. From the terrace, or even better from the top of the iwan or arched entrance portal, there are splendid views over Galilee and the Golan. As yet there is no accommodation in Umm Qais although there are plans to renovate and use some of the old Ottoman houses as a small hotel complex, in keeping with the character of the site. There are a couple of simple hotels at al-Himma in the Yarmuk valley below Umm Qais, but facilities are better in Irbid.

Steps lead down from the resthouse to the **Basilica Terrace**, an impressive Byzantine church complex which would have been visible from most parts of ancient Gadara and which makes striking use of the contrasting colours of the local black basalt and white limestone. On the east the terrace is cut into the bedrock and faced with a retaining wall of limestone blocks; its western edge is supported on a barrel-vaulted substructure. A colonnaded quadrangle of white limestone with a basalt outer passageway was the atrium for the basilical church to the south, a square enclosing a central octagon, a fairly common design in 5–6C Byzantine architecture. The Corinthian capitals of the atrium and the lovely basalt Corinthian columns in the central octagon and its narthex or porch come from earlier Roman buildings. Probably the octagon supported a semi-hemispherical dome. It was demarcated by chancel screens and inside a stone-lined depression with a semi-circular apse behind was the church's altar area or bema. Behind the apse, facing the east door of the church, is a pinkish marble column engraved with a cross. A shaft tomb was found inside the bema, with a stone ossuary or reliquary perhaps originally containing the remains of a Christian martyr. Around the church is a circular passageway with opus sectile paving—this symbolises the passage from the earthly to the heavenly realm.

South of the Basilica Terrace a path leads to the **West Theatre**, built entirely of black basalt, which is currently being cleared and restored. A tunnel through a vaulted passageway behind the seating emerges in the auditorium, which seated about 3000 spectators. Seats with high backrests were reserved for local dignitaries and their guests to enjoy plays, poetry and other entertainment.

> Gadara was renowned as a centre of the performing arts. Many poets, artists and intellectuals lived here: the satirist Menippus (3C BC) and poet Meleager (1C BC) were born in Gadara; Virgil and Horace were pupils of the 1C BC Gadarene philosopher and poet Philodemus, and the Roman emperor Tiberius was tutored in his youth by the Gadarene rhetorician Theodorus.

Behind the orchestra and remains of the stage building a **side street** intersected to the north with Gadara's main street, the Decumanus Maximus. This has been partly cleared below the Basilica Terrace where some of the original paving can be seen. Along the street is a row of **barrel-vaulted shops** faced with finely dressed ashlar masonry, their back walls supporting the foundations of the Basilica Terrace above.

Some sections of the colonnaded **Decumanus Maximus**, which crossed Gadara from east to west, have been excavated. Ruts of chariot wheels on the basalt paving show it was once a busy thoroughfare; pedestrians could use the pavements on either side. East of Gadara a Roman road connected the city with Abila and Bostra, to the west it descended to the Jordan valley, then crossed the river to Scythopolis and the Mediterranean ports. Shops and civic buildings lined the Decumanus. On the north side, c 100m west of the Basilica Terrace, is a curious structure with a niche in the rear wall flanked by steps and niches along its east and west sides. The original interpretation of this building as a **nymphaeum** or public fountain has been discarded. Although later converted into a cistern, the long barrel-vaulted chamber at the rear was not designed as such and the piping system below the street did not supply water to the monument. It was an elaborate building which clearly embellished the city centre—fragments of several fine Roman statues were found which were displayed in the niches—but its original purpose remains enigmatic.

Across the street is one of Gadara's **public baths** complexes. This has been excavated but is now much overgrown. Built in the 4C, the baths continued in use for some 300 years and comprised the usual apodyterium (changing room), frigidarium (cold room), tepidarium (warm room) and caldarium (hot room). During the Umayyad period (7–8C) the complex was converted into a series of smaller units. About 250m further along the Decumanus, in the fields to the north, is another very overgrown **bath-house**, now walled round and locked, although you can easily look in. According to an inscription it was built by a Gadarene nobleman named **Herakleides**, and its fine mosaics are now in the museum. Baths in antiquity were lively and hectic, places to relax and meet friends and acquaintances and hear the local gossip. Vendors and hawkers did brisk business as eating and drinking were part of the routine. North-east of the baths of Herakleides, little is left of the **North Mausoleum**, once a fine building on a podium.

About 200m south of the colonnaded street in this area is a large unexcavated building known locally as **al-Qasr**, 'the castle'. The line of the Decumanus continues for another 200m to a low circular monument of well-cut basalt blocks, originally the south tower of a free-standing barrel-vaulted gate which spanned the street. In the 4C it was dismantled to its present level and used as a water pool. Steps lead down to a **Roman hypogeum** or underground mausoleum which was reused in the Byzantine period, when the entrance hall, its ceiling supported on basalt columns, was added, and a three-aisled basilica built above the hypogeum, which then became the crypt of the church. Now there is nothing visible of this basilica except a few scanty remains of the foundations. Several Byzantine tombs were excavated in the underground entrance hall, one of which, covered by basalt slabs, is below the central arch of the porch. The mausoleum is kept locked, but the museum curator has the key. Basalt doors, now broken, open into a barrel-vaulted ante-chamber which is separated by another basalt door from the burial chamber. A vaulted passage or **cryptoporticus** ran above three sides of the burial chamber and was used as a depository for skeletons. In the area are several other mausolea.

About 200m west of the mausoleum excavations have uncovered part of Gadara's **West Gate** and adjoining **city wall**. The central gateway, flanked by two towers, may have been vaulted; it probably dates to the early 4C and was built over other structures. North-west of the northern gatetower are the basalt foundations of a substantial earlier building, perhaps a mausoleum. A fine road paved with well-cut basalt blocks laid diagonally and horizontally passed through the gate. Across the modern tarmac road, just beyond and to the south of the West Gate, a trench has revealed structures which may be connected to the **Hippodrome**. There is little to be seen of this stadium, which ran parallel to the Roman road for over 280m and was probably never finished. Just beyond its western end, where three Roman tombs were found, are the foundations of a splendid **Roman monumental triple gateway** flanked by towers, like Hadrian's Gate at Jarash, but probably built much later, at the beginning of the 3C. Clearly the gate was designed to impress visitors coming up to Gadara from the Jordan valley. Although the gateway was built of black basalt, much of the decoration was of white limestone; there is a nice collection of moulded elements from the gate on the ground nearby. West of the monumental gate the ground is at a much lower level. Investigations have shown that some time before the 8C the pavement of the Roman road was removed and a natural depression west of the gate was dug out and deepened to create a huge open air reservoir.

One of Gadara's strangest features is a **qanat** or underground aqueduct, cut into the soft local limestone, which brought drinking water to the city from **at-Turab spring** 12km to the east. Known locally as **Qanawat al-Far'aoun** or 'Pharoah's aqueduct' because it was thought that only Pharoah, the great black magician, was capable of such a wondrous feat, it is in fact a remarkable example of Roman engineering. It ends at the Basilica Terrace; somewhere in the vicinity there must have been a water distributor or reservoir. Many fragments of ribbed terracotta pipes were found when part of the tunnel was cleared but it is not obvious how the water was channelled. To explore the tunnel, which follows a very winding course, it is possible to go down a **manhole** beneath the floor of an old Ottoman house just behind the resthouse, for which the museum curator has the key. Descent is via a steep, rickety staircase and not for the faint-hearted. There is electric lighting, but it advisable to take a torch. The tunnel is high enough to stand up in and at intervals there are other manholes, now blocked with rubble. Small holes in the walls used to hold oil lamps for the engineers and labourers who dug the aqueduct and later for those responsible for clearance and maintenance. Exit is by the same rickety steps, but if you go down the tunnel with the museum curator, he may bring you out east of the museum, where the tunnel becomes an open channel cut out of the bed rock. Another similar tunnel under the acropolis of Gadara, also part of the city's water system, was not accessible to visitors at the time of writing.

Gadara's small **Museum** (open 8.00–17.00 Apr–Oct, 8.00–16.00 Nov–Mar, closed Tuesdays) is in the two-storey **Beit Rusan**, arranged around a pretty courtyard planted with pomegranate trees. Formerly the home of the Ottoman representative at Umm Qais who was from a rich merchant family, it is one of the largest houses in the village, and has been restored as part of a project sponsored by the Federal Republic of Germany. Exhibits are displayed on the ground floor and rooms on the upper floor are used for sorting and cataloguing finds from recent excavations. Left of the entrance a small shop sells postcards, books and souvenirs.

Basalt blocks in the museum at Umm Qais

The museum entrance opens onto a terrace with a covered reception area on the right displaying a white marble statue of **Tyche**, city goddess of Gadara, seated on a lion throne and holding a cornucopia filled with fruits in her left hand. Found headless in the orchestra of the West Theatre, the statue may have tumbled down from a shrine to the goddess above the auditorium. Tyche is represented on many Roman coins from Gadara.

On the wall left of Tyche is a **mosaic** from a tomb in the entrance porch of the underground mausoleum which names **Valentinianos**, **Eustathia** and **Protogenia** as the deceased buried there. Opposite the mosaic is a small room with a number of interesting exhibits including small pieces of **sculpture, glass** and **metal objects, pottery** and **piping** from the underground aqueduct. Above the display cases are limestone and basalt portrait busts and along the side wall pieces of **basalt sculpture** in typical Gadarene style, characterised by very schematic features. Some finds come from a cave near Gadara known locally as 'Seven Sleepers Cave'.

In the museum courtyard, particularly lovely when the pomegranate trees are in blossom, are sarcophagi, millstones, column drums and capitals. Under cover on the far wall are geometric **mosaics from the Baths of Herakleides**. Some fine **sculpture** is exhibited in the former stables of the Beit Rusan. The marble statuette of **enthroned Zeus** was found on a terrace beyond the North Theatre. Many coins from Gadara show a temple of Zeus with the god enthroned. The torso of a young **athlete** is a Roman copy of a Greek original; chubby **Harpocrates** holding up the front of his garment comes from the Baths of Herakleides. A broken statuette of **Artemis of Ephesus** ('Diana of the Ephesians' of Paul's epistle) is a long way from home. She is covered with rows of what have been variously interpreted as breasts, eggs or bulls' testicles, all symbols of fertility. Her garment is decorated with griffons and rosettes and on her arms are lions, always associated with mother goddesses in the Near East. Next to Artemis is the torso of a **satyr** with a pig skin and by the door is a **huge coiled snake**. Snakes symbolised constant renewal because they regularly shed their skin. Outside and opposite the sculpture hall is a three-line Greek inscription from the North Mausoleum which reads: 'To you I say, passer-by: As you are I was; as I am you will be. Use life as a mortal.'

From Umm Qais, past a military checkpoint (after which photographs are not allowed until you reach the Jordan valley), the road winds steeply down towards the Yarmuk gorge. In spring honeywort, anemones and anchusa pepper the hillsides and the bright yellow mimosa is in flower. At the 5km junction turn left for the Jordan valley or continue straight on to **al-Himma**, ancient **Hammath Gader**, a small town divided, with part in Jordan and part under Israeli occupation. Hammath Gader was famed in antiquity for its **sulphurous springs**—people came from all over the Roman empire to soak in the warm therapeutic waters and enjoy the luxurious **baths complex**. After bathing there was entertainment in a small theatre, or guests could retire to Gadara, to enjoy the cooler heights and the spectacles performed there. There are no ancient remains but many visitors still come to al-Himma to wallow in the waters, although the modern baths have seen better days.

Back on the main road a blown-up bridge, its twisted wreckage hanging dramatically over the Yarmuk gorge below, is a reminder of the heavy fighting in this strategically important area. Above tower the Golan Heights; in places the fence marking the border is but a short distance from the road. Past another checkpoint beyond which photographs are again permitted, the Jordan valley begins.

Rain is infrequent in the Jordan Valley, which is all below sea level, but the land is fertile and a sub-tropical climate and high humidity produce a 'greenhouse effect' excellent for agriculture. Villages dot the valley floor, which yields citrus fruits, loquats, grapes, date palms, olives, bananas and melons as well as tomatoes, cucumbers, aubergines and other vegetables. Mediterranean cypress, willow, carob and mimosa grow by the road and on the slopes of the eastern hills, which are scored by perennial wadis cutting down to the rift. Water is crucial for the valley's economy; a major canal which draws water from the Yarmuk flows alongside the road, part of a complex modern irrigation network. As it is some kilometres from the main road in most places, the deep-flowing River Jordan is not visible.

North Shuna, where the Wadi 'Arab enters the valley from the eastern plateau, is a thriving small town with an important archaeological site, today destroyed or obscured by modern buildings. Excavations showed that North Shuna was a farming settlement occupied almost continuously for over 1500 years during the Chalcolithic period and Early Bronze Age (late 5th–mid 3rd millennium BC). Today North Shuna is at the junction of a road linking Irbid with the main highway through the Jordan Valley. 9km south of Shuna a sign 'Jordan Valley Crossing Point' marks the road to c 2.5km **Sheikh Hussein Bridge**, one of the border points between Jordan and Israel. There is another road to Irbid after 2km and 8km further Tabaqat Fahl, ancient Pella, is signposted up a side road to the left.

TABAQAT FAHL—PELLA

Just beyond 2km **Tabaqat Fahl** village, on the left behind a fence as you approach the main mound of ancient **Pella**, is the **West Church (Area I)**, with three of the columns in the atrium re-erected. Now very overgrown, it dates to the late 5C or 6C and was on the eastern edge of a large cemetery. Connected with the building's north annex was a huge vaulted reservoir of the 7C, which could store 300,000 litres of water. Continue along the road skirting the main mound; in the valley to the left is a complex of **Abbasid buildings (Area XXIX)** occupied for around 250 years from after the 747 earthquake to c 1000. For a good view of Pella drive up the hill to the *resthouse*; from the terrace you can look down over the entire site and surrounding countryside.

■ Refreshments are served at the *resthouse*, which has toilet facilities. Excellent meals are available, slightly on the expensive side, but the food is very fresh. You may wish to taste the local 'St Peter's fish' from the Jordan River. Order before visiting the site and eat afterwards if you want to save time.

Pella is a huge site, comprising a main mound, 400m long, which has been subject to a number of archaeological soundings; the steep, largely natural hill of Tell Husn to the south and the Wadi Jirm between them. A perennial spring bubbles out from beneath the main mound and flows through the valley. Because of the abundant water the valley is green and in early spring the site is particularly beautiful, the hillsides covered in red anemones, calendula, spring groundsel, asphodel and other flowers.

History

Stone Age hunters roamed the hills around Pella as long ago as 250,000 BC, a number of camp sites dated 20,000–8000 BC were found in the nearby Wadi al-Hammeh, and by 5000 BC there was a Neolithic farming village at Pella itself. Remains of a Chalcolithic settlement were excavated on the slopes of Jabal Sartaba, east of Tell Husn, and in the Bronze Age Pella was a substantial walled town within the Canaanite cultural sphere. Although it is not mentioned in the Bible, Pella is referred to in other historical documents. Letters from el-Amarna in Egypt (14C BC) attest contact between the pharaohs and Pella's rulers, one of whom was called Mut-ba'alu. Known as Pihil in Egyptian texts, it supplied Egypt with a kind of wood used for spokes in chariot wheels (13C BC). At that time the hills around were thickly forested. Rich artefacts such as inlaid ivory boxes, imported pottery, alabaster perfume bottles and small objects overlaid with gold show that much of the Canaanite period was a time of prosperity when Pella traded widely throughout the eastern Mediterranean. Alexander the Great was credited with 'founding' Pella, but there is no evidence to substantiate the tradition; the town was not called after Pella in Macedonia, Alexander's birthplace, but the name came into use in the Hellenistic period as an approximation to the old Semitic name Pihil.

Pella's fortunes took a turn for the worse in 83 BC when the Hasmonaean ruler of Palestine, Alexander Jannaeus, crossed the Jordan and sacked the city. According to Josephus this was because its inhabitants refused to practise Jewish customs. Two Late Hellenistic fortresses on hills north-east and south-east of the city were perhaps built in response to the Hasmonaean threat. Pompey freed Pella from Hasmonaean oppression when he marched south and created the Roman province of Syria in 64 BC, and slowly the city revived. In the Roman period it was a member of the Decapolis (p 74) and connected by road to Gerasa, Abila and Scythopolis across the Jordan. Christianity probably reached Pella in the 1C; Eusebius relates how some early Christians fled to Pella in AD 70 to escape the Roman siege of Jerusalem. Certainly the new religion was established by the mid-2C and the Byzantine period, when Pella was part of the imperial province of Palestina Secunda, was one of the city's most prosperous. Churches were built, trade flourished and the population increased. By the 7C, however, decline had set in; alongside more widespread disruption of trade and communications, silting of the Wadi Jirm and perhaps the onset of plague adversely affected Pella. In 635 Islamic forces defeated the Byzantine army at the Battle of Fihl near Pella; thenceforth Christians and Muslims lived together in the town. Earthquakes in 717 and 747 caused severe damage, but there was still some occupation of the site in Abbasid and Mamluke times.

From the resthouse it is an easy walk down to the East Church and then to the main mound and the monuments in the valley, which can also be reached from the main road at the bottom of the hill. The **East Church** was built in the 5C in a former quarry on the eastern slope of Jabal Abu al-Khas overlooking the Pella basin. Originally it was approached by a monumental staircase from the wadi below. It is a triapsidal basilica and has a small colonnaded atrium with a hexagonal pool in the centre, presumably supplied from the rock-cut cistern to the north. A marble reliquary was found beneath the chancel. Some attractive marble and tile flooring is preserved in the portico between the atrium and the church.

Down in the valley is the city centre with a group of buildings known as the **Civic Complex** (IX). Most striking is the **Civic Complex Church**, possibly Pella's cathedral, constructed c 400 as a simple rectangular building with a **colonnaded atrium** to the west. Entrance was through the north wall of the atrium, which has a colonnade of 20 re-used Roman columns re-erected by the Department of Antiquities. On the east side the portico was paved with opus sectile and two greenish marble columns, one still standing, flanked the church entrance. Around the church were ancillary buildings. In the 6C the church was extended by the addition of three curved apses to the east adorned with glass windows, glass mosaic semi-domes, floor and wall stone mosaics and marble chancel screens. Two huge columns, perhaps from a Roman temple, were erected in front of the north entrance to the atrium. Final modifications were made in the 7C, when a **monumental staircase** was constructed leading to a new entrance in the west wall of the atrium framed with a limestone arch which is now on the ground nearby.

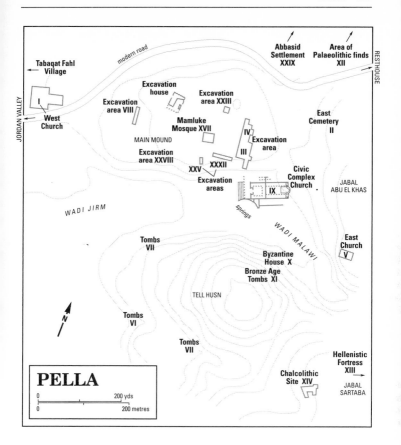

Few structures remain of earlier Roman Pella. Best preserved is the **small theatre** or **odeon** south of the Civic Complex Church built in the 1C for an audience of c 400. Many of its seating stones have been reused in later structures, including the monumental staircase up to the church. In front of the odeon a **paved forum** may have extended across the valley; soundings revealed paving stones and piping several metres below the present valley floor, suggesting that the stream was channelled beneath the forum. Roman remains in the wadi are unfortunately virtually inaccessible because of accumulated alluvium and a rise in the water table since antiquity. Somewhere in Pella were a nymphaeum, temples and various porticoes, all depicted on coins. A large building of the Herodian period, which may be a temple, has been partly exposed on the north face of Tell Husn. Above the odeon, where the Civic Complex Church was built, was a large paved court known as the **Parvis**, and to the west, partly covered by the later monumental staircase, are the remains of a **baths complex**, comprising an exedra and some vaulted sections into which clear water sometimes bubbles from the nearby spring. Texts from the 3–4C refer to people travelling to Pella to enjoy the warm baths.

Excavations on the **main mound** have been most productive and are continuing. Areas III and IV overlook the spring and Civic Complex. In **Area III**, a deep cut on the south slope of the mound, several phases of Bronze and Iron Age architecture were identified; there are two levels of stone wall, probably the city wall, of Early Bronze I–II (c 3400–2700 BC) and a section of a **massive mud-brick wall** with stone foundations on the outer side only, which surrounded the Middle Bronze Age city (c 1900 BC). In the same trench to the west is part of a Late Bronze Age civic building with a central courtyard which has been dubbed the '**Governor's Residence**'. On top of the mound in **Area IV** a deep sounding, scheduled to be back filled, reached levels of the 7th millennium BC (Pre-Pottery Neolithic B); alongside to the north a complex of **Byzantine-Umayyad houses** was cleared—the walls have been consolidated and a few columns reset. These houses were two-storeyed, stone below and unbaked mud bricks above; people lived upstairs and animals were stabled on the ground floor. Skeletons of animals and people were found, trapped during the earthquake of 747.

Area XXXII lies west of Areas III and IV. In the lower part is another section of the Early Bronze Age I–II stone wall that was excavated in Area III, and above it a monumental stone building of the 9C BC. North-west, on the flat summit of the mound, **Area XVII** is a small 13C–14C **Mamluke mosque**, now open to the sky; originally it had a roof supported on Roman-Byzantine column drums. Several other soundings have been made in the tell, and on the south slopes, overlooking the stream, natural weathering has exposed some sections of wall, mostly Byzantine.

Across the wadi is **Tell Husn**; on its slopes numerous Bronze Age, Roman and Byzantine tombs have been excavated, yielding interesting objects. Many of the **Roman tombs** were family mausolea, used for up to 300 years, with loculi radiating from a central chamber. The dead were often buried in wood or stone coffins and accompanied by funerary gifts such as figurines, jewellery and perfume bottles. Recent excavations on the top of Tell Husn have uncovered several interesting structures. Most obvious is a **6C Byzantine fortress** or military installation exposed mainly in the north-east trench, but also in other soundings. Courses of large stones alternate with courses of smaller ones in walls which are preserved to a considerable height. Probably this fort surrendered to the Muslim armies after the battle of Fihl. Also in the north-east trench there are strange stone platforms with evidence of burning from Early Bronze Age I (c 3000 BC); their function is unclear. On the opposite side of Tell Husn, in the south-west trench, is part of a Late Hellenistic/Early Roman temple stylobate with a single column base; a deep sounding shows the retaining wall of large well-cut blocks.

North-east of Tell Husn is **Jabal Sartaba**, which energetic visitors may wish to climb; the hike takes a good hour, some of the way along a tractor road, and the summit makes a lovely picnic spot. Pink and white hollyhocks bloom in spring and there are oaks and mimosa on the heights. On top of the mountain is a large, square **Hellenistic fortress**, constructed of rough mostly uncut blocks and perhaps never finished or used. It is thought to have been built early in the 1C BC in response to the military threat from the Hasmoneans in Palestine. There are four corner and four interval towers in the 1m-thick walls, where oak trees have now taken firm root, and two huge cisterns inside. As Jabal Sartaba is the highest hill in the vicinity, there are splendid views from the summit, across the Jordan Valley to the west, where the round hump of Mt Tabor sticks up prominently, and south-eastwards to Ajlun, where you can see the castle perched on the hill.

Ancient Tells in the Jordan Valley

Ancient tells (p 123) dot the valley floor as the road continues southwards. Approximately 17km from the turn-off to Pella a road branches right opposite a small mosque to the great double mound of **Tell as-Sa'idiyah**, which rises 40m above the plain and is one of the most prominent tells in the Jordan Valley. Sa'idiyah's location was no accident—it was on an important east–west route, where the Jordan valley is narrowest and there was a ford across the Jordan river. Two small outlying tells, one by the modern main road and one by the river, may have been outposts to monitor east–west traffic which passed by the town. Excavations were undertaken at Sa'idiyah by the University of Pennsylvania in the 1960s and resumed in 1985 by a team from the British Museum. On the lower tell part of a walled Early Bronze Age settlement including an industrial area for olive oil production has been cleared. It was destroyed c 2800 BC. Occupation resumed on the upper mound, during the Late Bronze Age (13C–12C BC), when Sa'idiyah was probably a border post of the Egyptian empire in Canaan. A **casemate defensive wall**, partly excavated, surrounded the settlement; on the east side was the main gate where a cobbled approach road entered the city through a vaulted mud-brick gatehouse. A large public building (12C BC) with Egyptian architectural features which was uncovered on the west side of the mound may have been a **governor's residence**. On the north slope is an impressive **stone staircase**, recently restored, leading down to an enclosed spring-fed pool which supplied the city with water. Surprisingly the spring has remained in the same place since antiquity. In the so-called governor's residence Egyptian style storage jars were found in a 'cool' room, where they may have been standing in water fed along a channel from the top of the staircase.

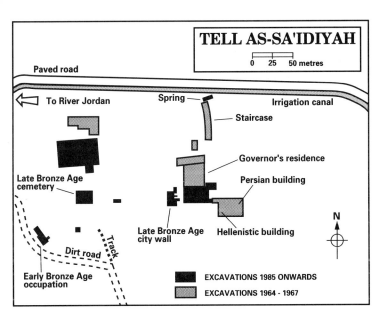

Outside the city wall, all over the lower mound, was the very intensively used **cemetery**; 80 per cent to 90 per cent of graves showed Egyptian influence and included Egyptian-style objects among the grave goods. Unusual burial types include 'double pithos burial' with the body inside two large storage jars placed shoulder to shoulder, reminiscent of Philistine anthropoid clay coffins, and many skeletons were tightly bound with Egyptian linen. A foreign population may be indicated, perhaps from the Aegean.

Sa'idiyah was violently destroyed c 1150/25 BC, towards the end of a period of great turmoil in the Near East partly connected with the arrival of new peoples, among them the Philistines. About 100 years later it was reoccupied and then inhabited almost continuously until the Roman period. In the 9C–8C BC (Iron Age II) Sa'idiyah was a well planned town, built to a grid plan; industrial activities included textile manufacture and olive and grape processing. Above the 12C BC city gate was an 8C BC gatehouse, comprising two stone towers flanking a wide roadway. On the summit of the main mound are the overgrown foundations of a public building of the Persian period, west of which is a fortress-like Hellenistic structure.

Another prominent mound, **Tell Mazar**, which was occupied during the Iron Age, is visible from the main road 6km south of the turn-off to Tell as-Sa'idiyah, and 3km further **Tell Deir 'Alla**, which means 'high monastery', is by the roadside on the right (west) in the village of the same name. It is often identified with biblical Succoth or Penuel, both of which refused to help Gideon when he was pursuing the defeated Midianites across Transjordan (Judges 8). Excavations by Dutch and Jordanian archaeologists since the 1960s have shown that the site was occupied from c 1700–400 BC; wall foundations and other features can be seen in the excavation trenches. On the north slope of the tell, where in the Late Bronze Age (c 1600 BC) the natural hill was extended northwards by an artificial clay terrace, there was a large **sanctuary**, in use for some 400 years until destroyed by earthquake and fire in the early 12C BC. As much foreign pottery was associated with the sanctuary it has been suggested that Deir 'Alla was a trading centre between Gilead and Egypt, where the gods received gifts and sanctioned commercial contracts. Support is lent to this hypothesis by tablets found in the sanctuary, several in an unreadable Aegean script. Remains of the 1st millennium BC Iron Age settlement, a complex of alleys and small rooms, some plastered, were cleared on the north-east part of the summit; one plastered wall was covered with an **inscription** in red and black ink, written in a local dialect of Aramaic, which concerns a prophecy of **Balaam, son of Beor**, also known from the Bible. Dated c 800 BC, it is now in the Amman Museum.

When the Israelite tribes were camped in the plains of Moab opposite Jericho, during the final stages of their journey to the 'Promised Land', Balak, king of Moab, afraid of so many foreigners in his territory, sent messengers to the prophet Balaam to elicit his help. Balaam came, but when asked to curse the Israelites insisted he could speak only God's words. He sacrificed bulls and rams to the Lord, who gave him a blessing for Israel rather than a curse, which he then proclaimed in spite of Balak's objections (Num. 22–24). Prophecy and divination were an integral part of ancient Near Eastern religions; the Deir 'Alla text, unfortunately poorly preserved, tells of oracles Balaam received from the gods at night, warning of coming disaster. It also contains a number of proverbs and curses.

ARCHAEOLOGY OF A TELL

Throughout the Near East there are thousands of mounds marking the site of ancient towns or villages, sometimes with a modern settlement or cemetery on top, sometimes abandoned. In Arabic these artificial mounds are known as *tells*. Tells are created by the accumulation of occupation debris over a long period of time and are characteristic of areas where **mud brick** was the commonest local building material. Mud brick is cheap, plentiful and has a limited life. When walls collapse a lot of debris is created, and as you cannot use mud bricks twice the simplest solution if you want to reuse the area is to level the surface of the ruined building and build another one on top. Thus the walls of the earlier building are preserved to a certain height together with anything which was buried in the rooms when the upper parts collapsed. In this way mounds grow up rapidly, composed of the superimposed remains of houses and other structures. Some tells, which cover important ancient towns or cities, may rise 35m or more above the plain.

It is for the archaeologist who digs down through the tell to distinguish the different occupation levels and sub-levels, to 'peel off the layers' and record the **stratigraphy** of the site, not always an easy task. Archaeological levels may represent distinct cultures and civilisations as a town or village is abandoned and reoccupied, and as people come and go. Sometimes one level is clearly marked off from the next by a layer of ash or burnt material, when the settlement has been destroyed by fire. Destruction levels are an archaeologist's dream, as the great scholar Sir Leonard Woolley explained: 'If the field archaeologist had his will, every ancient capital would have been overwhelmed by the ashes of a conveniently adjacent volcano. It is with green jealousy that the worker on other sites visits Pompeii and sees the marvellous preservation of its buildings ... and the furniture and household objects still in their places as the owners left them as they fled from disaster. Failing a volcano the best thing that can happen to a city, archaeologically speaking, is that it should be sacked and very thoroughly burnt by an enemy. The owners are not in a position to carry anything away, and the plunderers are only out after objects intrinsically valuable, the fire will destroy much, but by no means everything and will bring down on the top of what does remain so much in the way of ashes and broken brickwork that the survivors, if there are any, will not trouble to dig down into the ruins.'

As constraints of time and money make it impossible to excavate an entire tell, certain areas are chosen for investigation. A **step trench** cut into the slope of a mound, perhaps combined with a **sondage** or deep trench is useful to explore stratigraphy, then certain areas can be extended and new trenches opened up to uncover more of the **plan** of different levels. Usually the excavation area is divided into a grid of squares, with baulks between them (later removed), so the deposits can be seen in vertical **section**; the squares are aligned to a fixed measuring point on the tell. Digging is a process of destruction, so everything must be recorded accurately. Of course the site should be fitted into a regional context; a chronological framework is provided above all by **potsherds**, the broken pieces of pottery which are found in vast quantities on almost every tell. Levels at different sites which have the same pottery are roughly contemporary and can be fitted into the **pottery sequence** which has been painstakingly worked out by archaeologists.

10km south of Deir 'Alla a paved road to the left, before the Agricultural Research station, leads to the **Damiya dolmen field**, across the irrigation canal on a rocky ridge at the foot of the mountains. Dolmens are megalithic chamber tombs, found throughout Europe and the Middle East; typically a large horizontal capstone is placed on two or more upright stones which form the sides. Some of the Damiya dolmens were built in the Early Bronze Age (c 3000 BC); beneath the floor slabs is a small subterranean chamber which housed the body or bodies and grave goods. There are over 200 dolmens in the Damiya field, which is one of the largest in Jordan.

After 26.5km, past the first junction to South Shuna, the road branches right to King Hussein Bridge and left along Wadi Shu'aib to Salt. Turn right towards the modern town of **South Shuna**; nearby are a number of ancient tells, one of which, **Tell Nimrin** or **Tell South Shuna**, opposite the police centre, was cut through during the building of the modern road. Now there is little to see except for the impressive section towering above the road, but when excavated, a 6C Byzantine church with a mosaic pavement was uncovered, remodelled with new mosaic pavements in the Umayyad period (7C–8C). Some of the mosaics are in the small archaeological museum in Salt (p 59).

Nimrin was ancient **Bethnamaris** which came under the jurisdiction of the bishop of Livias 8km to the north. **Livias** is usually identified with the unexcavated **Tell Rama**, right of the main road in al-Rameh village 10km from South Shuna on the way to the Dead Sea. Herod the Great built a palace there, which was destroyed but rebuilt by Herod Antipas, who named the town Livias in honour of the empress Livia, Augustus' wife. Bethnambris (Bethnamaris) and Livias are both on the Madaba mosaic map; a Roman road connected Livias with Esbus (Hesban) and early pilgrims could turn off near the sixth milestone to visit the holy places of Mount Nebo.

After 1km, at the junction with the main Amman–Jerusalem road turn right (west) towards the Dead Sea. Soon Moses Memorial Church can be seen perched on top of Mount Nebo/Siyyagha to the south-east and on a clear morning you can also see Jerusalem. After c 6km, at a checkpoint, there is a left turn to Suwayma; straight ahead is King Abdullah Bridge and the West Bank, but the road is currently closed.

Take the road to Suwayma and c 200m past the junction follow the paved road on the left for 2km to a group of low mounds by a small farm on the right which mark the extensive Neolithic-Chalcolithic settlement of **Teleilat Ghassul**. Teleilat Ghassul means 'small mounds of the soap plant' a low scrub plant used by local people to make a kind of soap; archaeologically it is a most important site which spans the period between the Neolithic village cultures and the walled towns of the Early Bronze Age. Although investigations have been continuing for over 60 years and it is one of the largest late 5th–4th millennia sites in the Levant, there is little in the trenches for the visitor to see today except for wall foundations and storage pits. Among the most interesting finds were a series of wall paintings; one of these, perhaps representing a cult procession with masked figures approaching a shrine, is on display in the Amman Museum.

Dead Sea

6km from the Suwayma junction is a sign right to the **Dead Sea Resthouse**.

■ Here for a nominal fee you can use the beach facilities and discover for yourself the Dead Sea experience. Changing rooms are available and showers, essential to wash off the salt after bathing. There is a simple restaurant/snack bar but no overnight accommodation, although camping is permitted. Avoid Fridays if possible, when the facilities are crowded with day-trippers from Amman.

No-one can sink in the waters of the Dead Sea, which contain over 30 per cent salt and other minerals; not surprisingly its unusual buoyant properties have long excited interest and comment. Among the curious was Vespasian, on campaign in the Middle East before becoming emperor, who 'ordered some non-swimmers to be thrown with their hands behind them into deep water, and found that they all came to the surface as if blown upwards by a strong wind' (Josephus, *Jewish War* IV: 480). On the Madaba mosaic map (p 138–9) there are two boats on the lake, one carrying a whitish material, perhaps salt, the other transporting something yellowish, maybe wheat from the mountains of Moab. Near where the River Jordan flows into the Dead Sea a fish is shown frantically trying to swim away from the salty water, which spells death for all marine life.

Many 19C travellers went down to the barren shores, although not all dared bathe in the waters. One who did was the American John Lloyd Stephens, in 1836, accompanied not only by his companions, who 'lay like a parcel of corks upon its surface' but also by one of the horses, which obviously cared little for the experience: 'As soon as his body touched the water he was afloat, and turned over on his side; he struggled with all his force to preserve his equilibrium; but the moment he stopped moving he turned over on his side again, and almost on his back, kicking his feet out of the water and snorting with terror.' Mark Twain thought 'it was a funny bath' and tried various different positions but 'no position can be retained for long; you lose your balance and whirl over, first on your back and then on your face, and so on'. Today's tourists roll around in a similar fashion in the warm saline water or loll back reading their newspapers.

Stay for sunset if possible, when the Dead Sea is particularly beautiful. As the sun goes down and its warm glow shimmers across the water, look out for the tall minarets of the Dome of the Rock in Jerusalem silhouetted on the western skyline.

Beyond the resthouse is the 5km **Dead Sea Spa Hotel**.

■ Day visitors can use the beach, pools, terraces and other facilities; currently there is a charge of JD6, or JD12 with lunch or dinner, payable at reception. There is a restaurant, terrace and beach bars and a band in the evenings. Many hotel guests attend the **medical centre** which specialises in the treatment of skin diseases such as psoriasis and acne, for which Dead Sea water and mud are particularly beneficial. Various Dead Sea products, including lotions, shampoos and mud masks are on sale in the hotel shop.

As you continue southwards the desolate mountains of Moab rise steeply beside the road, cleft in places by wadis with clusters of bright green palms. **Zara Hot Springs** are 14km past the hotel, soon after the outlet of the Wadi Zarqa Ma'in. Unfortunately the stream is in need of a good clean-up, but there are several pools in which to paddle. Walk on a further 200m to the classical springs of **Kallirhoë** (beautiful springs), shown on the Madaba mosaic map with three buildings including a nymphaeum, and palm trees. **Herod the Great** built a baths complex here, not far from his palace at Machaerus (p 152), and it was to Kallirhoë that he came in search of a cure for his fatal disease, so graphically described by Josephus: 'a slight fever, an unbearable itching all over his body, constant pains in the lower bowel, swellings on the feet as in dropsy, inflammation of the abdomen and mortification of the genitals .. difficulty in breathing .. and spasms'. This his been variously diagnosed as psoriasis, arteriosclerosis and cancer.

Look for walls of volcanic tuff on the hillside east of the road opposite the pebbly beach. Within are a few column drums and excavations have revealed part of a deep plastered pool with a filter system and rooms around a courtyard. Doubtless there were a number of these pools in the Roman baths complex which appears to have been in use up to the time of the Jewish revolt. Later in the 4C part of the site was reoccupied and built over—Peter the Iberian took the waters here in the 5C. East of the pool is the iron nucleus of the spring which once fed the baths. The hillside here is full of mineral springs of different temperatures—there are over 60 of them and the hottest is 62˚C.

Walk down from the baths towards the sea where the remains of the broad stepped harbour wall can still be seen, though part of it has disappeared with the building of the road. Canon Tristram visited the site in the last century and thought it an excellent place for a baths because of 'the warm, salt sea in which, or rather on which, to disport and perform aquatic gymnastics', although he found the heat trying. It is now some distance from the shoreline, but once Herod's ships would have sailed here from the other side of the Dead Sea and a Roman road linked it with Machaerus and the springs at Zarqa Ma'in.

Beyond Kallirhoë the road cuts through the barren, rocky landscape with impressive views across the blue waters of the Dead Sea to the steep cliffs of Judaea on the other side. At 16km **Wadi Mujib** a bridge crosses the steep, narrow gorge, filled with water after the winter and spring rains. Soon the north end of the **Lisan Peninsula** *(lisan* means 'tongue' in Arabic) can be seen jutting far out into the Dead Sea. Here the lake is very shallow and in antiquity the southern basin may have been a plain, later submerged; there is evidence that in Roman times a road ran across the peninsula and connected with the western shore. From the Lisan peninsula to south of the Dead Sea salt flats is the area known as the **Southern Ghor**, literally 'southern depression', over 300m below sea level. Modern irrigation and agricultural techniques now enable crops to be grown on this once barren, salt-encrusted wasteland, and vast quantities of potash, one of Jordan's most important commodities, are reclaimed from the Dead Sea's waters. In antiquity it appears the land here was fertile, for scores of ancient sites have been recorded, and most scholars locate the biblical story of **Sodom and Gomorrah** in the Southern Ghor.

According to Genesis (13–14; 18–19), when Abraham and his nephew Lot were travelling with their flocks in southern Palestine conflict arose between their herdsmen over grazing grounds. They decided to separate and Abraham offered Lot first choice of land. Lot chose the fertile Jordan Rift valley and 'settled among the cities of the plain, pitching his tents on the outskirts of Sodom'. When four kings from the north swept down to attack the area, the allied forces of **Sodom**, **Gomorrah**, **Admah**, **Zeboiim** and **Zoar**—'**the five cities of the plain**'—were routed. Soon there was to be a worse calamity. 'The people of Sodom were vicious and great sinners' so Yahweh determined

Edward Lear's drawing of the Southern Dead Sea

their destruction. Lot was urged by two angels to flee with his wife and daughters, without stopping or looking behind. As they were entering Zoar catastrophe struck: 'Yahweh rained down on Sodom and Gomorrah brimstone and fire . He overthrew those cities and the whole plain, with all the people living in the cities'. Lot and his daughters were saved, but his wife was not so fortunate: she 'looked back and was turned into a pillar of salt'.

The destruction of Sodom and Gomorrah may preserve the memory of an earthquake, a not uncommon phenomenon in the Rift Valley, perhaps causing the bitumen there to ignite. As for Lot's wife, most travellers have managed to identify her somewhere among the strange crystalline salt formations. Not so Mark Twain, who wondered: 'Do you suppose Sodom and Gomorrah are under there yet? They must have floated to the top. Poor Lot's wife is gone—I never think of her without feeling sad. The cattle must have got her ... Peace to her sediment.' In the search for the cities of the plain, archaeological investigations have produced interesting results. **Five Early Bronze Age sites** were discovered, **Bab edh-Dhra'**, **Numeira**, **as-Safi**, **Feifeh** and **Khanazir**, all deserted around 2350 BC. Bab edh-Dhra', Numeira and Feifeh show signs of destruction by fire. A major problem with this equation, however, is that most scholars would date Abraham and Lot several centuries later.

27km south of Wadi Mujib is the Karak road junction. This is the main route from the interior to the southern Dead Sea, which descends dramatically alongside the Wadi Karak past a sign marking sea level to the Southern Ghor. **Bab edh-Dhra**, the preferred candidate for **Sodom** of the five Bronze Age tells, is c 1km east of the junction, on the left of the road by a small modern building and opposite a new housing complex for employees of the Arab Potash Company. Strategically sited overlooking the Wadi Karak, Bab edh-Dhra was a walled town which attained its greatest size and prosperity c 2600 BC; remains of the massive **town wall**, which was 5–7m thick with a mud brick superstructure on stone foundations, can be seen in the excavation trenches. A **sanctuary** was excavated by the wall in the south-east corner of the site. Bab edh-Dhra's enormous **cemetery** is along a track across the main road from the tell. Peppered with holes, the cemetery contains thousands of graves, the earliest dating to the end of the 4th millennium BC, long before Bab edh-Dhra was a fortified town. **Shaft tombs** with single or multiple chambers belong to this period; a typical chamber had a heap of bones in the centre with a row of skulls to one side and a number of ceramic vessels. During the period of the walled town burials were predominantly in rectangular mud brick buildings or 'charnel houses' and a small number of 'cairn burials', shallow pits filled with stones, may date to after the town's destruction c 2350 BC.

In **Wadi 'Isal**, c 7km south of the Karak junction, there are a number ancient sites, particularly of the Byzantine period. A few hundred metres from the road is a Byzantine structure associated with a water channel; some indications of copper smelting suggest this may have been a factory area. Further east on a hill, c 1km from the road, is another Byzantine structure, perhaps a watchtower; a large cemetery covers the hillsides nearby and there are graves in the hill below the tower. A Roman road which can still be traced followed Wadi 'Isal to modern Katrabba, perhaps biblical Luhith (Isaiah 15:5), on the plateau.

Numeira, tentatively equated by some with **Gomorrah**, is another large Bronze Age tell, with a modern pylon on it, on the left of the road 14km south of the Karak junction. Numeira was a walled town, perhaps inhabited for only 100 years or so before its destruction c 2350 BC. Its thick stone and mud brick walls can be seen surrounding the hill top; on the east are the remains of a massive stone tower, a later addition to the city's fortifications, possibly reflecting a worsening security situation shortly before the town's destruction. Within the walls are house foundations, now badly disturbed by recent trenching. **Rujm an-Numeira**, an unexcavated tower below the road to the right c 200m south of Tell Numeira, has much Nabatean pottery, and may be one of a series of Nabatean stations along Wadi Araba. About 5km further is the main entrance to the factory and solar evaporation pans of the Arab Potash Company.

For **Deir 'Ain 'Abata** or **Lot's Cave Monastery** turn left 4km beyond the potash factory and after 1km a blue sign 'Cave of Lot' marks the steep road to the site, currently under construction. A small concrete building just before the turn-off houses 'Ain 'Abata spring. Lot's Cave Monastery was discovered in the 1980s and is being excavated under British Museum sponsorship. From the parking area new steps go part of the way up to the site, which is perched on a steep cliff overlooking the Dead Sea; the final stretch must be scrambled up and is not recommended in the midday heat.

After leaving Zoar as fire and brimstone rained on the Cities of the Plain, **Lot and his daughters** settled in a cave in the mountains. Since they seemed to be the last people on earth, the girls were worried about not perpetuating the race, so they decided to get their father drunk and then have intercourse with him. Both became pregnant and gave birth to sons whom they named Moab and Ben-Ammi (Genesis 19:30–38). Thus the Bible explains the origins of the Moabite and Ammonite peoples. Lot's Cave, where the family traditionally took shelter, was a holy site from the Byzantine to Early Abbasid periods

Spring flowers at Jarash, Petra, Wadi Rum.
Above left Black Iris, Jordan's national flower

Left Sandstone, Petra. *Right* Sinai lizard

Above Qasr Burqu

Left Dancing Lady wall painting at Amra

Below left Foliate mask, Sweifiyeh church mosaic, Amman

Below right Mosaic detail, Sweifiyeh church, Amman

Golan Heights and Sea of Galilee, from Umm Qais

Civic Church Complex, Pella

Above Wadi Dana

Left Shepherdess, Disi, near Wadi Rum

Below Amman theatre

Rum – view from Burdah

Deir, Petra

Above Umm al-Jimal, Barracks

Left Bedouin milking sheep

Below Dolmen, Damiya

Cardo, Jarash

Araq al Habis, crusader caves

Treasury, Petra

Al Madras, Petra

(c 5C–8C), and there is evidence for earlier occupation going back to the Neolithic. Its associated church, described as (the sanctuary) of St Lot, is represented on the Madaba mosaic map just above Zoar.

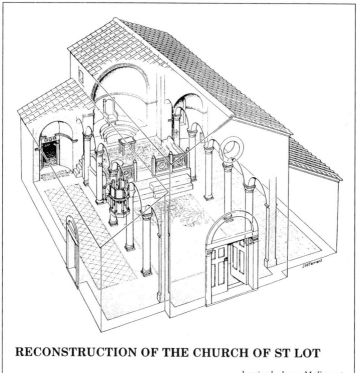

RECONSTRUCTION OF THE CHURCH OF ST LOT

drawing by James M. Farrant

Excavations revealed a three-apsed **basilica church** with the **cave** entered from the apse at the end of the north aisle. A four-line inscription before the cave entrance, dated April 606, refers to Bishop Jacobus and Abbot Sozomenus, and on the lintel above the door is a carved cross flanked by rosettes. Inside the cave is plastered and has a plain mosaic floor. In the main apse is a synthronon for the clergy with space for the bishop's chair; the nave and raised chancel were decorated with mosaic. An inscription in front of the chancel which gave a construction date of May 691 probably refers to a rebuilding or restoration of the church as earlier pottery was found below the mosaic floor. Among the many architectural fragments discovered during excavation was a reused block with a red-painted inscription invoking St Lot, confirming the dedication of the church. Around the church are the **domestic and kitchen areas** of the associated monastic complex. To the north is a deep **arched reservoir** and water catchment system.

As-Safi, identified with **Zoar** since Byzantine times, and on the Madaba mosaic map surrounded by date palms, is a modern town signed to the left after the Deir 'Ain 'Abata turn. Ancient ruins are few at as-Safi; for what remains there are turn left towards al-Nage 4km beyond the as-Safi road and after c 1.5km **Khirbet Sheikh Issa** is in the fields to the left and **Tawaheen as-Sukkar** is on the right.

Zoar from the Madaba mosaic map

Nothing is now visible at Khirbet Sheikh Issa, where limited excavations produced mainly Byzantine and Islamic artefacts.

At Tawaheen as-Sukkar, which means 'sugar mills' in Arabic, the standing remains are of Ayyubid/Mamluke sugar mills and an aqueduct which channelled water to drive the mills from nearby Wadi Hasa. All around the medieval site and stretching into the hills is a multi-period cemetery used first in the Early Bronze Age.

Feifeh, on the left-hand side of the main road, 10km south of the turn to al-Nage, is another Early Bronze Age walled town on a hilltop, much damaged in recent years. A heap of stones in the middle of the east part of the site may be a tower, and there is another possible tower on an outcrop to the west. Feifeh's final destruction was probably by fire, to judge from the thick layer of ash which covered the ruins. East of the site is a huge cemetery with cist graves; most are built with rounded stones and covered with slabs, some have upright slabs for the sides.

Khanazir, 6.5km south of Feifeh and just east of the main road, is the southernmost of the five Early Bronze Age towns which have been tentatively equated with the 'cities of the plain'. There is little to see beyond a large pile of stones on the hilltop, perhaps a tower, and a possible wall around the edge of the site.

South of Khanazir the road rises steeply as you leave the Dead Sea plain and the Southern Ghor and enter Wadi Araba.

Wadi Araba

Wadi Araba is c 150km long, from the edge of the Dead Sea plain to the Red Sea, and 10–30km wide between the mountains of Edom in the east and the Negev to the west. On average annual rainfall is a mere 20–30mm in this flat semi-desert valley, although there are rare heavy storms. Settlement was possible in the eastern foothills by careful water collection and storage, a skill at which the Nabateans in particular excelled.

CAMELS

Camels actually originated in America, but only relations like the llama now survive there. The Arabian camel, *C.Dromedarius*, unlike the Bactrian, has only one hump. It is extremely well adapted to the harsh conditions of the desert with a double row of eyelashes for protection against sand and wind and has a keen sense of sight and smell, though it can close its nostrils if necessary. In good times fat is stored in the hump for later use—it can also be converted to water which is why the camel can go for days without a drink. After a long period in the desert they will drink up to 25 gallons of water in a few minutes to replenish stocks!

They are not fussy about food, surviving, if necessary, on desert shrubs and thorns. Mark Twain remarked acerbically while visiting Palestine that 'Camels ... are not particular about their diet. They would eat a tombstone if they could bite it ... I expect it would be a real treat for a camel to have a keg of nails for supper.' They are prone to making extraordinary rumbling noises. According to Edward Lear, 'Some things in this world are not pleasant, to wit beetles in your hair ... fleas ... and the gulpyroarygroanery of camels.'

The Bedouin use their milk, meat and hides as well as riding them. The first biblical reference to camels comes from Judges 6:5 when the Midianites attacked the Israelites and 'their camels were without number'. Arabian camels are first actually depicted in the 8C BC on reliefs from Tiglath-Pileser III's palace at Nimrud, which are now in the British Museum. These show Assyrian troops pursuing Arabs who are mounted on camels, and also captured camels among the booty of one of the king's campaigns against Arab enemies. On a mosaic panel in the resthouse at the Moses Memorial Church there is a Ghassanid (Christian Arab tribesman) soldier with his camel. Camels were essential for the land trade routes: a large caravan might have up to 1000 camels, each carrying up to 500lb and travelling 20–30 miles a day, resting in the midday heat. They can walk at a speed of 8–10 mph all day and were essential to the raiding successes of the Arab forces in the First World War. Nowadays camel racing is a big sport, especially in the Gulf States, but the Bedouin usually use trucks and pickups instead of camels.

For **Qasr et-Telah** c 8.5km south of Khanazir turn east by a white dome-shaped monument with an inscribed stone and follow the foothills south for c 2km. Just north of a wadi beside a modern agricultural scheme which has destroyed the remains of an ancient field system recorded by Glueck in the 1930s there is a large **reservoir** and a small ruined **fort** or **caravanserai**. Water was channelled to the reservoir along a conduit from a spring up the wadi. Probably originally a Nabatean site, to judge from the vast amounts of Nabatean pottery found there, et-Telah has been identified with Roman **Toloha**, base of the **Ala Constantinia** referred to in the late 4C Notitia Dignitatum.

Continue southwards on the Araba road and after 10km or so look for a paved road signposted Fidan. Turn left along this road, bear right at a fork after c 16km and shortly after turn left along an unpaved track by the modern village of Fidan. A four-wheel drive vehicle is needed for the final 10km to **Feinan**, one of the most extensive ancient copper smelting centres in the Near East. The track runs to the left of a hill with a ruined building on top, passes two water tanks, the second with a reservoir, and then heads east up the wadi towards the mountains, for much of the way along the line of a black water pipe. When you reach the huge site cross Wadi Feinan and park on the north bank, by a blue sign, near the prominent central mound and surrounding ruins.

History

Research has shown that copper was mined and smelted intermittently in the greater Feinan region from the Chalcolithic to Byzantine periods (c 4000 BC–AD 650) as well as sporadically in Islamic times, notably under the Mamlukes and Ottomans. Copper deposits occur over a wide area, both high grade ore with manganese, mostly below ground, and lower grade ore in the Nubian sandstone. Vast amounts of slag attest to the industrial scale of the mining and smelting; a German survey has calculated 150,000–200,000 tons of slag in the Feinan area which may represent 15,000–20,000 tons of copper production. Feinan is the largest and most important of a number of copper smelting sites in this part of the Araba. It is often equated with biblical Punon; in the Roman and Byzantine periods it was known as Phaino and was the main town in the region. Under the Romans, according to Eusebius, convicts and Christians were sent as forced labour to work in the mines, which had up to four levels of galleries connected by shafts. In the early Byzantine period Phaino was a bishopric of Palaestina Tertia.

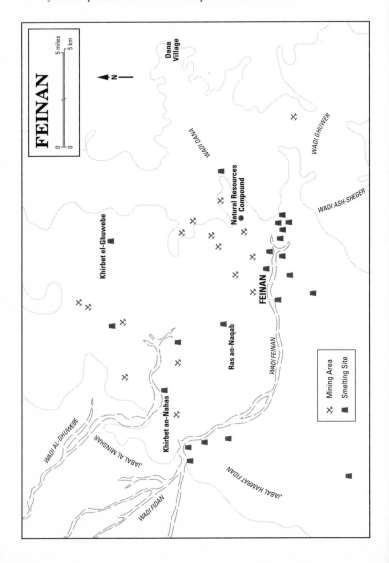

Most of the obvious ruins at Feinan are Roman and Byzantine. On the slopes of the main mound and the flatter area to the west are two **churches** and other ecclesiastical buildings, perhaps a monastery; a large structure on the summit may be Byzantine or earlier. Climb the hill for splendid views of the site and surrounding area. To the east are the high Shara mountains and routes through to 15km Dana (p 178) and Petra. Around the site are copper slag heaps and square plots of land delineated by stones which mark the remains of **ancient field systems**, irrigated from springs further up the wadi. Water was channelled along both sides of the Wadi Feinan; on the south side it was carried across Wadi ash-Sheger on a Romano-Byzantine **aqueduct**, part of which still stands. From there it passed through an industrial area, where today there are vast heaps of copper slag, to a **reservoir**, still fairly well preserved. In the east wall is the water intake system with settling tank, and in the north-west corner there is an internal staircase supported on an arch. Beyond the reservoir the water channel continues to a vertical water-driven **mill**, ruined but still impressive, and further to fields which stretch for some distance to the west. Feinan must have had quite a large population, to judge from the size of its **cemeteries** to the north-west and south-east of the site. There are thousands of graves, each marked by a stone, engraved with a cross if the occupant was Christian. Bodies were placed in a tomb chamber roofed with stone slabs and accompanied by grave goods; unfortunately more and more graves are being rifled by local Bedouin hunting for gold.

Return to the Araba road and 22km further south turn left at a sign marked 'Bir Mathkoor 8km'. Follow the track to a large blue corrugated metal building then swing right towards the Bedouin Police post by 11km **Bir Mathkoor**. Bir Mathkoor was at the Araba end of an ancient route from Petra; note Jabal Haroun, 'Aaron's Mountain', crowned with a small white shrine, rising above the Petra mountains in the distance. Behind a small village of modern concrete houses, built for the Bedouin but almost deserted, is a very ruined Nabatean fort or caravanserai which originally had four corner towers. The north-east corner has been badly damaged. East of the fort is another ruined structure which Glueck thought was a reservoir and to the south are extensive ash deposits. Fine Nabatean pottery and coarser wares litter the site. A deep well, now concreted, lies just north of the fort.

Return to the main road and at 49km **Garandal** you will see an extraordinary pagoda, marked 'Garandal Tourism Park' which was erected by the Chinese company that built the Wadi Araba road. Turn left just after the pagoda, right where the road forks and 500m along on the left-hand side is another Nabatean/Roman fort or caravanserai now almost totally buried under the drifting sand. Here the road from Petra via Dilagha emerges into Wadi Araba.

From Garandal drive southwards past 63km Aqaba airport and 67km Tell Maquss (p 202) for 70km Aqaba town and the Red Sea.

KING'S HIGHWAY

From Amman to Petra the King's Highway winds south through some of Jordan's loveliest scenery and past a wealth of historical sites. It is an ancient route, which follows the ridge of mountains east of the Dead Sea rift along a line of fresh water springs, and has been used throughout history by armies, traders and pilgrims, all of whom have left their mark. One of the first references to the King's Highway is in the Book of Numbers when the Israelites request passage through Edom, but are refused. 'We will go by the king's highway', they said, 'we will not turn to the right hand nor to the left, until we have passed thy borders' (Num. 21:17). A better translation than King's Highway is probably 'royal road', a generic term often used in the ancient Near East to describe a main transit route.

In the 1st millennium BC the Transjordanian 'royal road' linked the kingdoms of Ammon, Moab and Edom, and later the Nabateans used it to transport luxury goods from Arabia, particularly frankincense and other aromatics and spices. After Rome took over Nabatea, Trajan remodelled the road to facilitate the passage of troops and called it the **Via Nova Traiana**. A number of holy sites near the King's Highway attracted early Christian pilgrims and under the Crusaders, who built fine castles along it, the ancient road became the main thoroughfare of 'Oultrejourdain'. Muslim pilgrims used the King's Highway until the Ottomans developed the **Tariq al-Bint** (Desert Highway) as the main Haj route to Mecca in the 16C.

From Amman (Sixth Circle) take the airport road, turn right towards Naur and before Naur follow the signs to Madaba for 22km **Hesban**. A huge tell, which looms up on the right of the main road as you enter the modern village, marks the ancient site.

History
Hesban, biblical Heshbon, is described in the Book of Numbers as the city of Sihon, king of the Amorites, whose land was conquered by the Israelites under Moses (Num. 21). After the conquest of Canaan, Heshbon was allotted to the tribe of Reuben, but by the 8C BC the city was under firm Moabite control. In the Graeco-Roman period it was called **Hesbus** or **Esbus**; according to Josephus (Ant. XV, 294) it was fortified by Herod the Great and settled with veterans, perhaps to protect his border with the Nabateans. Esbus was at the key junction of the Via Nova Traiana and another Roman road which linked the town with Livias, Jericho and Jerusalem. At the beginning of the 3C it was raised to municipal status by Elagabalus and minted its own coins. In the Byzantine period Hesbus was an important bishopric; it is represented among the towns of Transjordan in the 8C mosaic pavement of the church of St Stephen at Umm ar-Rasas (p 150) and again in a mosaic from the 8C Acropolis church at Ma'in, now exhibited in the Madaba Archaeological Park (p 140). Despite fairly scant occupation in the Islamic period, Hesban flourished again after the Crusades and in the 14C became the capital of the Belqa district.

Excavations on the tell have revealed structures from various periods of Hesban's long occupation. Climbing from the south to the upper slopes of the mound a deep trench on the left contains a structure cut into bedrock and plastered, part of an **Iron Age reservoir** (9C–8C BC). Beyond is a **Roman monumental stairway**

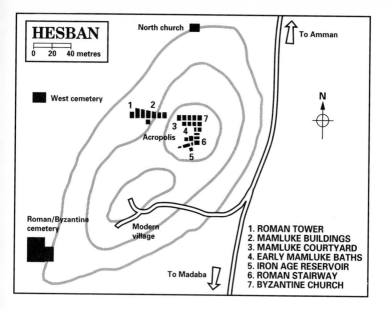

HESBAN

0   20   40 metres

North church ■   ⬆ To Amman

West cemetery ■

N

1   2
■▪▪▪▪▪■   7
3   ■■■■▪
Acropolis   4   ■■■
■▪■   6
5

Roman/Byzantine cemetery

Modern village

To Madaba   ⬇

1. ROMAN TOWER
2. MAMLUKE BUILDINGS
3. MAMLUKE COURTYARD
4. EARLY MAMLUKE BATHS
5. IRON AGE RESERVOIR
6. ROMAN STAIRWAY
7. BYZANTINE CHURCH

which originally led to a small temple on the acropolis. On the acropolis now is a basilica-type **Byzantine church**; another church was built below the tell to the north. Two levels of mosaic floor were discovered in the presbytery of this **North Church**; the upper mosaic, showing two trees and a pot sprouting grape vines, is displayed in the garden of the Madaba Museum. West of the church on the acropolis is an **Early Mamluke bathhouse** perhaps associated with **vaulted rooms** of the same period further down the slope of the mound. It has been suggested that this complex was an inn for travellers and their animals on the route from Karak to Damascus. West of the Mamluke buildings in a deep cut on the edge of the mound is a well-built **Roman tower**; from here across the valley you can see the **West Cemetery**.

Madaba

Continue on to 10km **Madaba** and follow signs up the hill to the **Church of the Map**. This pleasant town is situated on a rise on top of the old Roman and Byzantine remains: the mosaic floors for which it is famous date mainly from its Byzantine past. The *resthouse* near the Church of the Map provides meals but no accommodation. Money can be changed at the nearby Housing Bank. The **Tourist Office**, which is signposted, is a short distance further down the street from the church on the site of the **Burnt Palace**, a building decorated with mosaics which was destroyed by fire at some time in the late Byzantine period. At first it was assumed to be a church, but it is now known that it was a private house. The mosaics discovered here depict pastoral and hunting scenes within acanthus roundels framed by a grid of flowers and animals. A section of Roman road, also visible on the site of the **Madaba Archaeological Park,** runs along the south side of the building. The Park, an American-Jordanian joint project, is due to open shortly. This is the site of the **Church of the Virgin**, the **Hippolytus Hall** and the **Church of Elias** and also displays other mosaic plates from the area. The **Apostles' Church** will open in a second phase. Madaba's **Roman reservoir** is still visible near the Apostles' Church, although houses are being built inside it. The nearby offices of the Department of Antiquities house a nice little museum and the Church of the Map should not be missed. A good day's outing might include visits to the nearby **Moses Memorial Church** at **Siyagha/Mt Nebo**, the **Church of SS Lot and Procopius** and the churches of **St Sergius** and **St Stephen** at **Umm ar-Rasas**.

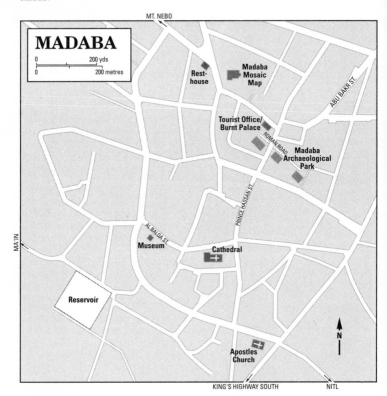

MT. NEBO

MADABA

0   200 yds
0   200 metres

Rest-house

Madaba Mosaic Map

ABU BAKR ST.

Tourist Office/Burnt Palace

ROMAN ROAD

Madaba Archaeological Park

PRINCE HASSAN ST.

AL BALQA ST.

Museum

Cathedral

MAIN

Reservoir

N

Apostles Church

KING'S HIGHWAY SOUTH   NITL

History

Madaba has a long history: it was part of the land of Moab, was taken by the Israelites (Num. 21:30) and later reclaimed by King Mesha of Moab who, on the **Mesha stele** (p 28), claims to have rebuilt the town. Nearby Mt Nebo is reputed to be the place from which God showed Moses the promised land. Later Madaba came under the control of the Jewish leader John Hyrcanus, was surrendered to the Nabateans and then passed to the Romans, who arrived in AD 106. The Third Cyrenaica Legion had a garrison here. Christianity spread to the region, the town had its own bishop by the 6C and flourished, but with the advent of Islam a slow decline set in. It was abandoned in Mamluke times and was resettled in 1880 by Christian families from Karak. When these families began building houses for themselves many long-buried mosaics emerged: most date from the Byzantine period and were found in churches, but some, such as the Hippolytus Hall belonged to private houses. The museum and Archaeological Park display a number of these floors in situ.

Weddings and services are still conducted at the **Church of the Map** (open 8.30–18.00, 10.30–18.00 on Sundays and Fridays); roughly half the population of Madaba is Christian, mostly Greek Orthodox. The famous map which the church houses was discovered in 1884 in the rubble of a former Byzantine church when resettled Christians began to build the present Greek Orthodox Church of St George. Dated to the 6C, probably to the time of the Emperor Justinian (527–565), it is the oldest extant map of Palestine and the source of some fascinating historical insights. It has survived despite damage over the years by fire, iconoclasts, collapse and rebuilding. The map is also a record of Church history, depicting biblically important sites in the Holy Land. Like the church, it is oriented to the east, so north is to your left, which may at first be confusing. Lack of space caused some problems for the mosaicists and there are some inaccuracies, particularly in Egypt, due both to stylistic requirements, the dictates of biblical history and lack of knowledge; but most of the towns it portrays have been identified. The map was probably based on a number of sources including the Bible, Eusebius' Onomasticon, a lexicon of biblical place names, road maps like the one known as the Peutinger Table and local knowledge, especially of the area around the Jordan. Towns, villages, churches and sites of biblical interest are all portrayed, Greek inscriptions give their names and quote from the Bible.

The map lies between the first three columns from the apse, mainly in the nave and south aisle. If it is covered by a carpet ask the attendant to roll it back. The original rectangle showed an area from Tyre and Sidon on the Mediterranean down to Egypt and across to Jordan; today only two fragments remain to the north of the main section which shows the Nile Delta, the river Jordan and the Holy Land. The central feature of the map is oval-shaped **Jerusalem (1)**, which has luckily survived almost intact. The city walls have 19 towers, the main colonnaded street runs south from the **Damascus Gate (A)** (today's Bab al 'Amud). Half-way down on the west side is the **Church of the Holy Sepulchre (B)**, its size an indication of its importance. Further along and across the street is the **Nea Theotokos Church (C)** which helped to date the map since it is known to have been consecrated in 542 during Justininan's reign. **The Church of Mount Sion (D)** lies at the south end of the street; between this and the Holy Sepulchre are the **Jaffa Gate (E)** and the **Citadel (F)**. Above Jerusalem is the expanse of the **Dead Sea (2)** and the **river Jordan (3)**. Two fish are swimming back up the Jordan and away from the lethal waters of The Dead Sea while another heads unwittingly to its death! There are two ferries across the river, the lower one, perhaps near the site of the present King Hussein Bridge, with a watch-tower on the West Bank. Nearby an almost obliterated lion chases its prey—a reminder that lions did once roam the Jordan valley. Iconoclasts have damaged the crew of the boats on the Dead Sea; between and above them an inscription reads 'Salt, also Pitch Lake, also the Dead Sea'. To the left, over the Wadi Mujib (biblical Arnon) are the hot springs of **Kallirhoë (6)** and **Baaras (7)** (now the site of the Zarqa Ma'in Hotel). At the top, across the mountains of Moab, is the walled city of **Karak (9)** (the XMΩBA of [XAP]AXMΩB[A] Charachmoba remains). Still on the east bank the **Church of the Sanctuary of Lot (11)** (TOTOYAΓIαΛ) is marked at the south end of the Dead Sea

1 Jerusalem	21 Askalon
2 Dead Sea	22 Gaza
3 River Jordan	23 Beersheba
4 Bethnambris	24 Mampsis
5 Livias	25 The Nile
6 Kallirhoë	26 its Pelusian arm
7 Baaras	27 its Sebennitic arm
8 Betomarsea (Maiumas)	28 Pelusium
9 Karak	29 Athribis
10 Zared (Wadi Hasa)	30 Tanis
11 Lot's Sanctuary	31 Sais
12 Zoar	32 Zois
13 Jericho	33 Rhinokolura
14 Nablus	34 Mediterranean
15 Gethsemane	A Damascus Gate
16 Bethlehem	B Church of Holy Sepulchre
17 Nikopolis (Emmaus)	C Nea Theotokos Church
18 Terebinth of Mamred	D Church of Mount Sion
19 Ashdod	E Jaffa Gate
20 Ashdod by the Sea	F Citadel

THE MADABA
MOSAIC MAP

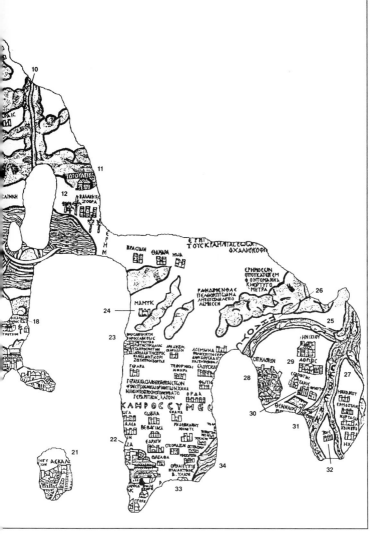

above the town of Balak, 'also Segor, now Zoora'. On the west bank is **Jericho (13)** with its palm trees, just left of the large area of damage. Below left and on the edge of the existing map is the damaged depiction of **Nablus (14)** (ΝΕΑΠΟΛΙC), shown as a large town with a colonnaded street, walls and towers. Just right of Jerusalem is **Bethlehem (16)** and the **Church of the Nativity**. The **Terebinth of Mamre (18)** ([ΑΡΒΩ] Η ΚΑΙ [ΤΕ]ΡΕΒΙΝθΟC) where Abraham met the Lord and was told that he and Sarah would have a child in their old age (Gen. 18) is on the far right of this section, but nearby Hebron is lost. An isolated fragment to the west shows part of **Ashkelon (21)** (ΑCΚΑΛ[ΩΝ]).

Further south lie the desert, the **Nile Delta (25)** and a glimpse of the **Mediterranean (34)**. This section, apparently based on Herodotus' description, is inaccurate: the coastline should turn west not east here, but presumably the mosaicist had no room to do this. Nor does the Nile flow in the right direction, but as a river of Paradise which, according to Genesis, was located to the east, and because of the constraints of space it has to run from east to west on the map. Just below the three mountain ranges on the left is **Beersheba (23)**, the limit of the Promised Land 'from Dan to Beersheba' and a large Roman garrison town. The large city in the bottom left corner of this section is **Gaza (22)** ([Γ]ΑΖΑ), then an important trading centre.

From the church it is a ten minute walk down to the **Madaba Museum** (open till 17.00pm, closed Tuesdays). The museum is temporarily closed for renovation but should reopen in 1996. It houses a collection of mosaics, a few rooms of ethnic costumes and archaeological finds. Some of the mosaics were found on site in the 1950s when the occupants of these houses were laying new floors.

Opposite the ticket office are some mosaic plates from the **'Cathedral'**—a large church only partly excavated and since damaged by modern construction. Down steps on the left is a house with a damaged mosaic floor showing part of a **Bacchic procession** with a Maenad and a naked satyr and four panels including one of deer and peacocks around a vase. This is currently covered while restoration of the room is underway. In the far top corner of the upper courtyard is the upper pavement of a small **presbytery** from Hesban's North Church dated c 550–600 and some gravestones, both Christian and Islamic. From here descend some steps to a small mosaic of animals from the early 6C **Lower Baptistery** floor of the 'Cathedral'. To the right is the **house of Farid el-Masri** where a mosaic floor shows a central medallion of a man's head and the popular design of pairs of animals between four fruit trees; the lion and ox are a symbolic reference from Isaiah 65:25 to paradise, where 'the lion shall eat straw like the bullock'. Two more rooms at this level display costume, including a Salt double dress, jewellery and coffee-making utensils. Continuing down past a faded mosaic of a tree with registers of cows and sheep nibbling at its leaves you reach the lowest level where two rooms are devoted to local archaeological finds with a number of cases of pottery, bronze, glass and lamps. Beyond are the mosaics of the **Twal family chapel** which cover two levels and were once divided by a chancel screen. They consist of a large pavement (somewhat damaged) of animals and designs in a square knot, including some very life-like cocks and a bird in a cage and, in the raised presbytery, a floral grid and a central medallion of a lamb grazing under a tree.

From here walk up to the **Madaba Archaeological Park** in Abu Bakr St past some fine old Ottoman houses on Prince Hassan St. On entering you will see part of the oldest mosaic found in Jordan, from Herod's Palace at Machaerus, hanging on the wall opposite. Immediately to the left is a fascinating example of iconoclastic damage: a mosaic from the Ma'in **Church on the Acropolis** where all that remains of an ox are the hooves and tail, the rest has been carefully blocked out and replaced by a large tree. The care with which this has been done suggests that this may have been the work of Christian iconoclasts, bent on correction not destruction. Further round on this side are mosaic vignettes of Hesban and Gadaron (Salt) from the border of this church. On the right of the entrance are mosaics from the church at Massuh, 10km north of Madaba.

Mosaic detail: Madaba Archaeological Park

Behind the Machaerus mosaic is the hangar over the mosaics of the **Hippolytus Hall** and the circular nave of the **Church of the Virgin** (Note. Work was not complete on the mosaic display at the time of writing) which has a mosaic floor rebuilt from a late 6C pavement of the same date as the church and of which only traces remain. A pattern of geometric knots, circles and squares encloses a dedicatory inscription within the central medallion which urges churchgoers to 'purify ... mind, flesh and works' before looking on Mary—this probably refers to an image of the virgin somewhere in the church. According to a second inscription east of the nave the mosaic was laid in the time of Bishop Theophane, 'Thanks to the zeal and ardour of the people who love Christ in this city of Madaba, for the salvation and assistance and remission of sins of those who have made offerings, and of those who will make offerings to this holy place.'

The early 6C Hippolytus Hall, named after the subject of its mosaic floor, lies west of the church and was partly covered by its vestibule. The hall in turn overlies an earlier Roman temple. The irregular rectangular floor is framed by a border of acanthus scrolls with hunting and pastoral scenes and personifications of the seasons as Tyches in the corners. Within the border the mosaic is divided into three sections: to the west a diamond grid contains water-fowl, trees and plants. The later addition of a wall damaged the central section which shows figures from the legend of Phaedra and Hippolytus including Phaedra herself. This theme continues above with Aphrodite and Adonis, identified by inscription, the three Graces chasing cupids and a peasant girl on the left. Above and outside the border next to two fish-tailed monsters are three Tyche figures: personifications of the cities of Rome, Madaba and Gregoria. Cross a section of paved **Roman road** to reach the **Church the Prophet Elias** of which little remains beside the **Crypt of Elianos** below. Both were decorated with mosaic floors, that of the church dated by inscription to 607/8 and the crypt mosaic to 595/6.

Situated at a crossroads in the south-east of the town the **Apostles' Church** is due to reopen shortly. An inscription now lost dated 'the holy place of the apostles' to 578, and somehow its mosaics, which show considerable classical influence, were spared from iconoclastic damage. It is famed for the personification of the sea (Thalassa) placed in the central medallion of the rectangular **nave**. The bare-breasted woman, reminiscent of the Nereid Thetis and clutching an oar, rises from the sea surrounded by fish, sharks, a sea monster and even a small jelly-fish. Round the medallion an **inscription** reads 'Oh Lord God, who has made the heavens and the earth, give life to Anastasius, to Thomas and Theodora' and identifies the mosaicist Salaman. Facing birds form a grid pattern in the rest of the nave. The acanthus leaf border, damaged on the south side, is notable for its chubby little boys and foliate masks. Geometrical patterns decorate the **side-aisles** and **inter-columnar spaces**. At the east and west ends pairs of animals face each other around trees or urns. Two **side chapels** also with mosaics lie adjacent to the north aisle. In the north-west corner here a small panel with a brief inscription mentioning Bishop John shows sheep and gazelle between pomegranate and apple trees. The larger chapel is irregularly shaped and divided by a step into two sections. To the west four fruit trees face diagonally inwards. Pairs of animals face each other on three sides and the inscription on the east side refers to the offerings given in memory of priest John 'for the zeal of Deacon Anastasius'. Above this a floral grid within a border contains birds and flowers.

Madaba to Mukhayyat, Moses Memorial Church and 'Ain Musa

7km north-west of Madaba on the way to the Moses Memorial Church at Mt Nebo a little road bears left. Follow it through orchards and farm land and you will come to 2km **Khirbet el-Mukhayyat**, reputedly the location of the Old Testament town of Nebo. The site of a little cluster of churches, it is well worth the detour to see the fine mosaic floor at **SS Lot and Procopius**. The guardian should be there daily until 17.00.

A corrugated iron roof marks the church of SS Lot and Procopius, named after early Christian martyrs, and protects an attractive, well-preserved **mosaic** discovered in 1913. Built under Bishop John in the mid-6C the raised **presbytery** has a bordered mosaic with sheep on either side of a tree—a fairly common religious motif. A dedicatory **inscription** runs below the step and dates the work to 557; the translation is given on the entrance wall. The inscription at the top of the **south aisle** begs St Lot to receive the prayers of Rome and Porphyria and Mary.

The main pavement has two sections: a twisting vine laden with grapes springing from acanthus plants in each corner divides the central panel into delightful vignettes of daily life. In keeping with the vine motif the grape features heavily: its harvest, pressing and treading are all carefully drawn, although fire damage has blackened a small section. Some of the finest work is in the inter-columnar spaces: a charming picture by the entrance shows a man rowing a boatful of amphorae, a church and a fisherman hooking a fish. This is a good example of Jordanian mosaic work where Nilotic influences merge with more familiar daily scenes and buildings. Opposite is a scene of ducks, waterlilies and fish, full of colour and movement. Next to the fisherman come two extraordinary animals with fish tails, opposite them are two deer and next to the deer a very life-like pair of geese.

At the west end the second section shows pairs of animals between four fruit trees. There are two hares, two stags drinking and two bullocks facing an altar, the **inscription** quotes Psalm 51:19: 'Then shall they offer bullocks upon thy altar' in a reference to sacrifice. The benefactress 'the lowly Epiphania' is also mentioned. Around the walls are mosaic panels from the nearby **Church of St George** which was built on the highest point here—a ten minute walk south-west. Dated by inscription to 536 its mosaics are no longer in situ, but the view down the Wadi Afrit to the Dead Sea is wonderful.

Mosaic from the Church on the Acropolis, Ma'in, showing iconoclastic 'repairs'

MOSAIC ART

Jordan has many mosaics from Roman, Byzantine and Umayyad times. The art of mosaic-making reached a climax in the 6C, when the centre of these developments was Constantinople, but skilled craftsmen also operated in the provinces. Mosaics in these outlying areas often depict subjects from everyday life (wildlife, hunting scenes, foliage designs) and can be charmingly informal. Byzantine art was primarily Christian art and many of Jordan's mosaics are from churches, but the secular tradition persisted and classical motifs remained fashionable: for example, in the use of personifications of the seasons, portraits of benefactors and pastoral scenes. Egyptian influences appear in the Nilotic scenes. Depictions of towns and places are particularly associated with Byzantine mosaics in Jordan—above all in the Madaba Map.

Mosaic artists probably worked from pattern books, hence the recurring themes. They laid the stone tesserae in a layer of wet lime over a bed of gravel in *terra rossa*, covered by a layer of lime and ash. The only mosaics which survive in Jordan are stone floor mosaics, but traces of glass mosaics used to cover walls have also been found.

Many mosaics suffered at the hands of Iconoclasts: the controversy over the worship of idols raged in Byzantium in the 7C–9C. During hard times many attributed the empire's plight to idolatry. Even the coinage was affected—Justinian had introduced Christ's face onto the gold solidus, but religious images disappeared from the coinage under the Iconoclastic Emperors. Sadly parts of and even whole mosaics were destroyed in Jordan in this period, although it is not clear who was responsible for this. Jews and Muslims were also wary of portraying the figure—the

Old Testament inveighs against the graven image, and a *hadith* (tradition) attributed to Mohammed says that God is the only creator. However, the wall paintings in the early Islamic baths at **Qusayr Amra** portray figures and the anti-iconoclast John of Damascus (700–750) does not mention Muslims as being iconoclastic. Several Jordanian mosaic floors laid well into the Umayyad period are further proof of Muslim tolerance of Christianity. Caliph Yazid II (719–724) apparently ordered the destruction of images, but the care with which some church mosaics have had the figures blocked out may imply that local Christians were themselves responsible.

Church mosaics use symbols and biblical references: early Christian art emphasised symbols such as the fish (the Greek letters IXΘYΣ matched the first letters of the phrase Jesus Christ, Son of God, Saviour) and the lamb, often as a way round the vexed issue of whether it was blasphemous to portray God and therefore man, who was made in His image. Other symbols recur frequently in the later Jordanian mosaics: peacocks symbolise the immortal soul, the lion and the bullock may refer to paradise, and a sheep tied to a tree to sacrifice. Mosaic inscriptions help with dating by referring to historical figures like bishops. Furthermore, at a time when the vast majority of the population was illiterate, mosaics often also served as visual explanations of Bible history and Christian teachings.

There are a few more churches in this valley, but none with mosaics visible. Below SS Lot and Procopius is the oldest church here, the 5C **Church of SS Amos and Casiseos**. Identified by an inscription on two pilasters, now lost, it had only a stone-flagged floor. Alongside to the north is the late 6C **Chapel of Priest John** which was found to have two mosaic floors, one above the other. A 15 minute walk east and south across the wadi brings you to **el-Keniseh** where the apse of a chapel and adjacent rooms to the north are visible.

Return to the main road and turn left. After 3km bear right through green gates to the **Moses Memorial Church**.

History

Perched 700m above the Jordan Valley, the view west from the Moses Memorial Church at Siyagha is breathtaking. On a clear day you can see the Dead Sea and the dark green of the Jordan Valley with Jericho just visible beyond. From these heights Moses is said to have been shown the Promised Land: 'And Moses went up from the plains of Moab unto the mountain of Nebo, that is Pisgah, that is over against Jericho. And the Lord showed him all the land of Gilead, unto Dan.'(Deut. 34:1). Egeria, the indefatigable 4C pilgrim, was shown the tomb of Moses inside the church and the view: 'From there you can see most of Palestine... To our left was the whole country of the Sodomites... We were also shown the place where Lot's wife had her memorial... The pillar itself, they say, has been submerged in the Dead Sea.' The modern sculpture outside refers to both the Old and the New Testament: 'And as Moses lifted up the serpent in the wilderness, even so must the son of man be lifted up' (John 3: 14–17). The area of Mt Nebo, including nearby Mukhayyat, has long been inhabited; the **Mesha stele** boasts of a massacre of its inhabitants: 'I took it and slew all in it, seven thousand men and women.' Most recently it has been taken over by the Franciscan fathers who began excavating in 1933 and have been responsible for extensive restoration since then.

The church is a simple building with a corrugated iron roof and modern stained glass windows. In the **nave** stumps of pillars lead down towards the raised apse with **synthronon**, the oldest part of the church; foundations of the old wall were excavated by the second row of pillars from the front. The original triapsidal building, possibly converted from an earlier, pre-Christian structure, is of limestone and dates from the 4C. Six tombs were found in the rock under the floor, one of them in the centre. In the **presbytery** you will see remnants of mosaic floor from different periods. The 4C Greek inscription reads 'under the most reverend and most pious priest and abbot Alexios the holy place was renovated' and the braided cross on the wall at the east end of the south side aisle came from the south vestibule floor.

There have been many changes to the church over the years which have considerably altered its shape. Originally there were funeral chapels to the north and south of the **vestibule**, a courtyard to the west and the monastery to its south. A **baptistery** was later added on the north side.

North of the nave is the **Old Baptistery**, its floor 1m lower than the rest of the church. The central part of the baptistery floor contains a beautiful, mid-6C mosaic combining dramatic hunting scenes with a calmer, pastoral section. Reds, yellows and browns predominate, and the clear black outline emphasises the design-sense of the craftsmen **Soelos, Kaiamos** and **Elias** whose names are mentioned in the inscription below. The inscription at the top reads: 'By divine grace, at the time of our father and pastor Elias, beloved by God, the holy diaconicon of God was rebuilt and beautified with the basin of regeneration it contains, and with the splendid kiborion, by the good offices of Elias abbot and priest, under the consulate of Flavius Lampadius and Orestes, in the month of August, in the ninth indication of the year 425 of the Province (Arabia-AD 531). For the salvation of Mouselios advocate and Sergia his wife, and the salvation of Philadelphus advocate and Goti advocate, and of all their kinsfolk. Amen Lord.'

There are four registers within the plaited border of the mosaic. At the top is a zebu tethered to a tree while to its right a shepherd fights off a lion and a soldier spears a lioness. Next comes a beautifully drawn scene of two horsemen astride their mounts, their dogs leaping towards a bear and a boar. The third register is calmer: a shepherd sits under a tree facing a goat and three fat-tailed sheep grazing among fruit trees. Finally comes a black man distinctively dressed—the ribbons on his head are a typically Persian motif. The spotted camel is an imaginative rendering of a cameleopard or giraffe.

Further east is the cruciform **font** with steps into it. At some time in the 4C a semicircular basin for baptism was placed in its southern arm. The spaces between the arms are decorated with mosaic knots and a fishscale design runs around three sides. During extension work in the later 6C the floor level was raised to that of the rest of the church and a new mosaic floor (now displayed on its walls) covered the old one.

The original building became the **presbytery** and the **courtyard** and **vestibule** the **nave** and **aisles**, which were laid with mosaics framed with a grapevine border, still partly visible in the aisles and some of the central intercolumnar spaces. The work was completed in AD 597. An inscription in the south side nave reads: 'For the peace and welfare of your servant Anosas and all his blessed house.'

Mosaic panels from the church of St George line the central nave: to the north are the dedicatory inscriptions and north entrance pavement showing two peacocks, symbols of the immortal soul, a tree, a lion, a zebu and two figures, one of them a harvester. Opposite is a section from the presbytery with birds around the altar columns and a sheep by a bush. An interesting panel from the south auxilliary chapel with deer and doves around a date palm, bears the name of the benefactor Saolas in Greek and on the other side either the same name in Christo-Palestinian Aramaic or the *bisalameh* (greeting of peace) in Arabic, in which case this is the earliest example of Arabic script found in Jordan.

To the south the old **funerary chapel** was rebuilt and subsequently became a **baptistery**. The mosaic panel reading 'Peace to all' on the right wall as you enter from the nave came from the threshold. Two **dedicatory inscriptions** on circular panels on the side of the font refer to Bishop Sergius and 'the most pious abbot Martyrius'. In front a mosaic panel shows gazelle grazing under fruit-laden trees. Above them pairs of water fowl flank two circular inscriptions reading: 'With the help of our Lord Jesus Christ the construction of the holy church and the Baptistery was finished, under the most pious bishop Sergius and the most beloved by God the priest and hegumen Martyrius in the fifteenth of the year 492' (AD 597).

The **Theotokos (Mother of God) Chapel** in the south-west corner was added in the early 7C when the floor level was raised and some rooms in the monastery taken over. Like the baptistery, railings divided the nave from the apse. A rectangular mosaic before the **apse** shows a ciborium and altar with a bull on either side, flowers and gazelle. This is much damaged by iconoclasts, but a delightful gazelle with collar and bell can still be seen on the left. The Greek quotation above the bulls is from Psalm 51:19: 'Then shalt thou be pleased with the sacrifices of righteousness ... then shall they offer bullocks upon thine altar.' An ornamental border surrounds the remaining mosaics whose central panel showed a hunting scene. Below, a swastika design surrounds animals and plants. Currently this area is used for displays and this part of the floor may be covered with a carpet.

Near the car park is the *resthouse*, which contains a mosaic from the nave of the **Kayanos church** in the nearby valley of **'Ain Musa**. This is probably the earliest depiction of a Christian Arab (Ghassanid) soldier and his camel, armed with bow and sword. The other figures are the benefactors Fidus and John.

About 1km from Mt Nebo on the way back to Madaba a bumpy road bears left and steeply down to **Moses' spring**. Look out for a **dolmen** marked by a cairn on the left just after a grove of pines and for the remains of an ancient watchtower on the other side. Eucalyptus trees grow by an ugly pumping station at the spring; according to Egeria this is 'the water which flows from the rock, which Moses gave to the children of Israel when they were thirsty'. When she visited there was a community of monks here 'of the kind known as ascetics'. The Roman fort of el-Mehatta was near here: it guarded the Esbus-Livias road used by pilgrims.

From here the road worsens, but it is only a ten minute walk to the 6C **Church of Deacon Thomas** which lies on the left of the road. Its square presbytery and three aisles were decorated with mosaics, the nave comparable to that of **SS Lot and Procopius** with scenes of sheep and shepherds, wild animals and huntsmen in an acanthus frame. The mosaic in the *resthouse* at **Siyagha** comes from the west end of the nave of the 7C **Kayanos church**, located in the nearby vineyards. This was part of a monastery complex and had two mosaic pavements, the lower one being early 6C work.

EARLY PILGRIMS

Pilgrimage to the Holy Land began very early indeed: Constantine's mother Helena paid a visit to Jerusalem some time after 325 and was associated with the discovery of the True Cross. This encouraged a trend among devout and wealthy Christians—and devotion certainly was required. In those times a pilgrimage from Europe must have taken a good year and been at best an exhausting and dangerous journey. The earliest account we have of such a pilgrimage is that of Egeria who was there in the 380s and gives a lively account of her travels which included visits east of the Jordan. In the 5C the elderly Bishop Peter the Iberian visited and took the waters at Kallirhoë. Even in the times of the Crusaders safety of pilgrims was not assured: the 12C pilgrim Saewulf describes Saracens 'watching day and night and always on the lookout for those whom they can attack', adding that the bodies of those who died were left by the road, the ground being too rocky to bury them.

As the number of pilgrims increased an industry developed to meet their needs: they required food, accommodation and protection. Hostels were built and soldiers might have to escort the pilgrims in the wilder areas. Pilgrimage was generally beneficial to the economy: a flourishing trade developed in relics, flasks of holy oil and water from the Jordan and even shoemakers prospered. It was also a means of legitimising the new religion—in identifying and visiting the holy sites, pilgrims were asserting the truth of biblical history. Origen travelled the Holy Land in search of sites and the historian Eusebius included many in his Onomasticon, a list of places which was probably used by the makers of the Madaba mosaic map. Pilgrims used the Bible as travellers today use guidebooks. Bible stories were taken for the literal truth: Egeria was shown the rock on which Moses broke the stone tablets and was disappointed to hear that the pillar of salt which had been Lot's wife had disappeared into the sea some time before: 'It used to stand near the sixth milestone from Zoar'. In fact, the pillar had miraculously reappeared by the time of the 12C pilgrim Theoderich's visit here.

Pilgrimage, however, was eventually debased by the peddling of relics, sale of indulgences and by professional pilgrims who lived on alms. Crusaders too were encouraged by the offer of remission of both sins and taxes. *Piers Plowman*, written in the 14C, calls for a return to the true spirit of Christianity. Its Passus V paints an amusing picture of a pilgrim: 'on his hat were perched a hundred tiny phials, as well as tokens of shells from Galicia, cross-ornaments on his cloak, a model of the keys of Rome, and on his breast a vernicle. All these emblems were designed to inform the world at large of all the pilgrim-shrines he had visited'. Instead of pilgrimage a new emphasis was placed on the Christian's spiritual journey, particularly after the Reformation, as the desire grew for reform and an end to corruption.

Excursion from Madaba to Ma'in and Hammamat Ma'in

Ma'in (Ba'al Ma'on of the Bible) is a ten minute drive south-west of Madaba; from the Apostles' Church look for the **Roman reservoir** on the left on the way out. There is nothing much to see at Ma'in now, but a number of mosaics were found here, including one on the acropolis in an Umayyad period church dated to 719 which contained vignettes of towns like the one at Umm ar-Rasas; some of these are now in the Madaba Archaeological Park. A small 6C church decorated with geometric and floral mosaic patterns and a dated inscription and a three-room complex including a funerary chamber and crypt were also found, along with the remains of a pribaton (bath) and a pilgrim hostel on the north-west slope of the tell. South-west of the mound was a monastic complex. Across the valley south-west of Ma'in is another little church without mosaics.

There are lovely picnic spots down tracks which in spring are lined with asphodel, anchusa, purple thistles and giant fennel off the road between Ma'in and the hotel and hot springs at **Zarqa Ma'in**. These are the classical waters of Baaras—the valley is full of hot springs and Kallirhoë, where Herod was treated for his ailments, is only 8km west on the Dead Sea. Both sites feature on the Madaba map (Baaras above Kallirhoë). On the descent, views of the cerulean-blue Dead Sea against the black and white rock are stunning, especially in the early morning.

■ There is an entrance fee for day visitors to the complex: the *Ashtar Hotel* offers a range of therapeutic treatments including hot baths, mud packs and massage for ailments like rheumatism, asthma, skin complaints and sports injuries; it also has an outdoor swimming pool. Cheaper self-catering rooms are available near the entrance with cafés and a small shop. At 200m below sea level it can be very humid here. The springs now gush out in a waterfall below the hotel and are scalding hot. Families come bathing in the pools below, reached by a rickety bridge. Be aware of cultural differences—bikinis may cause a stir! The pools are not always as clean as they might be.

From Madaba you can either continue south along the King's Highway to Dhiban, branching right at 13km Libb to visit Herod's palace at Machaerus or detour to visit some extra sites including the beautiful mosaics at Umm ar-Rasas, rejoining the King's Highway at Dhiban.

Excursion from Madaba to Dhiban via Umm ar-Rasas
Follow signs for Jiza via 10km Nitl from the Apostles' Church crossroads. A left turn at the junction in Nitl will take you on a short detour to 3km **Umm al-Walid** where remains dating to the Bronze Age have been found on a small tell. This is the site of an 8C **Umayyad complex** adjacent to remains from the Roman-Byzantine period. The large **courtyard** with rooms around it had a portico along the eastern side. Also on this side was the entrance, flanked by **quarter-towers** while semi-circular **interval towers** and round **corner towers** punctuate the walls. Benches line the entrance. Note the water pipes just south of the entrance and latrine outflow outside the north wall. Further east is a square mosque oriented north–south. Four column bases still showing once supported arches. The site was probably abandoned in the Mamluke period.

Return to Nitl and continue straight on towards Umm ar-Rasas. At 5km **Za'faran** twin Moabite towers, later reused by the Romans, kept watch over Wadi Themed, a tributary of Wadi Wala, from the north bank. One tower is by the road on the right, the other shortly after and a little further from the road on the left. On the crest of the hill on the south bank of the wadi another Moabite fortress at 6km **ar-Rumail** dominates the surrounding region. An outer wall and ditch enclose a confusing jumble of stones and a ruined though fairly well-preserved rectangular watchtower still standing over 6m high in places. Dozens of forts like Za'faran and ar-Rumail dot ancient Moab to watch over the land and protect against invaders.

After 2km bear left and continue a further 5km before turning left down a track to see the peculiar **tower** just north of Umm ar-Rasas which may have been a watch-tower or even a Stylite tower. Nearby to the east is a little church with a raised apse. The tower, solid inside except for a room at the top, has Greek crosses on three sides and a niche on the east face. Some fine, but weathered cornice decoration remains at the top. 30m north are the remains of a three-storey building and behind are cisterns, two quarries and more unexcavated ruins. Continue on 2km to **Umm ar-Rasas** where the mosaics are housed in a pale green hangar outside the town walls.

Tower near Umm ar-Rasas from The Land of Moab *by H.B. Tristram*

History

The town of Kastron Mefaa, as it was known, was an important frontier station in classical times. According to the historian Eusebius a Roman army unit was stationed by the desert at Mefaat and Jeremiah included it in his cursing of Moab: Jer 48:21 'Judgement is come ... upon Mephaath.' If you scramble up the walls by the recently excavated South Gate you will find a desolate sea of rubble inside with only the odd arch still standing. There were entrances in all but the west wall, that in the east being the largest and earliest. Later the south and east gates were blocked up. Two churches in the east wall have been cleared and partly restored. Both date to the 6C and had mosaic floors. Archaeological work has concentrated on the churches here, four inside the walls and at least 11 in the north sector outside. Excavations are continuing on the site and more churches are being cleared including the 'Church of the Lions', named after its fine mosaic floor which includes two lions.

The mosaics of the two churches under the hangar are viewed from a platform. The **Church of Bishop Sergius**, of which only the **raised presbytery** can be seen, lies to the north. On a rectangular panel before the altar rams and pomegranate trees surround a central inscription dating the mosaics to the time of Bishop Sergius (587). Unfortunately, the nave with portraits of benefactors and personifications of the Sea and the Earth was much damaged by iconoclasts. However, one figure, depicting a season, was discovered hidden under the pulpit in the south-east corner. An **inscription** by the presbytery step quotes Psalm 87:2: 'The Lord loveth the gates of Zion more than all the dwellings of Jacob' and one in the first inter-columnar space on the north has the names of the mosaicists. North of the nave is a **sacristy**.

St Stephen's Church, the larger of the two, is c 1m higher and has a splendid mosaic floor. Like that of Bishop Sergius, it has a raised apse decorated with geometric and knot designs and built over an earlier mosaic. It was the **dedicatory inscription** at the step which identified Umm ar-Rasas as Kastron Mefaa: it dates the mosaic to 785, proof that churches were being built in Jordan well into the Islamic period. Under this are the effaced portraits of the benefactors among fruit trees, and south of the pulpit is a pear tree. The badly-damaged central nave showed typical pastoral and hunting scenes.

It is the broad frame of the **nave** which provides some of the finest remaining work here: mosaic bands running the length of both sides show 15 major towns of the time. Those on the north are from Palestine, those on the south from Jordan. Pride of place near the apse is reserved for **Jerusalem** (HAΓIA ΠΩΛIC) and **Kastron Mefaa** which has a double space and shows a pillar with a church at its foot. The others, from top to bottom, are Philadelphia (Amman), Madaba, Esbounta (Hesban), Belemounta (Ma'in), Areopolis (Rabba) and Charachmoba (Karak). Below Jerusalem are Nablus, Sebastis, Caesarea, Diospolis (Lidda), Eleutheropolis (Beit Gibrin), Askalon and Gaza. Inside is an equally broad Nilotic border full of boats, fish and *putti* fishermen, and with ten vignettes of towns of the Nile Delta including Alexandria in the south-west corner. Two more Jordanian towns, Limbon and Diblaton are at the top of the side aisles by a pear and a pomegranate tree. Limbon may be the village of Libb, the other possibly Dhiban.

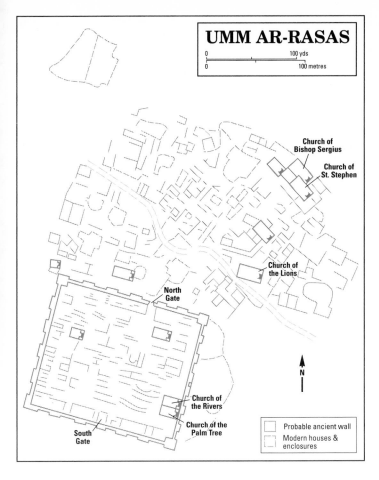

UMM AR-RASAS

0   100 yds
0   100 metres

Church of Bishop Sergius

Church of St. Stephen

Church of the Lions

North Gate

Church of the Rivers

Church of the Palm Tree

South Gate

N

     Probable ancient wall
     Modern houses & enclosures

From Umm ar-Rasas take the road to Dhiban, turning right at the junction just past the site and after c 7km, beyond a sign right to al-Meshrefeh, turn left along an asphalt road which is being repaved to 3.5km **Lehun**, a multi-period site with remains spread over a wide area. A small **Nabatean temple** on the left, down the slope from some modern houses, has recently been partly restored. Facing west, it is of finely tooled, embossed limestone blocks, with an altar against the back wall of the single chamber, and located towards the north-east of a large outer court-yard still visible in outline. There are other unexcavated Nabatean buildings in the vicinity.

When the asphalt road ends bear right along a dirt track to the **Moabite fortress** of Lehun, strategically sited on a bluff overlooking the Wadi Mujib (biblical Arnon) and offering magnificent views of the great canyon. Outside the main fortifications at the end of the plateau is an extensive **Iron Age village**. Curiously, some of the rooms in the typical courtyard houses have no door. A heavy lintel, replaced at a lower level, marks the entrance to the fortress proper, which is surrounded by a strong wall following the contour-line of the hill. On the south and west sides the outer wall has been plastered as protection against wind and rain, on the south-west and south-east it has been reinforced with corner towers. Perhaps, as suggested by the excavators, the fortress was used as a storage building to supply the garrison of King Mesha of Moab at Aroer, 3km west of Lehun.

To reach **Aroer** return to the main road to Dhiban, along which Jordan's national flower, the **black iris,** blooms in profusion in the spring, and turn left in c 7km, where pylons cross the road for the second time. Continue a further 2.5km, the last stretch unpaved, to the small mound visible from a distance alongside an isolated modern house. Aroer is in a commanding position on the northern slope of the Arnon valley.

History

After the Israelite conquest, according to the Bible, Aroer, which had formerly belonged to Sihon, king of Heshbon (Deut. 2:36), was occupied by the tribe of Reuben (Joshua 13:16) and was on the southern boundary of Israelite territory in Transjordan. Mesha, king of Moab, who reasserted Moabite independence from Israel c 850 BC, claims in his stele to have 'built Aroer and made the highway at the Arnon'. Excavations have revealed a new fortress of this period built over the earlier one, no doubt designed to control traffic on the King's Highway, which at that time crossed the Arnon gorge between Aroer and Balu', several kilometres east of the modern road. Nebuchadrezzar of Babylon destroyed the Moabite fortress in 582 BC; in the following centuries Aroer was occupied intermittently, but never regained its former importance.

North and north-west of the mound parts of Mesha's fortifications have been excavated; the north-west and north-east trenches show clearly the three parallel walls of Aroer's defences, which were further strengthened on the south-west and south-east sides by the steep cliffs of the Arnon gorge. Inside the fort are the remains of other walls, perhaps garrison buildings. On the south-west slope outside the walls are a number of cisterns.

Back at the main road turn left towards c 3km Dhiban to rejoin the King's Highway.

Madaba to Machaerus

If taking the King's Highway south from Madaba turn right in 13km **Libb**, Roman **Libona**, to see Herod's Palace of Machaerus. Pass the village of Mukawir where the Byzantine **Church of Bishop Malechius** has been excavated and was found to have a mosaic pavement. It lies on the left next to a small *resthouse* which offers accommodation. Two other churches were excavated a little further west, opposite the restaurant. Continue west 1.5km—the views over the Dead Sea are stunning before the conical hill on which the fort of **Machaerus** was built appears. Unfortunately it is being 'restored' and sparklingly new columns bristle from its top. Near the car park a little bar is being built where you can stop to admire the view before climbing to the fort: its Arabic name is ominous: *al-Mishnaqa* means gallows.

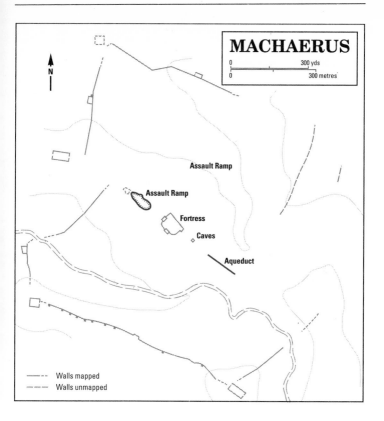

MACHAERUS

| 0 | | 300 yds |
| 0 | | 300 metres |

N

Assault Ramp

Assault Ramp

Fortress

Caves

Aqueduct

```
------ --   Walls mapped
------ ---  Walls unmapped
```

History

Machaerus' story begins with the Maccabean revolt against the Seleucids although there may already have been a small fortification on the hilltop. The Hasmonaean dynasty, which managed to carve out a substantial Jewish state during this revolt, peaked under the expansionist Alexander Jannaeus (103–76 BC) who established and maintained a number of forts to protect his territory; Machaerus was one, Masada another. On his death his widow, Salome Alexandra, succeeded him and ruled wisely. His son Hyrcanus became High Priest, but there was trouble from the beginning with the younger son, the ambitious Aristobulus who sought to seize power, proclaiming himself king. Both sides appealed to the Romans, but Pompey was evidently worried by Aristobulus and pursued him to Jerusalem, taking it with great loss of life in 63 BC. Aristobulus' son Alexander escaped and raised an army, taking control in various forts including Machaerus, prompting an attack by the Roman General Gabinius. A wily Idumean called Antipater, father of Herod the Great, fought with the Romans, having allied himself with Hyrcanus. Machaerus was probably razed in 56 BC, although Aristobulus now escaped and had one last attempt to rally troops from its ruins before being captured and sent back to Rome. After further trouble with this branch of the family, Antipater's son

Herod was proclaimed King from Rome and, having quelled the unrest, married a Hasmonaean and proceeded to consolidate power. Despite his blood-thirsty reputation (Octavian is reputed to have said of him that he would rather be his pig than his son, the implication being that this was safer!), Herod was responsible for great building projects and was a considerable patron of the arts. East of the Dead Sea he built himself a palace at Machaerus and developed the port at Zara, by the baths of Kallirhoë, where he could take the waters for his illness (p 126). Herod died in 4 BC and his kingdom was divided up among his sons, Herod Antipas becoming tetrarch of Galilee and Perea. According to the historian Josephus it was at Machaerus that Salome danced for Herod and asked for the head of John the Baptist. In AD 66 the Jewish revolt began and Jewish zealots took Machaerus from the Roman garrison there. Six years later the Romans under L. Bassus retook it after making elaborate siege preparations to storm the well-defended fort which Josephus describes in *The Jewish War*—ultimately these were not required as the Jews surrendered on the loss of one of their leaders, a young man called Eleazar. Once again Machaerus was destroyed, as was any hope of Jewish independence under the Romans.

Walk down the steps looking for the line of the aqueduct which runs up to the summit—the stones were used in the siege preparations by the Romans. There are a number of **caves** on the north-east side at the base of the hill and John the Baptist is reputed to have been held in one of them. This was also the side where the lower town grew up. It was inhabited by local people while the citadel was occupied by Jewish zealots who seized it during the revolt. Now scramble to the top, passing the outer wall which surrounded the **acropolis**. The 110 x 60m palace enclosure built over the original Hasmonaean fortress was divided into two blocks by a corridor. The east block had a courtyard which was probably flanked by reception rooms; the Romans, however, thoroughly razed the building on retaking it so not much evidence is left. On the south side are the remains of a **baths complex** where the oldest mosaic so far discovered in Jordan was found in the apodyterium. Part of it can now be seen in the entrance to the Madaba Archaeological Park. Most rooms of the palace probably had mosaic floors, the caldarium floor was in opus sectile. Looking back towards the car park the line of the **aqueduct** is very clear. For a good illustration of Roman siege tactics turn to the western edge and look down: the huge mass of rubble on the ridge to the west is the remains of the assault ramp. Further south, on a ridge running east–west is the circumvallatory wall up to 2m wide in places; the siege camps are marked by piles of stones at either end. The Romans certainly took this siege seriously and must have been relieved that in the end they were able to take Machaerus with such ease—the siege of Masada on the far side of the Dead Sea was to prove far harder and more tragic.

Wadi Wala, Dhiban and Wadi Mujib

About 23km from Madaba and 10km after the turning to Mukawir the road begins its descent to Wadi Wala; on the right, in a prominent position overlooking the wadi is **Khirbet Iskander**, a large Early Bronze Age site reached by a road signposted Al Nuzha on a sharp bend. Three main areas have been excavated and work is continuing. Khirbet Iskander is the first known fortified site in this part of the Middle East of the Early Bronze IV period (c 2350–2000 BC), usually considered a

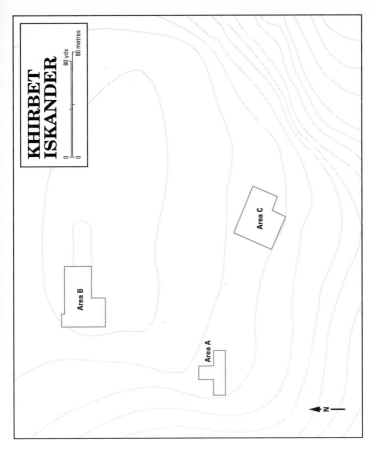

'nomadic interlude' between earlier and later urban cultures. Part of a multiphase **defensive wall** can be seen in Area 'B' in the north-west corner of the site; after the earlier inner wall collapsed in an earthquake, an outer wall was built and the gap between filled with rubble. Also in Area 'B' several occupation levels have been excavated; interesting features include a bench-lined room with whole pottery vessels adjacent to a room with a plastered stone bin containing botanical remains, a hearth, a firepit, a bovine hoof in a painted dish and two goat horns. The excavators suggest this was part of a larger complex which comprised both a storage and a cult area. Area 'C' at the south-east corner of the mound may be a **gateway** associated with the fortifications. It is a monumental complex approached by steps, comprising two chambers, perhaps guardrooms, which flank a plastered passageway with benches either side. Outside the walls three **cemeteries** have been explored; the dead were buried with pottery in shaft tombs.

A perennial stream runs through the pretty **Wadi Wala**, a tributary of Wadi Mujib, a fertile valley with pine and eucalyptus trees, lemon and olive groves and vineyards. As the road approaches the top of its southern slope, at a bend before the sign to Al Mesherfeh, you can see a stretch of the **Via Nova Traiana** and several **Roman milestones** in the valley bottom.

Next of interest is **Dhiban**, biblical Dibon, 20km from Libb, which comprises two hills; the southern hill is now covered by the modern town, the northern hill, which can be reached by a right turn in town, has been partly excavated.

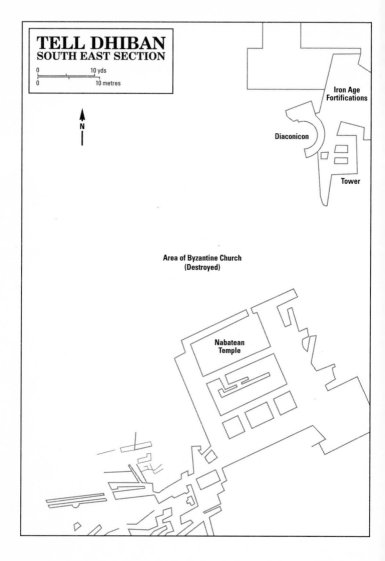

TELL DHIBAN
SOUTH EAST SECTION

0   10 yds
0   10 metres

N

Iron Age
Fortifications

Diaconicon

Tower

Area of Byzantine Church
(Destroyed)

Nabatean
Temple

History

Dibon owes its main claim to fame to being a capital of the Iron Age kingdom of Moab, although excavations have shown that there was an Early Bronze Age town here in the 3rd millennium BC. Mesha, king of Moab, whose stela was found at the south end of the tell in 1868, claims that after throwing off the yoke of Israel (c 850 BC) he rebuilt the city walls, gates and towers of his native town, ensured the water supply and constructed a royal palace. In the new quarter, called Qarhoh, Mesha also built a 'high place' in honour of Kemosh, the principal god of the Moabites, as did King Solomon outside Jerusalem, led astray, according to the Old Testament writer, by his many foreign wives! After Mesha, Dibon and the rest of Moab paid tribute to the great military power of Assyria and in the early 6C BC, under Nebuchadrezzar, Moab became a Babylonian province. Prosperity returned to Dibon under the Nabateans, who built a fine temple at the south-east corner of the tell. Under the Romans Dibon may have been a fortified post on the Via Nova Traiana; after the Byzantine period it declined and in the 19C the village transferred to the south hill, using the ancient tell as a burial ground.

Excavations at Dhiban in the 1950s and 1960s focused primarily on the eastern part of the huge mound, and although it is now rather overgrown the site is well worth a brief visit. Begin at the south-east, where there is an obvious 'entrance' to the tell; the area is much disturbed by digging and later structures, but a broad, open staircase once led up to the **Nabatean temple** platform on the right. This temple, its entrance to the north, consisted of a broad pronaos and naos and a tripartite sanctuary, and is similar in plan to the much larger Qasr al-Bint at Petra. Below the temple to the south and east are the impressive retaining walls of the surrounding raised platform. Dhiban's imposing **Iron Age fortifications** are preserved in part in this area, but can be seen most clearly in a trench to the north-east. Moab's capital was protected by a massive sloping battered stone rampart; behind the wall, at the bottom of the trench, are the foundations of a tower which may be associated with an earlier inner wall. Also in this area, above the walls, note part of an apse which belonged to the diaconicon of a **Byzantine church** built north of the Nabatean temple and now destroyed. A short distance further north is the Moabite **North Gate** to the city, rebuilt by the Nabateans: since excavation much of the gate and associated structures have collapsed, so the plan is unclear.

MOAB

Located east of the Dead Sea on the Transjordanian plateau between Ammon and Edom, the Iron Age Kingdom of Moab, which arose c 1200 BC, was centred around the spectacular gorge of the Wadi Mujib (biblical Arnon). Its southern boundary was Wadi Hasa (biblical Zered), in the north the border varied, but the Moabites usually controlled the Madaba area and the 'plains of Moab' opposite Jericho where the Israelites camped before entering the Promised Land. According to biblical tradition the Moabites and Israelites were related; the Moabites were descended from Abraham's nephew Lot (p 128). Originally ruled by a number of local princes, Moab was subject to Israel for some 150 years until the death of Ahab c 850 BC when a certain Mesha, from Dhiban, who describes himself as king of Moab, liberated his country and probably unified it at the same time. His deeds are recorded on a black basalt stele, which was set up in the capital Dhiban and is now in the Louvre. It is the longest inscription in Moabite, a language closely related to Hebrew. Much of Mesha's kingdom was good agricultural and pasture land and famous. As the Bible tells us, 'Mesha king of Moab was a sheepmaster, and rendered unto the king of Israel an hundred thousand lambs, and an hundred thousand rams, with the wool' (2 Kings 3:4). Even allowing for exaggeration this sounds rather extortionate; no wonder Mesha rebelled! Although they shared a common cultural heritage, Israel and the Transjordanian kingdoms were often in conflict as each state sought to defend and expand its borders. This is reflected in the vitriolic attacks of the Old Testament prophets: 'Moab shall be as Sodom ... the breeding of nettles, and salt pits, and a perpetual desolation' warns Zephaniah (2:9). 'There shall be lamentation upon all the housetops of Moab ... for I have broken Moab like a vessel wherein is no pleasure' thunders Jeremiah (48:38). Ironically the conquerors came from the east; five years after he sacked Jerusalem (587 BC), Nebuchadrezzar made Moab part of a Babylonian province.

Soon after Dhiban begins the spectacular descent to the **Wadi Mujib**, the biblical Arnon, one of the country's most dramatic geographical features. Aptly dubbed Jordan's Grand Canyon, the gorge is some 4km wide at the top and nearly 400m in depth. A viewpoint on the descent enables the visitor to stop and take in the breathtaking scenery, a product of the geological upheavals millions of years ago which also formed the Great Rift Valley. After snaking down the steep cliffs for c 9km the road crosses the river bed on a modern bridge near a spot near where a Roman bridge once carried the Via Nova Traiana. By the bridge is a lone post office, usually closed.

Below the road on the right, 3km from the bridge, is a terrace with a well cleared cistern and beyond it by the edge of the wadi the badly ruined walls of an almost square Roman fort, dubbed earlier this century **Muhattet al-Haj** or 'station of the pilgrimage'. This fort guarded the bridge over the Wadi Mujib and controlled traffic along the Via Nova as well as movement along the wadi.

Further up the road on the right are two fallen **milestones** of the Via Nova, their inscriptions visible, and at the top of the southern bank of the valley, left along a track opposite a few modern houses, is the **Upper Muhattet al-Haj**, called Karakun by the locals, with good views across the wadi. It is built of basalt and limestone and though ruined you can make out four angle towers, a gate flanked by two towers in the south-west wall and single interval towers in the other walls. Together the Muhattet al-Haj forts would have monitored the key Arnon crossing, essential in such wild country as described graphically c AD 300 by Eusebius: 'To this day is known a very treacherous place with ravines, called the Arnonas, extending north of Areopolis, in which garrisons of soldiers keep guard everywhere due to the terrifying nature of the region' (Onomasticon 212).

After the winding ascent the King's Highway continues straight across the fertile Moabite plateau, one of the areas where the black iris blooms in springtime. About 15km from the Wadi Mujib just before Al-Qasr village turn right, bear right immediately where the road forks and 2km along on the left you can see the ruins of **Khirbet Faris**, on good arable land overlooking Wadi al-Zuqiba and beautifully green in spring. Limited investigations suggest that the Khirbet Faris area was occupied intermittently from the late Iron Age. Throughout the Islamic period there was an agricultural settlement at Faris; the most obvious remains today are two large ruined Ottoman farmhouses and a small Muslim cemetery. There are reused older stones in the later buildings and two broken Roman milestones east of the site.

Return to **Al-Qasr**, where there is a **Nabatean temple** just east of the main road. It is a square building of standard Nabatean plan, similar to the Qasr al-Bint in Petra, with a tripartite cella, broad antecella and a portico in antis with four enormous columns. Steps led up to a second storey from the south adyton. Originally the temple was elaborately ornamented, to judge from decorated architectural pieces found built into houses of the modern village and scattered among the ruins. Opposite the entrance to the temple, by the fence which encloses the site, is a well-preserved arched cistern; as always the Nabateans ensured a good water supply.

Excursion to Balu'

From Al Qasr it is possible to make an excursion to 10km **Balu'** with a four-wheel drive vehicle. From north-east of the village an asphalt road runs for c 5km; where this gives way to a dirt road keep left and drive more or less straight on for another 4.5km to the black basalt ruins. Balu' is an enormous site, the largest known Moabite city, built entirely of basalt and strategically sited on the edge of the southern escarpment of Wadi al-Balu'. An important stela of the 12C BC, before Moab was unified under King Mesha, which is now in the Amman museum, was discovered here in 1930; it may represent a local Moabite king or chief flanked by a god and goddess and shows considerable Egyptian influence. It was from Balu' that the ancient King's Highway crossed the Arnon gorge to Aroer, hence the site's importance. Most of Balu' is a confusing jumble of stones, but there has been some excavation in recent years. The most impressive ruin is the so-called **Qasr**, or 'castle', its walls of huge, partly hewn blocks still standing 4–6m high. Along the northern edge of the plateau are the massive **fortifications**, a casemate defensive system, a short stretch of which has been cleared. Views from the escarpment are fabulous. Trenches have also been dug in a number of areas of domestic use, which have yielded everyday objects such as pottery, grinding stones, mortars and loom weights; in one unit the lintel has been replaced over a connecting door.

Back on the main road, continue to 5km **Rabba**, biblical **Rabbath Moab**, Roman **Areopolis**, another important town on the Via Nova Traiana, where a number of ancient columns have been re-erected in the middle of the modern road! The large coffee pot symbolises welcome and hospitality. By the roadside are the remains of the large settlement; part of a **street**, paved in black basalt and white limestone, a small **Byzantine church** among the ruins behind and a **Roman temple** with two niches on either side of the entrance. Inscriptions recorded that the temple was dedicated to the emperors Diocletian and Maximinian, whose statues were in the niches. During their joint reign (286–305) an elite cavalry unit, the *equites Mauri Illyriciani* was stationed at Areopolis.

12.5km beyond Rabba a road branches left towards the Desert Highway: this will get you to Petra more quickly than continuing along the King's Highway, which now winds down to c 5km Karak.

Karak

Descending from the King's Highway the **castle** dominates the skyline; the impressive **glacis** is currently under restoration. In the time of the infamous Reynald of Chatillon, prisoners were flung from the walls to their death, heads encased in wooden boxes to prevent them from losing consciousness until they met their end on the rocks below. Turn right beneath the castle and wind right

Tunnel entrance to Karak, an engraving from The Land of Moab, *H.B. Tristram*

round below the remains of the old town walls, and up through busy streets to park at the castle. Two tunnel entrances once led into Karak: one can be seen by turning right as you enter the town, passing on the right the square **tower** with an arched gate and inscribed band inside and continuing 100m down the road to an iron gate on the left. Behind is the tunnel which was still used to enter the town in the 19C. Karak is a busy administrative and agricultural centre with bustling streets; there are a few Christian tribes here—it is said to have had Christians living here long before the Crusaders arrived. The *resthouse* is next to the castle; its restaurant has lovely westward views. A torch is useful for visiting the castle. The castle museum is closed on Tuesdays.

History

Karak lies in the biblical land of Moab and was a Moabite stronghold long before the Crusaders built the castle for which it is famous today. Its biblical name is Kir-haraseth (II Kings 3:25) and it features as the walled city of Charachmoba on the Madaba mosaic map (p 138–9).

Although it was not the first crusader castle to be built east of the Jordan, its strength and location made Karak the most important of the defences guarding the Latin Kingdom's exposed eastern flank. Montreal (present day Shobak) was founded in 1115 to control the caravan routes between Syria, Egypt and Arabia and the following year King Baldwin I led an expedition down to the Red Sea adding a castle at Aila (Aqaba). Subsequently the energetic King Fulk (1131–43) created the lordship of Oultrejourdain and in 1142 its lord, Pagan the Butler, transferred his headquarters from Montreal to Karak—the early work dates from this period. According to the chronicler William of Tyre 'upon a very high mountain surrounded by deep valleys .... one Paganus ... built a castle on this site ... successors added a moat and towers.' In 1161 it was given to the De Milly family who completed the work on it.

The advantages of the site are obvious; surrounded by cliffs on three sides, the more vulnerable southern end was strengthened by the digging of a fosse and another ditch was added at the north (town) end. Reynald of Chatillon (aka the Elephant of Christ) was doubtless its most famous occupant. This ruthless adventurer came to the Holy Land to seek his fortune and acquired Karak in 1177 on his marriage to Etienette de Milly. He was famed for his courage, cruelty, untrustworthiness and daring exploits and it was he who led the army to victory over Saladin at Montgisart in 1177. At Karak the Dead Sea and Jerusalem were nearby and it was also well placed to overlook the lucrative trade and Meccan pilgrimage routes of the King's Highway. In 1183 de Chatillon had boats built here, transported to Aqaba and proceeded to

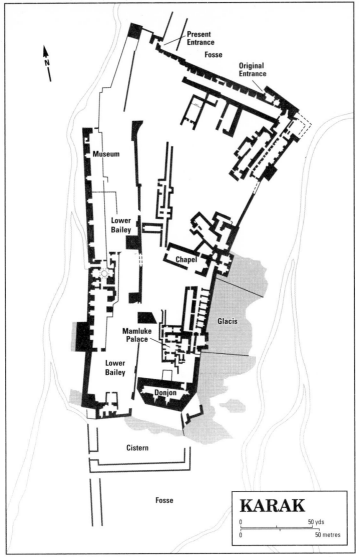

KARAK

0 — 50 yds
0 — 50 metres

terrorise Arab shipping on the Red Sea. However, it was his raid on a caravan in breach of a treaty with Saladin which so enraged the latter that he personally beheaded him after the battle of Hattin in 1187.

After the overwhelming defeat at Hattin, the Karak garrison must have realised that with no hope of relief they could not hold out forever. They put up a brave struggle, but capitulated in late 1188 after an eight month siege, having even sold their wives and children for food. Apparently Saladin was so impressed with their valour that he set them free. An earlier tale of Saladin's legendary chivalry also involves Karak: his armies besieged it in 1183 while a wedding was taking place inside. The bridegroom's mother sent out food to Saladin who responded by enquiring which tower the newly weds were lodged in and ordering it not to be attacked. Karak was given by Saladin to his brother who repaired and strengthened its defences. Subsequent occupants of the castle made substantial alterations to it, especially in the 13C and 14C; this work is finer than that of the Crusader period. During the Fourth Crusade in Egypt one of Saladin's descendants sent his treasure here for safe-keeping and it was only in 1264 that the Mamluke sultan Baybars managed to take it from the Ayubbids. He ordered extensions to the fortifications of the town, the building of the north bastion of the town wall and deepening of the moat. His device, the lion, can be seen on the circular tower on the east town wall. Karak suffered earthquake damage in 1293 and later became a place of exile.

Before entering the castle, look at the massive, rough-dressed masonry of the **north wall.** Compared to the much finer work of the Mamluke period visible inside, this was clearly built to a different specification: the Crusader's priorities were strong fortifications and they built at impressive speed. The original castle entrance, later altered to become a postern, lay further east in an angle of the wall. In plan Karak is an A shape: broader at the north (town) end it runs down a spur to the south tip. Most of the surviving Crusader work is on the east side, it is also apparent in the lower courses of the west wall of the upper bailey. The lower bailey on the west and the fine keep at the south end are later, mainly Mamluke additions. Cross the dry moat into the castle—it was once as much as 90 feet deep, but has since been filled up. The 14C writer Abu al-Fida tells of the occasion when a sultan and his retinue were crossing the drawbridge and it collapsed. The sultan's horse leapt to safety, but others were not so lucky. Tickets can be bought from the guardian inside.

Walk up the slope, then back towards the north wall and down the long, vaulted passage-way to the north-east corner. There are seven levels at Karak, the top one can be seen here as can a reused Nabatean block of a headless torso incorporated into the wall on the left. Follow the passage round to the right through **troops' quarters** and the **kitchens** on the right with an olive-press in the left corner and, in an inner room, the huge brick oven and chimney. Continue along the east wall and emerge facing the Mamluke keep. Walk past the remains of the ruined church where Irby and Mangles, who visited it early last century, saw frescoes of 'large groups of figures' on the walls. The fine **Mamluke keep** can be climbed for the view and to look down towards the reservoir behind it which could be used as a moat when the castle was under threat. Between the church and the keep on the west side are the remains of the **Mamluke Palace**, a complex which was probably built in the early 14C under Sultan al-Nasir Mohammed. Its central feature is a **reception hall** formed by a courtyard with barrel-vaulted rooms at each end and niches along the east and west sides. The room to the east may have been a mosque—there is a mihrab niche in the south wall.

From the church descend some steps just south of the apse. The carved stone panel at the bottom is Islamic. Directly opposite is a room with some reused Nabatean blocks built into the wall. Just past the entrance to this room turn right and down a few steps into the **dungeons** which were part of Reynald's extensions. Look for an arrow slit in the inner wall which shows that this was once part of the outer wall. At the far end of the dungeon corridor, with its cells on the left, the Mamluke Palace can be seen through a slit in the wall. Leave the dungeons and take the tunnel behind the carved stone panel which soon turns sharply right to run north past more troop quarters before emerging again near the entrance. From here descend to the **lower bailey** and turn right to find the little **museum** housed in one of the castle's vaulted storeys. The basalt block with the rear half of a lion in relief outside is dated to the Iron Age and was found in a house in Karak. The museum shows glass and pottery displays and a replica of the Mesha stela (p 28). Boards give details of recent excavations and there is a small exhibition on Gertrude Bell's visits to Jordan. You may persuade the guardian to accompany you to a lower level under this courtyard to see a fine Mamluke vaulted gallery running along the west wall.

THE CRUSADES

The First Crusade began with an appeal by the Byzantine emperor Alexius Comnenus at the Council of Piacenza for help against the Seljuk Turks. With the benefit of hindsight he might have regretted this since the Fourth Crusade was to sack Constantinople in 1204. On the 27 November 1095 Pope Urban II preached the Crusade at Clermont, calling men to arms against the enemies of God. There was a tremendous response to this emotive appeal and great numbers took the cross. Many were keen to visit the holy city of Jerusalem which they believed to be heaven on earth, though the offer of remission from sins, debts and taxes doubtless spurred them on.

The Crusades caused unimaginable upheaval as soldiers marched, fleets sailed and families were separated in the general hysteria. Jews were massacred as Crusader armies marched to Constantinople. Minor crusades had the most bizarre leaders: one group followed a goose which they firmly believed to be the Holy Spirit; the children's Crusade of 1212, like many others, never reached its destination. Anyone could go—Crusades were preached as, and called, pilgrimages; the word crusade was a later invention. Sadly the tremendous force of the movement turned easily to bad: a marked strain of anti-Semitism led to horrific Jewish pogroms in Central Europe and there were terrible massacres of Jews and Muslims when Jerusalem fell. Certainly the mixture of devotion, religious fervour, greed and cruelty was extraordinary.

Fortunately for the Crusaders, the Muslims were divided among themselves, which enabled the Crusaders to make speedier progress. Jerusalem fell to them on 15 July 1099 with an appalling massacre of its inhabitants (in marked contrast to Saladin's capture of the city nearly a century later). According to a witness of the scene, mounds of heads, hands and feet filled the streets and the pyres were like pyramids. The elected leader, Godfrey of Bouillon, refused the title of King, saying that he would not wear a crown in the city where Christ had worn a crown of thorns. He was installed instead as Defender of the Holy Sepulchre, but on his death a year later his brother Baldwin became king. Pursuing an expansionist policy he led an expedition across the Jordan in 1115 and founded the castle of Montreal (Shobak). It was during this period of consolidation after the First Crusade that the lordship of Oultrejourdain was established with a chain of castles running southwards to the Dead Sea. Although Jordan was never at the heart of the Crusader Kingdom it was strategically important in guarding the eastern flank of the territory from attack and for its control of trade and pilgrimage routes from Syria to the Red Sea and Egypt.

The Crusaders' grip on the territory they conquered was always tenuous: at its greatest extent their territory consisted of the Counties of Edessa and Tripoli, the Principality of Antioch and the Kingdom of Jerusalem. It was not an easy life. The king was never very wealthy and his main concern was the perennial shortage of manpower—disease and war were endemic, children died, wives lost their husbands in battle and others simply returned home having fulfilled their vows and gained pardon for sins. The king depended on his knights to provide him with fighting men in times of need (and there was almost constant fighting). The emergence of the Military Orders, the Knights of the Temple and of St John, also known as the Hospitallers, in the 12C provided a ready supply of knights and financial resources from huge endowments and possessions in Europe.

The first nail in the Crusader coffin was the loss of Edessa as early as 1144. Pope Eugenius III called for a Crusade in response, but the resulting Second Crusade was a fiasco. More troubling was the rise of a strong, united Muslim force under Zengi, Lord of Mosul and Aleppo, followed by his son Nur al-Din and finally Saladin (p 77), who consolidated power carefully, uniting the Muslims, encircling and eroding the Crusader territories. This process culminated in the battle of Hattin in 1187 and the rout of the Crusaders. The king and many knights were captured or killed, although Saladin behaved most chivalrously towards them apart from Reynald of Chatillon, whom he immediately beheaded for his crimes. Jerusalem fell in October 1187 and many Crusader possessions followed suit. The Transjordanian possessions had no hope of relief and it is amazing that they managed to hold on as long as they did—Karak until late 1188 and Shobak until spring of 1189. During the Third Crusade Richard the Lionheart twice came within a few miles of Jerusalem, but the city only returned to the Crusaders, and then briefly, in the 13C. The fall of Acre in 1291 heralded the end of their time in the Holy Land.

The word Crusader evokes visions of knights on horseback, but the knights themselves were in the minority. Others contributed as much to the achievements of those years: the stunning castles built with such speed and solidity and the battles won—all, ultimately, to so little avail. In Europe the rise of nation states signalled a loss of interest in a pan-national movement. The myth of the Crusades lived on, however, in the European consciousness. Tales of Saracens and chivalry abounded, Saladin and Richard Coeur de Lion were potent symbols. There were other, less obvious effects. The banking system and money economy developed as the Military Orders lent money for Crusades and so grew increasingly powerful. Medicine, science and architecture all benefited as Eastern knowledge reached the West.

The failure of the Crusades and decline of the Byzantine empire also marked a shift of focus from the East towards Western Europe. Nonetheless they left a lasting mark in the Middle East—impressive castles in varying states of repair are to be found from Turkey to the Red Sea. Whether or not one agrees with Voltaire's remark that the Crusades were an 'epidemic fury' which came 'that there might be no possible scourge which had not afflicted the human race', there is no denying the energy and power of the movement which was one of the stranger episodes of Western history.

Excursion to Lejjun

An excursion can be made from Karak to 24km **Lejjun**, the most important military site on the Roman Arabian frontier. Take the road to the Desert Highway and 22km from Karak Castle is a sign to 2km Al-Lajjun. On a ridge to the left of this road are Turkish Military Barracks built with stone robbed from the Roman fort. Lejjun legionary fortress is on the right beside the Wadi al-Lajjun, in a green fertile valley with a perennial spring, carpeted with flowers in the springtime.

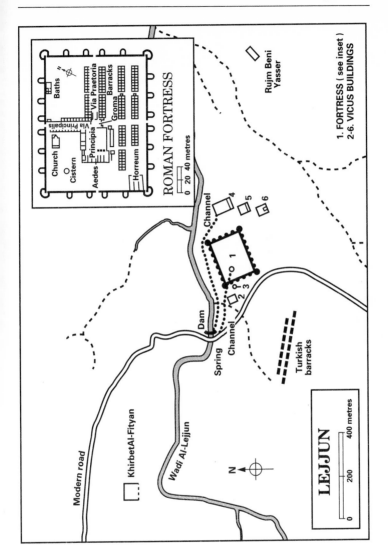

History

Lejjun was probably constructed in the reign of Diocletian, c 300, as part of his strengthening of defences to counter the incursions of nomadic Arab raiders, and became a key post in the Roman fortified frontier, the Limes Arabicus. **Legio IV Martia**, created around this time, was stationed here; possibly the proximity of Areopolis, 'city of Mars' (modern Rabba), influenced the choice of the unit's name. Arabic Lejjun may be a corruption of Latin 'legio', the ancient name of the site was almost certainly **Betthorus**. Around

2000 soldiers garrisoned the fortress initially, but following an earthquake in 363 there is evidence of a sharp reduction in the legion's strength. By the early 6C the garrison was severely run down and may even have been demobilised by Justinian, who seriously neglected the eastern frontier. All permanent occupation at Lejjun ceased after an earthquake in 551.

Lejjun is a typical late Roman fortress: a rectangular enclosure surrounded by a wall with four gates connected by two intersecting streets. Four circular angle towers and 20 U-shaped interval towers project from the wall. Beginning at the north-west corner where an angle tower, interval tower and section of wall have been excavated, walk around the walls to appreciate the plan of the fortress. All towers were entered from inside; the corner towers had two, possibly three storeys connected by a staircase, the interval towers had two storeys. The wall was composed of two faces of ashlar limestone filled with rubble. Part of the north gate has been cleared, it is triple entry and constructed of huge limestone blocks. Inside, the largest structure is the **prinicipia** or 'headquarters building', west of the **groma**, a four-sided monumental gateway at the centre crossroads. Behind a central courtyard is a transverse **basilical hall** with raised **tribunals** or speaker's platforms at either end, and a row of official buildings, including the **aedes** or shrine of the legionary standards which once had a barred iron gate across the entrance. Soldiers could view the sacred standards, but not enter the aedes, which in many forts served as the soldiers' bank. Rows of barracks fill the eastern half of the fortress, among other structures are a cistern, a church built c 500 near the north gate, a baths complex abutting the north wall and a **horreum** or granary. Outside the fortress a **vicus** or civilian settlement grew up. Excavated buildings include a Roman temple to the east, built at the same time as the fort, but soon abandoned.

Two observation posts were probably manned by detachments from Lejjun. About 1.5km past Lejjun, up the hill and along a track on the left is **Khirbet al-Fityan castellum**, built on top of an earlier Moabite fort. Located on the steep northern bank of the wadi, it commands a splendid view in all directions. Although it is ruined and the south wall has tumbled down the escarpment, the line of the other walls is visible and a sounding has cleared part of the north gate. From Khirbet al-Fityan you can see the watchtower of **Rujm Beni Yasser** on top of a hill east of Lejjun which protected the fortress against surprise attack from that direction.

South of Karak the road crosses the plateau to 11km **Mu'ta** where in 629 an army of some 3000 Muslims commanded by the Prophet's adopted son Zaid bin Haritha was defeated by local forces in the first major clash between Byzantium and Islam. Zaid himself, his second in command Ja'far bin Abi Talib and general Abdulla bin Ruaha were all killed and it was left to Khalid bin al-Walid, who later became one of Islam's greatest commanders, to lead the remnants of the army back to Medina. The Muslim dead were buried in 3km **Ma'zar**, where a modern mosque, distinguished by three green domes, contains the tomb of Ja'far. Zaid's tomb is in a small garden to the south-east. Left of the entrance a small museum contains gravestones, Koranic inscriptions, pottery, swords, coins etc.

Excursion to Wadi Hasa via Dhat Ras

As a pleasant alternative to the new Wadi Hasa road, turn left c 5km south of Mazar at a sign to Zat Ras (Dhat Ras), right at another sign, continue straight on where the road forks and c 5km from the main road turn left at a bus shelter towards the ruins of **Dhat Ras**, visible on the hill in the modern village. Part of a wall with engaged columns and roundels in typical Nabatean style still stands to a considerable height, the remains of a temple complex now much obscured by abandoned Late Ottoman houses. Some 300m lower down, by the roadside, is a small, well-preserved Nabatean temple, also described as a Roman mausoleum. The entrance is locked, but visitors can see through to the broad, arched cella at the back, from which a stairway led to a barrel-vaulted room above and up to the roof.

Nabatean temple at Dhat Ras

Continue towards **Shuqairah**, keeping straight on after 3km where the road bears left. Shuqairah is a modern village over a Nabatean-Roman settlement with few obvious remains except an ancient reservoir 500m on the right, which has been restored for local use. From here there are impressive views across the lovely **Wadi Hasa** to the mountains of Edom. The old road winds down to the valley bottom past the picturesque, semi-deserted village of **Al 'Aina**, green and well-watered from the local springs and surrounded by orchards, vineyards, olive groves and cacti, joining the new road for the ascent out of Wadi Hasa.

Wadi Hasa and Khirbet Tannur

A few kilometres from Mazar the road begins its descent to the **Wadi Hasa**, the biblical Zered, the border between Moab and Edom, where the limestone plateau

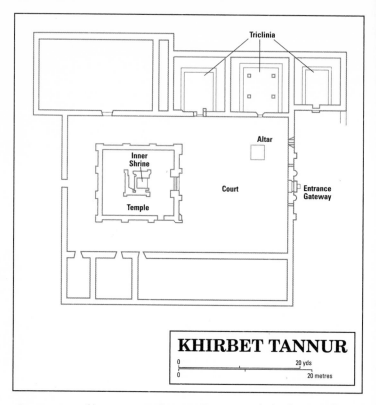

Triclinia

Altar

Inner
Shrine

Court

Entrance
Gateway

Temple

KHIRBET TANNUR

0   20 yds

0   20 metres

gives way to a wilder, more rugged terrain. Dominating the landscape as the road climbs out of the valley is a dark, brooding, extinct volcano beyond which, on the opposite side of the valley, is **Khirbet Tannur**, a high, cone-shaped hill with the ruins of a Nabatean temple on top. A dirt track branches right off the main road near a broken concrete signboard which marks the site. You can drive along it for c 1km and from there it is a 20–30 minute climb to the ridge on the left and up to the summit. Excavations during the 1930s revealed an impressive temple complex and a wealth of sculpture now displayed in the Amman Archaeological Museum and the Cincinnati Art Museum. Stripped of its ornament the site is rather bare, but it is worth the climb for the view and for the atmosphere of this remote 'high place' where the Nabateans paid homage to their gods.

There was an altar or small shrine on the mountain by the 1C BC; the temple complex in its final form dates to the 2C and comprised an outer courtyard flanked by rooms which enclosed the temple proper, on a platform, and the shrine within it. Building stones litter the site, but it is possible to make out the main features. In antiquity worshippers probably ascended the sacred mountain from the east via a stairway, then passed through a gateway into the walled outer court, which still retains some of its original paving and the podium of an altar in the north-east. A raised portico two steps high surrounded the court; ritual banquets were celebrated in three triclinia to the north.

At the west end of the court a flight of steps framed by engaged columns led up to the temple entrance. Over the doorway a huge bust of Atargatis as vegetation goddess, surrounded by vines and pomegranates, symbols of fertility, was crowned by an eagle finial representing her consort, Zeus-Hadad. She is now on show in the Amman museum. Above the columns was a frieze of busts portraying the planets with Tyche figures at each end. The heavenly bodies were important in the worship at Tannur; another relief depicts Tyche surrounded by a circle of zodiac symbols.

On the raised platform are the foundations of a small shrine oriented due east with steps on the south side which ascended to a rooftop altar. Quantities of animal bones found attest to regular burnt offerings. The pilasters on the east façade of the shrine carried relief busts of Atargatis with dolphins on her head veil or arrayed with ears of corn, and a central niche probably contained sandstone figures of Atargatis flanked by lions and Zeus-Hadad seated between two bulls. Zeus-Hadad is in Amman, but only fragments of Atargatis and her attendant lions were retrieved from the temple ruins. In the early morning, as they looked eastwards over the mysterious dark volcano, itself surely the embodiment of a supernatural power, the gods of Khirbet Tannur, in their white limestone temple, were lit up by the rays of the rising sun.

Atargatis, the paramount deity at Khirbet Tannur, was popular throughout the Hellenised Orient. Lucian, in the 2C, wrote a satirical treatise (De Syria Dea, 'The Syrian Goddess') on her cult at Hierapolis-Bambyce in north Syria. Queen of the heavens, she borrowed traits from other goddesses, such as Hera and Aphrodite and assumed a variety of forms. Temples in Syria and Asia Minor were often devoted to Atargatis as goddess of vegetation, the mother of nature and source of fertility. As grain goddess she guaranteed good harvests. A dolphin goddess far from the sea might seem incongruous, but the Nabateans were great traders and ventured to distant lands. As dolphins guide seafarers to safe havens, so Atargatis in this guise assured a safe journey across land and water and through the unknown regions of the after-life.

Atargatis as vegetation goddess at Khirbet Tannur

Excursion to Hammamat Borbita and Hammamat Afra

Where the King's Highway crosses Wadi La'ban 2km south of Khirbet Tannur, Hammamat Afra and Hammamat Borbita are signposted to the right. Descend the south side of the wadi to the green valley floor and 7km from the turn-off fork right to the springs of **Borbita**. Note the number of springs here, distinguishable by the patches of green; continue along the road which soon deteriorates, but is passable with care until it ends abruptly 13km from the turn-off where it has collapsed into the stream. Walk down to the stream and turn left up the pebbly bed; the hot water, rusty red from the high iron content, emits a strong smell of sulphur. In places the valley walls are striped bright red and brilliant green. A short way up are the **Afra** 'baths' where men have one pool and women a separate, rock-cut pool within, but you may prefer to walk on further, soothing your feet in pools of different temperatures; in places the water can be scalding. To rejoin the King's Highway retrace the road to the Wadi La'ban bridge and turn right.

Detail of Nabatean carving at Qasr adh-Darih

Wadi La'ban, Qasr adh-Dharih and Tafila

Research has shown that **Wadi La'ban**, which contains more springs further up the valley, was densely populated in the Nabatean period. Near 'Ain La'ban, the main perennial water source, a major sanctuary, **Qasr adh-Dharih**, was constructed and a magistrate, recorded in an inscription of 7 BC from Khirbet Tannur, regulated the water supply at the springs. To reach Qasr adh-Dharih, on the east bank of the Wadi La'ban, follow an unpaved road left across the wadi c 4km from the bridge, turn immediately left and then right, keep to the winding track through olive groves and finally drive down a steep slope and turn left to the ruins, c 2.5km from the main road. Dharih flourished between the 1C BC and the 4C AD, although there was also earlier and later occupation. It is currently undergoing excavation. Entering the site on the left is the basement of a large building with the springings of arches and a row of niches in the back wall. Carved stone blocks nearby and the temple beyond are decorated with acanthus, vines, grapes and pomegranates in Nabatean style.

Overlooking the Wadi La'ban, a beautiful north–south oriented **Nabatean temple**, once surrounded by a temenos wall, dominates the site, although later Byzantine modifications, when the central section may have been converted into a church oriented east–west, somewhat confuse the plan. This was tripartite: a closed porch, an ante-cella and a raised colonnaded cella with 'heart-shaped' angular piers, accessed from the front by lateral stairs, with a surrounding passage and side chambers. Vegetal designs and figures decorated the outer façade; a similar profusion of vegetal motifs covered the façade of the cult podium. Lions' heads carved on

Nabatean temple at Qasr adh-Dharih

the capitals suggest that the temple may have been dedicated to Atargatis, like the sanctuary at Khirbet Tannur. Perhaps the same craftsmen decorated the neighbouring temples; the carving is remarkably similar.

South of the temple a built-up area shows much reuse of Nabatean blocks and beyond, on higher ground, is a complex of rooms and courts. Towards the southern end of this area the excavators uncovered an **oil factory** where olives were pressed and oil decanted. Interestingly, this belies Strabo's statement that sesame oil was used everywhere in Nabatea because there were no olive trees. Several perforated circular stones on the site belonged to the factory machinery.

Dharih's **cemetery** was on the hillside south-east of the temple. One monumental tomb, in use from 110 to 360, is particularly impressive; it has six shafts, each with room for several superimposed burials.

Beyond Dharih the King's Highway winds uphill, offering lovely views of the site and Wadi La'ban below, and finally emerges onto a small plain, at the end of which a turning to the east goes to the Desert Highway. This was the site of the **Battle of Tafila**, the only pitched battle of the Arab uprising, described by Lawrence in *Seven Pillars of Wisdom* (Chs 85–6). Soon the road descends to the small town of **Tafila**, where terraces of olive groves and orchards cascade down the hillside, one of the most picturesque settings in all Jordan. Tafila, identified by some scholars with biblical Tophel (Deut. 1:1), was inhabited from the Iron Age until the Byzantine period, then more or less deserted until settlers came from Shobak in Ottoman times. **'Tafila Castle'**, on the edge of the valley, is a Mamluke and Ottoman tower which may rest on Roman foundations. There are plans to convert it into a small museum, but for the time being it remains locked.

■ There are no hotels in Tafila, but several small restaurants, including the *Tadmor Restaurant* on the main street, sell simple Arabic food. If you prefer a picnic there are food stores in the town centre.

From Tafila you can continue down the King's Highway to Petra or opt for a number of excursions along the way.

Excursion to Sela

Energetic visitors may wish to explore the remote mountain refuge of **Sela**, signposted from the village of Al 'Ain al-Beidha, 10km south of Tafila. Modern Sela, a charming little settlement with several old houses, is 4km from the King's Highway; from here the road descends precipitously towards the ancient site on the massive sandstone outcrop in the valley below. Access is via a stairway carved in the deepest cleft in the rock.

■ An excursion to Sela will take a couple of hours; the ascent is steep, but not difficult. It is advisable to take a good supply of water and the summit makes a lovely picnic spot.

History

Sela, which means 'rock' in Hebrew, has been equated with the site of the same name mentioned in the Book of Kings. According to the biblical account, Amaziah of Judah (796–767 BC) attacked Edom, defeated an army of 10,000 in the Valley of Salt and captured Sela (2 Kings 14:7). Chronicles (II 25:6ff) relates that another 10,000 Edomites were cast down from the 'rock' and slaughtered. Some scholars believe that the 'rock' is Umm al-Biyara in Petra where there is an Edomite settlement, but Sela seems a more likely candidate as it is in the heartland of Edom, close to the capital Bozrah and strategically located near the caravan route to the southern Dead Sea, Beersheba and Gaza. There has been no archaeological excavation at Sela, but surface pottery attests activity from the Early Bronze Age (c 3000 BC) to the Mamluke era (14/15C), with the Edomite Iron Age period represented. Nabatean pottery is rarer, although the stairway and rock cuttings on the summit are Nabatean in style. Diodorus mentions a 'strong, unwalled rock' where their elders, women and children took refuge when the Nabateans, at that time still nomadic, were attacked by the Seleucid king Antigonus I in 312 BC. Was this Sela or Umm al-Biyara? Did Sela ever support a permanent settlement or was it just a temporary mountain refuge in unstable times? More investigation of this important site is urgently needed.

Sela is approached through the second defile on the right past a large niche in the rock at ground level as the road swings round towards the bottom of the hill. Worn Nabatean steps show the well-trodden route and a **Nabatean dam** spans a gully to the right as the path descends to an open area. Recently a most important discovery was made here at Sela. On a smooth section of the rock face opposite, below a ledge about half-way up the cliff, you may be able to make out a rectangle containing relief carvings chiselled into the rock. It is difficult to spot with the naked eye but through binoculars you should be able to see it more clearly. On the left is a figure in long robes, presumably a king, while above him to the right are three divine symbols—a star, a winged disc and possibly a crescent in a circle. A **cuneiform inscription** fills the rest of the surface. This is the first cuneiform monumental

Cuneiform inscription at Sela

inscription found in Jordan; at the time of writing it was not published, but presumably it records the deeds of a Mesopotamian monarch, perhaps Nebuchadrezzar or Nabonidus, who passed by Sela with his conquering army. He is accompanied by the king of the gods—represented by the winged disc—by the star of Ishtar, goddess of love and war and perhaps by the crescent of the moon god Sin.

Bear slightly right across the open space to the **processional stairway** which winds steeply upwards to the mountain stronghold, entered through a **rock-cut gateway** up the gully on the left overlooked by a 'tower' of rock strengthened by stone walling. Slots behind the gateway, the only entrance to the natural fortress, may have held a wooden bolt. A piriform cistern is hollowed into the top of the 'gate-tower' and of particular interest are several **rock-cut houses** reached by climbing up on the left just beyond the gateway to the east end of the ridge. In the courtyard of the best-preserved house a settling tank and channel are connected to a large plastered cistern and there is a small step up to a vaulted room which still has traces of greeny-blue, red and brown painted plaster. Return to the deep passage which leads from the gate and climb up to the opposite side where, a short distance further, there are a couple of large caves looking west to Sela village. One of these has many 'cup holes' inside and hewn out of the back wall is a large block of rock with a step which has suggested to some a rock-cut 'throne'; it is very blackened from recent use. Higher up on the plateau 12 steps lead up to a platform on a small isolated rock c 3m high, perhaps an altar or 'high place'. Sela's summit is riddled with other Nabatean cuttings and cisterns, many still plastered; as always with the Nabateans water storage was a primary concern. Take time to wander around—views from the plateau of the surrounding mountains and valleys, once intensely cultivated but now wild and desolate, are magnificent.

Excursion to Wadi Hasa and the Via Nova Traiana

Garandal is signposted to the left c 3km south of Al 'Ain al-Beidha. Where the road forks turn right, immediately left, left again then right and the recently excavated site is on the left. Later Islamic buildings covered a well-preserved Byzantine church with a narthex, nave, side aisles and a raised chancel area. Geometric mosaics decorated the narthex and side aisles; the nave was paved with plain stone slabs.

Continue through Garandal on the road to Jurf ad-Darawish and after 12km fork left to 3km **Duwana**, a huge, unexcavated site which straddles the road and the wadi. On a ridge to the right of the road is a large building of well-cut limestone blocks which may be Nabatean. Its three sections are interconnected by doors. Most of the structures on the left hand side of the road are Islamic. Some 4km further turn left and immediately right: at the junction here is a Roman milestone of the **Via Nova Traiana** which can now be easily followed much of the way for

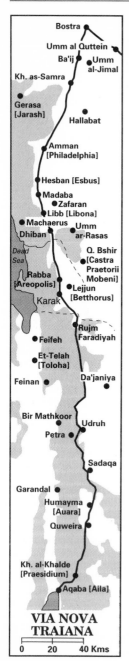

Bostra

Umm al Quttein

Ba'ij ● Umm
al-Jimal

Kh. as-Samra

Gerasa
[Jarash]

Hallabat

Amman
[Philadelphia]

Hesban [Esbus]

Madaba
●Zafaran
Libb [Libona]
● Machaerus
Dhiban   Umm
                ar-Rasas
Dead
Sea
                Q. Bshir
                ●[Castra
                Praetorii
Rabba   \ Mobeni]
[Areopolis] ●Lejjun
Karak   [Betthorus]

                Rujm \
●Feifeh   Faradiyah

Et-Telah
[Toloha]

Feinan ●   Da'janiya

Bir Mathkoor
              Udruh
Petra ●

                Sadaqa

Garandal ●

Humayma
[Auara]
              Quweira

Kh. al-Khalde
[Praesidium]
              ●Aqaba [Aila]

**VIA NOVA
TRAIANA**

0   20   40 Kms

the next 18km to the edge of the Wadi Hasa. This is one of the most interesting and best-preserved sections of Roman road in Jordan. The roadway, 20 Roman feet wide, has a foundation of fieldstones laid between raised curbs and a central spine. Regular **milestations**, often with clusters of milestones, mark the distance; there are good examples at 5km, 10km and 11.5km past the junction. Bear left along a graded track 13km after the junction, pass more milestones and a small tower and after 3.5km, just beyond the 58th milestone from Petra, note the fort of **Rujm Faridiyah** left of the road. Faridiyah, a square structure with an entrance facing the Via Nova, is strategically located above Wadi Ja'is to the west, where there is a perennial spring, and presumably monitored traffic along the highway. About 2km north of the fort, past another milestation, the Via Nova begins its descent to Wadi Hasa and can no longer be followed by car. With a gradient of between 6 per cent and 10 per cent the road descended 500m from the plateau to the wadi bed and crossed the Hasa on an arched bridge about 10km upstream from the King's Highway.

VIA NOVA TRAIANA

One of Trajan's first concerns after annexing Nabatea in 106 was to ensure good communications and the Via Nova Traiana, a grand trunk road which bore the emperor's name, formed the backbone of his new Province of Arabia. Completed between 111 and 114, it ran between the provincial capital Bostra and the port of Aila (Aqaba) on the Red Sea, *a finibus Syriae usque ad Mare Rubrum* ('from the boundaries of Syria as far as the Red Sea') as some of the milestones proclaim, a distance of some 400km. Many milestones name C. Claudius Severus, governor of Provincia Arabia throughout the period of building. For much of its length the Via Nova followed the King's Highway although in certain areas, for example at the key crossings of the Wadis Mujib and Hasa, the Roman engineers opted for different routes some distance from the old road. Forts and watchtowers along the way were garrisoned with soldiers who protected settlements and commercial traffic. Regular maintenance of such a busy and important artery as the Via Nova was essential and groups of milestones at some milestations, erected under successive emperors, demonstrate the commitment of the Roman authorities to the upkeep of the road. The latest group of milestones from Arabia show that repairs continued at least until the reign of Julian (360–363).

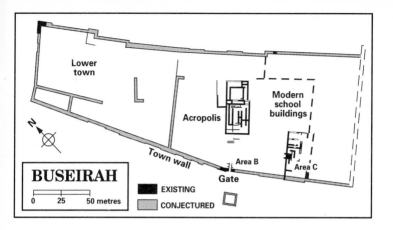

BUSEIRAH

Lower town

Acropolis

Modern school buildings

Town wall

Area B

Gate

Area C

■ EXISTING
▨ CONJECTURED

N

0   25   50 metres

BUSEIRAH

Back on the King's Highway, just after the left turn to Garandal, there is a sign right to **Buseirah**, 4km to the west, on a promontory surrounded by deep ravines. Past the 'town' centre on the left the deserted houses of the Late Ottoman period, with flat roofs and arched interiors, were spacious enough to house extended families. Ancient Buseirah is north of the village, at the end of the road, behind the modern school and playground.

History

Buseirah is usually identified with biblical Bozrah, capital of the Kingdom of Edom and target of the wrath of several Old Testment prophets. 'The sword of the Lord is filled with blood', warned Isaiah, one of the most vitriolic, '... for the Lord hath a sacrifice in Bozrah and a great slaughter in the land of Idumea'. According to the archaeological evidence Buseirah flourished only for a short time, from the 7C BC until the Persian period (mid-6C BC). Excavations have shown that it covered a substantial area, divided into an 'Acropolis' and Lower Town and fortified by a city wall. Settlement in this region was probably linked to the mining of copper, Edom's most important commodity. There is evidence for extensive Edomite copper mining and smelting in the desolate Wadi Feinan region (biblical Punon), south-west of Buseirah. Edom was no doubt an important source of copper for the Assyrians, who may have stimulated copper production; indeed the earliest archaeological evidence for Edomite settlement coincided with the western campaigns of the Assyrian king Tiglath-Pileser III (biblical Pul) in the later 8C BC. At the junction of the King's Highway and a major caravan route to the Wadi Araba and Gaza, Buseirah was also strategically sited for transit trade, particularly in spices and aromatics from Arabia.

Buseirah was excavated for several seasons, from 1971–74 and in 1980, but the site is now overgrown and difficult to interpret. Left (west) of the school playground is the archaeologists' **Area C**, a complex of rooms and courts with plastered floors and walls including a 'bathroom' with tub and possible lavatory. **Area B**, to the north-west, has revealed various phases of the casemate town wall. Steps led up from a postern gate in the wall to a gateway in the defences surrounding the '**Acropolis**', which is directly behind the school. Two major buildings overlie each other on the Acropolis, massive structures built of roughly hewn stone. Steps connected an outer courtyard to the earlier building; they can still be seen, badly cracked by fire and slightly pinkish in colour, with plinths on either side. The north-east wall of the later building has blocked the original entrance. These buildings may be part of a palace or temple complex; the excavators believe they show Assyrian influence.

EDOM

Edom, the largest of the three Transjordanian Iron Age kingdoms, initially comprised the region south of Wadi Hasa (biblical Zered) down to Wadi Hisma (north of Wadi Rum) and later also extended west across Wadi Araba. According to the Bible, the Edomites were descendants of Lot's brother-in-law, Esau, who is also related to the people of Seir, west of Wadi Araba. By describing Esau as 'red' (Hebrew 'admoni) and 'hairy' (Hebrew sa'ir) the biblical author alludes to Edom and Seir (Genesis 25:25). Edom was a wild, mountainous land and its people may have remained largely nomadic until the 7C BC, when the archaeological record shows a massive increase of agricultural settlements on the Edomite plateau. Agriculture is only feasible in this rather inhospitable land with well-organised water storage and distribution systems. Like their successors the Nabateans, who no doubt learned much from them, the Edomites became expert hydrologists. Also like the Nabateans they had a special relationship with their mountains; Edomite mountain strongholds include Umm al-Biyara (p 238), Ba'ja (p 250) and Umm al-Ala (p242), all in and around Petra, and Sela (p 172) near the Edomite capital Bozrah.

Copper was Edom's most important commodity, exploited in the Wadi Araba where the Feinan (p 131) deposits were heavily worked during the 7C BC. Edom also traded in luxury goods from further afield, including aromatics from Arabia and controlled an important settlement on the Red Sea (Tell al-Khaleifeh) and the outlet to the Mediterranean port city of Gaza in Philistia. Ezekiel refers to trade in luxury items between Edom and the Phoenician city of Tyre: 'Edom traded with you for the sake of your many manufactured goods, exchanging purple garnets, embroideries, fine linen, coral and red jaspar for your goods' (27:16). Amos alludes to slave trading between Edom and Gaza and Tyre.

There are few inscriptions in Edomite, a language closely related to Moabite, Ammonite and Hebrew, and except for the name of the main god Qaus, Edomite religion is virtually unknown. Several Old Testament passages, however, suggest that Edom was renowned in antiquity for her wisdom.

Probably the Babylonian king Nabonidus removed the Edomite monarchy in 552 BC on his way to Arabia, perhaps wanting direct control of the lucrative Arabian trade. Since the 7C BC the Edomites had been expanding westwards and when the Persians, successors to the Babylonians in the region, reorganised their border with Egypt c 400 BC southern Palestine became the hyparchy of Idumea, thus preserving the name of Edom. Edom proper became the nucleus of an Arab state, the Nabatean kingdom.

Excursion to Dana Nature Reserve via 'Ain Lahda

Return to the King's Highway or alternatively, before reaching the main road, turn right south-west of Buseirah and drive up into the hills for beautiful views back to the ancient site and modern village. Left along a dirt track towards the top of the hill and left again at the junction is **Nasraniyah**, which can be seen on a rise from the main asphalt road. It is completely unexcavated, but in a most picturesque location and worth spending a short time exploring. Most of the remains are of the Byzantine period. Among the jumble of stones are walls and doorways; three circles and a cross are carved on one of the finely tooled blocks.

Return along the same dirt track, continue straight ahead at the junction and the track meets the asphalt road just before 0.8km 'Ain Lahda, a cool spring where local shepherds water their flocks.

If you are driving from the King's Highway turn right at a sign to 'Ain Lahda, 4.5km south of the Buseirah junction and follow the road just over 3km to the spring, turning right at a sign to Dana campsite.

Dana Nature Reserve campsite is well signed from here: the entrance to it is 3km from the spring. There is a 2JD entrance fee to the reserve where you can hike through the oak and pine woods, camp or simply enjoy the wonderful mountain landscape. The reserve is run by the Royal Society for the Conservation of Nature (RSCN) and and is open from March to November. Tents, mattresses and blankets can be hired, a four-man tent costs 14JD, and the facilities are good.

Mosaic in the Hippolytus Hall, Madaba

WILDLIFE

Hunting, overgrazing, deforestation and development have sadly reduced Jordan's wildlife, particularly the larger mammals. Since its establishment in 1966, however, the RSCN has been working to conserve and protect threatened species such as the ibex, a small number of which live in the Dana reserve. At Shaumari oryx, onager, gazelle and ostrich are being bred in captivity. There are a few leopard left in the wild, wolves are now very rare, but striped hyena, jackal and foxes are occasionally seen. Badgers, hares, hedgehogs, jerbils and jerboas are also found, although you are unlikely to spot them.

Birds have also been affected by development—the pumping of water from the Azraq pools has severely reduced the number of migratory visitors as well as local species which were once so plentiful to judge from their frequent depiction in Byzantine and Umayyad mosaics. However, owls, woodpeckers, larks, wheatears, partridge, hawks and buzzards are among others to be seen here.

Snakes, including some poisonous species, are shy of noise, but look out for the blue Sinai lizard, a striking sight against the red Petra sandstone. There are also scorpions, especially in the desert.

Return to the King's Highway turning right at 'Ain Lahda and continue south passing the Qadisiyeh cement factory on your left.

Excursion to Dana Village and Wadi Dana

For **Dana village** turn right 1km after Qadisiyeh village and drive the 3km down to the old Ottoman settlement. By turning left in 1km and driving down towards the valley you can detour to see the outcrop of **Sheikh ar-Rish**, its summit covered with round hillocks, below to the right. Sheikh ar-Rish is difficult of access and has not been properly explored, but like Sela it is riddled with cisterns and water channels and may have been used from Nabatean to Byzantine times.

Dana village is the focus of an integrated conservation project and its setting, on the edge of the cliffs overlooking the Wadi Dana, is magnificent. Old Ottoman houses are being restored in traditional style, and electricity and water will be provided as an incentive for villagers to stay. An administrative and research centre is being built and training in various handicrafts and skills is being given. If you can arrange to be met at the other end it is a 3 hour walk westwards straight down **Wadi Dana** to **Feinan**. Starting in the orchards of the village descend through a changing landscape to the arid setting of the ancient copper-smelting town. Birds abound, especially in spring: there are cuckoos, doves, woodpeckers and noisy partridges and the gregarious Tristram's grackle. White broom and phlomis gradually give way to sea squill and scrub. Rounded white sandstone changes to red sandstone where manganese and copper deposits are found and finally to granite at the bottom. Although Wadi Dana must have been an important route from the plateau to the copper mines at Feinan, the valley was virtually uninhabited in antiquity and today, but for a few bedouin, there is little settlement beyond Dana village. As you approach Feinan, look out for the buildings of a Natural Resources compound which has facilities for scientists and archaeologists investigating the area. The extensive remains of ancient Feinan (p 131) straddle the wadi and hillsides beyond.

Shobak Castle

18km from Qadisiyeh bear right for Petra and right again to **Shobak Castle** in 4km. Drive through the modern village and round the castle to the present entrance on the north-east.

History

Founded in 1115 by King Baldwin I, Montreal was the first castle to be built in Oultrejourdain although Karak was later to replace it as administrative centre. The strategic hilltop site was well chosen and with water supplies assured it held out longer than Karak after the battle of Hattin, only surrendering in spring 1189, when its starved garrison had gone blind from malnutrition. Nowadays little remains of the Crusader period beyond a church and a chapel. Shobak then passed to Saladin's brother and remained in Ayubbid hands until Baybars took it and strengthened the fortifications. In the late 13C it was badly damaged and was largely rebuilt by the Mamlukes. After a mid-16C revolt Shobak kept its independence from the Ottomans until the late 19C. Later rebuilding, damage by Ibrahim Pasha's retreating troops, and the Ottoman village which occupied the ruins until modern times, have further obscured its architectural history, although the remaining walls and towers are impressive.

The castle walls and towers date to the Mamluke occupation; the 13C German pilgrim Thietmar visited Shobak and marvelled at its strength. The original entrance was on the north-west, but no sign of this remains. The tower right of the entrance bears an inscription referring to Sultan Husam al-Din Lajin (1297–98): this and two other inscriptions on towers to the north and west refer to rebuilding work after the destruction of 1293. On entering keep left and in c 30m turn left down into a vaulted room and through a doorway into the barrel-vaulted **chapel**. Two niches flank the shallow apse and steps at the west end lead to an unusual little room with square pits and a channel and the remains of older arches probably related to the chapel. Continue along the track to a cross-vaulted gatehouse with benches on either side. North of this and adjacent to a second gatehouse is the way down to the castle's ingenious water supply system—down 375 steps are spring-filled cisterns which would have helped the inhabitants withstand a siege. The climb down is not for the faint-hearted! Walk north through the second gatehouse and past ranges of arched rooms on both sides before turning left at a barrel-vaulted building with three arched entrances and then right again past a wide, vaulted room of much rougher masonry and down a corridor. At the end is the cross-vaulted round **tower** with four arched bays, machicolation and an inscribed band outside referring to restoration work done in the late 13C.

To reach the partly restored **Ayubbid Palace complex** turn east and in 20m right through a narrow vaulted pasage. Although the date is uncertain it is thought most likely to have been built in the early 13C under al-Mu'azzam 'Isa ibn al-'Adil. The complex consisits of a large **Reception Hall** with chambers off. The central *iwan* is missing, but those on either side of it are still there. Piers supported arches across the rectangular hall and at the far end are three small arched niches. Moving back toward the entrance you will pass the **baths** on the right, also an Islamic addition—Crusaders were apparently not so concerned with personal hygiene! Note the flagged floor and underfloor water channel. A small basin and some marble are visible in one room. Above is a confused jumble of Ottoman housing. Continue on and down some steps to a building which is thought to have been a **church**, later converted. There are three entrances to the rectangular room lined with columns, some still with arches between.

MEDIEVAL WARFARE

The Crusaders were were at war with one or more of their Muslim neighbours during most of their time in the Holy Land. In those 194 years there were many developments in the art of war as both sides learnt from observation and experience. Problem-solving of this sort accounts for many of the technological innovations of those years. The learning process began immediately—certainly the Crusaders were much struck by the mighty walls and massive defences of Constantinople which they saw en route to the Holy Land. For the Arabs the novel sight of a charge by hundreds of heavily-armoured knights on horseback was terrifying. Consequently they adapted their tactics, either ambushing the invaders or luring them onto unsuitable terrain—feigned retreat after attack was a favoured ploy.

For armour the Crusaders wore mail shirts, stockings and helmets and carried sword, mace and lance. A contemporary account claims that the Bedouin viewed armour with contempt since 'they believe that no man can die before the appointed day, and for this reason refuse to wear any sort of armour ... [saying] ... Be accursed like a Frank, who puts on armour for fear of death.' Coats of mail and helmets were, however, used by the Arabs and their swords were originally straight: the curved scimitar becoming popular only in the 15C.

The Crusaders immediately began building castles: due to their constant shortage of men the castle lay at the heart of their strategy. They chose strategic sites which were easier to hold with fewer men. As timber was in short supply greater use was made of stone, which they used with consummate skill to build such strong defences that many castles are still standing after many wars and earthquakes over the centuries. Wars and sieges often became bogged down—quite literally if a campaign dragged on into the winter rains. Therefore spring and summer were the campaigning months, winter was a time for rest, recovery and preparations for the next season's fighting.

In a siege the attacking side had a number of options: 30m, iron-tipped rams, worked by teams of up to 60 men under protective cover, could wreak considerable damage to the walls, but might be pinned or pulled sideways by the defending forces. Scaling ladders were an alternative, but these could be thrown off if there were sufficient hands on the walls. A Frankish speciality was the siege tower: an enormous, unwieldy, wooden contraption which was hauled up to the walls once the ground and moat had been levelled. At the siege of Tyre in 1111 one such tower was 24m tall. Mangonels and trebuchets were machines which hurled rocks and missiles. The mangonel—a huge sling—was a Byzantine idea. It was not very accurate although the Franks used it effectively. The trebuchet appeared after the First Crusade. Using the principle of the counterpoise (seesaw with weights) it could be adjusted to give a more precise aim. It could hurl stones weighing up to 300kg over 100m. The historian William of Tyre gives a dramatic description of what it was like to be on the receiving end of an attack: 'The very walls shook ... millstones and huge rocks hurled from the machines fell into the midst of the citadel ... rocks and all kinds of missiles were hurled ... their nights were sleepless, while during the day their strength was further exhausted by never ending combat.'

Castles might also have their own artillery engines set on sturdy platforms with which to counterattack. The Saracens were skilled at mining castles by digging a tunnel under the walls and then setting fire to the wooden props supporting it with the result that the tunnel would cave in bringing the wall down with it. Countermining—digging down to try and find the miners—was possible, but difficult. They were also fond of another Byzantine invention—Greek fire: 'the tail of fire that streamed behind it was as long as the shaft of a great lance. The noise it made in coming was like that of a thunderbolt falling from the skies; it seemed like a dragon flying through the air.'

The psychology of defence was important: castles which had strongholds within on which to fall back might be stronger, but men fighting in the outer parts who knew they could retreat might not try as hard as others with their backs to the wall. In defence archers were needed to provide flanking fire for sorties or to repel attackers. Postern gates were carefully positioned for sorties re-entering the castle and consideration was given to exposing the attackers' right (less well-protected) side. The balista was a giant crossbow using iron bolts four times the size of a normal arrow—at Crac des Chevaliers there are special balista embrasures. Tower design was controversial: the Knights of St John preferred round ones, Templars liked them square. Round towers were more resistant to attack by bombardment and mining, but less convenient for living in. Another Byzantine idea was machicolation—overhead holes through which to drop stones, missiles or hot oil. A bent entrance delayed the invaders and the Crusaders introduced the portcullis. Famine was a risk, but the attackers also had to feed their troops and castles could hold enough stocks for years: Crac des Chevaliers had nine cisterns and a windmill.

Medieval warfare depicted in an old stained glass window in St-Denis, Paris, (from Montfaucon)

Finally there were the conventions of chivalry: anecdotes abound of women spared and foes given quarter: Saladin is reputed to have offered Richard the Lionheart a fresh mount in battle. Against this individual magnanimity, one must set the broken pledges and appalling massacres, such as that of the fall of Jerusalem in 1099 when Jews and Muslims were slaughtered without mercy.

Continue on to Petra either retracing your steps or by taking the road west of the castle which leads you to modern Shobak in 2.5km. The best view of the castle can be had from this road. Turn right in Shobak for Petra. In 16km a sign right to Abdalia offers an alternative and striking route into Petra. This road is not in good condition and may soon be impassable, but has beautiful views of the Petra mountains if you drive a few kilometres along it to the crest of the hill. It emerges 11km on at the junction near **Beidha** from where you can turn left, pass the Bdul village and arrive in **Wadi Musa** near the Petra Forum Hotel. Otherwise continue straight on for 12km Wadi Musa.

DESERT HIGHWAY TO WADI RUM AND AQABA

This is the faster, less scenic route south. Its way lies through the desert, and although it may not be as attractive as the King's Highway, there are a number of good sites to visit if you have your own transport. Most are on the west side and therefore easier to reach driving southwards. This route is older than it might appear: the modern highway coincides largely with both the Hijaz Railway, built to transport *haj* pilgrims from Damascus to Medina, and the earlier Ottoman pilgrim's route (**Darb el Haj**) from Damascus. The road, also called the **Tariq al Bint** (Maiden's Way), after the Ottoman princess who reputedly preferred it to the King's Highway route used under the Mamlukes, was dotted with fortified way-stations which guarded the water supply for the pilgrims. Many of these Ottoman forts are still standing, the best-preserved is at Qatrana, while the railway is now used for transporting phosphates mined in the desert and the occasional tourist charter. A number of Roman forts lie just west of the Desert Highway, including an extremely well-preserved one at Bshir, a reminder that this was once Roman frontier country. The road ends at the Red Sea port of Aqaba, terminus of the Via Nova Traiana, and nowadays a beach resort. The best place for lunch is the *Qatrana Resthouse*. Accommodation is only available in Amman, Aqaba, or Karak Resthouse 40km from Qatrana. There is a campsite at Wadi Rum.

Qastal, an engraving from The Land of Moab *by H.B. Tristram*

Take the airport road out of Amman and 5km after the Madaba turn-off, take a slip-road right signed **Qastal**. Follow it for 4km parallel to the highway to park by the ruins, visible on a rise just left of a large building which has most unfortunately destroyed the north-west corner of the 68m square limestone complex. Numerous reoccupations and re-building make this a confusing site— it is thought that it may have originally been a Roman fort, the name a corruption of *castellum*. Rebuilt in the 8C, the audience hall is mentioned in Umayyad writings of this time.

The best-preserved area is the south-east where a circular **corner tower** is clear as are the semi-circular **interval towers** of the south side—there were four on each side. The entrance to the east, still visible with a decorated door jamb, was flanked by two interval towers and led into a **gatehouse** with stairs up both sides. Inside suites of rooms were organised around a central **courtyard** and sections of mosaic floor; the tesserae found here give some idea of its decoration.

There is a **postern gate** on the north side across the road from which is a peculiar **mosque**. The round angle tower just north of it may have been a minaret. Enter the cross-vaulted rectangular hall from the north, the *mihrab* niche is opposite. Since Gertrude Bell described this area in *The Desert and the Sown* there has been considerable deterioration. She assumed, as did Brünnow and Domaszewski, that this was a praetorium. 'It consists of an immense vaulted chamber, with a walled court in front of it and a round tower at the south-west corner. The tower has a winding stair inside it and a band of decoration about the exterior, rinceaux above and fluted triglyphs below, with narrow blank metopes between them.' Water was provided by a number of cisterns in the area including one which had been a quarry for the stone. Behind the modern building is an **Ottoman cemetery** with some interesting tombs. Continue along the slip road to rejoin the Desert Highway just before the airport turn-off.

North of the airport runway is the Umayyad palace of **Mshatta**. To reach it by car from the Desert Highway, take the airport turning and bear right at the Alia Gateway Hotel. Skirt the perimeter fence passing through a checkpoint where you may have to surrender your passport and continue round to the north side. After c10km turn right, pass another checkpoint and Mshatta is just around the corner.

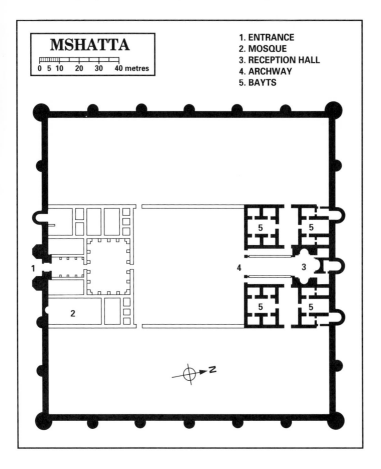

MSHATTA

0 5 10   20   30   40 metres

1. ENTRANCE
2. MOSQUE
3. RECEPTION HALL
4. ARCHWAY
5. BAYTS

History

Mshatta may well be the first site you see in Jordan—its barrel vaults can be seen as you come in to land at the airport, just north of the perimeter fence. Built in the late Umayyad period, probably under Walid II (743–44), it was planned on a magnificent scale, but never finished. The intricate carving of the stone shows persisting classical influences: naturalistic acanthus and vine-scroll feature prominently, as do animals and figures, although these were probably omitted from the area next to the mosque. Much of the elaborate façade of the outer wall is today in the Pergamon Museum in Berlin, the gift of the Ottoman sultan to Kaiser Wilhelm shortly before the First World War.

In plan, Mshatta is 144m square with 25 semi-circular **interval towers** and round **corner towers**. The only remaining stretch of decorated wall is right of the entrance: note how the Islamic fascination with pattern mingles here with earlier classical tradition in a typically Umayyad fusion. The sections now in Berlin show a bold design of triangles around interlaced foliage and central rosettes: 'Every inch of their surface...carved...Lions, winged lions, buffaloes, gazelle, panthers, lynx, men...peacocks, partridges, parrots', was Canon Tristram's description of Mshatta's ornament written last century. Not all the façade was decorated—work was never completed on Mshatta. Walk through the entrance which is flanked by **semi-octagonal towers**. The **mosque** is inside on the right, its *mihrab* niche jutting into the south wall. Passing a small pool or reservoir on the left walk down towards the trefoil reception hall surrounded by *bayts* (suites of rooms), some of which have the barrel-vaulted ceilings still in place. Mshatta, like Tuba is built of bright-coloured brick and stone. A **triple archway** spanned the entrance to the *iwan* or reception hall, with a **colonnade** behind it. Parts of the entablature, capitals and voussoirs lie around its stone columns. If you step through the doorways at the back of the hall you will see an interesting glimpse of life behind the scenes: Mshatta's latrines, which project out of the wall. Water probably came from Qastal or nearby Jiza. For all its splendour Mshatta was never finished, possibly because of the death of Walid II, but it is an interesting complement to the other Umayyad monuments in Jordan, similar in many respects to the more remote Qasr Tuba.

Return to the Highway and continue to 2km **Jiza** where there is a **Mamluke fort** and **Roman reservoir**, one of the largest in Jordan, just west of the road. Roman Zizia is mentioned in the *Notitia Dignitatum* as being garrisoned by the *equites Dalmatae Illyriciani*, although nothing beyond the reservoir remains of the Roman period. The present fort, a stop on the Haj route mentioned by the great 14C traveller Ibn Battuta, is still in military hands. It lies in the grounds of a military police post, whose permission must be asked to visit it. Inside it is dilapidated and the long barrel-vaulted ground floor room is used for storage. However, if you climb the rickety stairs to the first floor you will find evidence of transition over the years: Greek crosses in the lintel stones of a doorway in the south and a blocked arch on the west side. Probably in origin a Mamluke fort, it was repaired by the Ottomans in the 16C. Ibrahim Pasha's troops occupied it and did considerable damage before rebuilding work later in the 19C, when the triple-arched window in the south room upstairs was presumably added. Stairs led up to the roof top. An adjacent structure was still standing in the 19C when the Tristram expedition called here, but this has since disappeared.

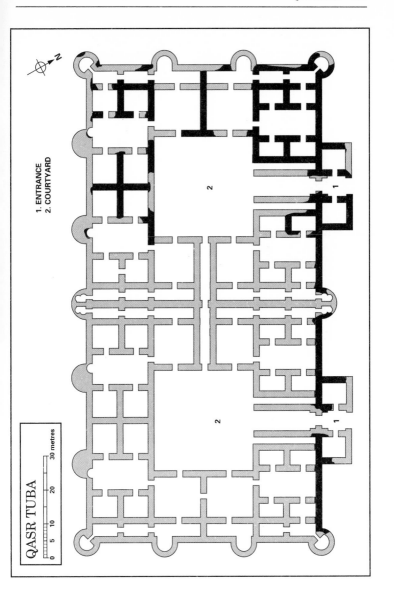

QASR TUBA

1. ENTRANCE
2. COURTYARD

0 5 10   20   30 metres

Excursion to Qasr Tuba

To reach the remote Umayyad site of **Qasr Tuba**, a four-wheel drive and guide are needed. Desert tracks lead there from south of Azraq, from Qasr Kharana and Qatrana. From the Desert Highway, 14km north of Qatrana, a graded track by a pylon leads east into the desert. Tuba is c 45 km from here. Branch left along a rough track for the last 6km, keeping south of the wadi and looking ahead for the barrel vaults of Tuba.

The most isolated of the Umayyad desert complexes, Tuba, like Mshatta, is unfinished and rather ruined, but makes an exciting trip into the desert. Planned as a double enclosure of two 70m square interlinked complexes, only the northern half was actually built. Its barrel-vaulted roofs and arched doorways are very similar to those of Mshatta. Begun in the late Umayyad period (743–744) it is built of mud-baked brick on stone. Much of the enclosure walls on the north and east still stands. The east wall had two entrances with square **flanking towers;** part of a semi-circular **interval tower** remains between them. The other walls had semi-circular interval towers, two east and west and five on the long south wall. The **corner towers** were round. Tuba may have been a caravanserai: like Mshatta, it does not appear to have served any defensive purpose. Water came from stone wells by the nearby wadi.

Shortly before Qatrana is the turning to **Bshir** which lies 12km from the Highway. Although the road to this beautiful and very well-preserved Roman fort is being graded, four-wheel drive is still needed to cover the last 7km. If in doubt ask for the reservoir (*birka*)—the Bedouin still use it. Just before a small tyre shop/garage on the northern outskirts of Qatrana, turn right onto a paved road and head west, crossing two sets of pylons. At 4km the road, now unmetalled, swings north up and along a ridge. Look out for red-painted stones marking the way. Turn west at c 7km and descend the slope. Bear right in 2km at a fork and continue for 2.5km.The impressive remains of the fort should be in view before then.

Qasr Bshir is one of the best-preserved Roman castella on the Arabian frontier, about one day's march (c 15km) north-east of the legionary fortress at Lejjun (p 164). Although Lejjun is not visible from Bshir, the forts were linked by road and signals could be transmitted rapidly via a number of watchtowers in the vicinity. Movement in the surrounding region was easily monitored from Bshir's towers, which commanded excellent views across the plain and hills to the east.

History

According to the Latin inscription above the gate, Qasr Bshir, described as **Castra Praetorii Mobeni**, was built from the ground up (*a fundamentis*), during the period 293–305, by Aurelius Asclepiades, Governor of the Roman Province of Arabia. Evidence for earlier occupation of the site is limited to Iron Age pottery (11C–10C BC) and the foundations of a Nabatean watchtower, now incorporated into the small Roman building west of the fort. Construction of the castellum was part of a major upgrading of the defences of the Arabian frontier during the late 3C and early 4C. It has been suggested that a local cavalry unit was stationed at Bshir, as there are mangers in several ground floor rooms and cavalry would certainly have been appropriate for the open, undulating terrain. In the 5C the site was abandoned. It was briefly reoccupied during the Umayyad period, when it may have served as a caravanserai, but subsequently fell into disuse following an earthquake in the 8C.

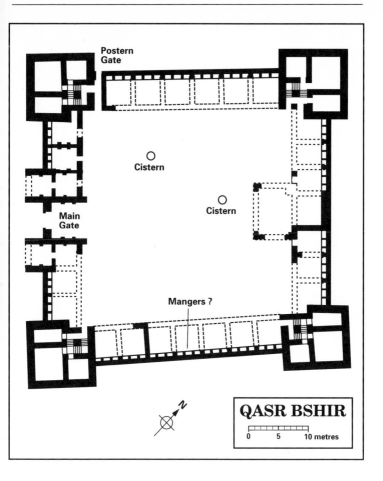

Postern
Gate

Cistern

Cistern

Main
Gate

Mangers ?

QASR BSHIR

0   5   10 metres

Bshir is an almost square **quadriburgium,** with projecting towers at the four corners and flanking the gate, a style typical of the late 3C and early 4C on the eastern frontier. Above the **main gateway** in the south-west wall are a relieving arch and a flat lintel stone bearing the **dedicatory inscription** in a tabula ansata which dates the fort's construction to the Tetrarchy, under the Augusti Diocletian and Maximianus and Caesars Flavius Valerius Constantius and Galerius Valerius Maximianus. Inside, the fort has a large **courtyard** lined by two-storey rooms, many now blocked by fallen masonry. Most of the ground floor rooms had three niches, interpreted as mangers, built into the walls, suggesting they were used as **stables;** at one manger per horse there were enough for 69 horses. Rooms on the upper floor may have been **barracks** for the troops. Probably most rooms were plastered inside; there are still traces of plaster on some walls. The well-preserved **angle towers** have three storeys with three rooms per storey and a staircase constructed round a central pier. Missiles could be fired from slit windows in the upper storeys. By the western angle tower in the north-west wall is a small **postern gate** and on top of the walls was a walkway accessed from the corner towers and protected by a crenellated rampart. Bshir's water supply was provided by two **plastered cisterns** inside the courtyard, possibly connected to the channel which enters the fort from the north, two further cisterns outside the walls and a large **reservoir** to the west which has been repaired and is still in use. Water was therefore ample not only for the garrison, but also for the horses and other animals stabled in the castellum.

Qatrana Resthouse and petrol station are only 2km south of the Bshir exit. This is the best stop on the Highway for refreshments. From Qatrana you can also visit the Roman legionary fortress at 21km Lejjun. Qatrana's small limestone **Ottoman fort** lies a further 2km south just west of the road. The **reservoir** is close by and was therefore easier to protect from marauding Bedouin. Restored in the 1970s, the fort was built in the time of Süleyman the Magnificent (1520–66). The entrance is in the south wall. The walls are crenellated and there is **machicolation** on all sides. The east and west walls have three slit windows with decorated lintels, the north and south four. Inside, stairs run up to the first floor and rooftop around a small courtyard with a number of rooms off. On the first floor some rooms have *iwan* entrances.

THE PILGRIMAGE TO MECCA

The main event of the Muslim calendar is the pilgrimage to Mecca and under the Ottomans the route from Damascus was one of the most popular, requiring tremendous organisation by the authorities. It is every Muslim's duty, once in a lifetime, to perform the *haj*. Pilgrims from all over would congregate in Damascus, crowding the *suqs* to buy provisions for the journey. According to the eccentric Victorian Charles Doughty, who travelled with the pilgrims, 'haj caravan drivers ... hold insolently their path through the narrow bazaars...ferocious young men, whose mouths are full of horrible cursings'. The Amir al-Haj, an official appointed by the Sultan, was a most prestigious post. He escorted the pilgrimage, bearing the standard of the haj to the first stop. Isobel Burton gives a lively account of its departure from Damascus. Pilgrims began arriving in Damascus in early Ramadan when they would sell their horses to buy camels. A date was set for departure as it was safer to travel together and everyone would assemble outside the city to see the gorgeous pageant. There were bands, parades, hawkers and even women of doubtful character. She also describes the careful order of the Caravan: '1.Guide. 2. Artillery. 3. Tents. 4. Bazar. 5. Sunni pilgrims. 6. Pasha's litter. 7. Irregular cavalry. 8. Mahmal (Ayesha's) camel. 9. Treasurer's litter. 10. More cavalry. 11. Shi'a pilgrims. 12. Dromedary riders.' One Mamluke Sultan apparently travelled with 40 camels carrying frames of growing vegetables and dispensed largesse as he travelled, but for the majority of pilgrims the trip was a long and gruelling experience. Doubtless disease and fatigue took its toll of the faithful in the harsh conditions of the desert.

Continue on to c 52km **Hasa**—what look like great sand pits along the way are in fact phosphate mines. A lesser known, dilapidated, but atmospheric Haj fort lies 5km west of Hasa and is visible on a fine day from the highway. To reach it turn right 300m before the flyover bridge and head west along a paved road for 3km to a small pumping station. From here you can see the fort near a line of pylons to the west, but it is a futher 2km on a desert track to reach it.

Like Fassua south of Ma'an, the Hasa fort lies by the wadi. A fine stretch of

stone-paved pilgrims' road runs just west of it crossing the river by an old **bridge**, now partly destroyed. The **reservoir** lies on the east and the entrance is in the north wall, which has almost completely collapsed, although the barrel-vaulted **gateway** and first floor window are still standing. In the centre of the **courtyard** with steps up to it and a side entrance is a c12m deep **cistern**. On the east and west sides, two *iwans* flank a smaller door and a single long room with three entrances runs the length of the south wall. Two sets of steps lead up to the first floor from here, which has a fine *iwan* in the centre of this side and next to it a curiously large window. On the east side steps led up to the roof. Outside a **false machicolation** decorates the west wall. Sir Richard Burton's description of a Cairo caravanserai vividly evokes the atmosphere of such way stations: 'in the courtyard the poorer sort of travellers consort with tethered beasts of burden, beggars howl, and slaves lie basking and scratching themselves upon mountainous heaps of cotton bales and other merchandise'. Water was the essential requirement at these stops, effectively fortified watering places. They were often two days' journey apart and Charles Doughty reports many complaints on his journey with the haj about the lack of adequate supplies: 'all the birkets (cisterns) leak and there is no water for the hajjaj; every year there is money paid out ...for the maintenance of the buildings; these embezzling pashas swallow the public silver'. A large part of the haj budget was devoted to paying off the sheikhs through whose territory it passed, not always to much effect.

Return to the road and after c 39km between the villages of Husayniya and Hashemiya look west for the Roman fort of **Da'janiya**. A glimpse of the low black line of the ruins c 3km away will give you the direction. Turn right into Hashemiya village by a white bus station and head north-west for 5km on the desert track, keeping a careful eye out for wadis. Da'janiya is one of the largest castella on the Arabian frontier, c 30km north-east of the great military fortress at 'Udruh (p 251), on the branch road which ran east of the Via Nova Traiana from 'Udruh to Jurf ad-Darawish. A long stretch of Roman road is well preserved to the south-west, between the fort and the road to Shobak. In the late 19C Doughty found that Da'janiya was 'often a lurking place of land-loping Bduw'. Today shepherds still graze their flocks among the jumbled basalt and limestone ruins and use the large **reservoir** south of the fort, originally Roman, but recently rebuilt.

Da'janiya is c 100m square, much smaller than a late legionary fortress, but larger than typical Arabian *quadriburgia* like Qasr Bshir or Deir al-Kahf. Angle towers project from each corner and there are two interval towers in each wall apart from the south-east, which has four towers, two flanking the **main gate**. There is another gate opposite, in the north-west wall, and a smaller, arched **postern** in the south-west wall. Inside the fort most structures have collapsed, but some areas have been cleared. Between the two main gates is the *via principalis*, with a large cistern, partly rock-cut towards its northern end. In the centre, east of the street, is the *principia* or headquarters building. Excavation has revealed the *aedes* or shrine of the standards at the back. Much of the rest of the interior is filled with **barrack blocks**, while some long rooms against the enclosure wall may have been **stables** and other, larger ones perhaps were **granaries**.

No inscriptions have been found at Da'janiya, so its date, ancient name and garrison are unknown. As forts with projecting towers are usually no earlier than the Severan era, it was probably built in the 3–4C, and its garrison, perhaps a cavalry vexillation, would have guarded the road against incursions from the eastern desert. Like so many other forts on the Arabian frontier Da'janiya was abandoned by the early 6C.

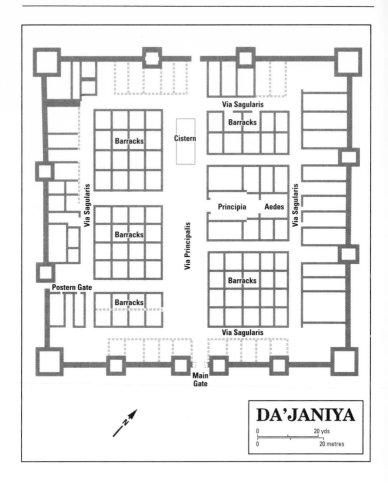

DA'JANIYA

0   20 yds

0   20 metres

THE LIMES ARABICUS

From its original meaning of path or road, the word *limes* by the late 1C had come to describe the frontier between the Roman empire and the barbarian world. In the East the *limes arabicus*, the Arabian frontier created when Trajan annexed the Nabatean kingdom in 106, was a broad fortified zone except for c 100km of the southern sector through the Hisma to Aila (Aqaba), which was guarded by a single line of forts along the *Via Nova Traiana* (p 174) supplemented by Rome's Thamudic tribal allies (p 199) who patrolled the desert to the south-east. Rome's main aim on the Arabian frontier was to monitor the movements and control the raids of nomadic Arab tribes. In their new province of Arabia the Romans took over the Nabatean defensive system and constructed new forts of their own both along the Via Nova Traiana, completed by 114, and further east. The Roman army of Arabia, the *Exercitus Arabicus*, originally consisted of a single legion of 5000 men, *legio III Cyrenaica*, based at the provincial capital of Bostra in the north, plus an equal number of auxiliaries. Legionary detachments were scattered throughout the province and local units included camel corps. During Diocletian's reorganisation of the eastern frontier (p 105) (late 3C–early 4C) many new forts were constructed, including the legionary fortress of Lejjun (p 164) for *Legio IV Martia* and *quadriburgia* like Qasr Bshir (p 186). South of Wadi Hasa Arabia was joined with Sinai and the Negev to become the province of *Palaestina Salutaris* (also known as *Palaestina Tertia*) and *Legio X Fretensis* was transferred from Jerusalem to Aila. In the 4C, when the frontier was most heavily fortified. Ammianus Marcellinus writes that 'Arabia ... is rich from a variety of products and studded with strong fortresses and castles'. Following the mid-5C there began an era of decline. Some forts were abandoned, many frontier forces (*limitanei*) became little more than a peasant militia and local defence shifted increasingly to Arab chieftains. After Justinian concluded peace with Persia in 532, all military construction along the Arabian frontier ceased. Such policies proved disastrous. Heraclius (610–641) was unable to organise an effective defence to oppose the Muslim armies in the 630s and their decisive victory at the Yarmuk in 636 sealed the fate of Palestine, Transjordan and Syria.

The ruined Haj fort of **Anaiza** lies right of the road immediately after the turn-off to Shobak and Petra just south of Hashemiya. Built of limestone and basalt the vaulted entrance still stands. The inside is reminiscent of a khan with vaulted rooms on three sides and a cistern in the courtyard. The desert highway now bypasses c 30km Ma'an and heads south-west to begin the descent of the **Ras an-Naqab** escarpment.

Excursion to Fassua and Mudawwara Haj Forts

In **Ma'an** itself there is not much to see, but there are two more Haj forts on the road to the Saudi border from Ma'an. With a four-wheel drive vehicle and a guide it is possible to visit them and then head west across the desert for a two to three hour drive on rough track to Disi, near Rum. Shortly after leaving Ma'an a turning for Jafr and Azraq is signed. Continue past it and southwards for c 55km. To reach the fort at **Fassua** (four-wheel drive necessary) take a track westwards immediately past an army post and cross the 2km railway south of the old station. The fort is hidden in a dip 2km on, charmingly located by a little wadi full of spring-flowering white broom; its yellowing mortar stands out in the stony black desert. Fassua was built in the mid to late 18C by Uthman Pasha whose name is mentioned in the inscription over the entrance in the north wall. Relatively unaltered, it stands in contrast to Mudawwara which was repaired and occupied by the army this century. **Twin reservoirs** lie 20m north of the fort, each with two sets of steps down. The courtyard **cistern** has been renovated during recent occupation of the fort when animals were kept here. Pass through the barrel-vaulted entrance noting the boltholes inside the door. The steps on either side of the courtyard as you enter have collapsed. The rooms on the west are arched while those opposite have been altered by the modern occupants. On the south there are *iwans* on both floors, with the lower arch being larger. Upstairs the east side rooms have collapsed. Decorative **machicolation** adorns the outside corners; the south wall has an extra one.

Continue 57km along the main road through the desert and hills passing various halts on the railway to a station on the left by a red and white pylon and wind pump. Turn right and after 2km follow a blue sign for **Disi**. **Mudawwara Fort** is north of the road 1km on. Surrounded by a fallen barbed wire fence and somewhat dilapidated inside despite renovation and occupation by the army earlier this century, the fort was built in the 1730s. A structure 50m east may have been a pen for animals, and there was a small circular cistern outside on the west. The entrance is on the east with a large iwan opposite. Inside, steps led upstairs off the entrance **vestibule**; those on the right can still be climbed with due caution. Upstairs a **mosque** and **minaret** have been added in the south-west corner and decorated with the Jordanian flag. The small domed room on the west may have been an oven.

Return to the Desert Highway and continue southwards c 30km to the sharp descent of the **Ras an-Naqab.** The views are spectacular, but drivers should concentrate on this notorious stretch of road—the heavy lorries using it, combined with the steep slope and fine landscape ahead, make it a dramatic drive. Part way down a sign to old Humayma leads to the right. Follow the track westwards for c 11km to an ancient aqueduct alongside which the track continues south-westwards to the extensive ruins of **Humayma**, the largest ancient site in the Hisma, a region of sandy desert that extends into Saudi Arabia. In this arid and inhospitable terrain water is essential, and Humayma's engineers devised a remarkable water collection and water storage system. Water at Humayma would have made the site a vital stopping point for travellers and some of the ancient collection points are still in use today, a testament to the skill of their builders.

History

Humayma's history begins with the Nabateans. It has been identified with **Auara,** a town which, according to Uranius' *Arabica* was founded by the Nabatean king Aretas III (87–62 BC) in response to an oracle given to his father bidding him seek out a place *auara*, meaning white in Arabic or Syrian. Aretas founded the town where he saw a vision of a man in white riding a white camel and Auara became the only major settlement between Petra and the port of Aila (Aqaba). Situated on a major trade route from the Red Sea to Petra, Auara must have prospered from the passage of traders and caravans through the Nabatean kingdom. When the Romans created the province of Arabia in 106, Auara became an important station on the Via Nova Traiana; it is mentioned in Ptolemy's list of settlements in Arabia Petraea (early 2C) and in the Peutinger Table, which locates it 20 Roman miles south of Zadagatta (Sadaqa, p 251) and 23 Roman miles north of Praesidio (Khirbet al-Khalde, p 201). These distances are exact. From the Notitia Dignitatum we know that in the late 4C or early 5C Humayma, listed as Haua(r)ae, was garrisoned by the *equites sagitarii indigenae*, a locally recruited unit of mounted cavalry. Clearly it was a prosperous military post in the Byzantine period. In the Beersheba Edict, which lists the annual taxes payable to the dux of Palaestina Tertia, Auara was assessed at 43 gold pieces, the highest sum of any Transjordanian town apart from the large military fortress of 'Udruh (p 251). In 687 Auara was sold to an Islamic dignitary, who constructed a fortified residence and it was from here, in the mid-8C that the Abbasids allegedly plotted the overthrow of the Umayyads.

Humayma's **aqueduct** is a masterpiece of Nabatean engineering, a ground level channel made of blocks of yellow marl or white limestone covered with limestone slabs which brought water from three springs to the north-east on the Shara escarpment. The main channel runs for almost 19km to 'Ain al-Qanah; a 7.6km long branch line connected 'Ain al-Jamam and 'Ain ash-Shara. At Humayma the

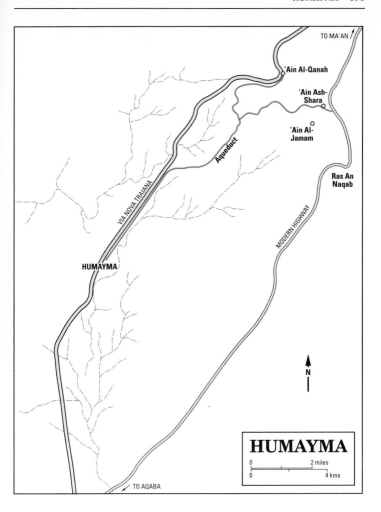

TO MA'AN

'Ain Al-Qanah

'Ain Ash-Shara

'Ain Al-Jamam

Ras An Naqab

VIA NOVA TRAIANA

Aqueduct

MODERN HIGHWAY

HUMAYMA

N

HUMAYMA

0   2 miles
0   4 kms

TO AQABA

aqueduct feeds into **two open reservoirs** of a similar size, one Nabatean, west of the road, and a later Roman reservoir, east of the road in the north-west corner of a large **military camp**. Limited excavations of the camp have cleared the East Gate, flanked by two towers, the south-east angle tower and various sections of wall. The camp's capacity has been estimated at around 2000 infantry or a large cavalry force.

South-west of the camp are the ruins of an extensive settlement. A **Roman baths complex** excavated south of the Nabatean reservoir has seven rooms

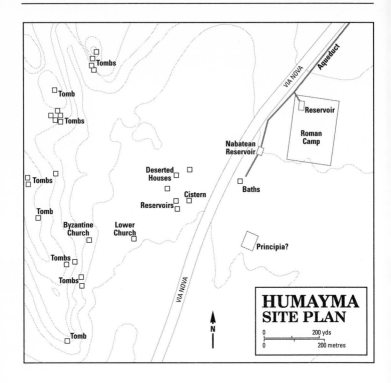

HUMAYMA SITE PLAN

0 _____ 200 yds

0 _____ 200 metres

including a well-preserved vaulted furnace room built of bricks and a caldarium and laconium (sweat room) with hypocaust system, plastered walls and vertical flues with piping. South-west of the baths, an **underground cistern** with a small square opening is still used by local bedouin; nearby are **two reservoirs**, of which one has been renovated for modern use, while the other still retains its original roofing arches. Both were probably built by the Nabateans and were fed from a large run-off field north of the settlement. Excavations north of the reservoirs where there are deserted modern houses among the ruins of the ancient ones have revealed a complex of structures including an apsed room which was probably part of a Byzantine church. To the south-west the so-called **Lower Church** has been cleared. It is a standard three-apsed basilica with a nave and two side-aisles, separated by arched piers. On several of the square paving stones were crosses marking burials. Three steps lead up to the raised chancel which has slots for the pulpit. In the south-west corner of the church is a staircase and a niche or cupboard. Around the main building are several ancillary rooms; in one, sections of water channel are reused upside down as steps to an upper storey.

Nabatean cuttings and **necropoleis** with rock-cut shaft tombs in use from 1C–6C dot the countryside around Humayma. On a large sandstone outcrop to the west which is easily climbed, there are water channels, a cistern, a stone circle and several graves including a multiple shaft tomb. On the eastern slope is another **Byzantine church**.

Wadi Rum

Return to the highway and continue down to 10km **Quweira**. Here, just north of the rock of Jebel Quweira, in the grounds of the boy scouts centre, are the remains of a Roman fort, now almost buried in the sands and a renovated reservoir, cut from the rock, which may be Nabatean. 10km south of Quweira bear left for **Wadi Rum**. After 17.5km fork right and continue another 12km for Rum village and the resthouse.

■ An entrance fee to the reserve of 1JD, payable at the **resthouse**, entitles you to a tea or coffee. There is **camping** only at Rum: two-man tents with mattress and blankets cost 8JD a night and there is a good shower block with hot water behind the resthouse. All meals and drinks can be had at the resthouse, while basic provisions may be bought in the shop at Rum and fresh food at Quweirah. There is also a basic campsite with a well at Abu Aina 3.5km south of here. If you want to appreciate the beauty of Rum in peace and quiet you can find yourself a campsite further away, but keep an eye out for scorpions and the odd snake—according to T.E. Lawrence, local treatment for snakebite was 'to bind up the part with snake-skin plaster, and read chapters of the Koran to the sufferer till he died'! Make sure you leave no litter. The desert is a fragile ecosystem and a particular scourge in Jordan is the vast amount of plastic litter which is both ugly and dangerous to wildlife. The resthouse is comfortable and well-run, but can get very busy with coachloads of day-trippers.

■ A daily bus leaves for Petra at 6.30 am returning later in the morning. Pickups and drivers can be hired for trips around the area, but visitors should be aware that not all have the four-wheel drive which is recommended for desert-driving, particularly for remoter areas. Check prices beforehand, they are posted up in the resthouse. Tourist police and a representative of the Ministry of Tourism can also help with information. Trips with four-wheel drive vehicles on the Aqaba-Rum desert road here can be arranged from Aqaba by the resthouse management (Tel: 03-313930) among others, and it is also possible to arrange five day camel treks from Petra.

■ Two good guides to walks and climbs in Rum have been written by Tony Howard—the smaller one, on sale in Jordan, is particularly good for walks. Climbers may wish to contact Sabah Atieeq via the resthouse. He is a qualified guide and also organises camping trips.

Many visitors catch only a fleeting glance of Rum en route for Petra or Aqaba, but if you have the time and can get beyond the rather dismal village at Rum and the well run, but often crowded resthouse, this spectacular place certainly warrants it. Rum is the best known of the valleys, but there are equally beautiful landscapes north of Disi and in outlying areas. Rum is famous to British visitors as the setting of David Lean's epic film *Lawrence of Arabia*, but it has a long history. There are rocks covered in Thamudic inscriptions (p 199) here, a Nabatean temple and graffiti as well as later Islamic inscriptions. Huge, weathered rocks rear impressively out of the sands and stretch down avenues of wide sandy valleys as far as the eye can see. In *Seven Pillars of Wisdom*, Lawrence wrote: 'Of Azraq, as of Rumm, one said *Numen inest*. Both were magically haunted ... Rumm was vast and echoing and God-like ... even the unsentimental Howeitat had told me it was beautiful.' The dramatic combination of massive rocks and canyons, sandstones over basalt and granite weathered into weird shapes and colours surrounded by desert sands, rivals Petra in magnificence. After rain, the scrubby bushes are briefly green and in spring you may find the desert blooming. Broom and thorn bushes grow in the sand with tamarisk and other shrubs, many of them being used by the Bedouin for food, soap, teas and medicine.

LAWRENCE AND THE ARAB REVOLT

The name of T.E. Lawrence is inextricably linked with the Arab Revolt from Turkish domination during the First World War, in which the country that is today Jordan played an important part. The uprising, which began in the Holy City of Mecca in June 1916, was encouraged by the British who feared a Turkish attack on the Suez Canal and thought this might distract them. The real strength of the somewhat unorthodox Arab forces lay in their use of the 'hit and run' tactics more typical of a guerrilla army. The Turkish line of communications stretched thousands of miles south into the Hijaz and was vulnerable to attack. By blowing bridges and cutting the railway line the Arabs provided crucial support for the British fighting under Allenby in Palestine.

Lawrence has become such a legendary figure, particularly since the release of David Lean's film *Lawrence of Arabia*, that it is hard to distinguish between myth and reality. He himself was keen to play down his role in the Revolt, refusing decorations and even a knighthood from King George V who apparently took no offence, although the Queen, according to Lawrence, was 'very huffy!' It was only after the war, and largely thanks to the American journalist Lowell Thomas, that he became famous.

His background made him ideal for a posting in military intelligence in Cairo when the war broke out: he had gained a First at Oxford with a thesis on Crusader castles and started work as an archaeologist at the excavation of Carchemish. Here he learnt skills which were later to stand him in good stead: fluent Arabic and the use of dynamite in excavating—a technique not advocated by modern archaeologists! While mapping for the Palestine Exploration Fund Survey he acquired a knowledge of southern Palestine and of geology, which is revealed in his vivid descriptions in *Seven Pillars of Wisdom*, particularly of Wadi Rum, which was one his favourite places. In Cairo he worked on information reports, mapping, analysis and policy. Later he was appointed a liaison officer between the British and Feisal, son of the Emir of Mecca, and subsequently adopted Arab dress at Feisal's request to ensure his acceptance among the Arabs.

Aqaba fell to the Arabs in July 1917, coinciding with General Allenby's arrival to take command in Palestine and the progression northwards of the British front there. Allenby entered Jerusalem in December 1917. At a later stage the fortress of Azraq served Lawrence as winter headquarters and it was here that a force of a thousand Arabs met in September/October 1918 to launch the vital attack on the railway at Dera'a, junction of the tracks from Palestine, the south and Damascus.

The line was cut, Allenby's forces routed the Turks and Damascus finally fell in October.

From the beginning Lawrence had been committed to the Arab cause, with the vision of a Pan-Arab movement liberating the region from Ottoman oppression. This, however, was to cause him great torment, as he frequently felt torn between two masters. Nonetheless, his vast knowledge of the Arab peoples and cultures as well as his work in British intelligence made him a respected figure on both sides. There is no doubt that he played a crucial part in the planning and implementation of many dangerous raids throughout the campaign, often riding huge distances on camel across the desert with the Bedouin. Perhaps his acheivements are best summed up in his own words: 'the dreamers of the day are dangerous men, for they may act their dream with open eyes to make it possible. This I did.'

After the war Lawrence worked to ensure an honourable solution was found to Arab demands for independence—no easy task given the need to juggle with French colonial ambitions in Syria, Arab nationalism and Zionism in Palestine and the British position on Palestine. As an adviser on Arab affairs to Churchill at the Colonial Office, he pushed for Mesopotamia to be made an Arab kingdom under Feisal. Feisal's brother Abdullah (grandfather of King Hussein) later became ruler and then King of Transjordan. Lawrence then enlisted in the RAF as a private. On 13 May 1935, at the age of 46, he died in a motorcycle accident.

Possibilities abound for walks and climbs, but take a guide if in any doubt about the way. The mountain across the valley from the resthouse is **Umm Ishrin**. Explanations of the name, which means 'mother of twenty', include the legend of a clever young woman who killed 19 suitors before the twentieth outwitted her and she married him. **Jabal Rum**, the highest peak here at 1754m, lies behind the rest-house: a day can be spent walking around it. A **Nabatean temple** nestles against its slopes a five minute walk from the resthouse, surrounded by other Nabatean buildings. Inscriptions on the temple walls record that it was dedicated to **Allat**, the great goddess of the people of 'Iram'. Probably the temple was built in the early 1C, during the reign of Aretas IV, although some scholars date it much later to the mid-2C. In plan the building resembles other Nabatean sanctuaries such as the Winged Lions' Temple at Petra or the temple at Khirbet Tannur. Entered from the east through a columned portico, the cella has engaged columns around the walls and a small raised shrine in the centre. The columns had moulded bases and were clad in fluted plaster painted red, blue and yellow; coloured geometric designs decorated the walls. Rooms are ranged around the main hall; in the south-west corner was a staircase to the roof and behind the shrine steps led up to a small back entrance. At some point, perhaps in the late 2C or early 3C, the Temple of Allat was taken over by Thamudic tribes and **Thamudic graffiti** some scratched over earlier Nabatean inscriptions, cover the walls and columns.

Rum was on a major caravan route from the Jordanian plateau to South Arabia and important because of its fresh water springs. Neolithic flints, Iron Age pottery and Minaean graffiti of the Hellenistic era show that the springs allowed settlement in the valleys long before the Nabateans arrived. From the modern water tank south of the Temple of Allat a short walk up the hillside on a well-used track brings you to **'Ain ash-Shallaleh**, the 'Spring of the Waterfall', also known as Lawrence's Well. Mint grows all around and scents the air, but the natural beauty is rather marred by a cement wall and modern graffiti. Here was a small Nabatean shrine to Allat; on the rock face are many Nabatean inscriptions and niches, and along the east side of the small wadi runs a Nabatean stone aqueduct which chan-

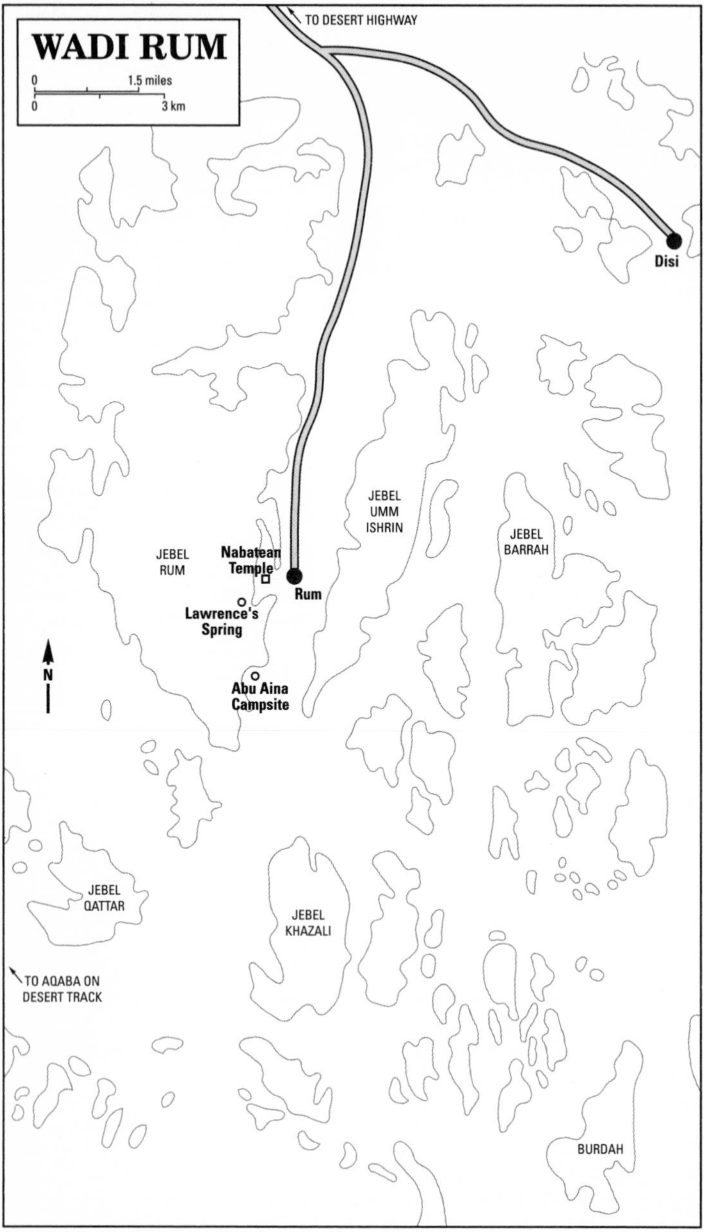

WADI RUM

0 _____ 1.5 miles
0 _____ 3 km

TO DESERT HIGHWAY

Disi

JEBEL
UMM
ISHRIN

JEBEL
BARRAH

JEBEL
RUM

Nabatean
Temple

Rum

Lawrence's
Spring

Abu Aina
Campsite

N

JEBEL
QATTAR

JEBEL
KHAZALI

TO AQABA ON
DESERT TRACK

BURDAH

nelled water from the spring to a reservoir in the valley below.

From here you can walk south to the campsite at **Abu Aina** in approximately one hour keeping at about this level and crossing two cols. Look out for Thamudic inscriptions and drawings of camels along the way. South-east across the valley from Abu Aina is **Jabal Khazali**, its northern face split by a canyon in which are many more Thamudic inscriptions, elongated human figures and pairs of feet. It is possible to clamber some distance into the narrow canyon along a rock ledge.

Thamudic rock drawings

THAMUDIC INSCRIPTIONS

In Wadi Rum and neighbouring valleys, thousands of drawings and graffiti were engraved on rocks by Thamudic tribes from the Arabian desert who probably moved into the region in the early Christian era. Such inscriptions, mostly just personal names, also occur in the Arabian peninsula. The script belongs to the South Semitic group, represented by modern Ethiopic. Associated with the graffiti are simple but charming drawings of animals, particularly camels and ibex, large pairs of feet and stylised human beings with elongated bodies. Hunters on foot, horseback or riding camels wield lances and bows and arrows.

The Thamud first appear in history in 716 BC when with other Arab tribes of North Arabia they were defeated by the Assyrian king Sargon II. At that time they lived between Mecca and Teima. Many centuries later when the Nabateans policed the caravan routes which passed through Rum to Arabia, the nomadic Thamudic tribes had expanded northwards and lived in apparently peaceful symbiosis with their more settled Nabatean cousins. Thamudic graffiti from Rum show that they honoured the same deities: there are several petitions to the Nabatean-Arabian goddess Allat and a few mention the Nabatean god Dushara. When the Romans took over the Nabatean kingdom in 106 they established friendly relations with the Thamudic tribes, who were probably enlisted as *foederati* charged with the defence of certain areas of the Arabian frontier including Wadi Rum. By this time the tribes had united into a federation governed by elders. As a gesture of goodwill and in remuneration for the Thamud's protection of Rome's interests in North Arabia, the Romans sponsored the building of a tribal league sanctuary at Rawwafa in the Hejaz, c 75km south of Tabuk. Inscriptions in Greek and Nabatean record that the temple was dedicated to Marcus Aurelius and Lucius Verus between 166 and 169 under the supervision of the governor of Arabia. In architecture and style it is typically Nabatean, reflecting the acculturation of the Thamud. By the late 4C some of the Thamud were serving as regular auxiliary units in the Roman army; in the Notitia Dignitatum there is reference to the *equites Saraceni Thamudeni*, stationed on the Egyptian frontier.

For those with only an afternoon to spare there are a number of sunset points not too far from the resthouse from which to watch the display of changing colours

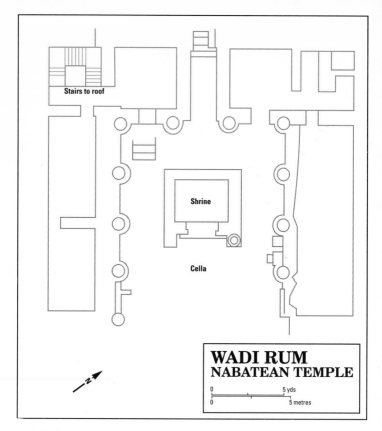

Stairs to roof

Shrine

Cella

WADI RUM
NABATEAN TEMPLE

0   5 yds

0   5 metres

and shadows as the sun goes down. Also in this direction, 8km south of the rest-house, is '**Ain Qattar**, meaning dripping of water, where there is a Nabatean well cut into the rock and fringed with moisture-loving ferns. Half-way there you pass two large boulders with Thamudic drawings on them. Less spoilt than 'Ain Shallaleh, this little oasis where the water seeps out of the rock has palm trees, wild figs and other flowers growing by it.

While there are a number of natural rock bridges at Rum, the highest and most striking is at 16km **Burdah**. The arch itself is visible from the east side of the mountain. A pleasant two- to three-hour scramble up to it starts near the north end of the west side and is fairly well marked by cairns. There are a couple of scrambles along the way, and one slightly exposed move just below the arch, so it is advisable to take a guide and rope with you for this, but well worth the trouble for the stupendous views from the arch.

Other possible excursions include the valleys north of **Disi**. At **Abu al Hawil** you can see the unusual rock-drawn figures, called Buddhas by the locals, or climb the small outcrop of Jabal Saluqi for the panorama and to see the dozens of Thamudic figures drawn on the rocks of the summit. North-east of Disi amid tumbled boulders at the foot of Jabal Amoud there is a a flat slab of rock two metres by one metre, covered with interconnected circles and lines which some suggest may be a map. The rocks around it are covered in Thamudic engravings.

10km south of the Rum junction and not far from the Desert Highway turn left for the remains of the Roman fort of **Khirbet al-Khalde**. To reach it (four-wheel drive needed) head east, skirting a rocky outcrop in the Wadi Yetm and cross the 2km railway. Look for the ruins which lie 2km south on a col and adjacent to the railway whose construction damaged the west towers of the fort. This is ancient **Praesidium** of the Peutinger Table, probably built by the Romans in the 3–4C on a site previously occupied by the Nabateans. Nabatean dressed stone is visible in the rooms on the west. According to the *Notitia Dignitatum*, in the late 4C Praesidium held a garrison of the *cohors quarta Frygum*.

The **entrance** to the rectangular granite fort is in the north wall. Rooms once surrounded the courtyard and are best preserved on the west despite the damage done to the **corner towers** here by the railway which passes only metres away. In places the walls still stand up to 4m. In the north-west corner two doorways at a lower level show very different stone and Nabatean masonry, indications of earlier Nabatean occupation. South of the fort is a smaller associated structure, thought to have been a caravanserai, with an entrance in the north wall and rooms visible all round the walls. Water was piped to the fort from cisterns higher uphill: the stones and sizeable remaining sections of the plaster pipe can be followed uphill from c 20m east of the fort.

RED SEA
The brilliant blue of the sea in the Gulf of Aqaba came as a disappointment to the Crusaders who arrived here on an expedition in 1116 fully expecting to find it red! The Red Sea is renowned for its marine life and the Gulf of Aqaba is no exception. From here scuba diving, snorkelling and other water-sports can be arranged, as can glass-bottom boat trips and a visit to the Aquarium for those who prefer to keep a safe distance from sea-life! Depths in the Gulf sink to 1800m. The best diving is south of the port area where the land falls away very steeply and there are wonderful coral reefs to visit, full of brightly coloured reef fish, sea grasses and corals. One-fifth of the species in the Red Sea are found nowhere else. Diving lessons, excursions and equipment hire can be arranged at the Royal Diving Centre 18km south of the fort and the Aquamarina I Hotel which also offers water-skiing, windsurfing and other water-sports. The Marine Science Centre and Aquarium are 9km south of Aqaba. Pharaoh's Island, also known as the Ile de Graye, is a short boat ride away.

Aqaba

From here the road follows the Wadi Yetm southwards through the mountains which now close in around it until you emerge at Aqaba, Jordan's only seaport. Not surprisingly, given its location at the north-east tip of the Gulf of Aqaba, it has a long history of occupation. Trade and pilgrimage routes over land and by sea led here from Egypt, Arabia and the north. Nowadays it is both a bustling port city and a tourist centre with a fine climate and beaches. The recent opening of the border with Israel has further encouraged tourism. A ferry runs between Aqaba and

Nuweibah in Egypt where you can visit the monastery at **St Catherine's**, built by a Christian from Aqaba. Trips can also be made to Petra and Wadi Rum.

There is a good **museum** (open 8.00–13.00 and 15.00–17.00, closed Tuesdays) in the Visitors Centre near to the **Mamluke fort**, and the open site of **medieval Aila** lies near the beach 1km north of here. Recent excavations have revealed walls of the earlier Byzantine town nearby and further west, in a restricted military zone is **Tell al-Khaleifeh**, once thought to be Solomon's port of Ezion Geber, but now dated only to the 8C BC.

■ Major **hotels**, many with private beaches, line the corniche road in Aqaba. More moderately-priced places are closer to the town centre as are the Post Office, banks, shops and restaurants. The **Tourist Office** by the fort is open 8.00–13.00 and 15.00–sunset. Staff here can help with information on accommodation, travel and tourism. There is a campsite on the way to the Saudi border, just past the public beach. For those wishing to visit **Egypt** on the twice daily ferry to Nuweibah, the Egyptian consulate on Istiqlal St is open daily 9.00–14.00 except Fridays. Visas currently cost 12JD; allow a day for issue. Tickets for the boat must currently be paid for in US dollars. On a note of caution be aware that the ferry is usually crowded and delays are frequent.

■ **Transport**. Taxis run from the Israeli border to 9km Aqaba, check the fare at the Tourist Office there. A bus service is planned for the future. Entry visas can be issued at the border which is open 8.00–18.30 and closed Fri–Sat. From Aqaba there are JETT buses (the JETT bus station is on the beach road), public buses and taxis to Amman, Petra and Rum. Trips can also be arranged to Rum by four-wheel drive on the desert road there. Royal Jordanian (offices at the Holiday International Hotel) have daily flights to and from Amman.

History

Its modern name is an abbreviation of **Aqabat Aila**, the pass of Aila, a reference to the route north to Ma'an through the Wadi Yetm gorge. In the past, however, Aqaba has been called many names, Aila, Haila, Ailana, Elim among others, as conquerors have come and gone, attracted by the fresh water only feet below ground by the shore and by its strategic location on a number of trade and pilgrimage routes.

Tell Maquss, a few kilometres south of the airport is the earliest excavated site in the area. Dating back to the Chalcolithic period, it may have been a secondary copper-processing site, but was abandoned for unknown reasons. Nothing much is known about Bronze Age occupation, but the settlement at **Tell al-Khaleifeh** on the border with Israel, appears to have been occupied 8C–4C BC. Solomon's port of Ezion-Geber must have been somewhere along the coast here: 1 Kings 9:26 describes it as being 'beside Eloth, on the shore of the Red Sea, in the land of Edom', but so far no conclusive evidence has linked it to Tell al-Khaleifeh, for which the earliest date of occupation is the 8C BC. The kingdoms of Judah and Edom were vying for control of the area at this time. Later, it came under Babylonian and then Persian rule. The Nabateans, originally nomads who grew rich on trade, had a presence here as they developed trade routes between the Hijaz, Syria and Egypt. According to both Diodorus and Strabo: 'these Nabateans ... later, by means of rafts, went plundering the vessels of people sailing to Egypt.'

In AD 106 Trajan annexed the Nabatean kingdom and immediately set to

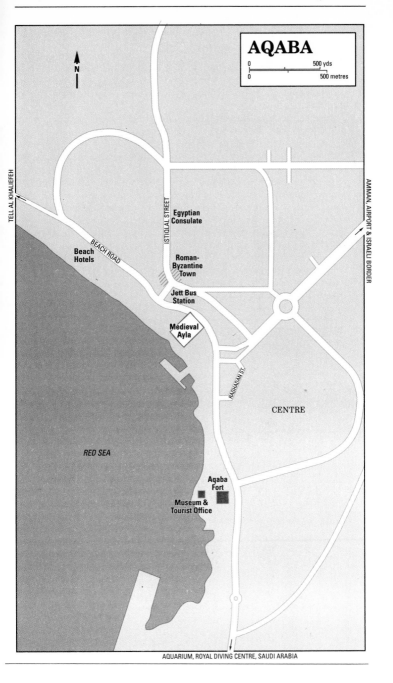

AQABA

| 0 | | 500 yds |
| 0 | | 500 metres |

TELL AL KHALIEFEH

AMMAN, AIRPORT & ISRAELI BORDER

BEACH ROAD

Beach
Hotels

ISTIQLAL STREET

Egyptian
Consulate

Roman-
Byzantine
Town

Jett Bus
Station

Medieval
Ayla

RED SEA

BAGHDADI ST.

CENTRE

Aqaba
Fort

Museum &
Tourist Office

AQUARIUM, ROYAL DIVING CENTRE, SAUDI ARABIA

work building a road from Bostra to Aqaba: *a finibus Syriae usque ad mare rubrum* read the inscriptions of the milestones which marked its length. The very first milestone of the way, now in Aqaba's museum, was found on the beach here. Diocletian's military reforms included the transfer of *Legio X Fretensis* to Ailana from Jerusalem in the late 3C–early 4C. Fragments of the dedicatory plaque from its camp were found near the Egyptian gate of medieval Aila.

A bishop of Aqaba attended the Council of Nicea. Not much has been found of Christian Aila, perhaps because stone from churches was reused in the Islamic town, but two capitals from a Byzantine church now in Amman Archaeological Museum show the soldier saints Theodore and Longinus, the centurion who guarded Christ on the cross. A Byzantine lintel similar to that at Deir 'Ain Abata was also found near the north-east gate of medieval Aila. Much remains under the sands, but recent excavations are bringing some light to bear on this period of Aqaba's history. It is possible that the Ile de Graye was occupied by this time. The Byzantine empire, preoccupied with its struggle against Persia, neglected its southern frontier and alliances and when the Muslims began to push northwards, Aqaba surrendered easily to them, signing a treaty with them in 630 which guaranteed its protection.

In the early Islamic period Aqaba continued to prosper. A new town or *misr* was laid out east of the old town. Comparable in size to the larger Umayyad complexes further north, excavations by the University of Chicago and the Department of Antiquities have unearthed much of the site of medieval Aila, revealing the city walls and a large congregational mosque among other structures. It appears to have been occupied from the 7C until the 11C when earthquake damage and tribal raiding overwhelmed the weakened Fatimid empire. In 1024 the *haj* was attacked, the pilgrims robbed and sold as slaves. Muqaddasi, the 10C Arab geographer, describes it as 'the port of Palestine and the storehouse of the Hijaz'. It was also, with its abundance of fresh water, an important stop on the *haj* route from Egypt.

No sooner had the Crusaders arrived in Jerusalem than they began looking east, both to secure their frontiers and in an attempt to control the trade passing to Syria and Egypt from Arabia. In 1116 Baldwin I led an expedition south founding castles at al Wu'eira in Petra and at Aqaba. No clear evidence remains of any building they may have done in Aqaba and the fortifications on the Ile de Graye, once thought to have been Crusader work, are more likely to have been built by the Muslims in the 12C. The Crusader presence in Aqaba was always a threat to the Islamic world and Saladin took the town from them in 1171. Reynald of Chatillon transported boats here in 1182–83 and briefly terrorised shipping on the Red Sea, but these and other exploits of his were counterproductive. The Muslims retaliated under Saladin, ultimately winning back even Jerusalem.

Writing in the 14C, Abu al Fida mentions a stronghold on the shore which may have been a predecessor to the present Mamluke fort here, built under the penultimate Mamluke Sultan. Later work on it was carried out under the Ottomans, when it was still an important pilgrimage stop. According to the 19C visitors Linant and Laborde the caravans would stay three days in Aqaba, but the opening up of new and faster routes by sea through the Suez canal and by railway from Damascus eventually sounded its death knell and the town dwindled into obscurity.

Aqaba was garrisoned with Ottoman troops during the First World War, presenting a potential threat to the British army in Egypt who were therefore quick to support the Arab Revolt which began in Mecca in 1916. Aqaba was a key target and it fell to the Arab forces on 6 July 1917—they had surprised the Turks by attacking from the north. The Sherif of Mecca subsequently spent six months here. Since then it has developed apace as the only Jordanian port and as a growing tourist centre.

Between the **Mamluke fort** and the sea is the attractive building which houses the Tourist Office, Department of Antiquities and the **Museum**. Some of the collection is being exhibited in Chicago, but is due to return shortly and there is still plenty to see including the Koranic inscription from the Egyptian Gate of Aila. Aqaba has always thrived on commerce: this is illustrated in the museum collection by the foreign pottery and coins found here. **Room 1** holds a collection of lamps, some of soapstone, Samarra ware and Chinese pottery and a capital carved from a block of coral. In a corner of the second room is the first milestone of the Via Nova, its inscription still clear: 'The Emperor Caesar, son of the divine Nerva ... reduced Aqaba to a province and opened and built this new road from the limits of Syria to the Red Sea, thanks to Caius Claudius Severus.' The section of fresco is from the Pavilion Building at Aila. **Room 3** contains various pieces of Coptic glazed wares from Egypt and coins from Iraq, Ethiopia and Egypt—evidence of the extent of trade. An 8C pot with two crosses on the base shows that there was still a Christian population in the town at the time. A Byzantine capital in the fourth room was later reused in the mosque. There is also a Byzantine inscribed lintel, a smaller capital with a cross and some pieces of lustre ware.

Just before leaving the museum on the left is the 'House of Sheikh Hussein bin Ali', the Sherif of Mecca, great-grandfather of King Hussein, who spent six months living here after the war. These rooms hold a collection of rifles, copper and silver bowls, coffee pots and mills, *mansaf* plates, embroidered dresses, harnesses and a camel saddle.

Behind the museum is the square **fort**, open daily till sunset. It is dated by inscription to the reign of the penultimate Mamluke Sultan, Qansawh el-Ghawri (1501–16) who, according to the Egyptian historian Ibn Iyas 'repaired the road to al-Aqaba ... where he built a khan with towers flanking its gates'. According to a second inscription found here, the Ottomans carried out some rebuilding in the time of Murat III (1574–95). The north-west tower was destroyed by shelling from British gunboats in the First World War. Inside it becomes clear that this is as much a caravanserai as a fort. Léon de Laborde, who stayed here in 1828, reported that there were only two ancient canon in the landward towers, none in the other two and that the gunner had converted the ruined mosque into a shop!

The projecting entrance, flanked by **semi-circular towers** each with an inscribed roundel including the *Bismillah* ('In the name of God', the customary introduction to prayer and a favourite calligraphic text), had a round arch which was later narrowed. The **machicolation** overhead now supports a decorative panel bearing the Hashemite arms. Inside the cross-vaulted **vestibule**, a lengthy inscription runs round the wall from right to left surmounted by roundels bearing the date AH 993. The main inscription, obscured at the beginning and end by later building work to narrow the entrance, reads on the right '... blessed and auspicious fort our Lord the ruling Sultan al-Malik al-Ashraf abu al-Nasar Qansawh al-Ghawri, Sultan of Islam and the Muslims, slayer (of the unbelievers and the polytheists)' and continues on the left 'reviver of justice in the universe ... the sultan ... may God glorify his victories through Mohammed and his house! This blessed fort was the work of the amir Khayir Bey al-'Ala ['] i the builder ... dated [in the year] ...'. The date given is unclear, it is either 1504/5 or 1514/5 (AH 920).

Pass under a second **machicolation** and narrow passageway with doors right and left to the second, domed **vestibule** and enter the large **courtyard**. There were rooms all round the walls, but those on the east are largely destroyed. Some restoration has been undertaken, particularly of the west wall where older alterations like the blocking of an arch are also visible. There is a **mosque** in the south wall. The hexagonal south-west tower is domed inside, whereas the two towers along the east wall are circular and bear some external decoration. On the north-east tower a carved square panel with a geometrical border contains a rosette and is surmounted by two leopards around a palm tree while the south-east tower has a better-preserved rosette also in a geometrical border. When Sir Richard Burton visited Aqaba on an expedition to Midian he reported that all the towers were round except 'the new polygon to the north-west'.

MEDIEVAL ISLAMIC AILA

Opposite the Miramar Hotel 1km north on the beach road is the site of medieval Islamic Aila where a team of archaeologists from the University of Chicago together with the Department of Antiquities have been excavating since 1986. The open site, in the sands near the shore, has good information boards describing the various sections. Four gates to the 140 x 170m city founded east of the earlier Roman-Byzantine site, have now been found, christened the Egyptian, the Syrian, the Hijaz and the Sea Gate. A wadi runs through the site, possibly along an earthquake fault. The ground water is very close to the surface here and has prevented excavations from going deeper in a number of places.

Begin at the **Egyptian Gate** on the north-west side. This is particularly interesting to look at because the changes it has undergone reflect the history of the city. Beginning as a round-arched gate 3m wide in the very early Islamic period before the Umayyads came to power, it was flanked by two projecting **semicircular towers**, later used as storerooms. The Koranic verse, known as the Ayat al-Kursi or Throne verse and still seen in Arab homes today, was inscribed in Kufic script over the gate, probably in the 8C. Later the arch was narrowed by the addition of a central column, the stump of which is still there. In the 9–10C, during the Abbasid period, the ground level rose and shops were added narrowing the street and a smaller pointed arch was built. Finally, as the city declined, the entire gate was blocked, leaving only a small drain-pipe exit.

The 2.5m **city wall**, made of stone with a rubble infill, was punctuated by **semicircular interval towers** and **corner towers**. Shops were built inside the gate narrowing the street and there were buildings against the walls. The style of earlier buildings is finer, with much reuse in later periods before a final reversion to mudbrick. Four axial streets divided the city into quarters and at the very centre is the large **Pavilion Building,** named after the discovery that at an earlier stage a structure with four large central arches constituted a tetrapylon pavilion structure. The present building is late Abbasid/Fatimid period rebuilt over an earlier building. The entrance steps on the north-west lead into a **courtyard** with a cistern and rooms around. There were also stairs up to the first floor. The **baths** were in the north corner while the west corner room was found to have been decorated with a wall painting. Now in the museum, it consisted of floral and geometric designs in red and black paint. Kufic graffiti had also been scratched here. Next to this room along the south-west wall is a central room which, in an earlier phase, had a large **arch** in the external wall, traces of which can still be seen. Remains of plaster floor and

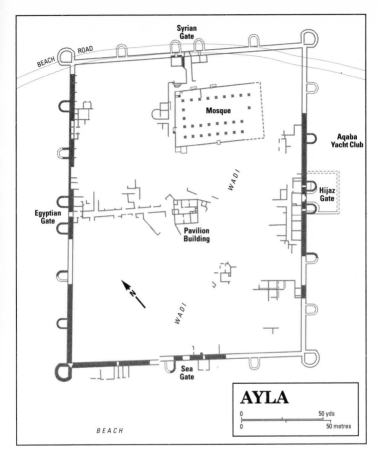

AYLA

another arch in the south-east wall suggest that this was once a pavilion and, judging from its central position, an important building in the early town.

30m north-east of the Pavilion Building are the remains of what was at first called the Large Enclosure and is now thought to have been the town's **congregational mosque**. Rebuilding has made this a very complex structure to understand, but the original building probably dates to the mid-7C and was rebuilt in the Abbasid era after an earthquake. Three **entrance platforms** lead to a **peristyle courtyard**. The rectangular design may be comparable to that of the Damascus mosque, with the double row of columns on the south-west side indicating a covered hall. The discovery of a niche, possibly the *mihrab*, in the south-west wall was confusing because it should face south towards Mecca. However, other cases of early mosques having incorrectly oriented *qibla* walls are known. A double row of columns on the south-west side face a single row of columns opposite. Glass tesserae found here suggest that wall mosaics decorated the mosque and a further platform in the south-west corner may have been the minaret base. The 8–9C Islamic school based here signifies Aqaba's importance at the time.

Behind the mosque and running under the beach road the **Syrian Gate** is just visible. Beyond it and under the hotel, there may have been a cemetery. A hoard of gold dinars minted in North Africa and presumably belonging to a merchant or pilgrim were found nearby. Excavations are underway at the **Hijaz Gate**, located within the grounds of the Aqaba Yacht Club, by its north-west boundary fence. Close to the shore the sea gate has also been excavated. A later square flanking tower to the right of the gate was built over a semi-circular base. Further west the outline of a circular **corner tower** is clear.

Recent excavations 200m north-west of here behind the JETT offices and garage, have so far revealed a 50m section of city wall with a projecting square tower from the earlier Roman-Byzantine city. Further domestic structures of this period, some with stone walls, others of mud-brick have emerged in the excavation trenches which spread over an area dissected by two streets. A trench near the beach road exposed a Nabatean cemetery where only the skeletons of children have been found.

Along the corniche past the hotels and the royal palace, **Tell Al-Khaleifeh** is some 500m from the sea in a restricted military zone by the border with Israel and cannot be visited at the moment. Excavated by Glueck between 1938 and 1940, the site has suffered the ravages of time. All structures were of mud brick and there were two main architectural phases; in the earlier phase a casemate fortification wall surrounded an open courtyard in the middle of which was a large building with three square rooms to the north and three larger rectangular rooms to the south. In Phase II, after the casemate fortress had been destroyed by fire, the settlement was considerably enlarged and surrounded by a double wall with a dry moat in between. Access was through a four-chambered gate to the south. Inside the area was filled with buildings, including the old six-room building, now in the north-west corner of the settlement. This earlier building is still identifiable, although it is very ruined. South and east of it are the foundations of buildings of the later phase. The fortification walls and southern part of the settlement, including the gate area, have disappeared beneath later diggings and shifting sand.

Glueck tentatively identified Tell al-Khaleifeh with Solomon's port of Ezion Geber on the Red Sea (1 Kings 9:26), which would place it in the 10C. Recently this identification has been challenged, because although dating Phase I of the site is difficult, pottery from Phase II is clearly 8C–early 6C BC Edomite ware. Small amounts of copper slag suggest some industrial activity. Edomite stamp impressions on some vessels which read 'belonging to Qaus'anal, servant of the King' have been dated to the late 7C or early 6C BC and there is scanty evidence of later occupation at the site through to the 4C BC. So it seems that Tell al-Khaleifeh was predominantly an Edomite settlement and Solomon's Ezion Geber must be sought elsewhere.

PETRA

In the heart of southern Jordan's Shara mountains lies **Petra**, capital of the Nabateans, who created in their lovely sandstone valleys a city unique in the ancient world. This remote desert stronghold with its extraordinary coloured rocks and carved façades has caught the imagination of travellers since it was 'rediscovered' in 1812, and despite tens of thousands of visitors a year it still retains its charm and mystery. Few will forget that first breathtaking sight of the 'Treasury' glowing in the sunlight on emerging from the gloom of the gorge which leads into the city; and it is but a short walk off the beaten track to avoid the crowds. To see Petra's main monuments at least two or three days are needed; spend longer to explore more outlying mountains and valleys or just to relax and enjoy the atmosphere and beauty of the site.

- **Information.** Tourist information and local guides are available from the Petra Visitors Centre (open 7.00–19.00 Summer; 7.00–16.00 Winter; tel: 03-336020/60), near the site entrance. For longer hikes with overnight camping in the Petra and Wadi Araba areas, Haroun Awad al Bdul is an excellent guide. Camel treks of two or more days can be arranged by Awadh Salama. Ask for Haroun at the Visitors' Centre or in the Bdul village 4km from Wadi Musa where Awadh may also be contacted. Trekkers should bring their own sleeping bags. For some areas at cooler times of year a tent is also needed.

- **Accommodation.** There is rapid building of new hotels and guest houses in and near Wadi Musa, the small town outside the Petra valleys, to cater for the growing number of visitors. Book beforehand and reconfirm if possible as demand often exceeds supply. Most expensive is the *Petra Forum*, with all facilities including swimming pool and conveniently close to the site entrance. Alongside is the *Petra Resthouse*, recently acquired by the Petra Forum. More modest hotels nearby include the *Edom*, *Petra Palace*, *Flowers*, and *Sunset*, with a large *Mövenpick* hotel under construction. There are several hotels and guesthouses in Wadi Musa centre and above the town near Moses' Spring. All hotels have restaurants and there are a few simple places to eat in town including the clean and friendly *Maroosh Restaurant*. Alcohol is expensive and only available in the larger hotels. Along the road from Wadi Musa to Ras an-Naqb more hotels are springing up; at 12km Tayba the old village has been tastefully restored and converted into the charming *Taybat Zaman* hotel complex with all facilities including craft shops.

- **Post Offices and Banks.** Near the roundabout in the town centre is the main Post Office and also a Housing Bank with exchange facilities (open 8.00–14.00 and 15.30–17.00 every day except Friday). There are bank facilities (open every day 8.00–12.00) and a Post Office (open every day 8.00–17.00) in the Visitors Centre; most hotels change foreign currency, the larger ones accept travellers' cheques.

- **Transport**. A JETT bus leaves Amman for Petra from the Abdali office 06.30 daily (journey time about 3hrs 30mins) and returns 16.00 from the Petra

Visitors' Centre. Slower local buses leave Amman twice daily between 09.00 and 13.00 (as soon as they have enough passengers) from Al-Wahdat Bus Station, Sharq al-Awsat Circle and return 06.00–07.00 and 13.00 from Wadi Musa usually via the Visitors' Centre. A Servis taxi leaves for Amman 05.00–06.00 daily. Two buses a day (06.30 and 07.30) leave Wadi Musa for Aqaba and return from the bus station near Aqaba Park between 09.00 and 12.00. Several buses a day run to and from Ma'an, one or two buses go to Shobak, and once a day at 06.30 a bus goes to Wadi Rum (journey time 2hrs) returning between 09.30 and 11.00. Always check timetables locally as they vary; Wadi Musa Bus Station is near the roundabout. Long distance by yellow taxi is much more expensive (prices are subject to discussion) and taxis will take you around Wadi Musa and the Petra region. Taxis: 1000 Taxi Service (next to Rock City Hotel, Tel: 336777); Petra Taxi (near Safe House Supermarket, tel: 336600).

■ **Shopping.** Wadi Musa has the usual souvenir shops—postcards, books, jewellery, sand bottles, clothing—and there are many stalls in Petra. Food stores, pharmacy (tel: 336444) and other shops are in the town centre.

History
Around 11,000 BC Stone Age man was already exploiting the abundant natural resources of the Petra region, particularly wild goats, and by 7000 BC some of the world's earliest farmers were living in a walled village at Beidha, cultivating cereals and collecting nuts and fruits. But Petra really came to prominence in the 7C BC when the Edomites settled on Umm al-Biyara and other mountain strongholds and built a town at Tawilan above 'Ain Musa in the hills to the north. Subject to Assyria, Babylonia, and then Persia, Edom in the 3C BC became the nucleus of an Arab state, the Nabatean kingdom, its capital at Petra. Originally from North Arabia, the **Nabateans** are first mentioned by the 1C BC historian Diodorus, who relates that in 312 BC Antigonus the One-Eyed sent his general Athenaeus against 'the land of the Arabs who are called Nabateans', at that time a nomadic people who raised cattle and sheep and could survive for long periods in the desert where they created a network of secret underground reservoirs. Athenaeus attacked a certain strong, though unwalled rock, perhaps the great massif of Umm al-Biyara at Petra, where the Nabateans had left their valuables, elders, women and children while celebrating a festival, killed some of the Arabs there and made off with vast quantities of frankincense, myrrh and silver. Some 150 years later the Nabateans had settled and Petra was the capital of an organised state.

On a branch road of the King's Highway, the great south–north route from Arabia to Syria, and at a point where the mountain ridge is pierced by a fault permitting east–west traffic to the Mediterranean ports of Gaza and Rhinocolura, Petra was ideally situated for trade and commerce. Furthermore it benefited from several fresh water springs. While still nomadic the Nabateans engaged in trade and it was from trade that Petra grew rich: metals, dyes, bitumen from the Dead Sea which went to Egypt for the mummification process; silks from India and China; and above all spices from Arabia—balsam, myrrh and especially frankincense. Smoked on every altar of the civilised world the quantities of frankincense consumed were enormous and the Nabateans controlled the routes from the Yemen, the sole source of world supply. With the wealth thus gained they embellished their capital city with splendid monuments, watercourses and gardens. Strabo records the impressions of Athenodorus who visited Petra at its zenith, in the late 1C BC: a cosmopolitan city with Romans and other foreigners mingling with the local inhabitants who lived in luxurious villas and a 'democratic' monarch who dwelt in a 'great house'.

The Nabateans, who used a distinctive form of Aramaic, have left few inscriptions. A list of kings beginning in the mid-2C BC has been reconstructed largely from coin evidence; the greatest was Aretas IV (9 BC–AD 40/44), 'the lover of his people', whose daughter was married to Herod Antipas. When Herod sent her packing because of his passion for the notorious Herodias (his niece and Philip the Tetrarch's wife) Aretas retaliated by launching an invasion to punish Herod and won a major victory. Another Herod, 'the Great', himself half Nabatean on his mother's side, had several military clashes with Aretas' predecessors Obodas II (30–9 BC) and Malichus I (62–30 BC). Throughout the 1C BC and 1C AD Petra prospered and the Nabateans were faithful allies of Rome. During the reign of Malichus II (40/44–70), however, the Romans occupied the Nabatean Red Sea port of Leuke Kome and began to divert the Arabian trade away from Petra to their own ports on the Egyptian side of the Red Sea. Rabbel II (70–106) recognised the consequences of changing trade patterns and moved his capital to Bostra in the Hauran. On Rabbel's death the Romans took over the Nabatean kingdom and the emperor Trajan made Bostra the capital of his new Provincia Arabia. Petra went into graceful decline, but was honoured by Trajan with the title metropolis and at least one Roman governor, Sextius Florentinus, elected to be buried there rather than at Bostra. Petra was a bishopric in the Byzantine period, but under Islam the city was virtually abandoned. Two Crusader forts show that in the 12C Petra was still an important stop on strategic caravan routes, but after the 13C, when Sultan Baybars passed through on his way to Karak, historical records cease. Petra was lost to the western world until rediscovered in 1812 by the Swiss traveller Jean-Louis Burckhardt, who found the inhabitants of Wadi Musa suspicious and unfriendly, but managed to see some of the antiquities which he aptly describes as 'amongst the most curious remains of ancient art'.

WADI MUSA

Petra really begins on entering Wadi Musa from the east, where a small white domed building by the roadside houses **'Ain Musa** (Moses' Spring), which provides water for the town. According to tradition this is where Moses, known locally as the great white magician, struck the rock and water gushed forth to slake the thirst of the Israelites (Num. 20) but it is difficult to match the location with the biblical account. **Wadi Musa** (Moses' Valley) cuts steeply through the town of the same name, formerly called Elji, home of the Liyatne tribe whose old stone houses, now deserted, cluster among neglected terraces down in the valley. Across the valley are the remains of an important Edomite settlement, **Tawilan**, in a commanding position overlooking the Petra mountains. Pottery, stone vessels, metal objects and beautiful gold jewellery were found at Tawilan; now only house foundations are visible in the excavation trenches. Much of modern Wadi Musa is built over a Nabatean settlement; there are many reused Nabatean blocks in the old houses, and in the lower part of the town up a road on the right past the Sunset Hotel a fenced area encloses **Nabatean kilns** where much pottery was unearthed. Nabatean pottery is among the finest in antiquity; the best is eggshell thin and deli-

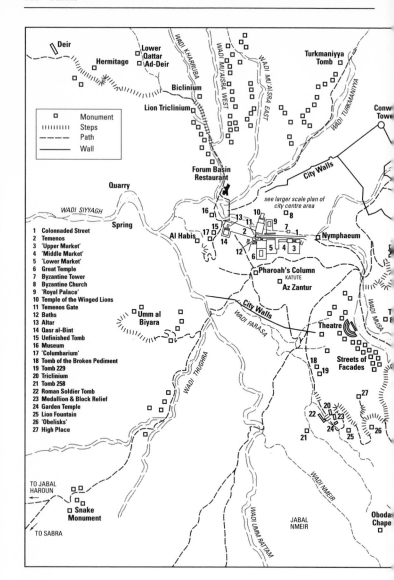

Deir

Lower Qattar
Hermitage   Ad-Deir

Biclinium

Lion Triclinium

	Monument
:::::::	Steps
- - - -	Path
——	Wall

Turkmaniyya Tomb

Conw Towe

Forum Basin Restaurant

Quarry

WADI SIYYAGH

Spring

1 Colonnaded Street
2 Temenos
3 'Upper Market'
4 'Middle Market'
5 'Lower Market'
6 Great Temple
7 Byzantine Tower
8 Byzantine Church
9 'Royal Palace'
10 Temple of the Winged Lions
11 Temenos Gate
12 Baths
13 Altar
14 Qasr al-Bint
15 Unfinished Tomb
16 Museum
17 'Columbarium'
18 Tomb of the Broken Pediment
19 Tomb 229
20 Triclinium
21 Tomb 258
22 Roman Soldier Tomb
23 Medallion & Block Relief
24 Garden Temple
25 Lion Fountain
26 'Obelisks'
27 High Place

see larger scale plan of city centre area

City Walls

Al Habis

Nymphaeum

Pharoah's Column
KATUTE
Az Zantur

Umm al Biyara

City Walls

WADI FARASA

Theatre

Streets of Facades

WADI THUGHRA

TO JABAL HAROUN

Snake Monument

TO SABRA

WADI NMEIR

JABAL NMEIR

WADI UMM RATTAM

Oboda Chape

cately decorated in brown or black on a terracotta background. Not far from the kilns, beside the Flowers Hotel, is a large **Nabatean reservoir** which collected water from the Wadi Musa area before it was channelled further into the Petra valleys.

■ Petra is entered through a gate near the Visitors' Centre where the ticket office is also located. Prices are high: currently 1 day JD20, 2 days JD25 and 3 days JD30.

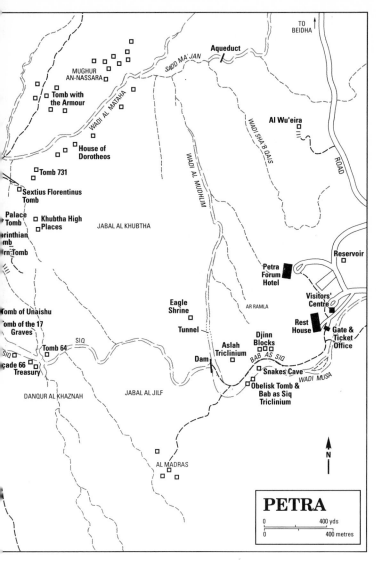

PETRA

0   400 yds

0   400 metres

The site is open from 7.00 or earlier until sunset. At the time of writing (although the system may change) you can ride a horse from the gate to the entrance to the Siq—this must be paid for (JD7 per return trip) in addition to the entrance fee. Recently the Ministry of Tourism has banned riding through the Siq to protect the monuments and prevent accidents as growing numbers of tourists enter the site through the narrow defile. Walking is a better option because you can stop to see the many interesting monuments on the way—from the gate to the Treasury it is an easy 2km walk. If you do take a horse and wish to return on horseback, note the horse's number and agree the return time with its owner. At the end of the return trip, or the outward trip if you only wish to ride one way, you are supposed to 'tip' a further JD3.

Djinn blocks at Petra

BAB AS-SIQ

Following the Wadi Musa a broad path runs through the area known as **Bab as-Siq** (Gate of the Siq) with several monuments along the watercourse and side valleys. Round the first bend, past a tomb with a simple crowstep façade, three huge cubes of stone come into view. Known as **Djinn blocks** because the locals believed they were the work of 'djinn' or spirits, they were probably funerary monuments; the middle one has two shaft graves inside. Explore the small side valleys for various tombs, water systems and cult niches and clamber higher to look over the beautiful moonscape of **Ar-Ramla** area. Opposite the Djinn blocks are three rounded rocks with caves; on the first is an obelisk in relief. Such obelisks, known as **nefesh** or 'spirit' stelae, were carved in memory of the dead whose names may be written below. There are two obelisks in the entrance passage to a cave on the same side c 20m further on, which has 12 shaft graves in the chamber. On the west wall are carved a horse with bridle and rider and two snakes attacking an animal. Appropriate in funerary context, serpents are powerful earth symbols, guardians and protectors, representing rebirth and renewal as they slough their skin.

Just beyond this tomb is the first major complex of Nabatean monuments, the

Obelisk Tomb and **Bab as-Siq Triclinium**, with associated **bilingual inscription** in large letters on the opposite side of the wadi. In Nabatean this reads: 'This is the burial place which 'Abdmank son of 'Akayus son of Shullay son of 'Utaih has chosen ... to build a tomb, for himself, for his successors and the successors of his [successors], for ever after: [he has done this in] his lifetime, in year ... of Malichus.' Below is a two-line summary in Greek: 'Abdomanchos son of Achaios has made the [funerary] monument for himself and his children.' The monuments date to either Malichus I (62–30 BC) or Malichus II (AD 40/44–70), probably the latter. Unique in Petra, the tomb derives its name from the four obelisks on the façade, perhaps representing the spirits of the dead within, flanking an eroded figure in a niche. Inside are loculi and shaft graves. Below the Obelisk Tomb and slightly off centre but carved at the same time is the Bab as-Siq Triclinium, a chamber with three benches for banquets in honour of the dead. In the rounded hills opposite are several caves, tombs and cisterns, and a group of 14 cult niches near the **Aslah Triclinium**, famous for the early Nabatean inscription on the back wall which reads: 'These are the halls and cistern made by Aslah son of Aslah, ... for Dushara, god of Mankatu, during the reign of Obodat, King of the Nabateans, son of Aretas, King of the Nabateans, in his first year.' Obodas, son of Aretas, ruled from 96/92 –86 BC.

Nabatean Kings

Aretas I c 168 BC	Malichus I 62–30 BC
[?Rabbel I]	Obodas II 30–9 BC
Aretas II c 100–96/92 BC	Aretas IV 9 BC–AD 40/44
Obodas I 96/92–86 BC	Malichus II AD 40/44–70
Aretas III Philhellenos 86–62 BC	Rabbel II AD 70–106

Just before the Siq the path rises over a modern **dam** where c AD 50 the Nabateans built a dam to deflect the flood waters of the Wadi Musa northwards through a tunnel and around Al-Khubtha mountain ensuring that the Siq was open all year as the main entrance to the city. Carved on the rocks across the wadi, bridged in Nabatean times as it is today, were a series of **'nefesh' stelae**, one of which commemorates a man who lived at Raqam but died and was buried at Garshu (Jarash). Josephus refers to Raqam as the capital of Arabia, hence it was almost certainly the Nabatean name for Petra. A solitary **djinn block** overlooks the wadi.

Eagle Shrine

A detour can be made here to the **Eagle Shrine**. Walk up past the djinn block, left across the roof of the tunnel to the other side of the wadi, then right, past the first side valley on the left and left up the next side valley. Climb up a short distance and carved in the cliff on the right are several niches. In one is a beautifully carved relief of an eagle, with open wings, symbol throughout the Hellenistic-Semitic world of the paramount male deity.

THE SIQ

Probably at the same time as the dam a **monumental arch** was built spanning the entrance to the Siq. Painted by David Roberts in 1839 and still standing in the late 19C, now only the supports remain, and a few voussoirs above the springing line. Here begins the Siq, that spectacular gorge about 1.2km long, a natural fault through the mountain, which was and is the principal entrance to Petra. Much of the way is in shadow, but occasionally a shaft of bright sunlight penetrates the high perpendicular walls. Two **water systems** channelled water from the large reservoir in Wadi Musa through the Siq. On the south side is a rock-cut channel covered with flat stones and on the north side water ran through ceramic pipes set in the cliff face.

> Among the many skills of the Nabateans was water engineering. Diodorus describes how in the desert while still nomadic they excavated subterranean concrete-lined reservoirs, with a small opening, and the water collection and supply systems of Petra are among the most elaborate of antiquity. Rainwater was collected behind dams and retaining walls and channelled into innumerable cisterns carved in the sandstone mountains and maximum use was made of the region's natural springs. Strabo writes that Petra had many springs for watering gardens and domestic purposes; today, apart from 'Ain Musa, there are but two perennial springs in the Petra valleys, one in Wadi Siyyagh the other in Wadi Abu 'Ullayqa.

Several sections of the **road** which originally paved the Siq are still intact. Opposite the first stretch is a **votive niche** with a god block, one of dozens of niches carved into the sides of the gorge. In the ancient Semitic tradition the Nabateans portrayed their deities in human and in aniconic form, as blocks of stone, usually rectangular. After c175m a **pedimented niche crowned with six god blocks** faces another section of the original road on the left. About 160m further, beside a wild fig tree on the longest stretch of paved road, a free standing sandstone block is carved with an **elaborate niche** facing west. It contains two different sized blocks on pedestals, both with schematic eyes and a nose although the smaller block is very worn.

Some 135m beyond you will see **ten blocks** of varying sizes carved on the right wall, and after another 100m, as the Siq bends again and narrows, various interesting reliefs and inscriptions decorate the southern cliff. Below a standing **god flanked by two animals**, probably bulls, a Greek inscription reads: 'Sabinus Alesandros, panegyriarches of Adraa, in piety dedicated'. As panegyriarch or 'president of festivals' Sabinus Alexandros probably came to Petra to participate in the 'Actia Dusaria', a festival with games in honour of the god Dusares, celebrated in Petra and Bostra every four years. Next to Sabinus' dedication is a **hemispheric god block** on a pedestal, which represents Dusares of Adraa near Bostra, below which is again engraved 'panegyriarches'. The two reliefs have been tentatively dated to the second half of the 2C AD. Right of the Adraa block are the Greek letters Γ KYP referring to the IIIrd Cyrenaica Legion which may have had a detachment in Petra at the time although its headquarters were at Bostra, capital of Provincia Arabia.

As the Siq continues it becomes very narrow and dark until turning a corner there is a strip of daylight and that first magical glimpse of Petra's grandest monument, the Treasury, immaculately carved from the warm red sandstone at the end of the ceremonial way and designed to impress. Take time to absorb the effect before emerging into the bright sunlight.

TREASURY
Carved deeply into the rock, its fine architectural detail beautifully preserved, although the figures have been defaced, the **Khaznat Far'oun** or **Pharoah's Treasury** derives its name from the huge urn surmounting the central tholos. According to local tradition Pharoah, the great black magician, created the

monuments of Petra and then deposited his treasure in the urn far from human reach. For many years the bedouin fired their rifles in vain at the much battered vessel hoping one day it would break open and shower the lucky marksman with gold and jewels.

Perhaps more than any other monument the Treasury expresses the eclectic nature of Nabatean culture and architecture, that dynamic blend of East and West expedited by Alexander the Great, whose conquests indelibly stamped the face of Greek culture on the ancient Orient. Hellenistic in style, with its elegant columns, floral capitals and classical mouldings, the Treasury is usually dated to the 1C BC. Probably a tomb, perhaps also a shrine, it has a subtle and complex iconography. On the lower storey two equestrian reliefs represent the **Dioskouroi**, the twins Castor and Pollux, sons of Zeus and the sister of Helen. Guides, companions, and helpers of man through life, they also accompany him after death. On the central acroterion crowning the pediment is the symbol of **Isis**, a disc between horns and ears of wheat; and the female figure above, holding a cornucopia, may also be Isis. Isis and the Dioskouroi were a popular group in the Hellenistic Orient, in some way linked with the individual and his salvation. Four figures below the broken pediments and two figures in the side bays of the tholos are brandishing what may be an axe above their heads; in the two back bays are **Winged Victories**. Four plump eagles, symbols of **Zeus-Hadad-Dushara**, the paramount male deity, crown the broken pediments; another eagle is in the pediment below the horns of Isis; and two lions, associated with the great **Goddess**, stand on each side of the lower entablature.

Inside, the Treasury is quite simple, a contrast to the façade. Steps between the two central columns, the left one restored, lead to a portico with side chambers which have unusual round windows above their decorated doorways. Another stairway leads to the main chamber which had huge wooden doors; note the massive sockets for the door frame and lintel. In the threshold is a circular hole with a recessed edge, originally covered, from which a channel runs to a basin by the staircase. Such an arrangement suggests libations, in the context of some long forgotten ritual. Three small rooms cut into the side and rear walls of the main chamber have framed and pedimented doorways, otherwise the interior is plain.

Two rows of vertical niches on either side of the Khaznah façade are difficult to explain; similar niches also occur in quarries near the High Place and in Wadi Siyyagh. Some writers suggest they are footholds used during the cutting of the façade.

Detail of the frieze on the Treasury, Petra

Alternative Routes from the Bab as-Siq

Although we recommend that on your first day at least you walk through the Siq there are other routes into Petra from the Bab as-Siq that the more agile and adventurous may like to try. Routes can also be done in reverse, but bear in mind that it can be harder climbing up than down!

AL-MADRAS

Just past the Obelisk tomb is a blue sign to **Al-Madras**, a 'suburb' of Petra in the hills south of the Siq. This can be visited as a short detour, preferably with a guide, or you can continue to the Treasury, avoiding the Siq, and further to the High Place. The path runs above and parallel to the Wadi Musa, bears right and continues, occasionally marked by cairns, through a manmade passage in the rock and alongside a smaller valley; below to the right is a rocky outcrop resembling a cob loaf. After some distance worn rock-cut stairs lead to a broad green hanging valley which was dammed by the Nabateans and around which are caves, a triclinium, water channels and basins. Beside the valley is a rock overhang at a higher level sheltering a small open court with benches and complex of water channels, basins, tank and cistern. Follow the ledge northwards around the mountain where another open area has cuttings, water channels, basins, niches and a dilapidated altar. Down some steps to a small clearing facing north is a large cave, now much blackened, where an inscription mentioning Dushara as 'god of al-Madrasa' was apparently found.

> In the Petra mountains and throughout Nabatea are dozens of cultic installations comprising a square or oblong rock-cut platform, usually with benches, a water tank, basin and channels, often an altar and other associated features. Such '**high places**' are part of the early West Semitic religious tradition; the biblical prophets vehemently condemned those of the Canaanites. No doubt the Nabateans smoked incense on their altars and poured libations. What other rituals they performed on their high places we can only imagine, but on the mountains they must surely have felt closer to their gods.

Looking back towards the way you came you should see a cluster of niches by some fallen boulders—alongside, facing west, are two caves with several Nabatean inscriptions. Cross over to these caves, and keeping them on your left follow the path alongside the rock face and down to the broad open tableland of **Jabal al-Jilf** with splendid views across to Jabal Haroun. It is a lovely walk southwestwards across the plateau to the **Danqur al Khaznah**, the high valley which descends to the Treasury at the end of the Siq. Scramble alongside and through the wadi and, where there is a Nabatean corridor hewn through the rock high on the left, keep right and climb along beside the cliff to emerge on a ledge opposite the Treasury. From here are fabulous views of the Treasury below and along the Outer Siq to the Theatre. Return to the corridor which leads to the ancient Nabatean stairway down to the Treasury; the descent is steep but not too difficult. Alternatively it is possible to go further back up the Danqur al-Khaznah and cross the plateau to the Great High Place on Jabal al-Madhbah.

WADI AL-MUDHLIM

When the Nabateans built the dam at the entrance to the Siq, they hewed a **tunnel** 88m long and c10m high through the solid rock to the right of the bridge to channel the flood waters of the Wadi Musa into the Wadi al-Mudhlim. It is a masterpiece of Nabatean engineering. A walk through the tunnel and along the wadi is a beautiful but somewhat difficult route to Petra city centre, quiet except for the occasional bird song and especially lovely when the oleanders are in bloom. It should only be attempted when the weather is clear and stable; flash floods are sudden and dangerous. Some distance after the tunnel the wadi bed veers left, passes the substantial remains of a Nabatean dam and then begins to narrow until a point where it is jammed by a large boulder. A drop of c 5m to the river bed below must be negotiated to continue. The wadi descends more steeply and after a sharp turn to the left becomes the narrow, colourful **Sadd Ma'jan**, sometimes hard to pass because of rock pools, sculpted by the eddying waters. In a circular basin the Nabateans cut a charming series of votive niches; the largest is beautifully carved with a segmented pediment, smaller ones have horns and a crescent. Further along are more niches and soon the wadi joins the broad **Wadi al-Mataha**. From here you can go straight towards the nymphaeum and the city centre or explore the area of Mughur an-Nasara (p 245) across the wadi.

OUTER SIQ

From the Treasury to the theatre the Wadi Musa is generally known as the Outer Siq and is lined with tombs. Note the continuation of the piped water system on the right-hand side. Many tombs are now partly below ground, as the level of the wadi has risen since antiquity. Diagonally opposite the Treasury steps go down behind a wall to Tomb 64, which contains interesting loculi and shaft graves. Multiple burials were common in Petra, for these are family tombs; a number of graves have more than one shelf, a feature also found in the early Arab tombs at Palmyra in the Syrian desert. For a good view of the Treasury, climb north alongside Tomb 64, cross a wall and double back to the rocks directly over the tomb. Alternatively, continue from the wall up the steep, broad gully to the top of the mountain from where the views are even more impressive, but this is a difficult climb. With a guide you can then go to the Khubtha (p 237) high places, continue above the Outer Siq for views of the theatre and city centre and descend by the Urn Tomb or Sextius Florentinus Tomb.

Past Tomb 64 steps lead to a very large cavern with benches on three sides; above on the rock is a tiny carved figure who seems to be holding a bow. Just beyond, on the opposite side behind a collapsed section of cliff, is the very broken **Façade 66**; you can still see the side pilasters and base of the niche alongside, decorated with diamonds and roundels. Originally this façade, which had collapsed by 1847, bore a poignant Greek funerary inscription:

> My name is Arrianos, and sacred Petra gave me birth, which was the metrop-
> olis of the land of Arabia. The citizens gave the prized honour of Ausonian
> laws. I was the first of a beloved family. While I was living through my twenty-
> seventh year a disease that subdues all took me away to Hades. One thing
> alone stings my heart, and that is that I have left to my aged mother ever-
> lasting grief.

Further down on the same side, past a series of rather top heavy façades, is an unusual tomb, partly free standing, with a row of stepped merlons on top. Beyond a couple of collapsed block tombs begins the stairway to the High Place; a cave along a path to the left has some of Petra's most strikingly coloured striated sandstone. In the corner of the cliff opposite the stairway is the **Tomb of the 17 Graves** (under restoration)—14 of these are in the floor and three are in the back wall. On the left wall are several nefesh obelisks, two with short inscriptions, one of which reads 'Nefesh of Zaid-Qawmo, son of Yaqum'.

Before the theatre the west cliffs are riddled with tombs on four different levels, the so-called **Streets of Façades**.

> **Nabatean tomb façades** (p 41) show considerable variation, but there are a number of standard styles which, contrary to what was once believed, do not represent a chronological development. Some of the simplest, well represented on the the Streets of Façades, have a single or double row of stepped merlons or 'crowsteps' in relief. Another style has a cavetto cornice surmounted by two half merlons or there may be a double cornice, the lower in plain classical style. Sometimes there are squat columns in the attic between. Cornice-type monuments often have pilasters with Nabatean capitals flanking the façade. Classical capitals are plain, with angular projecting corners and a central boss. Doorways may be simple rectilinear or surmounted by a triangular or occasionally arched pediment; some have a double door frame. Although most Nabatean tombs conform to these standard types, a number of monuments have more idiosyncratic façades and some of the more grandiose, like the Treasury, are highly elaborate.

THEATRE

Petra's **Main Theatre**, dated to the 1C AD, is unusual as it is almost entirely carved from the solid rock except towards the front on either side, where part of it was built free-standing. Yawning holes in the cliff above the seating are what remain of earlier tombs, their façades hacked away during construction. In style the theatre is Hellenistic, with a more than semicircular cavea and seating right down to the orchestra, which was cut into bedrock and covered with hard cement plaster. Partly restored by the Department of Antiquities, the stage had niches framed by pillars on the front; the scenae frons, two or three storeys high, was faced with marble and elaborately decorated. Fragments of mouldings were found, as well as column drums and capitals and a marble statue of Heracles, the most popular and widely-worshipped of Greek heroes. With 45 rows of seats, the theatre has a capacity of 6000–7000, a large audience. In the orchestra, steps lead up to what might be an altar, perhaps for burning incense to honour the gods. We can only hypothesise about performances staged in the theatre; classical drama seems unlikely because presumably most of the audience understood neither Latin nor Greek, but no doubt the Nabateans had an appropriate repertoire of their own to draw on at festival time.

MONUMENTS OF THE EAST CLIFF

Opposite the theatre and above the pretty souvenirs and refreshments cave are several large tomb façades. Most interesting is **Tomb 813** also known as the **Tomb of Unaishu**, reached by scrambling up the rocks at the end of the Outer Siq. It is a rare example of a complete Nabatean tomb complex (p 234). In front of the tomb, which has 11 loculi in the chamber, originally covered with stone slabs, is an open courtyard with porticoes to north and south. Remains of column bases are clear on the south side. On the north side of the court through a doorway is a triclinium which unusually has three loculi in the rear wall. Beyond Tomb 813 and at a slightly higher level is the well-preserved façade of **Tomb 808**, also a double cornice type with side pilasters. In 1896 the American traveller Gray Hill found in this tomb or in Tomb 813 part of a grave slab, since lost, with an inscription which read: 'Unaishu, brother of Shuqailat, queen of the Nabateans, son ...'. A plaster fragment with a broken inscription which could be restored to read 'Shuqailat' was found by Zayadine in Tomb 813, where he also believes the 'Unaishu inscription', belongs, hence the name of the tomb.

Queen Shuqailat I, second wife of Aretas IV (9 BC–AD 40/44), who appears with her husband on Nabatean coins in years 27–48 of his reign, could be the queen referred to in the Unaishu inscription. More probably, however, she is **Shuqailat II**, who ruled as regent for her son Rabbel II (70–106) in his first six years and who is described as 'sister' of the previous king Malichus II (40/44–70), although she is thought to have been his wife. Two other princesses, Gamilat and Hagiru, are called 'sister of the king' under Rabbel II (70–106). Usually the chief minister seems to have the title 'brother of the king', so possibly Unaishu, Shuqailat's 'brother', was minister during her regency. How far 'sister' and 'brother' denote actual kinship terms is unclear. Although as a quasi-independent ruler during the minority of her son Shuqailat II is so far unique among **Nabatean queens**, all queens were probably quite influential, in line with a strong Arab tradition which lasted until the advent of Islam. Shuqailat thus takes her place alongside such indomitable women as the Queen of Sheba and Zenobia of Palmyra. Women in general may have had a fairly high status in Nabatean society; married women could hold and bequeath property and there are hints that genealogy may have been traced through the female line.

Walking north and descending to the valley you pass several more tombs and caves, including one, heavily eroded, with magnificent multi-coloured rock. Part way down you can join the steps which ascend from the wadi to one of Petra's grandest monuments, the **Urn Tomb**, striking from afar because of its dominant position and the arched sub-vaults, some restored, which carry part of the colonnaded forecourt. The tomb derives its name from the urn finial crowning the pediment. Engaged columns and pilasters decorate the façade, between are three loculi, the centre one still partly closed with a portrait bust, perhaps of one of the tomb owners. Above the columns, in the main frieze, are four more busts, very weathered. Most interesting inside are the features dating from the time when the tomb was converted into a church. Near the left corner of the back wall is the Greek dedicatory inscription in red paint: 'In the time of the Most Holy Bishop Jason this place was dedicated on the fifth of Loos in the [year] 341, there being present a detachment of courageous troops of [...] and Deacon Julianos [...] to Christ the Saviour [...]' This is AD 446–47; the dating is according to the era which begins with the creation of the Roman Province of Arabia, in AD 106. Several large holes drilled in the floor of the chamber probably date from the same time. Two lines of three extend from the central niche in the rear wall, a cross line of six probably held up a chancel screen, four in front could have supported a pulpit and four larger holes in the centre of the chancel area may have been for the ciborium over the altar. Five holes in the niche are more difficult to interpret, possibly a table for preparation of the Eucharist. The other niches, perhaps curtained, could have served as treasuries, vestries or for ecclesiastical paraphernalia, while the holes in the walls we may imagine holding hooks for icons, hangings, or lamps.

Before leaving the Urn Tomb take time to enjoy the superb view from the fore-court: Petra city centre, Umm al-Biyara, the urn on top of the Deir, the High Place. Below the Urn Tomb, on a rock terrace overlooking the Wadi Musa, are the remains of a **private house** with a clay oven, of the 1C BC, one of few to have been excavated in the Petra valleys.

Further along the east cliff are other grandiose monuments. Beyond a weathered façade notable for its beautiful colours is a large tomb which has some similarities to, but none of the beauty of, the Khaznah. Its common designation, **Corinthian Tomb**, is a total misnomer. Above, a central tholos is framed by a broken pediment, below, the façade is curiously asymmetrical with three different doorways. Alongside is a most unusual monument, one of the largest in Petra, inappropriately named the **Palace Tomb**. There are five superimposed orders, and much of the upper façade, now badly damaged, was free-standing because the cliff into which it was carved was too low. Best preserved is the right-hand side, protected by the projecting cliff. Stylistically, comparison with the inner façade of the central temple at Qasrawet, a caravan station in northern Sinai, is interesting. Six irregular niches in the second storey, from one of which (third from the left) a vertical shaft leads to the top of the cliff, perhaps held portrait busts or commemorative stelae. Inside there are four chambers, but only the middle two connect.

Often described as **Royal Tombs**, although there is no evidence for this, the monuments of the east cliff were obviously special, as they are not only imposing but are also in a prime position in central Petra; the 'Corinthian Tomb' is in direct alignment with the main colonnaded street. Beginning with Urn Tomb, they were carved in chronological order, moving north round the mountainside. Many have described the architecture, the colours of the rock, the glorious sunset, but none perhaps so lyrically as **Edward Lear** who visited Petra in 1858 with his servant Giorgio Kokali from Corfu:

'Wonderful is the effect of the east cliff as we approach it with its colours and carved architecture, the tint of the stone being brilliant and gay beyond my anticipation. "Oh master", said Giorgio (who is prone to culinary similies), "we have come into a world of chocolate, ham, curry powder and salmon" ... As the sun went down, the great eastern cliff became one solid wall of fiery-red stone, rose-coloured piles of cloud resting on it and on the higher hills beyond it like a new poem-world betwixt earth and heaven. Purple and darkling the shadows lengthened among the overgrown buildings and over the orange, red and chocolate rocks of the foreground ... Silent and ghostly terrible rose darker and darker the western cliffs ... till the dim pale lights fading away from the myriad crags around left this strange tomb-world to death-like quiet and the gray gloom of the night'.

A rough path goes from the east cliff to the Wadi Musa and Petra city centre, alternatively continue around the cliff across the city walls to the Sextius Florentinus Tomb and the area of Mughur an-Nasara (p 245).

CITY CENTRE

Petra may seem to many visitors to suffer a surfeit of tombs, it has even been described as the 'sarcophagus of an ancient civilisation', but in antiquity the city centre and surrounding valleys boasted a fine array of free-standing public buildings, temples and private residences. Most of these collapsed long ago in a series of earthquakes, but even a cursory glance at the hillsides reveals a jumble of finely

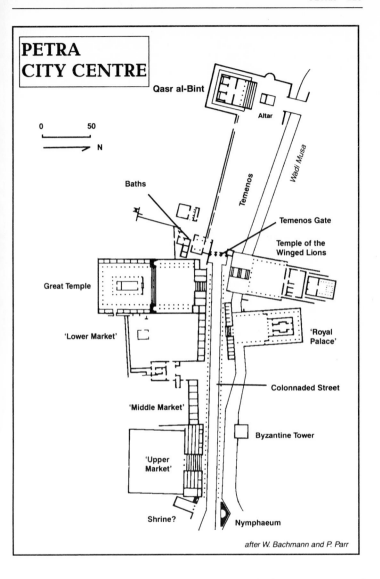

PETRA CITY CENTRE

Qasr al-Bint

Altar

0   50

N

Baths

Temenos

Wadi Musa

Temenos Gate

Temple of the Winged Lions

Great Temple

'Lower Market'

'Royal Palace'

Colonnaded Street

'Middle Market'

Byzantine Tower

'Upper Market'

Shrine?

Nymphaeum

after W. Bachmann and P. Parr

tooled stone blocks, the occasional wall and a mass of broken pottery. Some of these buildings are now being excavated and the results are spectacular.

East–west through the city centre alongside the Wadi Musa ran an elegant **Colonnaded Street**; a few columns have been re-erected, one with a pseudo-Ionic capital which belongs elsewhere. In places the marble paving is intact, but shows no wear marks from wheeled vehicles. Contrary to other grand cities of the Orient it seems only people and animals used Petra's main thoroughfare. Beside the street and beneath a large terebinth tree, where the Wadi Mataha meets the Wadi Musa in a riot of fiery-coloured sandstone, are the solid foundations of the **Nymphaeum**, the public fountain dedicated to the water nymphs found in cities throughout the Graeco-Roman world. A cistern beside the Palace Tomb perhaps provided the water with a head of pressure. West of the Nymphaeum on the south side of the street a staircase leads up to an unexcavated area dubbed **'Upper Market'** by the German scholar Bachmann early this century. Two broken plinths on the pavement in front of the staircase carried a free-standing arch with a dedication in Greek to the emperor Trajan dated 114. Beside the steps lie three blocks of the incomplete inscription, which records that Petra was honoured by Trajan as metropolis. Clearly inscribed at the bottom left of one of the blocks are the words [μη]τροπολιξ Πετρα. Although he made Bostra the capital of Provincia Arabia, Trajan was obviously aware of Petra's continuing importance in the southern part of his new province. Little rooms built of reused blocks along the southern colonnade may be Byzantine shops from the 4C or later; above are other unexcavated terraces, Bachmann's **'Middle Market'** and **'Lower Market'**. Beyond the 'Lower Market' is the stairway to a great **temple**, one of the largest complexes in Petra, currently under excavation and fenced round. Ascending terraces, one paved with fine hexagonal limestone slabs, lead to the portico, its four gigantic pillars now dramatically collapsed like a pack of cards. A colonnade surrounds the cella, which has steps at the back, and is constructed of finely tooled blocks. Beside the temple are various ancillary buildings.

On the north side of the Colonnaded Street, across the wadi, were other monumental buildings, accessed by bridges over the watercourse. Opposite the re-erected columns are the ruins of the so-called **'Byzantine Tower'** and high above, on a ridge, a **Byzantine Church** of the 5C–6C has been undergoing excavation and conservation by the American Center of Oriental Research since 1992. It is a tripartite basilica preceded by an atrium with marble paving in the nave and mosaics in the side aisles. In the north aisle people, animals, birds and various objects are depicted within red vine scrolls on a bright yellow background, in the south aisle personifications of Wisdom, Earth, Ocean and the Four Seasons, flanked by animals and fish, are set in a geometric mosaic. Fragments of glass wall and ceiling mosaics, marble relief screens and carved capitals attest the rich decoration of the church. Until the church has been properly consolidated and protected with a roof you may find you can only visit when the archaeologists are working.

Past an unexcavated structure called by Bachmann the **'Royal Palace'**, which was linked to the Colonnaded Street by a bridge of which the abutments still survive, is the **Temple of the Winged Lions**, one of the most exciting discoveries of recent years, partly fenced off while awaiting restoration. Tentatively dated to the reign of Aretas IV (9 BC–AD 40/44) on the evidence of an inscription of AD 27/8 found during excavation and now in the Forum Basin Museum, the temple derives its name from zoomorphic capitals with winged lions in place of volutes, one of which is in the Petra Museum, and from lovely relief carvings of winged lions facing small winged figures grasping snakes in each hand, now displayed in the garden of the Forum Basin restaurant. As lions are associated with the 'goddess' in the ancient Orient many scholars believe the sanctuary was dedicated to **Atargatis**, **Al-'Uzza** or **Allat**. Another suggestion, on the basis of statuettes of **Isis**, **Osiris** and **Zeus-Sarapis** found during excavations, is a sanctuary of the **Egyptian Gods**. A rectangular stone idol, displayed in the Forum Basin Museum, which has schematic eyes and nose and an inscription which reads 'goddess of

The 'goddess of Hayyan son of Nybat' from the Temple of the Winged Lions, now in the Forum Basin Museum, Petra

Hayyan son of Nybat' could have had the horns of Isis in the now empty hole in the centre of the floral wreath across the top. Due to the syncretistic nature of Nabatean religion the various possibilities are not mutually exclusive; the temple was almost certainly dedicated to a 'goddess' whatever her name or names, perhaps in association with her consort.

An elaborate approach comprising a propylon, bridge, and ascending terraces with double colonnades connected the temple with the Colonnaded Street. Part of the stepped bridge is still extant and zoomorphic Ionic capitals with elephant head volutes as well as several relief panels decorated with arms and armour discovered nearby are thought to come from the propylon. Three of these panels are in the Petra Museum and a couple of capitals, broken but still showing the elephants' wrinkled brows, are on the ground by the bridge. A portico *in antis*, its monumental columns now concertinaed down the hillside, was carried on arches and from there the worshipper passed into a square cella, with engaged half and coupled quarter columns along the walls and two rows of free-standing columns parallel to the east and west walls. Twelve columns with 'winged lion' capitals surrounded the altar platform, which is reached by steps to each side at the front. Behind the altar platform an opening leads down to a small chamber with shelves. In antiquity the temple was elaborately decorated. Niches between the engaged columns perhaps held statuettes, and the altar platform was paved in black and white marble while the cella floor had white and brown marble paving, set in cement. Loose remnants are lying around and there are pieces in situ in the doorway. Two phases of interior decoration were identified: in the earlier phase the plastered walls were painted with classical motifs such as garlands, putti and dolphins, symbols of Atargatis. Around the column bases was a ring of marble, which can still be seen in many places, the shafts were stuccoed with a floral pattern or had cabled fluting. Later the walls were pecked over, replastered and repainted in plain colours and the fluting on the columns filled in to give a smooth finish. Among the ancillary buildings to the temple, west of the portico, was a painter's workshop with paints and pigments still in their ceramic containers and a marble-cutter's workshop with over 1000 pieces of marble. Also west of the temple is a Byzantine domestic complex built over earlier structures. Note several millstones in the rooms.

NABATEAN PANTHEON

Nabatean religion must be understood within the context of the Hellenistic world, where East meets West, fostering cultural interaction and a syncretism of Oriental and Occidental gods and beliefs. Deities were worshipped in Nabatea in aniconic form, as **betyls** or stelae, sometimes with schematic eyes and nose, reflecting the traditions of the desert Arabs and other West Semitic peoples like the Canaanites, and in figurative form as in the Greek world and other parts of the Middle East. A multiplicity of names, drawn from different traditions and often describing 'aspects' of the same god, characterises the Nabatean pantheon.

DUSHARA, 'lord of the Shara-mountains', north of Petra, was the head of the pantheon, the national deity and patron of tribe and state. He was identified with the Greek **Zeus** and with **Hadad**, the great Syrian god who guaranteed the rains and fertility of the land. Among his symbols are the eagle and the bull. As **Dionysus** he is decorated with grapes and vine leaves, his favourite drink was wine, he was patron of the royal drinking societies. Possibly Dushara was also linked to the Egyptian deities **Osiris** and **Sarapis.**

ALLAT, an Arabian goddess, probably the original consort of Dushara. She may be identified wth the Greek **Athena**.

AL-UZZA, a goddess related to Allat in the Arab tribal pantheon. Allat, Al-'Uzza and another goddess Manat are mentioned in the Quran (Sura 53:19). Al-'Uzza becomes equated with the Greek **Aphrodite**. Al-Uzza/Aphrodite was sometimes assimilated to the Egyptian **Isis** whose cult is attested at Petra and whose rites and mysteries were so popular in the Hellenistic world.

ATARGATIS, the 'Syrian goddess' and great sky-mother, paramount deity along-side Dushara. One of her main sanctuaries was at Khirbet Tannur. As fertility goddess she is decorated with grains, vines and fruits, as dolphin goddess she was protectress of seafarers and synonymous with **Aphrodite**. Among her symbols is the lion.

BAAL-SHAMIN, 'lord of the heavens', originally a Phoenician god, whose cult became especially popular in northern Nabatea, where he had a splendid temple at Si in the Hauran. There was a temple to Baal-Shamin near the modern mosque in the centre of Wadi Musa.

AL-KUTBAY, god of writing, equated with the Greek **Hermes** and Assyrian **Nabu**.

SHAI' AL-QAUM , an ancient Arabian warrior god who abstains from wine, a custom also observed by the nomadic Nabateans of the 4C BC according to Diodorus.

QOS, chief god of the Edomites, also worshipped by the Nabateans.

At the monumental **Temenos Gate**, which marks the entrance to the precinct of the great free-standing temple beyond, the Colonnaded Street, which was completed before the gate, comes to an end. This arrangement was alien to the classical world; the grand colonnaded avenues, so typical of the Graeco-Roman Orient, normally ran north–south between the city's two main gates and were

The Temenos Gate, Petra

busy thoroughfares for both through traffic and local transport. Petra's arrangement is characteristically Nabatean and occurs again at Bostra, the northern
capital, where the main street runs east–west and ends at a 'Nabatean Gate' beyond
which was a precinct with monumental buildings.

Sockets for hinges and bolts indicate that the three openings in the Temenos Gate
once had doors. Pilasters flank the entrances; three blocks of a floral frieze survive
on the south pilaster of the south arch, and the pilasters flanking the centre
entrance were decorated with panels containing alternate floral motifs and busts.
Note the different bust on the left, which is a modern replacement. Of several pieces
of sculpture found nearby, a winged Tyche holding a palm branch and cornucopia,
now outside the Petra museum, probably once ornamented the gate. South of the
Temenos Gate are the partly excavated **Baths**, not properly accessible and rather
dirty. Two underground domed chambers, one of which is circular with engaged
columns and niches, and an adjacent staircase were cleared—if you climb up from
the Temenos gate you can look down into one domed room through a hole in the
roof.

Enclosing the **Temenos** or temple precinct was a boundary wall, collapsed into
the wadi to the north but well-preserved on the south side. Its main feature is a long
double row of benches topped by a plinth which used to carry statues. Cut into one

of the blocks in the western section c 30m from the Qasr al-Bint is a much weathered inscription dedicating a statue to Aretas IV (9 BC–AD 40/44); the boundary wall and the temple it encloses are therefore earlier than this king's reign. Most scholars date the **Qasr al-Bint al-Far'oun**, the 'Palace of Pharoah's Daughter' to the 1C BC; its local name derives from the tradition that Petra was built by Pharoah. It was in fact a huge temple, typically oriental in style, square with a tripartite adyton, broad cella and a broad portico, approached by a monumental staircase faced with marble, now much destroyed. Four massive pillars stood at the top of the staircase. From the portico an arched doorway which may have had a lintel below leads to the cella and triple sanctuary. Columns across the front of the east and west chambers supported a second storey reached by staircases in the walls; in the east wall is a large window which has been restored. The centre recess has engaged columns along the walls, a striking relieving arch at the back and a raised floor approached by steps at each side, where the main cult statue would have stood. The Qasr al-Bint is built of ashlar masonry with a rubble and mortar core; timber stringcourses, seen clearly in the portico and exterior walls, provided tensile reinforcement and the temple probably had a pitched wooden and tiled roof. At the top of the outer walls is a Doric frieze which had flowers or busts in the metopes, including the bust of 'Helios' in the Amman Museum, and there was much use of stucco decoration, well-preserved on the corner pilasters. Scholars have always assumed, although without proof, that the Qasr al-Bint was dedicated to Dushara. Part of a marble hand, several times life size, discovered in 1959, was believed to be part of a cult statue, c 7m tall, from the centre adyton, but the deity was unknown. Recently several finds have shed more light on the gods worshipped in the temple. Most important are two fragmentary inscriptions; one is a dedication which has been read as 'Zeus Hypsistos', synonymous with Dushara, the other has been restored as a dedication to Aphrodite. If the interpretation is correct, Dushara and Aphrodite were revered together in the great sanctuary. Ceremonies in this vast sacred area were surely spectacular; before the temple is a massive **altar**, approached by steps and once veneered in marble, where incense no doubt was smoked and animals perhaps sacrificed while crowds thronged the temenos and the gods watched from within.

Detail of the Doric frieze on Qasr al-Bint, Petra

■ Across the bridge from the Temenos precinct the *Forum Basin Restaurant* serves drinks (including alcohol except during Ramadan), snacks and buffet lunches. Nearby are several small cafés serving drinks and snacks; *Atalla's café-tent* in the Temenos area and *Haroun's café* below the museum will also provide packed lunches at a reasonable price, useful if you are planning a long day's hike.

Petra has two small **museums**, one recently opened and attached to the Forum Basin Restaurant and the other in a cave in the cliff face of al-Habis. Entrance is included in the price of the site ticket. A good selection of finds from in and around Petra including jewellery, pottery, coins, water piping, a statue of Aphrodite found in the theatre, a statue of Dionysus, and various architectural fragments are displayed in the newer museum. Boards have excellent descriptions of the geology, geography, history and archaeology of Petra. In the garden of the restaurant decorated capitals and relief sculpture are mostly from the Temple of the Winged Lions. Steps lead up to the other museum (closed Fridays), comprising three rock-cut chambers, originally a Nabatean house, with five windows above the door. Petra's inhabitants lived in rock-cut and free-standing houses; the east face of al-Habis has more rock-cut houses which accommodated visitors before there were any hotels in Wadi Musa. These are now used by the Department of Antiquities, which also carries out its work in the modern building between al-Habis and the Qasr al-Bint. Over the entrance to the museum is a magnificent bust of a god with curly hair and beard, perhaps Sarapis. Other interesting pieces inside include a bust with helmet and spear, which may be Ares, an eagle with outspread wings standing on a thunderbolt, symbol of Zeus, a winged head and a female sphinx. Most of the sculpture in the museum was found in the area of the Temenos Gate.

Past the museum the rock-cut path continues around the cliff to a more open area; note the lovely views down the Wadi Siyyagh with rock-cut houses in the cliffs. On the left a tomb has been converted into a charming 'house' with steps up to a forecourt and pretty garden; on the right is a Nabatean sacred area, centred around a sunken court. Caves and worn tomb façades are grouped around the court and above and behind the crow-stepped tomb is a high place. Just past the 'house', by a well-preserved tomb façade, it is possible to climb to the top of Al-Habis up a gully and worn Nabatean stairway, but the easiest route is from the Qasr al-Bint.

Behind the Qasr al-Bint, on the east face of al-Habis, is the so-called **Unfinished Tomb**, which shows clearly how the Nabateans carved their monuments from the top down. If completed it would have had two side pilasters and two free-standing columns across the front. Uphill from the Unfinished Tomb behind a large rock is the **Columbarium** or 'dovecote', a misleading name for one of Petra's more enigmatic monuments. Rows of small square niches, some still blocked with little stones, cover the walls. Horsfield, who worked at Petra in the 1930s, noted depressions marking the position of urns in the niches and traces of ashes. On this evidence it has been suggested that the Columbarium was a repository for cremation urns. A number of larger, shallow niches perhaps held portrait sculpture.

For the small **Crusader Fort of Al-Habis**—a 15 minute climb—follow the rock face further, at the top of the ridge turn right just before a sign to Al-Habis, and walk towards the cliff. Steps wind round to a rock platform on the west side and up past restored walls. A wooden footbridge with no railings must be negotiated on the way. Pass through the gate with a rock-cut bench and up again to a gatehouse. Pick your way up to the top; to the right, steps lead to the small upper bailey—under them is a small barrel-vaulted room. Opinions are divided as to the purpose of this small fort, possibly it was occupied after the loss of the larger castle at al-Wu'eira (p 247). Construction was dictated by the terrain and consequently there are a number of different levels, but the jumble of rock and fallen masonry has obscured the layout. From the summit there are excellent views over Petra; the east cliff tombs are particularly beautiful in the late afternoon sunlight. Directly below al-Habis to the east you have a bird's-eye view of some newish excavations, a complex of buildings with a lovely paved terrace.

Walks and climbs from Petra City Centre

Petra centre is the starting point for walks, hikes and climbs to other valleys and more outlying areas of the city. On most of these walks it is advisable to take a guide, although there are usually enough people on more frequented routes such as the 'Deir' and 'High Place' to point the way.

THE DEIR

From the Qasr al-Bint the path to the Deir goes along the Wadi Musa, across a bridge at the beginning of the Wadi as-Siyyagh and alongside the garden and terrace of the Forum Basin Restaurant, where there are usually some donkeys waiting for anyone who feels unable to manage the several hundred steps to the top. Prices are negotiable. We advise walking the ancient processional route; with stops on the way ascent takes about one hour. After some distance along a flat sandy valley with various carved chambers in the cliffs the stairway begins and soon there is a small wadi on the left with a sign to the **Lion Triclinium**. This rather weathered monument at the head of the wadi derives its name from the lions on both sides of the doorway, which had a circular window above, now eroded so that door and window join. At either end of the Doric frieze are 'medusa heads' and urns crown the pediment. Perhaps to complement the lions, symbols of Atargatis, a god block in a niche to the left of the triclinium may represent Dushara. Continue up the steps, underneath a large fallen boulder, to an open area, where another wadi, the Wadi Kharruba, joins the Wadi ad-Deir from the north. From the rocks to the left there is a good view down to the Lion Triclinium. Clamber for 5–10 minutes up the **Wadi Kharruba**, a lovely side valley with pretty flowers in spring, to see a fine **biclinium** with three urns on the pediment. As you look at the monument note Nabatean graffiti on the rock to the right below; inside there are two stepped benches, a square cupboard in the left wall and a ledge on the back wall with a rectangular cutting in the ground beneath.

After a flat stretch the stairway begins again; as it turns sharply left, the wadi to the right leads to the **Lower Qattar ad-Deir**. Keep to the left as the wadi narrows, clamber through and almost immediately double back left for the path which goes up and then bends back right to the broad ledge beneath a rock overhang above the ravine. Here water drips all year round, hence the description '*qattar*' from the Arabic root meaning 'drip' or 'trickle', and here the Nabateans carved a triclinium, tanks, various inscriptions and votive niches in one of which is a two-armed cross. In the half-light, as the water trickles onto the rock, it is easy to imagine why the Nabateans regarded this as a sacred place.

The way to the Deir winds upwards to another more open area from where there are stunning views back to the 'Royal Tombs'; a ledge runs north to the **Upper Qattar ad-Deir**, which is much smaller than the lower one and of little interest. Ahead is a deep, spectacular gorge down which in the distance rises the impressive massif of Umm al-Biyara. As the path continues to the right you catch a first welcome glimpse of the great urn on top of the Deir. A sign by the path announces the **Hermitage**, so called because of crosses carved in the caves above. To reach the caves bear right off the path then scramble up loose shale on the left—the first cave has a squarish niche in the back wall with a cross to the left and a worn Greek inscription on the right beginning IC XC; there is a hole through to the second cave with a cross in a circle on the right wall. Return to the path and across the valley note a keyhole-shaped cave high in the rock by some juniper trees, which is also carved with a cross. To reach this cave continue for c 40m and at the end of the

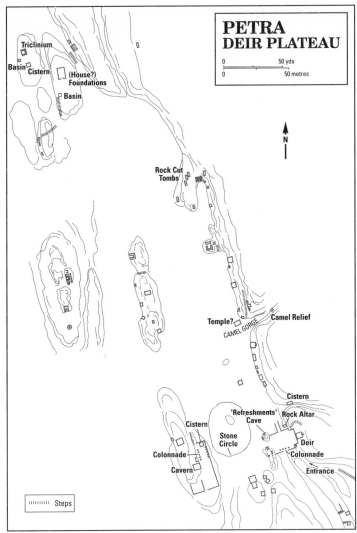

**PETRA
DEIR PLATEAU**

Triclinium

Basin Cistern (House?)
Foundations

Basin

N

Rock Cut
Tombs

Temple? Camel Relief
CAMEL GORGE

Cistern

'Refreshments' Rock Altar
Cistern Cave

Stone
Circle Deir

Colonnade Colonnade

Cavern Entrance

Steps

wide rock shelf bear left up a broad Nabatean stairway, then left through a gully with more steps and up to the cave. Right of the cave entrance is a nicely cut three-armed cross.

Back at the main path there are about 50 more steps upwards and a short descent to the Deir plateau. On the right is the great façade of the **Deir**, which is indeed, as Edward Lear so aptly wrote 'a fit crown to the marvels of the ascent'.

What the Deir lacks in beauty it gains in size. In design it is similar to the Treasury with two storeys crowned by a gigantic urn, but there is none of the delicate detail or architectural finesse. The rather plain façade, however, has the distinction of being the largest in Petra, 48m high by 47m wide, twice the width of the west front of Westminster Abbey, London. Deir means 'monastery' in Arabic and the monument probably earned its name from crosses scratched inside; several scholars believe that in antiquity it was a sacred hall maybe connected with the cult of one of the Nabatean kings, Obodas I (96/2–86 BC), who was buried at Avdat in the Negeb and deified after his death. An inscription in the cliff to the west reads 'Let be remembered 'Ubaydu son of Waqihel and his associates of the symposium of Obodat the god'. In the chamber are two low wide benches where members of the cultic association may have wined and dined and in the back wall is a recess for the image. Flanking the courtyard in front of the Deir was an elegant colonnade; look carefully to see the foundation wall and some columns clad in fluted stucco embedded in the ground to the south. North of the courtyard are the remains of an open air altar behind which steps lead the intrepid to the urn atop the monument. The steps go to a level area with ancient cuttings from where you clamber over to the gully at the back, turn right and scramble up a short distance to the 10m-high urn. Down below the people look minute and the view of the plateau and surrounding mountains is superb. On top of the far pediment is a mysterious geometric design with arcs and straight lines—perhaps an architect's plan. A middle line points to Mount Hor, the sacred mountain where Moses' brother Aaron is buried, crowned by its tiny white shrine. This is surely no coincidence, for all the signs are that the Deir plateau was an important sacred place, where Nabatean pilgrims once thronged for colourful ceremonies and rituals.

The Deir itself is only part of an even larger complex. Opposite is a large rocky outcrop with a gaping **square rock-cut cavern**. To reach it keep to the right of the 'refreshments cave' and cross a wide open space. Though not immediately obvious, this is a huge circle framed with dressed stones only clearly visible from a high vantage point. Climb the rocky outcrop from the right, behind a large Nabatean cistern, now dry, where part of the original stairway is still intact. The edge of the terrace in front of the cave shows the remains of a colonnade and from here is a good view of the Deir and the **stone circle**. This is where David Roberts did his painting of the Deir using artistic licence to include the 'Royal Tombs'. Inside the cave is a beautifully cut niche with a triangular pediment, now marred by modern graffiti. Holes in the base may have held clamps for a statue and the rectangular holes in the cave walls held metal hooks, probably for hanging devotional objects. On the right wall, near the entrance a lone foliate capital is inserted into a niche. The capital in the niche on the opposite wall was last seen in 1908. Above the cave, on top of the hill, are the jumbled remains of walls and buildings awaiting excavation. From here there are spectacular views across the mountains to the west.

To explore further return across the stone circle to the cliffs left of the Deir. Tombs and cliff dwellings, cisterns and water channels, attest a thriving community up here in the past. One of the larger cisterns, which usually contains ample water, is in the narrow gorge behind the rock altar of the Deir. It is easily accessible up an ancient water channel. Continue northwards, following the rock face, and on your right is the **'Camel Gorge'**. Climb up the rock, follow the gully round along a ledge under the overhang and a short distance along is a small cave. Right of the entrance is a weathered low relief of two men leading camels flanking two pedestals or altars. The men are wearing baggy 'Persian' trousers and the camels are dromedaries although one appears to have two humps due to a trick of the weathering. Camels were very important for the Nabateans, whose fabulous wealth was based on the trade in spices and other luxury goods from Arabia and the East.

The Greek geographer Strabo, describing the caravan traffic up the Incense Road, tells us that the aromatics were conveyed from one tribe to the next and if the odours made them drowsy they inhaled a stimulant of asphalt and a plant known as 'goat's beard'. Return to the entrance of the 'Camel Gorge' where there are the unexcavated remains of buildings, one perhaps a temple, littered with broken Nabatean pottery.

Head north, away from the Deir, keeping the deep gorge on your right. At the far end of the plateau on a spur of rock are the foundations of a building and a rectangular basin for collecting rainwater. Below and to the west of this rise a goat path leads to a small but perfectly preserved **'high place'** with benches on all sides, a basin and a large plastered cistern still used by the bedouin who have covered it with corrugated iron. It is worth pausing here a while to absorb the atmosphere on the edge of this Nabatean world—the stillness, the grandeur of the brooding basalt mountains and the enchanting views of the distant Wadi Araba.

Climb back up the goat track, continue straight ahead and you arrive back at the stone circle.

The Deir to Beidha
This route, which takes about two and a half hours, should not be undertaken without a guide; there are two short sections which could pose problems for the less agile and those with a fear of heights.

From the Deir walk north alongside the cliff, past the 'Camel Gorge', and keeping the broad gully on your left climb up and round the mountain. Just past a tree the path has broken away, but it possible to continue by crawling along a precipitous ledge above. Continue around the mountain on a shelf, fairly broad in most places, going down and up again where the shelf is broken until you are more than 180° from the starting point. There are stunning views across the Wadi Araba and beautiful rock formations along the way; where the descent begins is another rather difficult ledge, then a grassy area with wild thyme and sage which would be a lovely place for a picnic. Turn right along a rock-cut Nabatean road then walk across an undulating open area, cultivated in spring, past the beginning of the **Wadi Mu'aisra East** and turn left away from the mountains before **Wadi Mu'aisra West**. After some distance bear right down a broad valley which leads eventually to the Neolithic site at Beidha (p 249).

WADI FARASA AND THE HIGH PLACE
Of the two main routes to the High Place, one from near the theatre and the other along the Wadi Farasa, we opt here for climbing up via the Wadi Farasa, the longer but more interesting route, and descending to the theatre. Obviously the climb can be done in reverse.

From behind the Qasr al-Bint a clear track goes eastwards up the hillside to a lone column known locally as **Pharoah's Column** or **Pharoah's Phallus**, probably belonging to the portico of the unexcavated monumental building embedded in the hillside behind. Past the signs to Aaron's Tomb, Wadi Sabra and Naqb al-Ruba'i on the right the path continues to the area known as **Katute**. A **Nabatean villa** of the 1C excavated on the terrace beneath **az-Zantur** to the left shows that wealthy Petrans lived and entertained in style; part of the reception area had elegant columns and painted walls and outside the villa there was a garden. In the early 2C the Nabatean villa was destroyed and the terrace was not resettled until the early 4C, when two smaller houses were built over the ruins. A separate bakehouse to the east, with two ovens, was probably shared by the residents. Katute is crossed by the southern city walls (p 244), not easy for the untrained eye to trace; refuse was thrown over the walls forming a huge domestic rubbish dump. Accumulated rubbish, which includes masses of broken pottery, spans several centuries. Hundreds of cultic figurines and 'perfume bottles' found on Katute suggest a manufacturing area; perhaps the aromatics of Arabia, especially myrrh and balsams, were processed here into perfumes, cosmetics and ointments and sold in the characteristic little clay vessels.

Descending Katute the track crosses the valley bottom and continues towards the upper reaches of the **Wadi Farasa**, with several interesting monuments. Above the wadi on the left, the **Tomb of the Broken Pediment**, its doorway weathered to a strange keyhole shape, has a forecourt approached by a flight of steps, and is still sometimes used by local Bdul. Water cisterns related to the tomb were filled by runoff channelled from the mountain above. Some 50m further **Tomb 229** has an unusual segmental arch above the doorway carrying three urns with tall pointed lids. The main triangular pediment is crowned by three squat round urns.

Wadi Farasa West

Just after Tomb 229 turn right to make a short detour to a small enclosed wadi west of Wadi Farasa which contains several monuments worth visiting. As you walk up the wadi **Tomb 258** on the right has a façade similar to the Roman Soldier Tomb b but without the niches. Above the doorway is a triangular pediment and a Doric frieze with discs in the metopes. There are six loculi high up in the back wall of the tomb chamber. Two further tombs are carved in the west cliff, the second still retaining part of the blocking stone in the central loculus in the back wall. Water was channelled to a basin by the tomb from a cistern across the end of the wadi. East of the cistern, facing north, is a tomb with a worn but nicely coloured façade and interesting interior. In the rear wall are three loculi with floor graves, and in the left wall five cavities with engaged pilasters between. On the right wall the pilasters have been carved but there are no loculi.

NABATEAN TOMB COMPLEX

From the number of tombs in Petra and the care lavished on their façades it is clear that the Nabateans attached great importance to death and the funerary cult. Tombs were family mausolea used for multiple burials; a full Nabatean tomb complex comprised several elements, best described in a long, interesting inscription on a tomb in the Wadi Turkmaniyya: 'This tomb and the large and small chambers inside, and the graves fashioned as loculi, and the courtyard in front of the tomb, and the porticoes and the houses within it, and the gardens and the triclinium, the water cisterns, the terrace and the walls and the rest of all the property in these places, is the consecrated and inviolable property of Dushara...' From the rest of the inscription it is clear that ownership of the property was guaranteed by contract which also stipulated who could be buried there. Many different burial practices are attested at Petra, including ordinary inhumation, burial with lime, partial cremation, cremation, and possibly burial after exposure. Evidence for funerary rituals is sadly lacking but it is assumed that funeral banquets and perhaps feasts in honour of the ancestors were celebrated in the triclinia. No doubt the tombs and gardens were well looked after, perhaps by family members who lived in the houses mentioned in the Turkmaniyya inscription as part of the tomb complex.

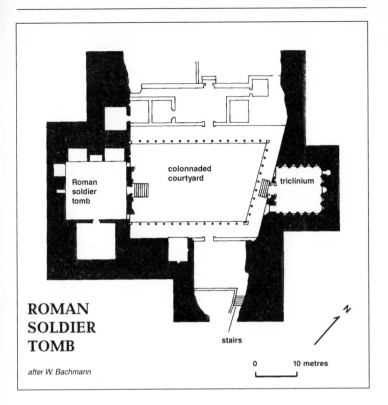

**ROMAN
SOLDIER
TOMB**

after W. Bachmann

colonnaded
courtyard

Roman
soldier
tomb

triclinium

stairs

0   10 metres

Roman Soldier Tomb Complex
Return to the main path and after a short distance steps lead up to the **Roman Soldier Tomb** and **Triclinium**, the best example in Petra of a full Nabatean tomb complex.

Going up the steps notice the well-tooled blocks of the retaining wall for the **courtyard** above, which is now very uneven but was originally surrounded by a **columned portico** except on the tomb side. There were several rooms behind the portico to the north and in the court we should imagine a garden. Three framed niches in the tomb façade have inset sculpture probably representing the tomb's occupants; the central headless figure wearing a cuirass has given the monument its name. Inside there are two large chambers; the main chamber, lit by windows high up on either side of the door, has a series of recesses in the walls. Towards the back is a long rectangular podium with slight traces of cement. Entered through the left side wall is the plain second chamber. Opposite the tomb, the triclinium is the most elaborate in Petra. Inside are broad benches with raised ledges along the front and the walls have partly fluted engaged columns with niches between. Stucco still adhering to the walls shows that the beautiful mauve, red and grey of the sandstone, which enhances the beauty of the monument today, was covered over in antiquity. Above the triclinium are a large **cistern** and now roofless rock-cut hall, only visible from higher up.

To the High Place

The processional way continues to the **Garden Temple**, a charming little monument with two free-standing columns and an open area in front, thought at one time to have been a garden, hence the name. Inside, the floor is not cleared and the walls have graffiti of gazelles and armed figures. Right of the temple is the retaining wall of the huge plastered cistern of the Roman Soldier Tomb complex, one of the most important in this part of the city. A large tree still takes advantage of the moist environment. A short distance further up the wadi, notable here for its beautiful colours, the real climb to the High Place begins. There are lovely views back to the Garden Temple, Umm al-Biyara and the city centre.

After a steep climb up a winding staircase you cross the wall of a Nabatean dam to an open area and straight ahead carved in the rock is the **Lion Fountain**, now without its head, which was perhaps made of metal. Water flowed down the carved channel then probably passed through a pipe and out of the lion's mouth. No doubt a place to stop and drink was welcome to worshippers on their way to the High Place; today an old Bdul lady may be there with a flask of sweet tea. Just beyond the Lion Fountain up on the left is a **rock-cut altar**, the path then cuts through a passage, and a short way down on the left is a rocky outcrop with an overhang which shelters a little sanctuary. Most interesting is the **Medallion and Block Relief**, which depicts Dushara both as a god block and as an anthropomorphic figure in the medallion above. From here there is a good view of the Roman Soldier Tomb below and the cistern and open hall above the Triclinium.

Before the next steps there is some **Nabatean graffiti** on the wall on the right; the path then goes up, down and up again past more graffiti and a **four-line Nabatean inscription** in big letters behind a tree. From here the track climbs steadily upwards, then doubles back left along a flatter stretch past a refreshments stall before the final ascent to the High Place. This passes through the substantial remains of a **high wall** or 'castle' of dubious age and function; at the top of the steps you must scramble up the rock on the right, past a large cistern, to reach the summit. Alternatively keep to the lower ground on the left, through a rock-cut passage, climb up to the shelf on the right and a short way along clamber up the original Nabatean steps to the central court. The **High Place** is the largest and most famous of many such cultic installations in and around Petra (p 218). Around the edge of the sunken court, aligned north–south, was a recessed 'bench', best preserved on the far (north) side; in the centre is a rectangular raised platform, aligned with the main altar. This is approached by four steps and has a recessed edge and a socket in the centre, probably for a stone stele representing the god. Left of the altar a basin is carved in the rock and beside it four steps lead to a shallow circular depression with a ridge around, perhaps for a cover, and a drain which discharged onto the steps. Facing the central court is another water tank.

Obviously the High Place was the venue for important ceremonies, during which priests and worshippers would have honoured the god, probably Dushara, with frankincense and libations, for these were the components of all Nabatean worship as the Greek geographer Strabo tells us: 'they honour the sun, setting up an altar in the house, making libation on it daily and using frankincense ...' Animal sacrifice may have been part of the ceremonies and perhaps the High Place was also used for funeral rites like the Canaanite high places. For Nabatean funeral customs the most controversial comment is made by Strabo, who reports that the Nabateans 'have the same regard for the dead as for dung ... and therefore they bury even their kings beside dung heaps'. A curious statement given the high esteem in which the Nabateans clearly held their defunct kinsmen! Similar statements occur elsewhere in the writings of both Strabo and Herodotus in connection with the funerary customs of the Bactrians, Sogdians and Massegetae—Iranian peoples who practised exposure of the dead in accordance with Zoroastrian tradition. For the Greeks this was clearly anathema. On this basis it has been suggested that the Nabateans may have practised something similar, if not for all, perhaps for royalty. In this context the High Place could be seen as an 'exposure platform' like those known from Iran.

Walk and climb down straight ahead from the High Place to the north edge of the ridge for fabulous views of Petra City Centre and return to the steps by the ruined wall along an easy path east of the summit. Ahead two **'Obelisks'** mark a Nabatean quarry where the mountain top was systematically hacked away for building blocks, perhaps for the 'fort' opposite. To return to the Outer Siq near the Theatre, turn left at the bottom of the steps and the route is clearly marked. On the way there are some beautiful views down the gorge.

Wadi Nmeir

With a guide you can descend from the High Place via **Wadi Nmeir**, which runs parallel to Wadi Farasa. Cross to the obelisks, walk straight ahead through a narrow pass and after a couple of minutes go right up a gully with tamarisks. As you emerge wind right and down to an open sandy area and continue down past beautifully coloured rock formations to a small clearing with caves. Straight ahead is the so-called **Obodas Chapel**, a yawning cavern with a rough cutting and tiny niche above. Inside there is a god block and a Nabatean inscription carved on a 'beam' in the ceiling from which the cave derives its name. Pass between the Obodas Chapel and the cave on the right which has a niche and cistern, and find steps down the narrow gully, which doubles back and emerges in an open grassy area. Ahead on the left looms the imposing bulk of **Jabal Nmeir**, up which the Nabateans carved a steep staircase. Continue down more steps, past a small god block and a large tomb chamber with two doors and follow the narrow valley, its high cliffs a magnificent array of colour. On the right is a rock ledge with shaft graves, then the path comes out at Wadi Umm Rattam, from where a track leads right towards Katute and the City Centre and left to Wadi Sabra (p 241).

Khubtha

There are several routes up **Jabal al-Khubtha**, the great massif which sits between Wadi Musa and Petra City Centre. From the broad gully north of the Treasury it is a short but steep scramble with one large boulder rather difficult to negotiate; there is also a way up from the Urn Tomb which we have not tried, and a third route from the Sextius Florentinus Tomb which is easy but a steep climb. In antiquity a Nabatean road led up the mountain from behind the Sextius Florentinus Tomb, but as this has collapsed in several places it is better to follow the goat path up the wadi to the left of the tomb. When you reach the Nabatean dam at the top turn right to the ridge overlooking the city centre for a number of high places. On the north edge of the ridge is a typical high place with recessed platform, basin, reservoir and channels, and just to the south a second high place has an unusual deep circular cutting with a lip. Steps alongside go up to the ruined remains of a free-standing building, and a large rock further south also has ruins and a cutting on top. Beyond is the most interesting of the cuttings. A staircase, now broken at the bottom, leads to a rock-cut gateway into a small court which has a rock altar attached to the western wall. Narrower steps go up to shallow 'benches' on either side of the cutting. It is not surprising that such a prominent mountain as Khubtha should have a series of high places, positioned to afford the devotee who worshipped there magnificent views over Petra city centre and the western mountains. Today's visitor should note especially the fine view from the ridge of the theatre carved in the hillside below.

WADI SIYYAGH

Wadi Siyyagh runs below the north side of al-Habis. Unfortunately a once pleasant walk has been spoiled by a jeep road along the valley bottom. In antiquity this was a residential area, for there are many rock-cut houses in the cliffs on either side, one of which has painted decoration. There are modern steps up but the house is kept locked for safety. At the junction of the Wadi Siyyagh and the Wadi Kharrubat ibn Jurayma, on the left, recent floods uncovered a triclinium with associated basins and channels; the area is now rather disturbed because of passing vehicles. From here the Wadi Siyyagh turns north and broadens out; where it describes a wide U-turn is a Nabatean quarry with roughly cut 'footholds' similar to those alongside the Treasury. Here you must pass through a fence to an area cultivated with olive trees, vines and figs. Further along as the wadi narrows slightly is 'Ain Siyyagh, one of only two perennial springs now in the Petra valleys, its former beauty marred by concrete walling. On the west cliff near the spring by a large fallen boulder are some Nabatean inscriptions.

UMM AL-BIYARA

A climb up Umm al-Biyara, the great massif which rises 300m from the Petra basin and dominates the city centre, is a must for the energetic visitor with time to spare. Take a guide for this moderate hike, which involves one slightly exposed move. It should take under an hour and is well worth the effort. In the 7C BC the summit of Umm al-Biyara was occupied by the Edomites, and for the Nabateans it was clearly a sacred mountain up which they carved a magnificent processional way.

Approach Umm al-Biyara from Pharoah's Pillar (p 233), following the path signed Wadi Sabra and Aaron's Tomb, cross Wadi Thughra at the bottom and head straight to the massif, keeping a large deeply cut single-divide crowstep tomb on your right. Umm al-Biyara's east face is peppered with a variety of façades at different levels, a combination of rock-cut houses and tombs. Near the large crow-step tomb is a blue sign 'Umm al-Biyara' and to the left is a gorge where the Nabatean processional way began. As the beginning of the ancient road is broken, it is easier to make a short detour to the south and go up behind a juniper tree where there are modern steps and cairns marking the way. Turn right (north) along the ledge, past a shallow cave with a very lightly carved obelisk on the south wall and a series of niches to the staircase up the gorge, which is part modern and part Nabatean. After a few steps you pass the remains of an arch, only preserved on the right-hand side, which once spanned the staircase. Beyond the staircase is a wide corridor which doubles back and divides into two very impressive rock-cut ramps. Take the southern ramp, which is better preserved, at the top turn right and follow the cairns. Most of the route to the summit, which winds up Nabatean steps and along ledges with the occasional short scramble over a few rocks, is well marked. From the summit, a trapezoidal rocky plateau that slopes from west to east, there are stunning views in all directions. Juniper trees dot the plateau, where wormwood, sea squill and phlomis also grow.

Straight ahead on reaching the top are the trenches and spoil heaps of excavations directed by the British archaeologist Crystal Bennett in the 1960s, which revealed part of a 7C BC **Edomite settlement**. A group of dry stone houses with

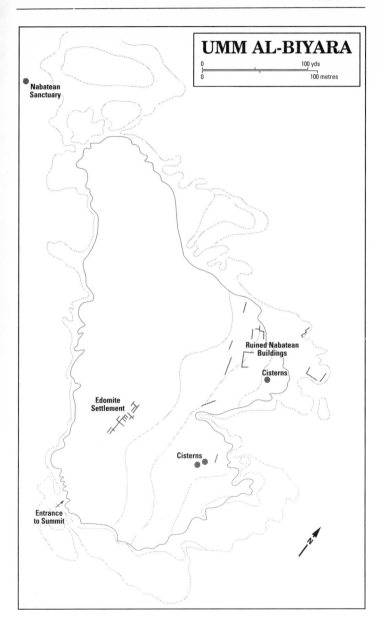

UMM AL-BIYARA

0   100 yds

0   100 metres

Nabatean
Sanctuary

Ruined Nabatean
Buildings

Cisterns

Edomite
Settlement

Cisterns

Entrance
to Summit

N

long corridor rooms and smaller square rooms leading off were uncovered. Most walls, built of flat uneven slabs of limestone easily chipped off the rocky outcrops on the mountain, still stand to a considerable height. Occupation was domestic and the main area was destroyed by fire. A seal impression found in one room has been restored to read 'Qos-Gabr, King of Edom', a king mentioned twice in Assyrian texts of the 7C BC. Umm al-Biyara has often been identified with biblical Sela from where Amaziah of Judah (c 79–781 BC) cast down 10,000 Edomites (II Chron.12). Excavation, however, revealed nothing from the early 8C BC, although as the Bible does not specifically mention occupation at Sela under Amaziah the question remains open. Amaziah renamed Sela Joktheel (II Kings 14:7) and Eusebius, writing in the 4C, equates Petra with Joktheel. Another candidate for biblical Sela is the mountain refuge of the same name near the Edomite capital Bozrah (p 172).

Umm al-Biyara means 'mother of cisterns' and there are several huge piriform plastered **cisterns** for rainwater collection cut into the rock north-east of the Edomite settlement. These could be Edomite but are more likely Nabatean and recall Diodorus' description of early Nabatean 'reservoirs lined with stucco ... the mouths of which they make very small, but by constantly increasing the width as they dig deeper, they finally make them of such size that each side has a length of one plethrum' (Diodorus XIX 94. 6–7). Diodorus also mentions a strong unwalled rock, perhaps Umm al-Biyara, where the Nabateans had left their valuables, elders, women and children, which was attacked and looted by Athenaeus in 312 BC (Diodorus XIX 95. 2–3).

Near the cisterns, on the eastern edge of the plateau, are ruined Nabatean buildings. It has been suggested that there was a temple on the summit, a fitting climax to the ceremonial ascent. At the north-west corner of the plateau, go down steps to a clearing then clamber down a gully to the left to see a charming **Nabatean sanctuary** beneath a rock overhang facing west, with a series of seven votive niches. Four niches are empty, two have god blocks on high pedestals and one niche contains a horned altar carved with a small god block. Among inscriptions and graffiti on the walls of the sanctuary are a worn Greek and Nabatean inscription on a tabula ansata below the second niche from the left, and a Greek inscription in large letters which includes the word IEPΩN 'holy'.

SNAKE MONUMENT

From Pharoah's Pillar, follow the signs to Aaron's tomb and Wadi Sabra and the path leads down to the **Wadi ath-Thughra**. Ahead is Umm al-Biyara with numerous tombs and houses carved into the base of the rock. A broad track then follows the wadi southwards away from the city centre until after c 30 minutes the **Snake Monument** becomes visible on the rocks above. Climb up the rocks for a clear view of this unique monument and the tombs associated with it. In a prominent position overlooking the 'suburb' below, the fat serpent, symbol of immortality and endless renewal, is coiled around a central block on top of a square pedestal, as though it were guardian of the area. Local Bdul still live in the caves and tombs around and use the large **Nabatean Cistern**, which has steps leading down to it and associated water channels and basins. Higher up is the **biggest cistern in Petra**, not immediately obvious as such because of the small opening, near some caves and the 'farm', a flat cultivated area with trees, fenced around.

■ From the Snake Monument excursions can be made to Sabra, as-Sadeh and the Jabal Haroun. Sabra and Jabal Haroun are each a day-trip from Wadi Musa and we recommend you take food, water and a guide. For as-Sadeh, which combines with Sabra, two days are needed with one night camping. It is also possible to drive to as-Sadeh with a four-wheel drive vehicle.

SABRA

At the 'farm' above the Snake Monument the way to Sabra is signposted and bears left across the plateau towards the Sabra mountains visible through a gap between two hills. Heading towards the gap you soon come to a very large cistern known as the **Birkat ad-Darb** or 'Way Cistern' with steps down and a filter system. On the right is Jabal Haroun, crowned by a little white shrine, which is lost from sight as you go through the pass between the hills to the **Btahi** area. Here and beyond is the home of the **Saidiyeen** tribe, related to the **Bdul** of the Petra valleys but less affected by tourism. You may still see their herds of camels and traditional black and white goat hair tents. The path descends to the broad sandy wadi bottom where you bear left and follow the valley for some distance until it joins the **Wadi Sabra** which becomes progressively greener as you approach the ancient ruins of **Sabra**. Here the Nabateans had a flourishing agricultural and industrial settlement which is still relatively uninvestigated. Hewn into the cliff on the left is the **theatre**; the rock-cut steps capped with stone seats are best preserved on the south side of the auditorium. Apparently the uppermost row of seating stones had backrests and were rounded at the front upper edge, making them particularly comfortable. Above this top row, in the middle of the auditorium, is the retaining wall of a **reservoir** above the theatre, part of a complex water channelling system from the mountains above. An unusual feature of the Sabra theatre is the fallen rock left by the Nabatean builders at the back of the orchestra; beneath is a water basin reached by eight steps. On both sides of the wadi are the remains of an extensive settlement; a short distance past the theatre there is a cult niche in the cliff and just beyond is the perennial spring, **'Ain Sabra**. On the north-west side of the wadi above the spring the ruins of a monumental building with large columns, distinctive Nabatean decoration and walls clad in marble at the base, may have been a temple. Heaps of **copper ore slag** on top of the wadi embankment attest extensive Nabatean mining and smelting activities. Cupriferous sandstone deposits and iron ore further along the wadi, the constant supply of water from the spring and the proximity of Petra make it likely that Sabra was one of the most important Nabatean metal-working centres.

To return to the centre of Petra it is possible to take a slightly different route by retracing your steps part of the way then branching right after Btahi past **Wadi Umm Rattam**, **Wadi Nmeir** and **Wadi Farasa** to Wadi Musa below the Urn Tomb.

Another very lovely route to **Sabra**, but which we do not recommend for the return trip because it is so steep, starts on the Ras an-Naqb road south of the Grand View Hotel. Head west towards the Sabra mountains, down fields and a tractor road, and before the flat-topped **Tabqa mountains** turn south down the gorge of **Ras Sabra**, along a well-defined track through an area of beautiful variegated sandstone. The wadi widens and not far from the Sabra theatre the way from Petra joins it from the north.

AS-SADEH

From Sabra it is a 3–4 hour trek to as-Sadeh. Alternatively if you have a four-wheel drive vehicle take a local guide who knows the way, follow the road from Wadi Musa towards Ras an-Naqab, turn right after 15km at a sign to Dlagha, and after some distance, at the bottom of a steep descent, turn right again at Wadi Msheith towards Wadi as-Sadeh. As-Sadeh and its surroundings have been used by man in many different periods. On a rise before the wadi a roughly built structure, perhaps a tower, has yielded Nabatean and later pottery and below in the valley is a ruined Nabatean village with some round houses. Further east on the south slope of the valley an Early Bronze Age settlement (mid 3rd millennium BC) has some two dozen dwellings with double walls to insulate against heat and cold. Beyond and overlooking Wadi as-Sadeh on the south side, the high plateau of Umm al-Ala mountain was settled by the Edomites in the 7C BC. As on Umm al-Biyara (p 238) and Ba'ja (p 250) these enigmatic Iron Age people seem to have needed the security of an easily defensible mountain stronghold, although what they were afraid of is unclear. During the Nabatean period the north slopes were covered with walled terraces, some still used, watered from 'Ain as-Sadeh at the head of the wadi. Water was channelled from the spring along the mountainside via a well preserved stone-built aqueduct, a good example of Nabatean hydraulic engineering. In one place two elegant arches supported the aqueduct, of which one remains. Nearby part of the wadi is deeply cut by flood waters; at one point where it drops c10m the rock is beautifully striped with bands of soft greeny-blue and hard red-pink stone.

If you have a vehicle you can return to the 'main' road and back to Wadi Musa or continue westwards until the road meets the Araba at Wadi Abu Khusheibah not far south of the Nabatean caravan station of Bir Mathkoor (p 133). A beautiful drive back to Petra is up Wadi Namala, south of Feinan (p 131), where some of the mountains are covered with juniper and the rocks are a splendid array of white, black, red, pink and brown. Nearer Petra the road runs into Siq Um al-Alda, guarded by two giant obelisks and continues past Beidha before reaching the Bdul village and Wadi Musa.

JABAL HAROUN

Jabal Haroun is most easily reached on a track which runs south-west from the 'farm' by the Snake Monument alongside the mountain. From the Snake Monument the walk should take 1–2 hours. Follow the track down to the Wadi Maqtal ad-Dikh past the Bdul cemetery on the right beneath a juniper tree and then head upwards on a path with steps and rock ledges, towards the top. For much of the way you can see the white shrine on the mountain. When the path reaches a high plateau south of the summit turn right and a short distance further begin the final ascent from the south. On the way up the staircase is a large reservoir, once roofed. According to tradition the small white domed mosque on the summit houses **Aaron's tomb**. It was rebuilt in the 14C and has a Koranic inscription over the entrance. Although a guardian should be there to unlock the door to pilgrims, visitors should not be disappointed if there is no one around.

According to Biblical tradition **Moses** and his elder brother **Aaron** were denied entry to the Promised Land because they had doubted in the Lord. At Yahweh's bidding and as the Israelites looked on, Moses took Aaron and his son Eleazar up Mount Hor, 'by the coast of the land of Edom', put Aaron's garments on his son and Aaron died on the mountain (Num. 20). Moses then led the Israelites around Edom, whose king refused them passage through his land, to the plains of Moab opposite Jericho. A different route for the Israelites is given in Numbers 33, but both versions make it difficult to equate Mount Hor with Jabal Haroun, which is in the very heart of Edom, although the link has become firmly established in local belief. Aaron is also an important prophet in the Islamic tradition and is mentioned several times in the Koran.

Muslim, Jewish and Christian pilgrims all climb the mountain to pay their respects at the shrine.

Jabal Haroun has long been a holy mountain; the Nabateans have left a god block and several inscriptions and possibly a Byzantine monastery was located here, the precursor of the Muslim shrine. Views from the summit are stunning: east to the Sabra mountains and beyond, west across the Wadi Araba and most striking of all north to the Jabal ad-Deir on which is clearly incised the tiny but perfect façade of Petra's largest monument.

JEAN LOUIS BURCKHARDT AND THE REDISCOVERY OF PETRA

For over 600 years, from the time of the Crusades until the beginning of the 19C, Petra's whereabouts was unknown to the West. Credit for its 'rediscovery' goes to Jean Louis Burckhardt, well educated son of a wealthy Swiss colonel in the French army. When the family fortunes took a downturn Burckhardt left continental Europe for England where he offered his services as an explorer to Sir Joseph Banks of the Association for Promoting the Discovery of the Interior Parts of Africa. It was decided he should go to Mecca and then cross the Sahara as part of the returning pilgrims' caravan. To do so he was to disguise himself as a Muslim trader from India, which would excuse any strange accent and mistakes in his Arabic. Before leaving England he studied Arabic at Cambridge, then spent a while in Malta, and eventually made his way to Aleppo where he stayed two years perfecting his Arabic and studying the Koran. In 1812 he set out for Cairo. At Karak, believed by the clergy at Jerusalem to be Petra, his interest was excited by rumours of a city in the mountains. For 20 days Burckhardt was kept by the sheikh at Karak, on the pretext of protection, but finally they set off south, with the sheikh demanding further 'protection' money. As he kept his resources hidden on his person and thus seemed to have no money Burckhardt was compelled to give his good saddle in exchange for the sheikh's. His stirrups were duly demanded and so in considerable discomfort he travelled on, passing from the protection of one tribe to another, losing ever more apparel as bribes or payment for provisions, among which was a goat. At each encampment he heard talk of buildings hidden in Wadi Musa. Recalling a reference in Eusebius to Aaron's tomb near Petra, and knowing the tribesmen did not want to take him to the ruins, which they believed concealed ancient treasure, Burckhardt announced that he had made a vow to sacrifice to the prophet Aaron. His guide Hamid, hired at Elji (Wadi Musa) and paid with a pair of old horse shoes, had little option but to lead him there with his goat, through the Siq to the Treasury, and thence towards Mount Hor. It was 22 August 1812. Hamid was very distressed and anxious, and when Louis, who had already examined a number of tombs, turned off the path towards the Qasr al-Bint his suspicions were thoroughly aroused. 'I see now that you are an infidel', he said 'who has some particular business amongst the ruins of the city of your forefathers; but depend on it we shall not suffer you to take out a single part of the treasures hidden therein ...!' Louis replied it was mere curiosity that prompted him but Hamid remained darkly suspicious so he dared not explore further. When they reached the foot of Aaron's mountain the sun had set so Burckhardt agreed to sacrifice his goat there in sight of the tomb. They slept for a while then retraced their steps in the darkness. Burckhardt travelled on to Cairo, thence to Nubia, went to Mecca and Medina and finally died of dysentery in Cairo in October 1817. He was only 32 years old. His book *Travels in Syria and the Holy Land* recounting his journey to Petra was published posthumously in 1822.

Returning along the same route from the Jabal Haroun an interesting detour may be made to **Wadi Abu 'Ullayqa**. When you reach the place where the track crosses Wadi Maqtal ad-Dikh turn left down to Wadi Waqidh and left again to the deep gorge of Wadi Abu 'Ullayqa, where carvings and inscriptions attest a popular Nabatean sanctuary. Along a ledge on the south side of the wadi are lots of inscriptions and 'pecked feet' and a niche containing a seated female figure, her head missing, who is probably the goddess Isis, popular throughout the Hellenistic and Roman world. She wears flowing robes and is facing Jabal Haroun. Further down the wadi on the same side towards Jabal Barra which rises impressively in the near distance a small cistern is known as Abu Dallu. Dallu means 'bucket' in Arabic and the cistern is so-called because local people believe a bucket was lowered from there to raise water from a dam in the gorge below.

Alternative routes out of Petra

Adventurous visitors may like to leave Petra via routes other than the Siq and Bab as-Siq; we suggest a few possibilities, all of which can also be done in reverse and combined with other walks.

MUGHUR AN-NASARA AND SHA'B QAIS ROUTE

This route starts at the east cliff, goes around al-Khubtha mountain and ends at the Petra Forum Hotel. From the 'Palace Tomb' continue north around the mountain and cross the remains of the inner line of the **North City Walls**. Further round is the **Tomb of Sextius Florentinus**, Roman governor of the Province of Arabia, who died probably AD 128 or 129. His tomb is one of the latest in Petra, and it is rather surprising that he was buried there as Bostra was the capital of the province he governed. A Latin inscription below the curved pediment informs us that the tomb was built by his son and gives a summary of Sextius Florentinus' career:

> 'To Lucius ... ninius, son of Lucius Papirius Sextius Florentinus, Triumvir for coining gold and silver, Military Tribune of Legion I Minerva, Quaestor of the Province of Achaia, Tribune of the Plebs, Legate of Legion VIII Hispania, Proconsul of the Province of Narbonensis, Legate of Augustus, Propraetor of the Province of Arabia, most dutiful father, in accordance with his own will.'

A worn bust in the centre of the curved pediment may be a Medusa. She has something knotted around the neck and wind-blown locks and tendrils, perhaps snakes, on either side. Above the pediment is a very weathered eagle. An urn crowns the upper triangular pediment. Inside is a long chamber with several loculi.

From here cross the wadi to explore the outer line of the **North City Walls**, best preserved near the **Conway Tower**, a strongpoint on a high rock, with flanking curtain walls and bastions.

> Petra was protected to the east and west by mountains and defended by **walls** to the north and south, probably built in the 1C BC. The southern wall ran from al-Habis across Katute to near the theatre; the northern wall had a main outer system which ran north-east along the Wadi Abu 'Ullayqa to the Conway Tower. A later, inner line of fortifications, built over earlier houses, which dates perhaps to the 3C or 4C AD when the city had shrunk in size, ran

from the Wadi Abu 'Ullayqa to near the 'Palace Tomb'. Note that many of Petra's tombs are outside the city walls of the 1C BC, on the edge of the inhabited area.

North of the Sextius Florentinus Tomb, **Tomb No. 731** is distinguished by its strikingly coloured façade, a rich carmine colour with bands of grey-blue and white. Oleanders blooming before the tomb in spring and summer add their own touch of colour. Further along the **Wadi al-Mataha** in the north face of al-Khubtha a complex of rock-cut houses is known as the **House of Dorotheos** because the name is twice inscribed in Greek in a huge triclinium with three doors and windows which is part of the complex. Above the House of Dorotheos and running in a straight line along the mountain is the channel which brought water from Wadi Musa to a cistern beside the 'Palace Tomb'. On the opposite side of the wadi the rambling rocky moonscape of **Mughur an-Nasara** or 'Caves of the Christians', is so-called because of crosses carved in some of the caves. Nabatean cuttings, caves and tombs abound. Most interesting is **Tomb No. 649**, high above the path used by the Bdul to go to and from their village but not immediately obvious as it is partly concealed behind rocks. This large tomb, which faces west and has a court in front, is also called the **Tomb with the Armour** because of the frieze between the dwarf pilasters. In each outer bay is a bearded mask-like face, very worn, and in the centre bay is the armour which includes shields and a cuirass. Inside the tomb are several loculi. Spend a while exploring this area if possible as there is much to discover and some fantastic rock formations; if you walk north and cross Wadi Umm Sayhun you can reach the Bdul village.

Continuing along Wadi al-Mataha you pass another area of tombs on the left— some still used for storage and penning animals—and on the right is the entrance to **Sadd al-Ma'jan** and **Wadi al-Mudhlim** (p 218). Further along, where the wadi opens out, climb up on the right towards rocks that look iron stained and cross over into the adjacent wadi. As you walk across you can see the remains of a charming little **aqueduct** up the valley on the left, part of the system which channelled water from Wadi Musa into the city. To reach the Petra Forum Hotel keep the valley with the aqueduct on your left and walk straight ahead along the right side of **Wadi Sha'b Qais**. The most difficult part of the walk is where a large boulder has fallen into the valley, blocking the path—it is just possible to squeeze between the boulder and the cliff face. Further along cross through oleander bushes to the left side of the wadi, walk alongside a well-cut water channel and soon the Petra Forum Hotel appears in the distance.

WADI TURKMANIYYA
Between the Qasr al-Bint and Forum Basin Restaurant a motorable service road comes into Petra. Follow the road along **Wadi Abu 'Ullayqa**, also called **Wadi Turkmaniyya** until after about 15 minutes the façade of the **Turkmaniyya Tomb** is on the left, the bottom half entirely broken away. Between the two central pilasters is a very important Nabatean inscription, the longest found in Petra, which lists the different components of a Nabatean tomb complex (p 234) and certain associated legal provisions.

Nabatean was a dialect of Aramaic with strong Arabic influence, written in a semi-cursive script which can be rather difficult to read. It has some resemblance to the Hebrew script of the time. Unfortunately there are few Nabatean inscriptions of any length. The longest are contained in papyri found in caves at Nahal Hever, overlooking the west side of the Dead Sea; they concern ownership of property in Nabatea by various Judaeans. Another Nabatean papyrus, from a cave of the Wadi Murabba'at near Qumran, deals with a land transaction between two Judaeans who for some reason had employed a Nabatean scribe. Most scholars believe that the early Arabic script derived from Nabatean.

The road then continues past a checkpoint to the modern Bdul village, 4km from Wadi Musa.

WADI MU'AISRA EAST TO BEIDHA

Walk towards the Qasr al-Bint from the Forum Basin Restaurant and on the left is the green valley of **Wadi Abu 'Ullayqa** with clusters of oleanders and **'Ain Abu 'Ullayqa**, its perennial spring. Follow the path alongside the wadi for c 200m and by a row of four bricked-up houses on the right cross the wadi towards two more houses and then scramble up the rocks left or right of the deep cleft where **Wadi Mu'aisra East** joins Wadi Abu 'Ullayqa. At the top begin walking along the wadi bed, looking back towards the city centre for excellent views of the Qasr al-Bint and Pharoah's Pillar. Along the valley on the left is an area of tombs including several with curved pediments; further on the valley narrows and for part of the way the path then follows the old Nabatean road, cut deep into the rock. A lone single-divide crow-step tomb overlooks the road. Higher up the wadi behind a fence on the left is a deep plastered **reservoir**, the base stones of its original arched roof still in place, and a little further is an unusual **circular cistern** with steps leading down. About 10–15 minutes' walk from here the wadi emerges into open undulating country, part of the **Beidha** area, where in springtime white broom, red poppies, daisies, grape hyacinths and mallow bloom among the wheat. Around the mountain to the east is a rocky outcrop with steps to a small court containing a votive niche and water basin. A short distance north across the fields, surrounded by a modern wall, there is a most interesting **Nabatean grape press**, one of many in the outlying agricultural areas of the Petra region. From the paved press the liquid passed into a square settling tank and thence into the deep round vat, reached by steps.

> **Cultivation of the vine** was important in ancient Nabatea and research suggests that a quicker crop was produced by planting the vines on top of round stones covered with sand, thereby encouraging the roots to spread horizontally. Dushara, the paramount Nabatean god, was assimilated to Dionysus, god of wine, who was the patron of the extensive wine-producing area of the Hauran in northern Nabatea. We know from Strabo that the Nabateans celebrated *symposia* (a term which implies wine-drinking parties) in groups of 13, with two singing girls, limiting each person's consumption to 11 cups.

Five minutes' walk east of the grape press are two large reservoirs, the second with fruit trees planted in it; if you continue eastwards you will reach the road to 6km Wadi Musa about 2km from the Bdul village. It is also possible to walk from Wadi Mu'aisra East to the Neolithic site at Beidha (p 249) and Siq al-Barid (p 248) by bearing left at the end of the wadi, then right across the area known as Shamasa and down a broad valley.

Excursions from Wadi Musa

There are many interesting historical sites and areas of natural beauty in the Petra region. The following are a few suggestions, best done by car from Wadi Musa, except for al-Wu'eira which can easily be reached on foot. Beyond Beidha you need a four-wheel drive vehicle.

AL-WU'EIRA CRUSADER CASTLE

Straddling a ridge west of the road to the Bdul village, c 1.5km from the Petra Forum hotel is **Al-Wu'eira Crusader Castle**. Turn left off the tarmac road at an open sandy area and head for a large square tomb. The way down follows a gully 20m left of this, but if you are in doubt about your bearings the castle is actually visible a little further along the road. About 20m below road level is the **gatehouse**, the only entrance— follow the occasionally stepped gully down and round towards it. The rock-cut gatehouse spectacularly bridges the deep ravine. Steep gorges surround al-Wu'eira on all sides, making this a very defensible site.

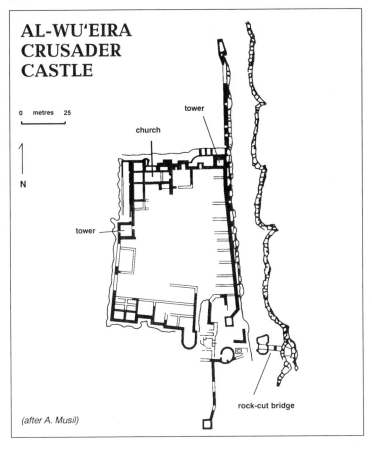

AL-WU'EIRA
CRUSADER
CASTLE

0   metres   25

N

tower

church

tower

rock-cut bridge

(after A. Musil)

History

Their southern defences were important to the Crusaders, both to protect their exposed flank and to keep control of the trade and pilgrimage routes through Aqaba. Baldwin I led an expedition down to these parts in 1115 and founded the castle of Montreal (Shobak). Construction began at al-Wu'eira, called Le Vaux Moise (Moses Valley), the next year and probably at Aila/Aqaba too. In 1144 the castle was seized from the Franks. The Franks, unable to recapture the castle by military means, had to resort to burning the olive groves on which the Turks who had seized it were dependent. It fell to Saladin in 1188.

Pass through the gatehouse arch noting the benches and niche on the left and make your way up to the castle. The Crusader work is all 12C, but there is also evidence of Nabatean occupation: steps, basins and chambers cut into the protruding bedrock and an unusual example of a rock-cut 'house' at the end of the southern ridge, reused by the Crusaders as a watchtower. The main enclosure is c 100m x 35m with an extension running north from the north-east tower: the walls cling to the precipitous and slippery edges, making this an impossible site to storm. Inside there are traces of a few rooms. The best-preserved tower is in the middle of the west wall. Head towards the corner tower on the north-east passing the chapel on your way: the small apse is still there with a niche in the wall to its right. The **north-east tower** is barrel-vaulted with a slit window. The east tower has now disappeared.

BEIDHA/SIQ AL-BARID

Continue north to the 2.5km **Bdul village**, home of the Bdul families who were moved by the government out of the caves and tombs of Petra during the early 1980s. After c 5km a signed road forks left to Beidha, 200m along on the right there is a huge **Nabatean Cistern** up a staircase and behind a modern wall, which is still used by local people. All over this area are carved steps, channels and cisterns, which collected water for drinking and irrigation; in antiquity the Beidha region was intensively cultivated, as it is again today.

The road ends at the entrance to the **Siq al-Barid**, the 'Cold Siq', so-called because little sun permeates the narrow gorge. Right of the entrance is **Façade 846**, a lovely 'classical' façade with a terrace in front reached by steps: the unusual interior is simply a long recess which is the same height and width as the doorway. Wearmarks in the door sockets indicated that the doors were opened many times. Sockets attest an original gate at the entrance to the gorge, which is about 350m long and has three open areas with narrower sections between. In the first area is a striking rock-carved chamber with two pilasters and two free-standing columns across the front, usually described as a **temple**, below which is a rock-cut house with three chambers, one a 'kitchen' with three recessed shelves in the walls. The second open area is notable for four large **triclinia**, three on the right and one on the left; these triclinia were not associated with tomb complexes and may have been used for hosting banquets for special guests and for the traditional 'symposia' which were a regular part of Nabatean life. An inscription at Beidha, north of Siq al-Barid, refers to a symposiarch. Further along on the left a rebuilt staircase goes up to the famous **Painted House**, a biclinium with stucco on the walls painted to imitate masonry and an arched recess with a plastered and painted ceiling. The ceiling painting is rather blackened, it is easier to make out the main features with the aid of a torch. Birds rest among flowering vines; on the left side a 'Pan' figure plays a flute and a winged 'cupid' pulls a bow; on the right another little figure runs through the foliage. There is fine interior tooling, parallel lines across the ceiling and lines at 45° on the walls. On the evidence of such tooling it has been suggested that the Nabateans used a type of three-pronged chisel to finish their cut surfaces. At the end of the third open area of the Siq al-Barid a rock-cut staircase leads through a narrow gap to a broad rock ledge from which there is a fine view; the Nabatean path goes down to the wadi leading ultimately to Petra if you turn left, and Jabal Qarun (p 250) and Wadi Araba if you turn right.

Many scholars consider the Siq al-Barid as a caravan station of greater Petra, where traders would halt and conduct their business. The fertile land around would be ideal for grazing the animals, there was ample water, and the huge triclinia would have been perfect to host guests and do business. Traffic from the great emporia of Alexandria, Rhinocolura and Gaza would cross the Negeb and arrive here via the Nabatean caravanserai of Bir Mathkoor in the Wadi Araba.

Detail of the decorations in the Painted House, Siq al-Barid, Petra

Beidha Neolithic site

Facing the entrance to the Siq al-Barid follow the track left around the mountain and a 15-minute walk brings you to **Beidha**, one of the oldest excavated Neolithic villages, dating between c 7200 BC and 6500 BC. Much of the site has eroded into the wadi but enough remains to give a good picture of life in this part of Jordan in what archaeologists call the Pre-Pottery Neolithic period when man was first experimenting with agriculture. After camping in temporary huts for a while, the people of Beidha built a retaining wall around their village, clearly visible to the south, and semi-subterranean round houses with stone walls around an inner framework of wooden posts which supported a reed and clay roof. Inside the retaining wall to the south-west note the sunken foundations of these houses with slots in the walls for the posts. Animal and plant remains which have been analyzed show that the Beidha people hunted and probably herded various animals—in particular wild goat—gathered pistachio nuts, and cultivated emmer wheat and wild barley; querns and grinders for cereals and flints for cutting are still scattered around the site. About 6650 BC the village was destroyed by fire. After it was rebuilt, the people constructed rectangular houses alongside the round ones; a group of these can be seen on the higher ground at the centre of the village. Outside the boundary wall to the east is a complex of structures which the excavator believes had a religious or ceremonial function. They are characterised by large slabs of stone set on edge or laid on the floor with an associated basin. For no apparent reason Beidha and other sites in Palestine and Jordan were abandoned c 6500 BC; a climatic change has been suggested or even an epidemic of plague although there is no evidence of either. Beidha was never re-inhabited.

JABAL QARUN

At the left turn to Beidha and Siq al-Barid fork right along the main road and then turn immediately left at the sign to Hesha. On the right-hand side is **'Ain Dibdibah**, an important spring from which water was channelled, part of the way through clay piping, to the northern areas of Petra. This is the road from Petra to Wadi Araba via **Siq Umm al-Alda** and after the first few kilometres is only passable by four-wheel drive vehicles. On the left, about 6km past the Bdul village, there are two huge, beautifully carved **obelisks** in relief on a single plinth in a niche; a little further on steps lead up to a cave which one could easily imagine as a checkpoint to control traffic on this important route. The broad valley here is beautiful, with clusters of holly oaks and the sound of birdsong. Some 2.5km past the obelisks turn left across the mountain with the Wadi Jabu on the right, cross the wadi, then bear right towards a deserted village where there is a very deep **Nabatean cistern**. After c 500m drive left up the lower slopes of the **Jabal Qarun** which overlooks Wadi Musa as it descends to the Araba. From here there are fabulous views over the Araba mountains and beyond. According to local legend the tomb of Moses' brother Qarun is on the top of the mountain; ruins and Nabatean pottery suggest there may have been a sanctuary there.

There is a lovely walk along old routes from Jabal Qarun to Siq al-Barid. Follow the track back past the deserted houses, and c 2km from the mountain where the track forks, take the right turn and then bear left down the rocks towards the wadi. From here the walk takes about 45 minutes. The track goes down steeply, part of the way along the old Nabatean road. After c 20 minutes leave the valley, climb up left via a narrow Nabatean cutting and at the top of the defile turn right and squeeze past a very large rock on the right to cross into the next valley. Along the valley to the right is another way to Jabal Qarun, for Beidha bear left down the hill, noting a number of **Nabatean dams** in the valley bottom. Walk along the wadi, and past a dam where there are large trees is the Nabatean staircase up to the west end of **Siq al-Barid**. Continue along the wadi for **Beidha Neolithic site** (p 249) and for Petra via **Wadi Mu'aisra East** (p 246) or the **Deir Plateau** (p 230).

BA'JA

On the Wadi Araba road, 1km after the turn-off to Jabal Qarun, a track leads right to 1km **Ba'ja** and comes to an end by a small glen near a little modern building. Facing the mountain, walk right, down to **Siq Ba'ja**, where there was a Nabatean agricultural settlement. Part of the dam built across the gorge still stands, and channels lead water to cisterns below the village. Several grape presses, with treading floors, settling tanks and vats, attest ancient vineyards as at Beidha. On the mountain top above the village is an **Edomite mountain stronghold** with house foundations, cisterns and rock-cut steps. Ascent starts c 40m north of Siq Ba'ja, past the small glen, and is via a series of chimneys and fissures, only negotiable for someone with climbing experience. Our attempt was a failure!

Return to Wadi Musa by the same route or with a four-wheel drive vehicle continue down Wadi Namala to Wadi Araba, a lovely scenic drive which emerges near the important copper smelting site of Feinan (p 131).

SITES SOUTH AND EAST OF WADI MUSA
South and east of Wadi Musa are a number of small sites which can be combined with a scenic drive. From Wadi Musa take the road to Tayba and Ras an-Naqb and not far out of the town on the right is '**Ain al-Braq**, the spring which supplied al-Madras and the High Place with water. Recent excavations in the area of the spring have brought to light a large and well built multi-roomed complex of the Nabatean period with a flagged courtyard and columns. From here and further along the road are lovely views over Petra, and 12km from Wadi Musa centre the road to Taybat Zaman is signposted, where an old stone village has been tastefully converted into a hotel complex. Some 15km from Wadi Musa is a sign right to Dlagha. This is another road to Wadi Araba which can be passed with a four-wheel drive vehicle. Along this road you can also reach as-Sadeh (p 241), a 'suburb' of Petra about 15km from the city centre. Take the road on the left to **as-Sadaqa**, ancient Zadagatta, where a Nabatean and Roman watchtower, **Rujm as-Sadaqa**, crowns a high hill east of the village. Under the Romans, Zadagatta was a station on the Via Nova Traiana, garrisoned, according to the Notitia Dignitatum, by a unit of *equites promoti indigenae*. Most of the unit would be in a settlement below the hill while a detachment manned the tower from where they could observe both the Via Nova and the eastern desert. Continue to c 7.5km **Ail**, also on the Via Nova, where the Roman castellum recorded earlier this century has been almost entirely destroyed. Only the south-east corner is visible in the picturesque old village, now almost deserted in favour of the modern settlement nearby.

Keep on the road which runs due north of Ail, after 2km turn right at a blue sign to Betar and c 500m along, after entering **Basta** village turn right again to the **Pre-Pottery Neolithic site**. Dated in the 7th millennium BC, Basta is partly contemporary with Beidha, and is remarkably well preserved. Alleyways separate small stone houses with tiny windows still intact. A network of channels may be part of a drainage system. Basta's inhabitants cultivated emmer wheat and barley and kept goats. Gazelle, wild cattle and other animals were hunted, and fruits and nuts, particularly pistachios and almonds, were gathered in large quantities. In their village the people of Basta made bone and stone implements, beads of sandstone, turquoise, malachite and shell, and they carved pieces of mother-of-pearl which were probably sewn on clothing. Finds from other contemporary sites attest an important mother-of-pearl industry in the region.

'Udruh
North of Basta, at the Wadi Musa junction, turn right to c 10km '**Udruh**, one of the most important Roman military sites in Transjordan, the ruins of which are beside the road on the right in the modern village.

History
In the Nabatean period 'Udruh was a town and watering place where caravans coming from Aila (Aqaba), which did not want to negotiate the steep route down to Petra, could halt on their way north to the Mediterranean and

Damascus. When the Romans took over the Nabataean kingdom in AD 106 they constructed a large fortress at 'Udruh, alongside their grand trunk road the Via Nova Traiana. The original garrison unit of 'Udruh is unknown, but it is possible that legio VI Ferrata was moved there during Diocletian's reorganisation of the eastern frontier at the end of the 3C and beginning of the 4C. There seems to have been building activity at the site until the 6C; c 630 the town surrendered to the Muslim forces without resistance and some occupation continued throughout the Islamic period.

'Udruh fortress is trapezoidal in shape, with four circular **angle towers** at the corners and 20 U-shaped **interval towers**, which are not bonded into the enclosure wall, so may be later than the wall. Excavation of the **south-western angle tower** has revealed three rooms at ground floor level and a staircase that winds around a central pier. Umayyad rebuilding is evident in the upper storey. Outside the south-west corner of the fortress the large building is probably a **Byzantine church**. In the middle of each wall of the fort there is one main gateway; best preserved are the south and west gates. Inside is mostly a jumble of stones, but in the western part of the fortress a building has been cleared which the excavator believes is the **principia**, or headquarters building, later converted into a church. Adjacent to the wall east of the north gate is a late Islamic, possibly Ottoman, fort and outside the wall, near the north-east corner, is the perennial spring which has attracted settlement throughout the ages. From 'Udruh there is a good view of the eastern desert.

Return to Wadi Musa along the same road, entering the town from the east, by Moses' Spring.

Illustration from the Notitia Dignitatum showing Ziza (Jiza), Arcopolis (Rabba), Speluncis (Deir al-Kahf?) and Mefa (Umm ar-Rasa) now in the Bodleian Library

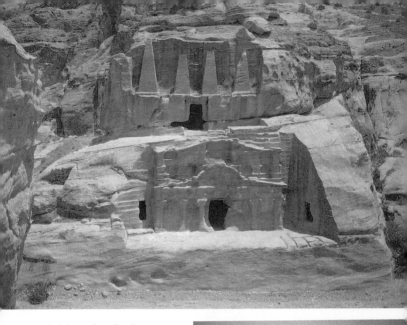

Petra: Obelisk Tomb and Bab
as-Siq Tricilinium *above*

Shobak Crusader Castle *right*

Karak Crusader Castle from
the east *left* & Qasr Bshir *right*

INDEX